THE ART OF IRAN

BY THE SAME AUTHOR

Les Antiquités bouddhiques de Bāmiyān, *Ars Asiatica*, Van OEst, Paris, 1928. In collaboration with Mme Y. A. Godard and J. Hackin.

Bronzes du Luristān, *Ars Asiatica*, Van OEst, Paris, 1931.

L'art de la Perse ancienne, *Histoire universelle de l'art*, 1932.

Les monuments de Marāgha, Paris, 1934.

The Tāri-Khāna, Damghan, *Gazette des Beaux-Arts*, December 1934.

Abarkūh, *Athār-é Iran*, 1936–1.

Natanz, *Athār-é Iran*, 1936–1.

The Towers of Lādjin and Resget, *Athār-é Iran*, 1936–1.

The ancient mosques of Iran, *Athār-é Iran*, 1936–2.

History of the Masdjid-i-Jāmi, Ispahān, *Athār-é Iran*, 1936–2.

Ardistān and Zawaré, *Athār-é Iran*, 1936–2.

Ispahān, *Athār-é Iran*, 1937–1.

The Parthian statues at Shāmi, *Athār-é Iran*, 1937–2.

The fire monuments, *Athār-é Iran*, 1938–1.

The tomb of Sultan Uljāitū Khodābenda at Sultaniya, *A Survey of Persian Art*, vol. I, London, 1938.

Gunbad-i-Kābūs, *A Survey of Persian Art*, vol. I, 1938.

Khorāsān, *Athār-é Iran*, 1949–1.

Ispahān. The tomb of Bābā Kasem and the Imāmī madrasa, *Athār-é Iran*, 1949–1.

Iranian vaults, *Athār-é Iran*, 1949–2.

Le Trésor de Ziwiyè, Haarlem, 1950.

Le tombeau de Mawlānā Hasan Kāshī à Sultānīye, *Les arts asiatiques*, 1954.

L'art musulman at les génies nationaux, *Cahiers d'histoire mondiale*, January 1954.

Unesco collection of world art: *Iran, Persian Miniatures, in the Imperial Library*, Teheran.

'Essays and lectures', *Orientalia Romana*, Roma, 1958.

Persepolis, *Bible et Terre sainte*, May 1961.

L'architecture iranienne à l'époque islamique, *Jardin des Arts*, October 1961.

ANDRÉ GODARD

Former Director-General of Antiquities in Iran

THE ART OF
IRAN

TRANSLATED FROM THE FRENCH BY MICHAEL HERON

EDITED BY MICHAEL ROGERS

London

GEORGE ALLEN & UNWIN LTD

PRINTED IN GREAT BRITAIN
in 11 point Plantin type
BY SIMSON SHAND LTD
LONDON, HERTFORD AND HARLOW

I dedicate this book to my wife Y. A. GODARD
my courageous companion for many years,
always ready to give a helping hand, and also
to our friend M. T. ULLENS DE SCHOOTEN *who has*
shown us deep and constant affection at all times.

PREFACE

I N this study of Iranian civilization, or more accurately of the art which is its visual expression, I have concentrated on five aspects: the formation and evolution of Iranian architecture, which is not well known and can only be properly examined and understood in the country itself, the sculpture which was its normal accompaniment up to the Islamic period, the glazed ceramic decoration which subsequently fulfilled the same role, the metalwork and the extremely informative numismatics. I have dealt more briefly with ceramics, fabrics, carpets and painting, because both Europe and America possess excellent collections which have been the subject of authoritative books. Instead, I have tried to retrace the continuous line of Iranian art which went on beneath superimposed foreign fashions and influences.

It may well be that what has given us the best idea of the artistic significance of Islam and its effects on ancient Iranian civilization is the re-appearance of traditional Iranian works of architecture in the Muhammadan period. However, until 1926, when H.M. Riza Shāh Pahlawī acceded to the throne, the art of Iran was only represented in the eyes of the world by the minor arts, masterpieces of which occupy the showcases of the great national museums of the world, both public and private. Nothing or almost nothing was known, even in Iran, about Iranian architecture, because of the indifference of the country's inhabitants to the vestiges of their ancient civilization as well as a fanaticism which prohibited foreigners from entering religious buildings. Because of the difficulty of travelling, in the not so distant time of caravans and atrocious roads, the few monuments described by travellers were nearly always the same: those they found on the two routes which traverse Iran in the shape of a cross, from Tabrīz to Būshīr, via Sultānīya, Qazwīn, Qum, Isfahān and Shīrāz, and from Qasr-i Shīrīn to Mashhad, via Kirmānshāh, Hamadhān, Qazwīn, Teheran, Dāmghān and Nīshāpūr. In addition I should point out that the descriptions and drawings brought back by these travellers are by no means compatible with one another.

On the other hand during the reign of H.M. Riza Shāh Pahlawī, i.e. from 1926 to 1941, it was possible to enter and work in all the monuments in Iran, even in the particularly holy cities of Mashhad and Qum. Moreover numerous roads were built which made possible the discovery of hitherto unknown monuments.

Since 1942 the work of reconnaissance and study on the spot has become less easy. Once more the mullahs are trying to forbid foreigners access to religious monuments, but the fact remains that for fifteen years it was possible to examine at leisure, draw, photograph and measure several hundred ancient monuments—in other words enough buildings for a detailed study of Iranian architecture. Obviously we are still only at the stage of monographs and hypotheses, but already many basic problems have been solved. Now we can trace through the maze of influences discernible in them the history of monuments, from as far back as we can see to the most recent times, which have been restored and modified for better or worse on countless occasions. In the process we can gradually reconstitute the history of Iranian art as a whole.

However I feel that this book might not be properly understood if I did not begin by introducing the reader to the actors and also the places and circumstances of the events related in it. So the reader will find a historical summary at the beginning of each of the five parts of this work, intended to mitigate this difficulty, as well as a historical map of the period.

In addition I have annexed detailed notes to certain parts of the text: those, for example, which are intended to define the religious context—primitive Mazdaism, Zoroastrianism, Sassanid Mazdaism, Manichaeism and Mazdakism, the Sunnite and Shi'ite doctrines—or those which deal with recent finds made at Hāsānlū, south-west of Lake Urmiya, or in the villages of Uman, Daylamān and Pir Kūh situated in the Zagrus Mountains, to which the principal means of access is the route from Amlash, which has given its name to a great number of antiquities produced over a period of more than a thousand years and discovered scattered over an enormous area.

To facilitate the understanding of the more technical passages I have introduced a number of plans and drawings into the text. They will be particularly useful in the first part, which deals with a prehistoric period for which archaeological objects, in the absence of archives, are the only existing documents, and in the last three parts, where they will make it easier to grasp the development of Islamic architecture from its Parthian and Sassanid origins.

On the other hand the inset black and coloured plates express the purely plastic qualities of Iranian art. The documentation assembled here witnesses to an originality peculiar to each period and yet to the permanence of the Iranian spirit through the centuries.

At the end of the book will be found a general map of the country, a bibliography and detailed tables.

In conclusion I should like to express my warmest thanks to everybody who has helped me to assemble the iconography of the book, especially the Keepers of Teheran Museum, the Louvre, the Cabinet de Médailles of the Bibliothèque Nationale, the Musée des Arts décoratifs and Baghdad Museum, as well as Mr Erich F. Schmidt of the Oriental Institute of Chicago and all the private collectors who have preferred to remain anonymous.

A. G.

Paris, February 1962

NOTE ON TRANSLITERATION

In the earlier sections of this book, up to and including the Parthian period, either the Classical name has been given or, where this is not in common use and would confuse, a phonetic equivalent in standard English. From the Sassanians onwards, however, the position changes considerably owing to the fact that our knowledge of names depends first partly and later totally on Islamic authorities.

Although Arabic script was adopted in Iran fairly soon after the Conquest and has remained, with a few trivial modifications, the written script of Iran, it is a commonplace that it is ill-adapted for the transcription of Persian. In particular, the Arabic distinction between long vowels which are written out and which may play also a consonantal role and short vowels which are pronounced but which are not generally written out, is one which suits a Semitic, consonant-rooted language but which is not at all appropriate to an Indo-European language, like Persian, in which vowel-changes are of fundamental importance. The consequence is that pronunciation and stress in Persian tend to be very different from the indications which the spelling would otherwise give. It is, therefore, impossible to provide a system of transliteration which will satisfy both the phonetician and the philologist. The only possible criterion we can use is consistency.

Since this book is meant for students of the art of Iran and not its language the complex apparatus of diacritical marks which are customarily used in the transliteration of Arabic would be confusing and unnecessary. A compromise, therefore, has been effected, in that at least the long vowels have been indicated; this, while far from perfect, will aid both spelling and pronunciation to a certain degree.

In general English phonetic equivalents may be assumed, with the following exceptions:

ā, ī and ū are pronounced *ah*, *ee* and *oo* respectively, short *a* is usually pronounced *e* as in b*e*ck; *i* and *u* are as in b*i*t and b*o*tched

dj is pronounced as in *jazz*

g and *dj* are phonetically interchangeable (e.g. *Gūrgān* has the alternative *Djurdjān*)

gh is the voiced equivalent of the *ch* in the Scottish *loch*; it sounds rather like a guttural French *r*

h, more or less, as in *hat*

k as in *keeper*

kh, which is the unvoiced equivalent of *gh*, is pronounced like the *ch* in *loch*

n before *b* is pronounced *mb* (*Gunbad*, dome or tomb, is for this reason sometimes written as *Gumbad*)

p is strongly aspirated

q is a more guttural *k*, as in king*c*up

w is midway between the English *v* and the English *w* (*aw* is, however, pronounced *ow*)

Notwithstanding this programme, when the spelling which this system produces differs *very* widely from its traditional English equivalent, the 'English' has been given in brackets. And in a few cases, for example, Teheran, it was felt that the result would be merely confusing. These names have, therefore, been left as they are.

CONTENTS

ILLUSTRATIONS

FIGURES

MAPS

1. CARBONIFEROUS POTTERY JAR
Alburz. *c.* 2400–2200 BC. Height: 8½ in. Private collection.
This vase, decorated with lozenges, is shaped like a female bust with breasts very close together, which have prominent orifices so that the water spurts out when the vase is filled. Other pieces of grey pottery have been found on the same site.

2. SMALL VASE: BURNISHED CARBONIFEROUS POTTERY
Alburz. *c.* 2400–2200 BC. Length: 5¼ in. Private collection.
This egg-shaped vase is pointed at each end and has a neck which broadens out. A snake in relief decorates the spine. The body is fine and well worked. This rare and highly original piece comes from the same site as the jar in plate 1.

3. SMALL PERFUME-BOTTLE
Susa. 3000–2800 BC. Length: 2¾ in. Louvre.
This alabaster dove was no doubt used to hold some precious liquid.

4. LIMESTONE STATUETTE
Susa. *c.* 3000–2800 BC. Height: 4½ in. Louvre.
This statue represents a man squatting; on his knees he holds a jar for holding perfume.

5. A CYLINDER OF THE AKKADIAN PERIOD
Provenance unknown, possibly Mesopotamia. 2400–2200 BC. Height: about ¼ in.; diameter about ⅛ in. Rietberg Museum, Zurich.
Fight between the hero Gilgamesh and a water-buffalo. This theme, repeated antithetically, is accompanied by the motif of a lion rampant attacking a rampant bull. Unlike the water-buffalo, the bull has quite small horns. This theme of animals fighting one another and of Gilgamesh fighting wild beasts is characteristic of the Akkadian period.

6. CERAMIC CUP
Necropolis, Susa. *c.* 3200 BC. Diameter: 7½ in. Louvre.
This cup has a fine cream-coloured body. The interior is decorated with three comb-like motifs. In the centre a triangle encloses a triple cross.

7. VASE FOR LIBATIONS
Necropolis B, Siyalk. 1000–800 BC. Height: 5⅞ in.; length, including spout: 12⅜ in. Coiffard collection. Louvre.
A pink vase with a long beak-like spout and handle. On each side are seen moufflon in profile painted in aubergine slip. The rest of the decoration, also in aubergine, is geometrical. Vases with long spouts generally come from necropolises where they were no doubt used for funeral rites.

8. TRIPODAL JAR
Luristān region. *c.* 1100–900 BC. Height: 4¾ in. Coiffard collection. Louvre.
This wide-mouthed jar is of a gritty, coarse body. It could be hung up by its two handles. The belly is decorated in aubergine with geometrical motifs.

9. TERRA-COTTA REVETMENT TILES
Susa. *c.* 1165–1151 BC. Height: 4 ft 5 in. Louvre.
These three panels decorated a temple built at Susa by Kutir-Nahunta and his brother Shilak-Inshushinak, King of Anzhan and Susa.

I

2

3

4

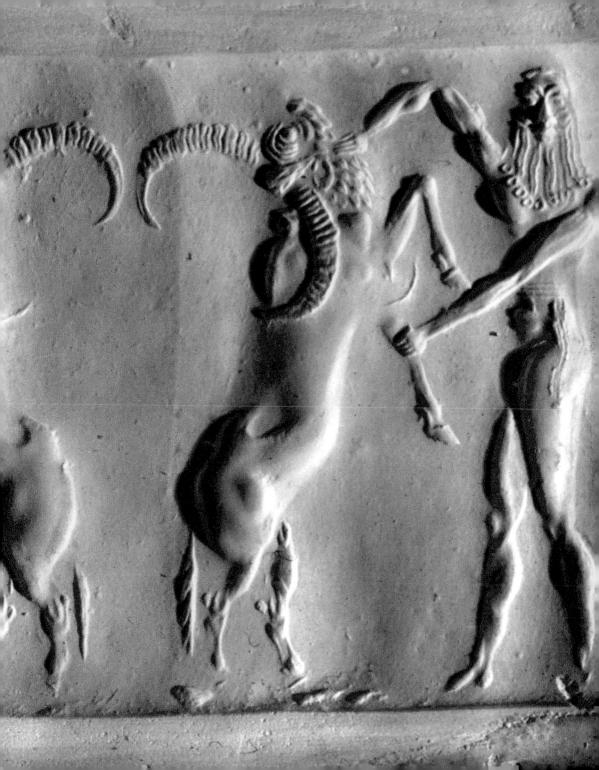

6

7

8

PART ONE

ANCIENT IRAN

CHAPTER 1

THE IRANIAN PLATEAU AND
THE ZAGRUS MOUNTAINS

I RAN is an enormous plateau surrounded by gigantic mountains. The interior of
this virtual fortress, the lofty battlements of which almost totally exclude the passage of rain clouds, is a rocky wilderness, almost a desert. The outer provinces are
humid and fever is rampant. For several months of the year they suffer from intense
heat. In the absence of easy communications, the rural centres are mainly villages or
agricultural market towns, sometimes still surrounded by ancient defensive walls. The
principal towns lie on the plain, at the foot of the mountains on the periphery, along an
irregular line of oases which have formed or been exploited at the mouths of spring
torrents and streams from deep ravines where the winter snows melt slowly. However,
these oases are few in number and small in size and although Isfahān—an exception—
has become a large industrial town, the chief manufacturing town of Iran, it is because
it has a river, the Zanda Rūd, which is almost dry in summer, but is a river nevertheless. In an attempt to increase its volume, part of the course of an affluent of the River
Kārūn, which rises nearby, has been connected with it. A few years ago, Teheran, the
capital of Iran, where large-scale works for increasing the water supply are now going
on, was only able to exist thanks to some forty underground culverts called qanats,
which brought water from sources in the Alburz Mountains about eleven miles away.
Yazd, another industrial town, is supplied in the same primitive fashion. Kirmān,
Gulpāygān, Sāwi, Dāmghān, Samnān, etc., are even worse off for water.

In other words there is a constant shortage of water on the Iranian plateau and the
small amount there is is found only in the narrow fringe of vegetation which runs
along the foot of the more important mountain ranges; even then it is frequently only
represented by scattered green patches on the edge of the desert. But in the ranges of
mountains around the edge of the plateau, especially in the Alburz and Zagrus (Zagros)
ranges to the west and north of Iran, there are enormous, beautiful valleys. They are
richly endowed by nature and in them a great part, much more than was previously
believed, of the ancient history of Iran unfolded. The Zagrus range, about 725 miles
long and more than seventy-five miles wide, is made up of regular parallel folds of more
or less the same height. They are separated by depressions thirty or even sixty miles
long, which are sometimes as much as fifteen miles wide. The only means of communica-

tion between them is by precipitous paths, where only skilled mountaineers dare
venture, and passes at a height of more than 9,000 feet. Every kind of extreme of
climate can be found there, from the stifling heat of the low valleys to the acute cold of
the perpetually snow-clad peaks. As a result, therefore, of these variations in altitude,
which make it possible to grow the most varied crops, as a result of the rainfall on the
slopes of the mountains which face towards the sea, and the heat which this region experiences because of its comparatively southerly altitude, the Zagrus range, which will
be frequently mentioned in the first part of this book, is a region of multiple resources,
suitable for raising livestock in every season. But the exploitation of these resources
imposes a very special way of life on the inhabitants of the region. As soon as spring
comes the heat drives the flocks and their keepers from the low valleys, where they
have spent the winter, and forces them to make for the peaks where they stay until the
late autumn snows send them down again. Nomadism is the rule in these mountains;
not, of course, fundamental nomadism, when whole tribes are constantly on the move
with their flocks in search of subsistence, but what we might call a localized nomadism
(or transhumance), from the mountains to the valleys and vice versa. In addition only a
part of the population of the tribes accompanies the flocks when they move. The old
people, young children and the infirm are settled, as are, more or less continuously, the
craftsmen; weavers, smelters, blacksmiths, leather dressers, goldsmiths and farmers.
As a rule they live fairly high up in the mountains, at about 4,500 feet, the level of
staple crops, around vast organized sites where the shepherds and their flocks stop and
rest on their way up or down. There is no doubt that, towards the end of the second
millennium BC, a great number of the famous Luristān bronzes were executed up
there, in these villages which controlled comings and goings in the mountains.

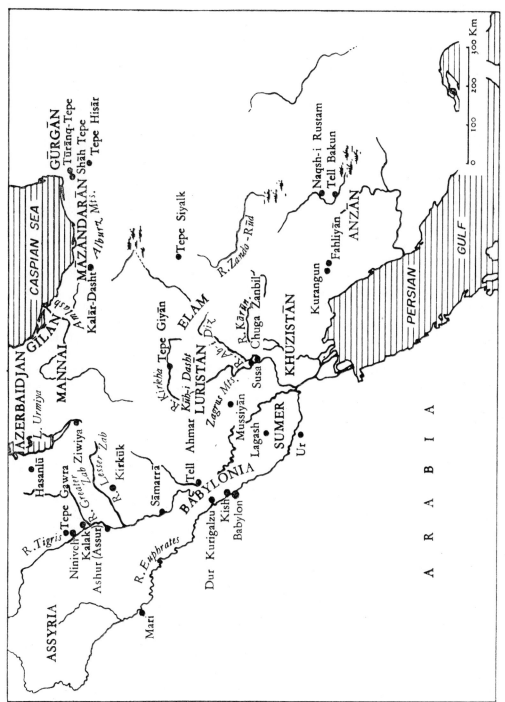

ANCIENT IRAN

CHAPTER 2

ANCIENT IRAN

T HE Zagrus region seems to have been occupied at a very remote time by peoples whose origin is still unknown. They are called Asianic, the term by which the inhabitants of this part of Asia in prehistoric times are generally designated.
It is probable that as early as the pre-historic period groups of these so-called Asianic peoples inhabited villages near the sources of rivers and that, even if they mainly subsisted by hunting, they gradually became farmers and stock raisers. They had domesticated some species of animals, including various sorts of sheep and oxen, and the large number of spindle-whorls of sunbaked clay found on the site of their first settlements is adequate proof that they had already mastered the art of weaving. They used the sling and the club rather than the bow, when hunting, and hoes of chipped stone and flint knives for farming. Metal had not yet made its appearance. Without a potter's wheel they made very simple vases which they baked in the open air on brush-wood fires. At least that is what we have learned from the archaeological excavations carried out in Iran over the last twenty-five years.[1]

Little primitive villages of sun-baked brick developed gradually as the inhabitants of the country devoted themselves increasingly to agriculture and the need for a larger supply of manpower was felt. The hunters who had become comparatively settled built kilns and discovered a method of moulding bricks, which considerably altered the aspect of their houses. Their taste improved and this was particularly obvious in the art of pottery. The shapes of their pots became more elegant. At first the decoration imitated basket-work, but later flights of birds and files of ibexes, depicted in a way which was at the same time naturalistic and schematic, were also used to ornament the vases.

Then metal-working appeared, although it only developed slowly among these villagers. Copper points began to replace carved bones as the heads of weapons, although flint and obsidian implements and stone clubs and axes were still in more or less general use. Tombs have yielded small pieces of jewellery made of copper, shells from the Persian Gulf, and cornelian and turquoise beads from the eastern regions bearing witness to a system of barter which was already highly developed.

[1] The principal Iranian sites of this period which have been excavated are: Susa (Khūzistān), Tepe Siyalk (near Kāshān), Tepe Hisar (near Dāmghān), Tepe Giyan (near Nihāwand), Tell Bakun (near Persepolis), Tūrān Tepe (Gūrgān) and Hāsānlū (Azerbaidjan).

These simple facts sum up several centuries of material evolution in the life of an agricultural race, which passed slowly from the stone to the bronze age and did so alone, without any outside contributions.

In the following period—still part of the fourth millennium BC—the progress of this rudimentary civilization became more rapid and more significant, but can still be considered as the result of normal local development. Ceramics are now richer and more varied (figs. 1 to 3). In the decoration use is made of further kinds of animals, chasing one another or fighting (figs. 4 and 5), and of a skilful geometry which, in the highly original workshops at Susa, Tell Bakun, Tepe Siyalk, etc., transforms basically animal shapes into what are virtually abstract patches and lines. The latter are more closely connected with the strange world of superstitions than simple decorative art (figs. 6 to 10 and pl. 6).

For ancient man, living a wretched and precarious existence, attributed the untoward events of his hard life to the action of evil powers, very much as our own Middle Ages accused the Devil of being the author of all its evils. He feared the 'evil eye', the fate which the baleful powers capriciously inflicted on humanity, and tried to protect himself against it with all sorts of talismans. Even today Iranians claim to preserve themselves from the selfsame terrors by carefully chosen amulets. These objects had— as they still have today—to accompany man throughout his daily existence, to surround him, so to speak, with their protection, and that is how we may explain primitive man's taste for representing the sun, for example, by its rays and its animal attributes: the eagle, the lion, the bull, different sorts of goat, and the various symbols with which he decorated his pottery.

No doubt the need for protective divinities also made itself felt, for at an early stage the storm, the river and the wild beasts which threatened man, his house, his flock and his crops were adored, and the tree, symbol of the forest, was deified. Even today almost every village in Iran preserves and looks piously after a large plane-tree which is looked upon as a kind of guardian angel. Sometimes a traveller sees an isolated tree right in the middle of the desert. Since trees normally only grow in naturally humid or artificially irrigated places, a tree which grows in the most arid place of all—miraculously as it seems—becomes sacred. On seeing it the man makes a wish, ties a nondescript rag to its branches, perhaps a reminder of ancient libations and ancient sacrifices, and goes on his way with his mind more at ease.

It was not surprising, therefore, that these primitive amulets underwent a gradual transformation into works of art. This was the case with idols (fig. 11 and pl. 1) which remained amorphous for a long time. These were the representation, in varying degrees of crudity, of a female personage, and have been found on a great number of archaeological sites. Nearly every religion has preserved the memory of the mother goddess in whose person people venerated the very principle of existence, the symbol of fertility and abundance and which this naïve image represents. Her cult was subsequently displaced by that of male deities, of whom she remained both wife and mother.

The decorative repertory of the pottery of the fourth millennium is made up of these various elements or parts of them: the horns of a bull or an ibex, a bird's wing, the

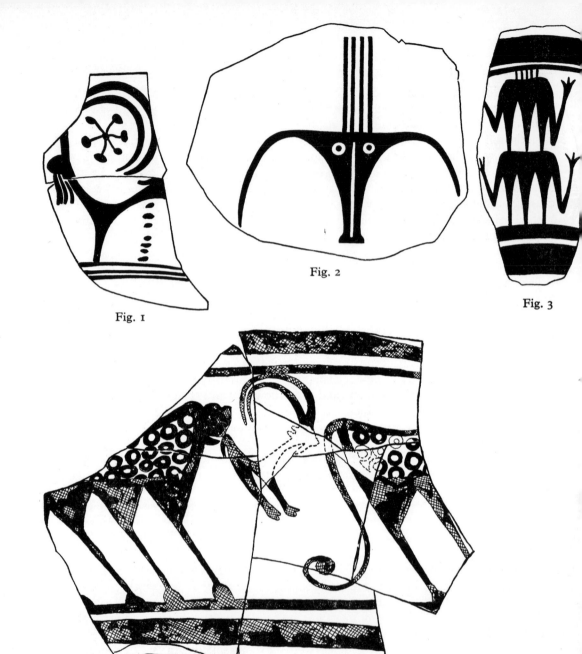

Fig. 1

Fig. 2

Fig. 3

Fig. 4

Fig. 5

Fig. 6

Fig. 7

Fig. 8

Fig. 9

Fig. 10

lion's head and the foot of some wading bird, to name a few examples. The energy and continuity of this art led to its diffusion over the whole of the high plateau and even beyond.

During this period metal-working developed even more rapidly, no doubt encouraged by the type of life which the possession of numerous flocks began to impose on a section of the population. In fact, it developed so rapidly and in such a way that perhaps we are justified in situating the home of metal-working in the range of mountains bordering the Iranian plateau. Metal-working, that vital discovery, could only have been the result of fortunate circumstances exploited by peoples who had rich mineral deposits and vast forests near their settlements. Now we know that the Iranian mountain dwellers had, within easy reach, vast quantities of the ores they had learnt to smelt and also of the firewood which they used to stoke their pottery kilns. Heavy weapons and instruments tend to disappear. Copper knives, daggers, cold chisels and arrowheads abound. Articles of adornment are made of cornelian and turquoise as before, but also of lapis-lazuli and there are long copper pins with hemi-spherical heads and necklaces of mother-of-pearl, rock-crystal and jade. Button- and later cylinder-seals (figs. 12a and b, and 13) appeared and their use spread quickly. They were made of rare local stones, sea-shells, turquoise and lapis-lazuli brought from increasingly distant areas where these precious materials were bartered for agricultural produce. 'During this period there is nothing to denote disturbances or radical changes caused by the appearance of foreign elements.' But at the end of the fourth millennium, as the result of events as yet unknown, possibly an Elamite invasion, the Caspian lands began to feel the influence of the civilization of their south-western neighbours. From the most remote periods and throughout the third millennium, Gilgamesh, the deified hero whose legend and epic have been so often quoted, was represented on cylinder-seals (fig. 14 and pl. 5).

At the end of the fourth millennium clay tablets with signs representing sounds and words appeared at Susa, Tepe Siyalk and Tepe Giyan. From that time onwards, as had happened earlier in Sumer, there were undoubtedly scribes in Iran whose main occupation was to keep the accounts of church property. These hieroglyphs, known as proto-Elamite, do not seem to have been followed up, whereas the Sumerian ones evolved naturally from pictography to the creation of a genuine syllabic language. This language made rapid progress during the third millennium: laws, prayers and invocations to the divinity were written down.

The need to express feelings accepted by these various peoples in common led to their diffusion throughout the high Caspian plateau. As for religion, it is still very difficult from the artistic point of view to specify the known data: belief in an after-life, fear of the mysterious beyond (pl. 4) and consequently the worship of chthonic divinities, of which the serpent is one of the animal attributes.

It appears that, in Iran, side by side with the age-old devotion to the great fertility gods, the cult of a snake god as a symbol of fecundity was particularly active from the fourth to the first millennium BC. That it remained active is shown by button-seals (figs. 12a and b), vases of grey carboniferous pottery (pl. 2), as well as important rock

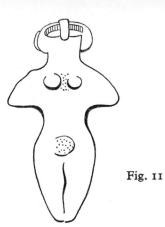

Fig. 11

(a)   (b)

Fig. 12

Fig. 13

Fig. 14

bas-reliefs of which traces can still be seen at Naqsh-i Rustam[1] and Kurangun[2] (fig. 15), for example.

Fig. 15

At the end of the third and during the second millennium bronze work was practised with increasing skill. Fine weapons were produced and examples have been found in the various archaeological excavations of the Fertile Crescent and Mesopotamia. It would seem that each of these human groups tried to improve or copy the weapons of its neighbour. In contrast the pottery on archaeological sites where numerous bronze objects have been discovered seems to be less beautiful and delicate.

Carboniferous pottery made its appearance in the course of the third millennium and is still used by the inhabitants of northern Iran. However, a variant of the grey carboniferous pottery with unusual shapes is found at Tūrān Tepe and Shāh Tepe (in the Astarābād-Gūrgān region), which are the very places where terra-cotta figurines have been discovered showing a certain skill in representing human beings in the round (fig. 16). These statuettes, the heads of which have a circular depression so that hair can be attached to them and which have deep sunken eyes meant to be filled with some white matter, are unknown on the plateau and are not found anywhere else in the world to the best of my knowledge, unless perhaps in the Aegean islands. We may suppose that they are the work of a people from the east who moved westwards along the Caspian Sea towards the middle of the second millennium without crossing the Alburz Mountains and ultimately ended their journey in the Aegean islands.

[1] A few miles north-west of Persepolis.
[2] On a rock overlooking the River Fahliyān, north of Būshūr.

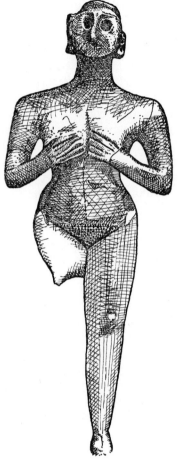

Fig. 16

THE LURISTĀN BRONZES

In the time of Samsu-Iluna,[1] the Kassites, who had overrun Iran, threatened the eastern frontier of the Babylonian kingdom, but were conquered and thrown back into their mountains. Around 1530 BC they seized their opportunity, reappeared on the plain, and a little later, in 1500 BC, founded a Kassite Babylonian dynasty which lasted for several centuries. In 1168 BC they were, however, decisively repulsed as far as the Zagrus Mountains by the King of Elam, Shutruk Nahhunta.[2] They then lost their political importance. But we must not lose sight of them: Assyrian texts mention the

[1] Son of Hammurabi, King of Babylon (1728–1685 BC), according to the chronology of Poebel and Cavaignac.
[2] Shutruk Nahhunta, c. 1200 BC.

Kashshu who clashed with the authority of the Kings of Assur, and later Greek historians frequently allude to those 'belligerent barbarian tribes renowned for their warlike
valour'. Alexander the Great had to fight them and we know that in 317 BC Antigonus,[1]
leaving Seleucus[2] to besiege Susa, entered the land of the Kosseans (or Kassites) without having agreed to pay them the customary tribute and that his troops, 'harassed by
these savage mountaineers', suffered a great deal.

In the middle of the second millennium, at the time of the conquest of Babylon,
they had already become a thriving people of peasants, nomadic stock raisers and
warriors who, according to Strabo, could 'put at the disposal of the Elymaids[3] on
occasion as many as 13,000 archers to help them when fighting the Susians and Babylonians'. They had intermarried with Aryans who had penetrated on to the plateau in
the course of remote and unrecorded migrations, but these Aryans had been so completely assimilated that one could not really say that they modified the fundamental
unity of the aboriginal population in the slightest.

For the greater part of the year most of them inhabited the high plains of the Dasht-i
Khawa, the Dasht-i Alishtar and the Māhī-Dasht, to the north of the Zagrus Mountains, living as nomads and devoting themselves to horse breeding. It is from their
tombs grouped near the springs by which they camped in these high plains of Luristān
that the numerous bronze, gold, silver and even iron objects which have been discovered since 1928 have come. These objects are both offensive and defensive weapons:
daggers, swords, maces, shields, axes, the heads of arrows and lances; items of harness
for horses: bits for everyday use (fig. 17), bits for breaking-in, ceremonial bits (pl. 24);
bracelets (figs. 18 and pl. 31), fibulae, buttons, mirrors, toilet accessories; vases of every
kind: vases for funerary libations (fig. 19), cups, goblets and even, at a later period,
situlae[4] (fig. 20) decorated with scenes borrowed from Assyrian mythology; cylinder
seals (fig. 21), representations of the Great God, the Great Goddess and especially
of the Mesopotamian hero Gilgamesh (figs. 22 and 23), as well as his companion
Enkidu.

From these two heroes Luristān borrowed fashions and created composite creatures
(see plates 16, 17, 18 and 19). During the time of the nomadic warriors and hunters we
believe to have been Kassites, the inhabitants of Luristān looked on these creatures as
protective spirits. Figure 32 shows the transfiguration of Enkidu when he took his
place in the pantheon of these mountain-dwelling Lurs.

The traditional hero of Mesopotamian art, Gilgamesh, shown in pl. 5, is well known.
However this character was completely transformed in Luristān and became a mere
talisman, an amulet which lost every trace of ceremonial character through constant

---

[1] Antigonus, known as Cyclops (the one-eyed), one of Alexander the Great's generals, satrap of
Pamphylia, Lycia and Greater Phrygia *c.* 323 BC, strategus of the Asian armies *c.* 321 BC. Proclaimed himself king *c.* 306 BC; killed *c.* 301 BC at Ipsus.

[2] Seleucus I, general of Alexander the Great, satrap and later king of Babylonia. Founder of the
Seleucid dynasty (*c.* 305–280 BC).

[3] The Greek name for the Elamites.

[4] In the art of the Zagrus Mountains, the *situla* was used for fetching the water required for various
ceremonies.

Fig. 17

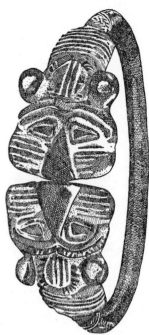

Fig. 18

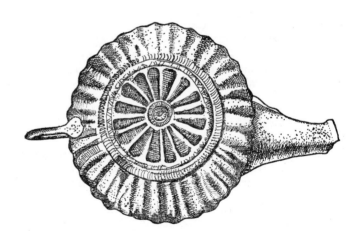

Fig. 19

Fig. 20

10. LEFT SIDE OF A BRONZE BIT

Luristān. 1200–1000 BC. Height: 7⅜ in. Coiffard collection. Louvre.
This object represents a winged monster. The human head is crowned with a sort of crescent moon or horned tiara. The wing ends in a grimacing animal head.

11. DETAIL OF THE BLADE OF A BRONZE DAGGER

Zagrus Mountains. c. 1000–900 BC. Length: 1 ft. 1 9/16 in.; width: 7 1/16 in. Coiffard collection. Louvre.
On this blade is engraved a deer with its feet folded under its body. Rosettes and intertwined ribbons form the decorative background.

12. HANDLE OF A WHETSTONE: BRONZE

Zagrus Mountains. 1100–900 BC. Height: 4 5/16 in. Coiffard collection. Louvre.
This object represents the fore-quarters of two paired ibexes carved in the round.
Whetstones were indispensable in the age of bronze weapons. All types of them were made, some of them very beautiful. They seem to have been, more or less, articles of male jewellery.

13. BRONZE AXE WITH DIGITATIONS

From a tomb in the region of Kirmānshāh (western Iran). Beginning of first millennium BC. Length: 5½ in. Archaeological Museum, Teheran.
One of the five digitations of this axe is replaced by a vulture's head. The blade is decorated in relief by a fantastic figure, wearing a kind of bonnet. In his arms he holds a fish, symbol of the Mesopotamian god Ea and the Canaanite god Dagon.

14. AXE OF A VERY ANCIENT TYPE

From excavations carried out by Professor Ghirshman at Chuga Zambil, an Elamite town situated near Susa. 1250 BC. Length: 4¾ in. Louvre.
The socket of this bronze axe is decorated with a gold or electrum animal, probably a wild boar. The blade, which bears an inscription in the name of the King of Elam, Untash-Huban, springs from a lion's head.

15. BRONZE HALBERD

The Harsin region south of Kirmānshāh (Luristān). End of second millennium BC. Width: 6 11/16 in.; height: 4⅛ in. Private collection.
The blade, its upper edge decorated with a row of guilloches, is joined to the socket by a bearded human head, seen full-face. The socket, encircled by three groups of bands, is surmounted by the stylized animal most frequently represented in Luristān.

16. SIDE-PIECE OF A CEREMONIAL BIT

Luristān region. c. 1200–1000 BC. Height: 6¼ in. Private collection.
This side-piece represents the 'protector of flocks', wearing the horned tiara. His arms hold apart two winged monsters with the heads of birds of prey on a stag's body.

17. HEAD OF BRONZE VOTIVE PIN

Luristān. 800 BC. Diameter: 3⅛ in.; height: 3 1/16 in. Private collection.
The upper part of this disc-headed pin represents the bust of the 'Protector' and two griffins, head downwards. The elongated necks of two fantastic animals enclose this composition in an oval; the pin itself was made of iron.

4

16

17

18

18. BRONZE DECORATION OF A BIT

Luristān. *c.* 1000–900 BC. Diameter: $2\frac{3}{4}$ in.; height: $3\frac{1}{8}$ in. Private collection.
This ornament, consisting of a wheel with six spokes, is surmounted by the head of the hero wearing the horned tiara. Two animals clinging to the outside of the wheel are turned towards him.

19. BRONZE IDOL

Luristān. *c.* 1000–800 BC. $6\frac{1}{8}$ in. Private collection.
This idol represents the protector of the flocks holding two monsters at arm's length. He himself is supported by a group of human heads and cocks' heads. We do not know what they symbolize.

20. DISC-SHAPED BRONZE PENDANT

Provenance unknown, but possibly from Luristān. End of second millennium BC. Height: $5\frac{1}{16}$ in.; width: $4\frac{9}{16}$ in. Musée du Cinquantenaire, Brussels.

Fig. 21

Fig. 22

Fig. 23

use. We might almost imagine that religiosity had given way to animal art as the result of an evolution, possibly as a result of Assyrian influence . . . or we might believe that art for art's sake was born in Luristān . . . but we know that art for art's sake never existed in ancient civilizations and that even if the panther, for example, appears on certain vases from Siyalk and Hisar, it was in the hope of rendering it harmless. So as to make this more credible, it was depicted with its head cut off.

In spite of the very pronounced Assyrian influence, we find something quite different in Luristān, the systematic exaggeration of the particular features of each animal: the elongated neck and bulging eyes of gazelles, for example (fig. 24), is to some extent their caricature, in the good sense of the word. In short, they show an imaginativeness and witty observation which did not exist in Assyria. Incidentally, this may not have been an innate gift of the Luristān craftsmen and was perhaps the contribution to the art of Zagrus of those Aryans who gradually mingled with the indigenous population and became its aristocracy.

In the settlements where stout stone walls effectively protected men and flocks from wild beasts, the hero,[1] in the form we know him, naked or almost so, is represented running at full speed with a snake in each hand (fig. 25). The snake was a familiar figure in ancient Iranian imagery. Ideal as a garland, it was used to decorate the edge of ancient pots (pl. 2) on which it appeared undulating on the ground like meandering water and disappearing mysteriously into itself. It became the symbol of good and evil, one of the representations of water, i.e. of abundance, and one of the animal attributes of the chthonic divinities.

We come across it throughout the art of Luristān, even during its latest period. Indeed we know several situlae on which the well-known vase spouting water is depicted, but with the two traditional jets of water represented as snakes.

Elsewhere the hero, always shown running, carries pomegranates, i.e. one of the symbols and perhaps, in Luristān, the main symbol of fertility (fig. 26). As well as a swift servant, actively devoted to the peasants' interests, bearer of the snake, the pomegranate and doubtless other symbols of the earth cult which is still obscure to us, he became yet another figure: the fecundator. To my personal knowledge two pins show him in this role. He is naked, horned and bearded; he carries a lamb in one hand, a goose in the other, and runs at full speed, as is his habit (fig. 26). On the other pin he appears impregnating a flower, yet still running.

However, he is not the god of fertility. In Luristān, as in the Mesopotamian plain, this god was most often identified with the principal creator of everything, the Great God or Great Goddess. At first the deity might be either because it appears that this principle, 'father and mother which created itself', 'mother and lord', was originally of indeterminate sex. Later, in Sumer, in the role of Great God, he is mainly depicted as 'the god of summits, storm and beneficent rain'. He bears different names according to the region. His animal attributes are the bull and various kinds of goat. The Great

---

[1] The legendary hero Gilgamesh, considered to have been the king of the very ancient town of Erech (Uruk-Warqā), a great hunter of wild animals, lions, bulls, boars, etc., became for this reason the protector of flocks, crops, in short a sort of fertility spirit.

Fig. 24

Fig. 25

Fig. 26

Fig. 27

Fig. 28

Goddess or earth goddess is his spouse. Sumer, Elam and Iran knew her as the 'naked goddess', but other countries, particularly Asia Minor, clothed her in a long dress.

In Sumer, where he is especially depicted as the god of vegetation, the Great God often holds branches which seem to sprout from his body and are cropped by goats or ibex, his animal attributes. He is thus represented on a bas-relief from Assur which like all Assyrian art can be traced back to Sumer and which Contenau describes in these terms (fig. 29): 'The god, seen full-face, is bearded, a domed tiara covers his head, his body seems to be naked down to the waist; there begins a sort of flared skirt which reaches to the ground . . . the god's arms are held to his chest; he holds two branches at an angle which terminate in three inflorescences in the form of pine-cones arranged in a trefoil shape thus framing his head. At waist height two similar branches seem to emerge from his hips and blossom forth on either side of the personage. To right and left of the god a rampant ibex is supported on the inflorescences of the lower branch cropping the tips of the upper branch.' This description is almost identical with that of the plaque from central Luristān depicted in figure 31. The principal figure, who has a beard, is also seen full-face, his body seems to be naked to the waist and from it there also starts a kind of flared skirt which reaches to the ground. He holds the stems of two small bushes. At waist height two branches also seem to spring from his hips. So the similarity between the two figures is striking. This detail, *inter alia*, is too unusual for it to be a matter of simple coincidence; it seems clear that it is indeed the Great God of fertility who is depicted on the Luristān plaque. As for the rampant animals which in this case are monsters and not ibexes, the animal attributes of the god, as on the stele from Assur, they reproduce another well-known motif from Assyrian sculpture, the guardians of the sacred tree. In Assyria these guardians were generally monsters—half-men, half-animals—from which we can deduce that the objects held by the monsters on our plaque, and which the god also holds, are branches of the sacred tree. Moreover there are two pins on which we find the two ibexes, animal attributes of the god, eating the tree (fig. 30), as well as the monsters which are its guardians (fig. 31).

The plaque probably belongs to the second half of the second millennium BC. Its technique seems to indicate this, as does the fact that the bas-relief from Assur which should be compared with it can be dated to the same period. The small curling plaits of the monsters do not invalidate this dating, for we find identical ones on another monument of the same period, the stele of Untash-Huban,[1] which is in the Louvre; nor do the four wings of the god, very clearly shown on a cylinder which E. Herzfeld published in his *Archäologische Mitteilungen aus Iran*, Berlin (1929–38), and dated to about 1250 BC.

But there is another solid argument for boldness in attributing this date to the plaque. We shall find it in comparing a pin which also comes from central Luristān (fig. 32) with the lower register of the stele of Untash-Huban (fig. 33). The figures on the pin and the stele are so similar that we cannot doubt their close kinship; and even if we hesitate to say which of the two objects was the older, we would tend to assign the

---

[1] Untash-Huban (or Untash Gal), King of Elam, *c.* 1250 BC.

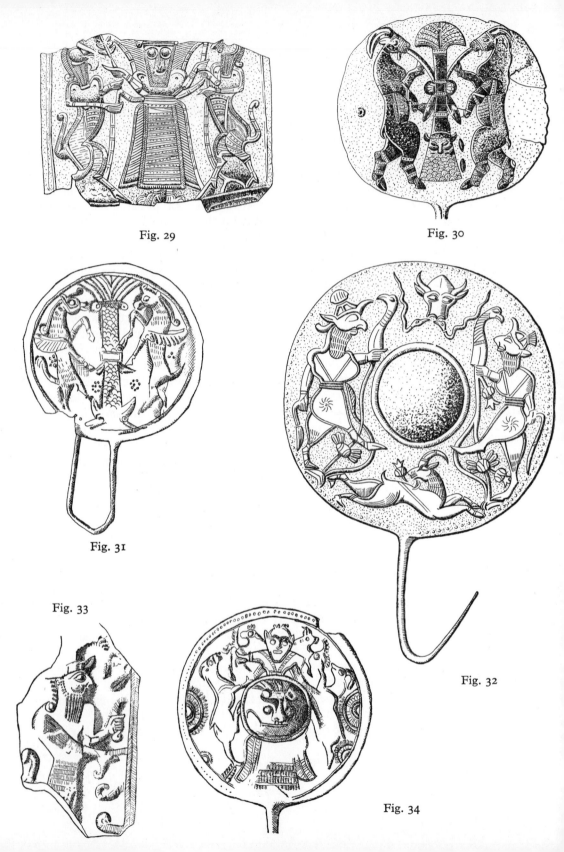

Fig. 29

Fig. 30

Fig. 31

Fig. 33

Fig. 32

Fig. 34

pin to the period of the Stele of the Vultures[1] in the Louvre or the bas-relief of the 'patesi' (ruler) Gudea[2] in the Berlin Museum which shows him led by two gods. This latter relief is admittedly much older, but in it we find the same decorative feeling, the same breadth of expression and the same depiction of the figures. The pin from Luristān represents two spirits in every way like those on the stele. The same typical nose, the same beard, the same thick plaits with their ends curled up, the same strange head-dress where the 'bull or goat' ear is even more marked than on the stele and the same animal hind-quarters. They also hold branches of the sacred trees. Judging by the stele bearing the names of Untash-Huban and his wife, Napir-Asu, who lived during the second half of the second millennium BC according to the chronology of Poebel and Cavaignac, I feel justified in dating our pin to the same period.

If we now compare our pin (fig. 32) with the plaque (fig. 29), we see a confirmation of this attribution in that the same type of art is involved, though a little cruder in the case of the plaque, and the same ideas expressed by means of the same decorative features. The god of fertility is absent from the pin, no doubt because of the *umbo*, or boss it contains, but in both specimens there are two spirits holding the branches of equally small bushes which grow from the soil at their feet. They are both bearded and both have extremely beaked noses. They wear short plaits and have animal hind-quarters.

So we have sound reasons for dating the bas-relief from Assur, the stele of Untash-Huban, the plaque and pin I have just mentioned to the same period, i.e. the second half of the second millennium BC. But the two last-named objects are not the only bronzes from central Luristān which exhibit the very personal accent of Elamite sculpture and glyptics in the time of King Untash-Huban. The pin in figure 34 is only one of many. This pin shows the god of fertility feeding ibexes, his animal attributes, with his substance, for here he is the 'tree god'. Branches appear to spring from his chest. He holds their leafy extremities which the ibexes are eating. This is what we saw on the bas-relief from Assur. The god wears a long fringed robe; the wings indicated in the lower part of the disc prove his divinity and on both his shoulders appears the sacred dragon, symbol of Nin-Gizzida.

Nin-Gizzida, the special god of the ruler Gudea, is the 'lord of the tree of life' of the Sumerian pantheon. Gudea built a temple for him. His son, Ur-Nin-Gursu,[3] dedicated a statue to him. He has been depicted several times, for example on the bas-relief in Berlin already mentioned which represents Gudea being led by two gods. One of these gods, the one who holds the patesi by the left wrist and on whose shoulders stand two dragon's heads, is Nin-Gizzida. We also see him in an analogous presentation scene which decorates a cylinder-seal of the same patesi Gudea (fig. 35). The king is led by a god whose shoulders bear two dragon's heads: Nin-Gizzida.

[1] This stele, one of the main monuments of the Sumerian period, commemorates the victory of a chief of the town of Lagash over the neighbouring town of Umma.

[2] Gudea, prince and ruler of Lagash (2060–2042 BC). Several statues and statuettes of this personage are in the Louvre.

[3] Ur-Nin-Girsu is the son of Gudea. He is not to be confused with the god Nin-Girsu. Ur-Nin-Girsu means 'the servant of the god Nin-Girsu'.

Fig. 35

Fig. 37

Fig. 36

Fig. 38

Fig. 39

It is clearly the 'lord of the tree of life', the 'tree god', who is depicted on the pin in figure 34. The branches which spring from his chest and which the ibexes are cropping classify it with the bas-relief which depicts the god Assur as god of fertility and seem clearly to date it as still in the second half of the second millennium BC.

Decorating another pin (fig. 36), we again find the combination of a standing figure along the main axis of the object with the same large grimacing head on the stomach. Once more it is a god of fertility, not Nin-Gizzida, but Nin-Girsu, 'lord of the beneficent rain', patron of Lagash, as he is represented on a cylinder from the time of Ur, characterized by the protoma of a lion[1] on each shoulder. Lord of the rain and not a tree god, he has no need to feed his ibexes, as Nin-Gizzida does, with branches issuing from himself. He would be carrying them nonchalantly by the hind leg if the maker of the object had known how to draw a closed fist. This clumsily executed pin clearly seems to be contemporary with the preceding one.

Figure 31 shows two winged animals facing each other on either side of a tree. Since the tree is a palm tree and the palm tree, which is unknown in the Kūh-i Dasht where the object was found, is the sacred tree of Sumer, it seems as if this scene, like the preceding ones, was directly borrowed from Sumerian mythology. I may add that it was probably executed at the same period as they were. The fact that the animals have wings does not invalidate this supposition, nor does the sort of capital with Ionic volutes which surmounts the tree trunk. The latter are merely the stylized portrayal of clusters of fruit which sculpture and glyptics usually depict on either side of the trunks of palm trees where the palms begin. These clusters, most commonly represented in the form of spheres, sometimes become volutes in the Kassite period. One can see examples of them in the study E. Herzfeld has devoted to the art of the second millennium in his *Archäologische Mitteilungen aus Iran*. So there is nothing to prevent this fine pin, with the scene it represents dating from the most remote antiquity, from coming in fact from the second half of this millennium—since technique and dimensions are those of the pins with which it was found, with no detail *apparently* later than the middle of the second millennium.

The sacred tree, sometimes presented as a god in its own right, flanked by animals which guard or eat it is, no doubt, the favourite decorative element or at any rate the most frequently found element in the art of western Asia from its origins down to modern times. It figures, as does the god of fertility, on many objects found in Luristān. As we have just seen, it is generally represented surrounded by animals or monsters. But it has also been found on some rare pins, all by itself and occupying the whole of the space to be decorated (fig. 37). On a very beautiful plaque from Kūh-i Dasht of which unfortunately only one half remains (fig. 38), it is flanked by two winged bulls, treated most remarkably, to judge by what is left. Their necks are thinner than a horse's and their hind-quarters are more like a greyhound's than massive and bovine. I have not found the like of this bull drawn in such a manner anywhere but in Luristān. But it could I think only have been invented during a very extensive and pure

---

[1] Forepart of an animal's body, used as a decorative motif in sculpture. See, for example, the protoma of a lion in Plate 36.

period of Sumerian art, obviously not that of Gudea which is far too remote, but that of Untash-Huban. Once again the tree is the sacred palm tree of Sumer. In the design of the object we can make out one of the two spherical clusters traditionally attached to the top of the trunk from which the palm fronds spring and something of the fronds themselves. Below the bull there are two intertwined snakes similar, *qua* snakes, to those which decorate the libationary vase of Gudea and, *qua* decorative motif, to the plait-work which can be seen in the Louvre on a bas-relief of bituminous clay which dates from about 2900 BC. Here they serve to underline the scene which they some-times frame; for example on the stele of Untash-Huban, on the 'unfinished Kudurru',[1] or 'anepigraphic Kudurru', or again on the 'Kudurru of King Marduk-Zakir-Shum'.[2] Between the neck of the bull and the tree there is a bird of prey which holds an animal in its talons.

The palm tree, the snakes, the bulls, which are all attributes of the Great God of fertility, take us back again to the Elam of Untash-Huban which definitely seems to have been the great inspirer of the bronze-founders of central Luristān during the second half of the second millennium BC.[3]

But just as the 'naked goddess' does not venture into the vast plains of northern Luristān without her masculine counterpart (pl. 26 and 27), so the Great God of fertility cannot go among the settled peoples without the goddess of fertility. As G. Contenau says, 'the union of the Great God and the Goddess is necessary to produce human unions, the reproduction of flocks and even the union of elements from which the rain will come, for example, by a kind of sympathetic magic'. However, although we are well acquainted with the Great Goddess of the horse breeders, we do not know what the goddess of the settled tribes looked like.

After the looting of the temple of Surkh Dum[4] by the Lurs a cornelian bead in the form of an olive has been found; on it is engraved the following inscription: 'Kurigalzu to the temple of the god Sin' (fig. 40). The period of the Kassite King Kurigalzu,[5] assuming that it is he, agrees perfectly with that of the manufacture of the majority of the objects I have already mentioned and shall refer to again. This inscription might be very important if it was established that it really came from Kūh-i Dasht. For one thing it would prove that there was at least one temple of the god Sin in this region, at Surkh Dum or elsewhere.

We have already seen some representations (fig. 32) of beings we may call 'spirits', half-men, half-animals, usually guardians of the sacred tree. Here are some others. One of them carries the sacred tree of Sumer, a palm tree, over his shoulder with one hand and with the other he carries an ibex, head downwards (fig. 41). He is bearded, has

---

[1] Stele or boundary-stone used to demarcate properties by placing them under the protection of the gods. It is analagous to the Hermae used as mile-stones and boundary-stones in Greece.

[2] For all these, cf. G. Contenau: *Manuel d'archéologie orientale*, pp. 900–909.

[3] Indeed it is Elam of the time of Untash-Huban which seems to have been the great inspirer of all the Luristān bronze-founders.

[4] The temple of Surkh Dum was discovered and excavated by E. Schmidt in the Kūh-i Dasht, a valley in central Luristān.

[5] The Kassite King Kurigalzu I reigned in Babylon about 1425 BC. North of Babylon he founded a royal residence bearing his name, Dur Kurigalzu, which acquired great importance.

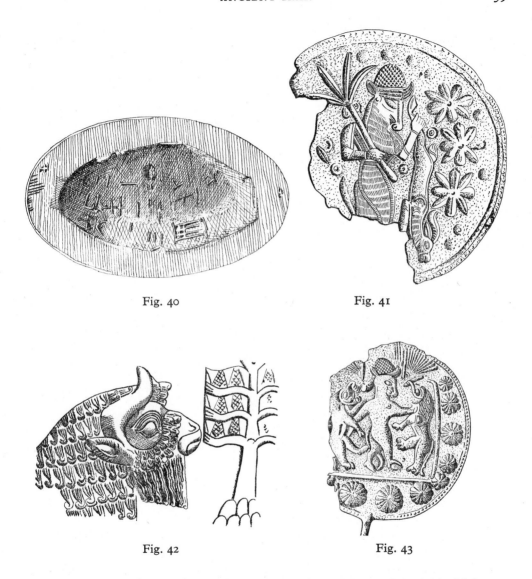

Fig. 40

Fig. 41

Fig. 42

Fig. 43

a trunk-shaped nose and wears the domed tiara of the god Assur, decorated with horns.
According to an established convention which a detail from a bowl of bituminous
stone dating from the middle of the third millennium (fig. 42) illustrates perfectly,
these horns are depicted in profile when they would naturally be full-face. We also see
that he has ears like those of the 'spirits' in figures 32 and 41. Now the pin shown in
figure 32 probably dates from the second half of the second millennium and we know
that the habit of carrying a small tree is current with the figures on a Karkūk[1] glyptics,

[1] Karkūk, the modern Kirkuk near Mosul in Iraq.

which correspond roughly to the middle of the second millennium. Moreover the eight-pointed stars, so to say, to be seen between the man and the edge of the disc have been studied by E. Herzfeld, who considers them as absolutely characteristic of the second millennium. So we find once again works influenced by Sumerian art, towards the end of the second millennium.

We come across the same figure, half-man, half-beast, with a nose like a trunk and wearing the domed horned tiara, in the decoration of the pin shown in figure 43. He is not shown as guardian of the tree, but in the attitude of the hero taming wild beasts. He is again depicted several times on the magnificent pin[1] which appears in figure 44.

Fig. 44

At the top and bottom of the disc, in pairs, four of these figures with animal hind-quarters hold sacred branches which end in birds' heads, as in figure 32. To right and left, also in pairs, four figures, identical with the first four down to the waist, hold the lance of Marduk;[2] but they wear skirts, have men's feet and are possibly priests.

Of the temple servants, it is reasonable to accept the bearers of palms in figures 45 and 48 as priests, as well as a priestess who is a sacred dancer (fig. 47). The two men in figure 48 each hold a palm in one hand. In the other, the figures on the left hold a snake by the tail. We do not know what the figure on the right is doing, because the pin, from the temple of Surkh Dum, had been damaged on that side, but it is likely

---

[1] Some parts of this beautiful pin, to left and right, are not authentic, but the rest of it is.
[2] This lance is the symbol of the god Marduk.

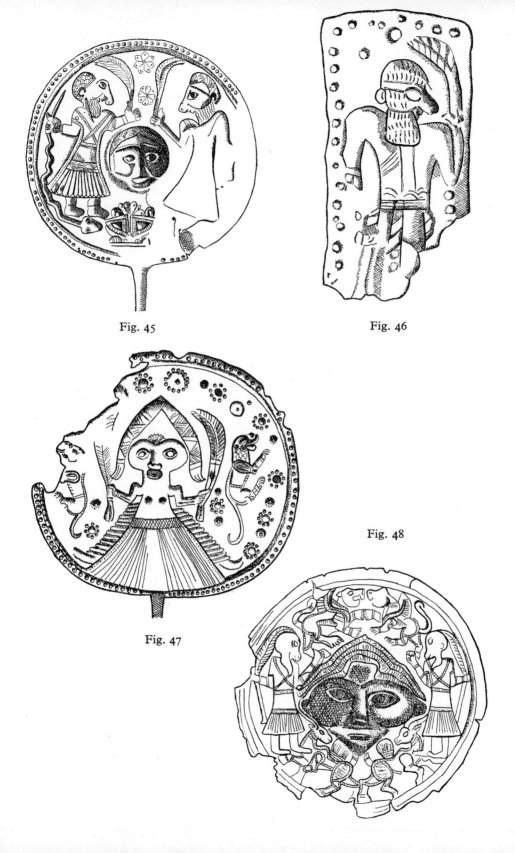

Fig. 45

Fig. 46

Fig. 48

Fig. 47

that he is making the same gesture. They are both dressed in robes which are flared and pleated at the bottom, like that of the Queen of Elam, Napir-Asu, in the Louvre, but shorter, for the Queen's dress only reached to the ground to ensure the stability of a bronze object weighing some 4 tons. Our men with the palms have the trunk-like nose we have already seen on the faces of a certain number of 'spirits' and on their heads wear the domed tiara with imbricated ornaments which we have already seen several times.

The scene represented has no relation to those in which we have seen the protective hero running with a snake in each hand (fig. 25). The figures on our pin do not run, the idea of running water is not expressed and the disrespectful way in which the snake is held is adequate proof that here we have a slain, dead snake. Yet why do the two men offer each other a palm so ceremoniously? I think that these palms, which are not fly-whisks, are rather like the bundle or *barsom*[1] of Mazdaism, implements of the local cult and that the scene depicted is a religious one, perhaps that of the destruction of the snake as a symbol of evil.

Another man bearing palms (fig. 46) is bearded and also has a trunk-like nose; he is bare-headed but his hair is bound by a sort of bandeau; he also bears a palm upright in front of him, like a candle. If we consider, as it is natural to do, that the figures with this characteristic nose date from the same period, we should consider the genii previously examined and our men with the palms as contemporary with each other. Now several of these genii were certainly executed before the end of the second millennium BC. Incidentally this attribution is confirmed, as regards our personages with the palms, by the fact that those in figure 45 wear a robe in the fashion of the time of Untash-Huban, i.e. as I have already mentioned, about 1250 BC.

Figure 47 doubtless represents a priestess, a servant of the goddess Nana,[2] performing a ritual dance, the 'rain dance', for example. She is clad in a long dress of light material with multiple pleats and wears a kind of wool bonnet like that of the head in figure 55. She too holds a palm in each hand. Two wild beasts and small repoussé rosettes are placed around her, no doubt to satisfy the traditional oriental *horror vacui*. This pin, from the Graeffe collection, is probably less ancient than the preceding ones. It will be dated by consideration of the following series of large female heads.

The faithful, the congregation using the temples, are not completely unknown to us, either. In fact Luristān has yielded, in the company of pins with religious subjects, a fairly large number of small figurines in the round, cast by the *cire perdue* method, generally only a few inches high. These can be grouped with those which have been discovered in Susa, as well as in Mesopotamia, about which there has never been much discussion. They are generally considered as representing 'worshippers'.

We must now consider the large female heads already mentioned, which in my opinion cannot be regarded as representations of astral deities. Like the preceding statuettes they simply seem to me to depict the temple worshippers. Apart from the fact that these female heads cannot symbolize the sun goddess or the moon god, they

---

[1] The fasces called the *barsom* was carried by the priests during certain ceremonies.
[2] Nana, or Anāhit, was considered as a goddess of springs, hence of fertility.

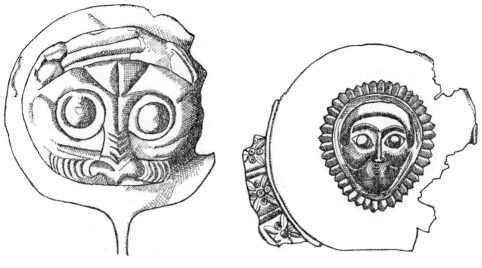

Fig. 49

Fig. 51

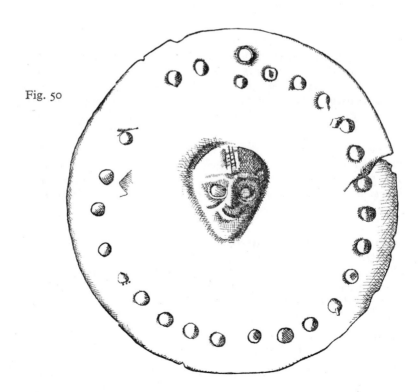

Fig. 50

21. FRAGMENT OF BRONZE PLAQUE

Luristān. End of second millennium BC. Height: 5$\frac{1}{16}$ in.; width: 4$\frac{9}{16}$ in. Rietburg Museum, Zurich.

A standing divinity, with arms outstretched, is in the centre of the composition. He is surrounded by two old men, no doubt priests, each holding a palm and thus forming a kind of arch above the divinity. Their facial appearance recalls that of the old men in plate 23.

22. BRONZE DISC PIN

Luristān. End of second millennium BC. Length: 11$\frac{1}{8}$ in.; diameter: 6 in. Coiffard collection. Louvre.

A human head in bold relief occupies the centre of this composition. It is surrounded by a circle of flutes which are repeated on the edge of the disc.

23. FRAGMENT OF A BRONZE DISC PIN

Luristān. *c.* 1200–1000 BC. Length: 8$\frac{1}{4}$ in.; diameter: 3$\frac{7}{8}$ in. Coiffard collection. Louvre.

In the centre of the disc is a head in bold relief like the one in plate 22. It is framed by two old men, doubtless priests, who hold palms. Their facial appearance recalls that of the old men in plate 21. The personage on the left holds a snake by the tail. Snake and palm were part of the Mesopotamian fertility rites. Below the central motif is a symbol the meaning of which is unknown. This sign resembles the Chinese t'ao-t'ieh, but seems to have preceded it. Plates 21, 22, 23 and 32 apparently belonged to the same culture.

24. BRONZE CEREMONIAL BIT

Luristān. 1200 BC. Height: 5$\frac{7}{16}$ in.; width: 6$\frac{9}{16}$ in. Coiffard collection. Louvre.

This bit represents two horses in motion. The head and necks of the animals are executed in the round. We notice an attempt at realism which seems to characterize the more ancient art of the bronze-founders of the end of the second millennium, whereas the art of the eighth and seventh centuries was expressed in skilful decorative formulae at some remove from nature (see plate 17).

25. BRONZE FIGURINE

Provenance unknown. 900 BC. Height: 4$\frac{13}{16}$ in.; width: 1$\frac{3}{16}$ in. Coiffard collection. Louvre.

This piece, possibly the handle of a whetstone, represents the fore-quarters of an animal with a human head surmounted by horns. The treatment of the face is similar to that of the statuette in plate 26.

26. DIVINITY: WHITE BRONZE

Luristān. 1000 BC. Height: 6 in. Private collection.

This fertility goddess wears the conical hat which formerly constituted the head of the iron pin which attached the figurine to its base. Composite idols are more commonly found in Luristān than fertility goddesses of this kind.

27. MALE DIVINITY: BRONZE

Luristān. 1000 BC. Height: 6$\frac{3}{16}$ in. Private collection.

This god wears a conical hat like the one in the previous plate.

26   27

28

28. BRONZE STATUETTE

The Pusht-i Kūh region in Luristān. *c.* 900–700 BC. Height: 1 ft. 3⅛ in. in its present state, i.e. without feet and the bronze slab which would have been its base. Archaeological Museum, Teheran.

This figurine, of unusually large dimensions, represents the guardian divinity of a town as yet unknown, which must have been displaced during a war, and then returned to its original home. The inscription engraved on the bottom of the skirt in neo-Babylonian cuneiform characters dates from 600 to 500 BC, whereas the statue looks older by several centuries.

COLOUR PLATE

I. GOLD GOBLET DECORATED WITH THREE LIONS IN SINGLE FILE

Necropolis of Kalar Dasht (Gīlān). Tenth century BC. 4$\frac{5}{16}$ in. by 5$\frac{1}{16}$ in.; weight: about 4 oz. Archaeological Museum, Teheran.

This gold goblet with a band of three lions in high relief, the strongly projecting heads of which were moulded in the round, inserted and fixed to the object by small rivets, bears witness to Nordic, Urartian or Hittite influences. There are two plaits, one round the rim and round the base. The base itself is decorated with more plaits and stars. It was found together with a gold dagger and various terra-cotta objects in the valley of Kalar Dasht not far from the Caspian Sea at an altitude of about 3,500 feet. Jacques de Morgan considered this region to enjoy one of the pleasantest climates in the world. And in fact it seems to have been inhabited in remote times by very rich peoples. The exhibition '7,000 years of art in Iran', which was held in the Petit Palais in Paris (autumn 1961), showed numerous objects from the archaeological sites of the Amlash region, which are not very far from Kalar Dasht.

C

have a character which is anything but religious, with their smart hats, their earrings and their necklaces. Moreover, we seem to know their origins, which have nothing very religious about them.

We know that, from the middle of the second millennium BC at least, Luristān made pins ornamented in the centre with a boss in high relief, sometimes plain (figs. 32 and 73), sometimes representing the head of an animal (figs. 34 and 36) or a human head (figs. 44, 45, 48, 50, 51 and 77). This sort of *umbo*[1] defined an annular surface which was particularly suitable for decoration, although at first it was seldom used, or if it was, ineptly. Very often the boss remained isolated in the centre of the disc, where figure-scenes were depicted composed as if the central boss did not exist. A certain symmetry was thus obtained, but in relation to the main axis of the object, not in relation to its centre, and sometimes, as in figures 34 and 36, serious difficulties of composition resulted.

It was no doubt at this time that pins came from the north via Assyria which also had bosses in high relief in the centre, the surround being decorated with those animal friezes of which the craftsmen of the neighbouring country were so fond. The Kūh-i Dasht seems to have given a favourable, even fervent welcome to this new kind of decoration, renouncing its own ornamentation, but as we shall see further on drew no profit from this new acquisition. However, it realized that a man's or an animal's head could become a decorative motif capable of ornamenting the whole disc of a pin on its own. The heads of wild beasts which the artists of Luristān knew well from having long decorated numerous objects with them; the bellies of long-necked vases, the ends of shafts, bracelets, handles of daggers, etc., immediately and unhesitatingly assumed an extraordinary importance in this new fashion (fig. 49). The impression produced by this extremely beautiful motif, curiously like the Chinese *t'ao-t'ieh*, is positively gripping. However it did not last and subsequently disappeared from the ancient Mesopotamian repertoire.

The motif of the human head seems to have met with resistance at first, undoubtedly because the Luristān decorators were less at ease with it than with the very ancient animal heads. The insignificant hemispherical mask of the early days gradually assumed a more special character (fig. 50), but progress was not great and the whole thing would not have come to much, indeed would probably have suffered the fate of the animal heads, if fashion had not taken a hand. For the ladies of Luristān acquired the habit of choosing those pins offered for barter which they found most novel or attractive, and which represented the ladies themselves with their hair dressed and wearing hats in the fashion of the day. Strange? No more than the discovery in the necropolises of Tanagra and Myrina of terra-cotta statuettes which showed the family and friends of the dead in contemporary costume.

The pins ornamented with large female heads, reproduced in figure 51 and plate 22, probably two of the most ancient, follow on quite well after the preceding one but are superior to it in every way. The three heads have the same shape, broad at the top and narrow at the chin. They all occupy the centre of the object and are surrounded by a

---

[1] An *umbo* was a central excrescence, like the bosses which occur on some shields.

Fig. 52

Fig. 53

Fig. 55

Fig. 54

Fig. 57

Fig. 56

Fig. 58

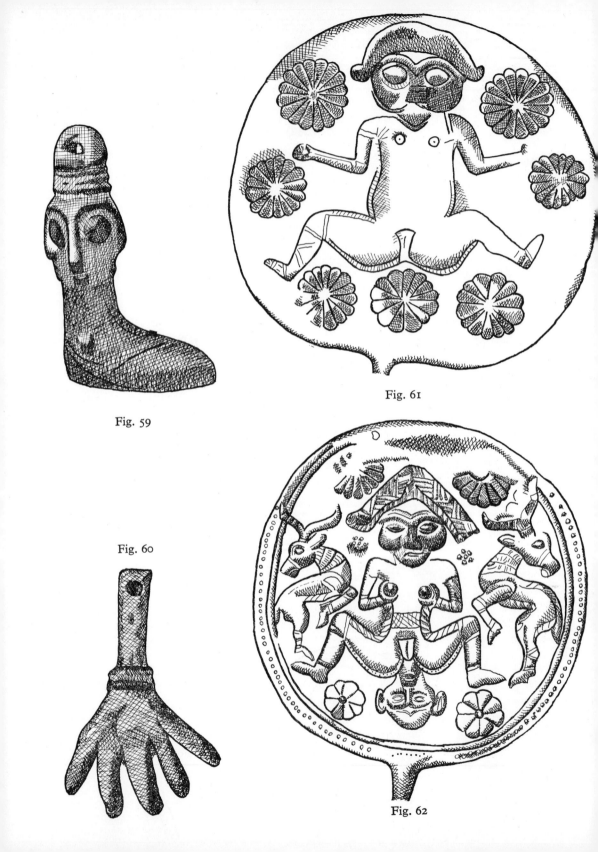

Fig. 59

Fig. 60

Fig. 61

Fig. 62

large undecorated space, but the proportions and arrangement of the whole are much better in figure 51 and plate 22 than in the other. The head itself is better modelled. Being larger it occupies the centre of the disc better, while an intermediary ornament between the figure and the background, composed of a sort of ovolo, gives the object a very satisfying decorative look.

Next appear some much more freely handled heads, of which I give a few typical examples here. Some, with their hair carefully dressed, have it separated by a centre parting (fig. 52), bouffant (fig. 53) or fringed, like the kouroi of archaic Greece (fig. 54). Others wear a kind of pointed bonnet which looks woollen (fig. 55), a round embroidered toque (fig. 56) or a hat ornamented with what appear to be scales (fig. 57). The faces differ considerably, some being thin and sharp-featured, others massive and even bloated. They often have the air of portraits rather than conventional representations.

These are all female heads. The next one is male (fig. 58). It seems to be a mere rough sketch. But I have seen a pin in the Coiffard collection on which the same head is depicted in the same way, by line alone.

On these pins, therefore, the image of the god seems to be replaced by that of the templegoer, the worshipper, who is also represented by the small bronze statuettes I mentioned previously. However, others have been found which correspond more exactly to our idea of an *ex voto*: those which were offered to the divinity to obtain his aid in certain circumstances. We recognize something similar in those pendants in the shape of a foot (fig. 59) or a hand (fig. 60) which the women of Luristān hung from their necklaces, but this explanation is perhaps not entirely adequate since figures 61 and 62 clearly represent pins offered to the temple in the hope of or in gratitude for successful childbirth.

I mentioned earlier that, among the settled peoples of central Luristān, the hero protecting the flocks became the messenger of the god of fertility and disappeared, or very nearly, from his role as conqueror of monsters. Two images (figs. 63 and 64) illustrate without words the history of this disappearance. However, there do exist scenes where the protector of flocks, the friend of beasts, has outlived the conqueror of monsters (fig. 65). On another pin, a sort of buffoon, who really no longer has anything in common with the athletic Gilgamesh, seems to be holding two performing wild beasts (fig. 66).

We can also no doubt recapture his memory in the hunting scenes found among both the settled peoples and those of the high pastures, but less frequently in the Kūh-i Dasht than among the horse breeders. The hunter, very badly drawn, fires his bow at unidentifiable animals often even more clumsily depicted (fig. 67), and then we see his game: the gazelle, wittily expressed simply by means of pieces of iron cut up and riveted together, articulated originally like a toy (fig. 70), the ibex (fig. 67, bottom half), the large partridge which one still often finds curled up in the dust of the road (fig. 69), a sort of guinea-fowl (fig. 70) and no doubt other small beasts of the same type. Small game! Already we are far from the days when a man choked a lion in each hand or seizing a furious bull by the horns threw it on its back with one jerk.

All the images we have just examined are clearly those of a religious, intelligent,

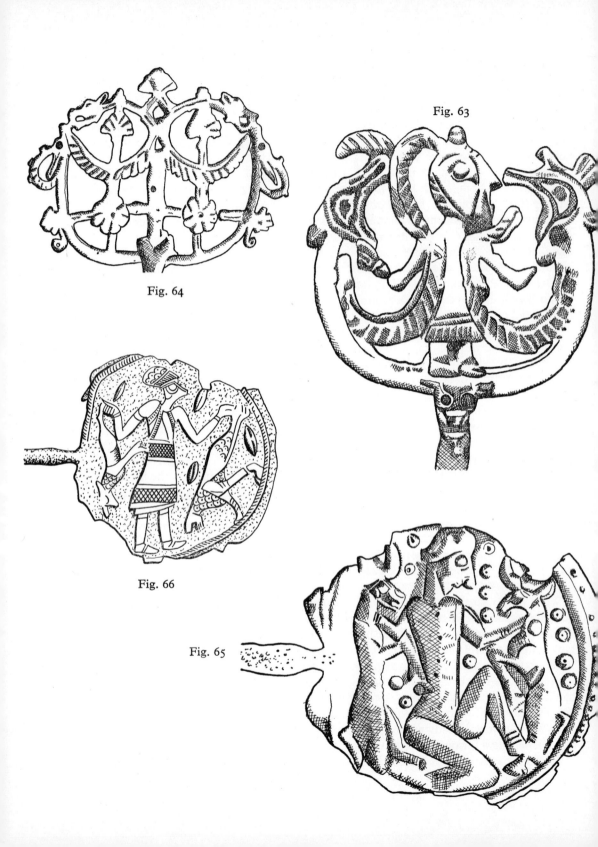

Fig. 63

Fig. 64

Fig. 66

Fig. 65

Fig. 67

settled people, neither warriors nor big game hunters, who loved elegant horses (fig. 77) and small dogs (fig. 72); they have all taught us something, they have all added a touch of colour to the picture we are trying to paint of a certain part of ancient Luristān. But there are others from the same finds which I must mention, not in my view significant, but merely well executed. Side by side with the first which are often clumsy and even crude, but always perfectly characteristic of the men, things and ideas of their time, they represent, so it seems, second-rate imported objects,[1] pretty, well made, but impersonal and without real interest.

One of these objects (fig. 73) is perfectly representative of a whole group of pieces on which we always see the same conventional animals at an impossible headlong gallop and the same sort of work by a skilful craftsman who shows only too clearly his boredom at executing the same winged monsters for the ten thousandth time. However, these mass-produced objects have a certain importance for us. We are familiar with those pins of almost pure copper, still intact in places, in figure 73. They are of the same period as the Assyrian, or so-called Assyrian, paterae, about which there was so much discussion some sixty years ago, i.e. from the first half of the first millennium BC, when 'a somewhat relaxed, industrial yet elegant style' flourished throughout western Asia. As to their place of provenance there can be no question of placing it in Phoenicia, Egypt or Mesopotamia, as has been done with the paterae. They are in the same vein as the embroidery carved on the royal garments of the Nimrud statues.

[1] There is no doubt that they were imported, not exported.

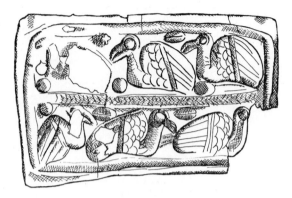

Fig. 69

Fig. 68

Fig. 71

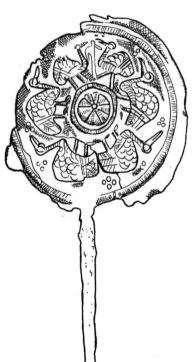

Fig. 70

Fig. 72

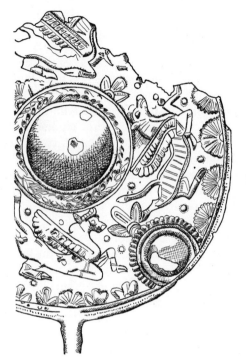

Fig. 73

Fig. 74

Fig. 75

They are clearly Assyrian, whether they were made in Assyria itself or in Luristān by craftsmen who were Assyrian or of Assyrian education. Incidentally this is not at all to contradict the first hypothesis, for we know that Assyria did considerable trade with Luristān.

The discovery for example of one of these in the Kūh-i Dasht[1] supports the hypothesis that Assyrian objects were imported into Luristān. It is a cup with a diameter of $4\frac{3}{4}$ inches and a height of $1\frac{9}{16}$ inches made of fairly well preserved brass. The base, like the centre of the disc on the majority of large pins from the Kūh-i Dasht, is decorated with a boss, surrounded by concentric rays, then by three circles of a thin plait-like ornament. Between the third circle and the sides of the cup there is an annular zone $1\frac{3}{16}$ inches wide, decorated with four animals in single file (fig. 74), alternating with four trees (fig. 75). The tree is the Assyrian palmetto resting on a double reversed volute. The animal, very skilfully drawn and typical of the elegant industrial style I have just mentioned, is the winged quadruped with a human head well known in Assyrian glyptics. As in many representations of the same period, one of the wings is pointed backwards, behind the head, the other forwards. The whole is markedly Assyrian, with characteristic animals following one another and the palmetto-trees, as well as the drawing, the engraving and even the material, which is fine brass. In it we obviously have a very characteristic example of the Assyrian objects imported into Luristān during the ninth and eighth centuries BC.

The pins of which figure 73 shows perhaps the most unmistakable type are, I think, roughly contemporary with the construction of the palace of Assurnasirpal II[2] at Kalah,[3] i.e. they could be dated from the first half of the ninth century BC. After them, I suppose, would come those which are a faithful imitation (fig. 76), then others which are sometimes still decorated with prancing winged animals, but on which Iranian subjects appear more and more, the small figure with the large nose in figure 77 for example. The beautiful dancer from the Graeffe collection (fig. 47) and the large female heads (figs. 51 to 57) would presumably belong to this series. Lastly would come a final group of objects from the end of the Assyrian period.

The pins and plaques with religious subjects, as well as the small figurines of worshippers, date, as we have already seen, from the second half of the second millennium BC. The objects from the Kūh-i Dasht would then be divided between two clear-cut artistic periods, one extending from the second half of the second millennium BC to the beginning of the ninth century BC, and the other from this date to the Achaemenid period, i.e. the sixth century BC, the first being influenced by the brilliant Elamite art of the time of Untash-Huban, the other by Assyrian art of the time of Assurnasirpal II.

This summary of the history of the Luristān bronzes omits any mention of the Kassite domination of Babylonia,[4] as if this astonishing adventure had in no way affected the art of the Zagrus region towards the end of the second millennium; and

---

[1] The cup in question is supposed to have been found in a tomb, together with the bronze socket of an iron halberd.

[2] Assurnasirpal II, King of Assyria, reigned from 884–860 BC.

[3] Kalah (Nimrud), on an affluent of the Greater Zab.

[4] Babylonia bordered on Assyria in the north, Sumer in the south and Elam in the east.

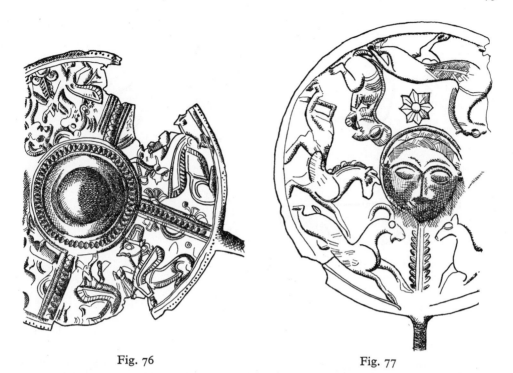

Fig. 76   Fig. 77

this does in fact seem to be true. So far no Luristān bronzes have been found in the Mesopotamian plain. The excavations carried out on the site of the Kassite town of Dur Kurigalzu[1] have not produced a single one. The few there are in the show-cases of the Baghdad Museum come from confiscations made by the customs at the country's frontiers or were bought commercially. I confirmed this from the Museum's register of acquisitions which the office of the Director-General of Antiquities in Iraq very kindly allowed me to consult.

How can we explain the complete absence of Luristān bronzes, i.e. bronzes possessing the very special character of the art of Luristān, in the Mesopotamian plain and the very great numbers of them in the Zagrus Mountains? It seems that there is only one possible answer to this question. The Luristān bronzes, with the exception of the weapons to be discussed and perhaps ordinary horse's bits, and some very simple artefacts—rings, arrow-heads, fibulae, bronze cups and goblets—did not exist at the time of the Kassite occupation of Babylonia. They did not appear until later, when the invaders had returned to their mountains.

I am convinced that the majority of the very ancient weapons which C. Schaeffer has assembled under the title *Archaic Luristan* were discovered in Luristān but in fact were made in the plain, in Elam or Mesopotamia, then introduced into the Zagrus

[1] Founded by the Kassite King Kurigalzu I, whose capital it was (present-day Agerguf).

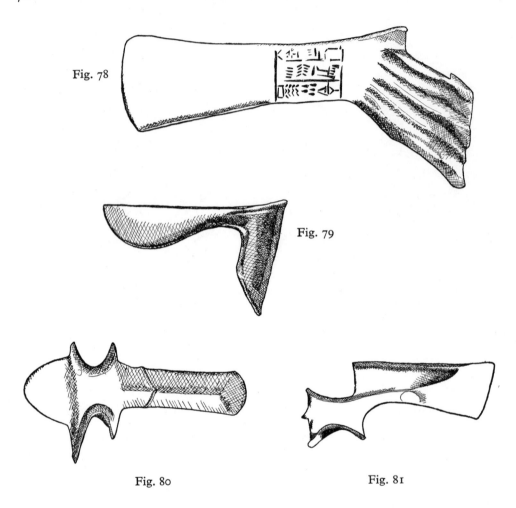

Fig. 78

Fig. 79

Fig. 80

Fig. 81

region by conquest or commerce, or that they are Kassite copies of them. In support
of this hypothesis one could quote almost all types of Luristān weapons.

There is for example an axe which comes from this area and belongs to the Teheran
Museum (fig. 78). It bears a Babylonian inscription in the name of a certain 'Beli Sar,
the powerful king, king of all' which can be dated to the Agade[1] period. It is identical with the one from Tell Ahmar[2] which Schaeffer dates to 2200–1900 BC.

The three axes found at Mussiān in the necropolis of Tepe 'Álīābād,[3] reproduced

---

[1] Agade is Akkad. The Akkadian dynasty begins with Sargon the Elder about 2400 BC and ends c. 2060
with Naram Sin, giving way to the Erech (or Uruk) dynasty.

[2] Tell Ahmar, the former Til-Barsip, is situated on the Euphrates a little below its confluence with
the Sadjur. The distance from Tell Ahmar to Karkemish is only about 10 miles.

[3] Mussiān is some 30 miles west of Susa.

together in the *Mémoires de la Délégation archéologique française en Perse*, Vol. VIII, and another axe of the same type belonging to the Baghdad Museum, dated to the third millennium BC, as well as the one of the same type in my possession (fig. 79), all seem to have the same origin. C. L. Woolley and A. Parrot have found several examples of them at Ur and Māri.

Fig. 80 shows a genuine Luristān axe similar to that of Naram Sin[1] as it appears on the stele in the Louvre, and thus dated to the middle of the third millennium BC which resembles the one found at Tepe Gawra[2] illustrated by Schaeffer in his *Stratigraphie* and dated by him to 2100/2000—1900/1700 BC. I would like to add two more axes to this series: one found at Tepe Gawra, too, and dated by Schaeffer to the same period, and the other actually from Luristān (fig. 81).

Now let us look at some axes of the best-known Susian type: one of them, belonging to the Teheran Museum, was found at Susa by M. de Mecquenem and dated by him to *c.* 2200 BC; another was also found at Susa in the deposit of offerings for the foundation of the temple of Shushinak. Figure 82 shows one from Luristān. It is identical in shape with the two preceding axes. The bronze has the same greyish patina and is just as rough in texture. It ought, therefore, to be sufficient to show an axe of the same type (fig. 83), also found in Luristān, but delicately worked in fine smooth bronze, to make it fairly clear that the former axes have the same Elamite origin and that only the last, from particularly dry ground, might be a product of the Zagrus region.

Further evidence is provided by a digitiform pick belonging to the Baghdad Museum where it is dated to the third millennium (fig. 84) and a similar one (fig. 85) found in Luristān and now in Teheran Museum. Another pick, with no digitations, from Luristān and now in the Louvre (fig. 86) is identical with the one from Tell Ahmar which Schaeffer dates to 2200–1900 BC. These four objects very probably came from the Mesopotamian plain. The same is I think true of two coiled picks in the possession of the Teheran Museum. One of them was found at Susa by M. de Mecquenem (fig. 87) who dated it to 2200 BC. The other one comes from Luristān.

The type of dagger most frequently used in Luristān was of bronze, often in one piece, with two fins clasping a decorated piece of wood or bone on both sides of the hilt (fig. 88). Examples have been found at Ras Shamra,[3] where Schaeffer dates them to between 1450 and 1365 BC, at Tepe Giyan (1550–1200 BC), and elsewhere.

Another, rarer dagger, also of pure bronze but with a round hilt the top of which is like the head of a nail (fig. 89), is identical with the one from Veri[4] dated by Schaeffer to between 1350 and 1200 BC.

Yet another, much rarer example is dated by Schaeffer to between 1350 and 1500 (fig. 90).

Lastly a typical dagger from Ur (fig. 91) and what Luristān made of it (fig. 92).

[1] Naram Sin, King of Akkad. Grandson of Sargon (after 2400 BC).
[2] Tepe Gawra, slightly to the east of Niniveh, the ancient Assyrian capital.
[3] Ras Shamra, the ancient Ugarit, on the Syrian coast, on a latitude with the northern tip of Cyprus.
[4] Veri, in Talysh in Russia.

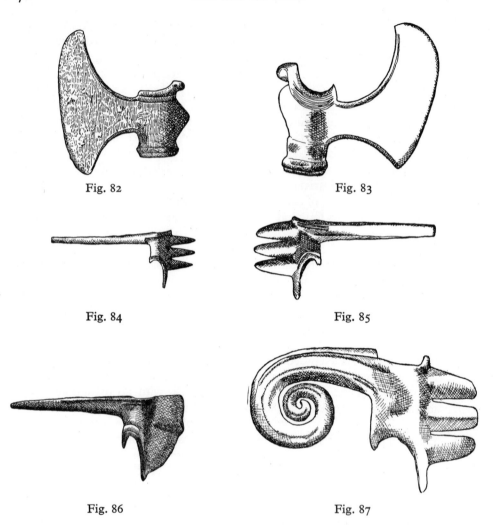

Fig. 82   Fig. 83

Fig. 84   Fig. 85

Fig. 86   Fig. 87

The whetstone, an essential accessory to the bronze dagger, must have existed at the same time (fig. 24) and it is no doubt for that reason that Schaeffer dates those I have published in *Bronzes du Luristān* to about 1500–1200 BC. The bronze handle of one of them, with its Kudurru or ibex head unknown in the mountains (fig. 93), was no doubt made in the plain. The handle of the other whetstone, neither better nor worse executed, probably has the same origin (fig. 94).

In other words axes, picks and daggers copied from the arms of neighbouring countries, whetstones and no doubt various simple tools and objects of adornment may have been made in the valleys of Luristān before and during the occupation of Babylonia by the Kassites. As for the objects of finely smelted metal, skilfully and vividly

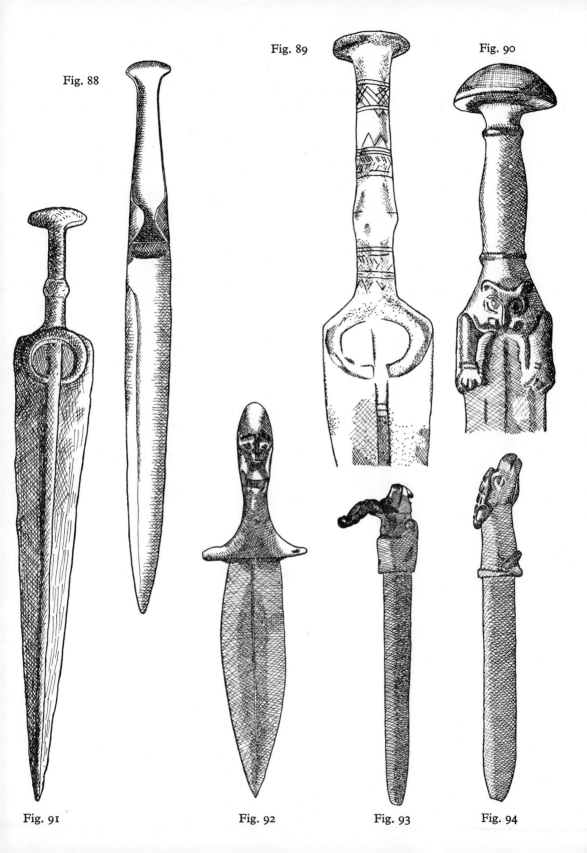

Fig. 88

Fig. 89

Fig. 90

Fig. 91

Fig. 92

Fig. 93

Fig. 94

29. HEAD OF A BIRD, PERHAPS A PARROT: GOLD
Ziwiya treasure. (Kurdistān, the ancient country of Manai.) Fifth century BC. Height: $3\frac{1}{8}$ in.
Archaeological Museum, Teheran.
The Ziwiya treasure was at first believed to have been buried in the eighth century BC, but according to Barnett the vat in which it was found belongs to the seventh or even the fifth century BC.

30. SILVER ORNAMENT FROM THE ZIWIYA TREASURE
Ziwiya. Seventh century BC. Height: $12\frac{11}{16}$ in. Archaeological Museum, Teheran.
This ornament, which was designed to be attached to some other material, as the holes surrounding it show, approaches both Assyrian and Etruscan art (cf. the gold fibula from the Regolini-Galassi tomb at Cerveteri).

31. ELECTRUM BRACELET
Luristān. Beginning of first millennium BC. Height: $3\frac{15}{16}$ in.; width: $3\frac{5}{8}$ in. Louvre.
Six lions' heads in relief adorn this bracelet.

32. DETAIL OF A GOLD PLAQUE
Luristān. *c.* 1000 BC. Length: $13\frac{3}{16}$ in.; height: $2\frac{1}{8}$ in. Private collection.
This gold plaque made to be sewn on to a leather band represents a scene of sacrifice and offering. The high priest is seated on a stool. Two sacrificers bring him some kind of deer. The type and clothing of these figures is similar to plates 21 and 23.

33. DETAILS OF THE GOLD PECTORAL FROM ZIWIYA (KURDISTAN)
Find made by farmers who divided it into fragments. *c.* 800–600 BC. Width of the pectoral: $13\frac{3}{16}$ in. Archaeological Museum, Teheran.
(a) In the upper part an ibex rampant mounts guard in front of a highly stylized tree of life. It turns its head towards a female sphinx wearing a sort of apron. (b) The lower part represents a winged bull, its head turned towards a figure with drooping wings and hands upraised as if it were a telamon supporting an entablature. The upper part of the 'telamon's' body is human, the lower part rests on bull's feet. These figures had a symbolical and prophylactic value: they were deemed to protect the wearer of the pectoral against misfortune.

34. ELECTRUM GOBLET
Western Iran. Beginning of first millennium BC. Height: $4\frac{5}{16}$ in.; diameter: $4\frac{5}{16}$ in. Louvre.
A two-headed monster decorates the goblet. Its breasts and the arms seem to be human, but its legs are covered with reptilian scales. Note the twisted lower part of the body, a feature of the Kassite period. The monster holds two antelopes by their hind legs in its outstretched arms; they are faithfully reproduced and very delicately executed. The motif is repeated four times.

35. FIRE ALTARS AT NAQSH-I RUSTAM, NEAR PERSEPOLIS
Pre-Achaemenid period (?). The larger is about 5 ft. 10 in. high and the smaller about 8 in. less.
These altars, built close together, were obviously used for the fire and water cult.

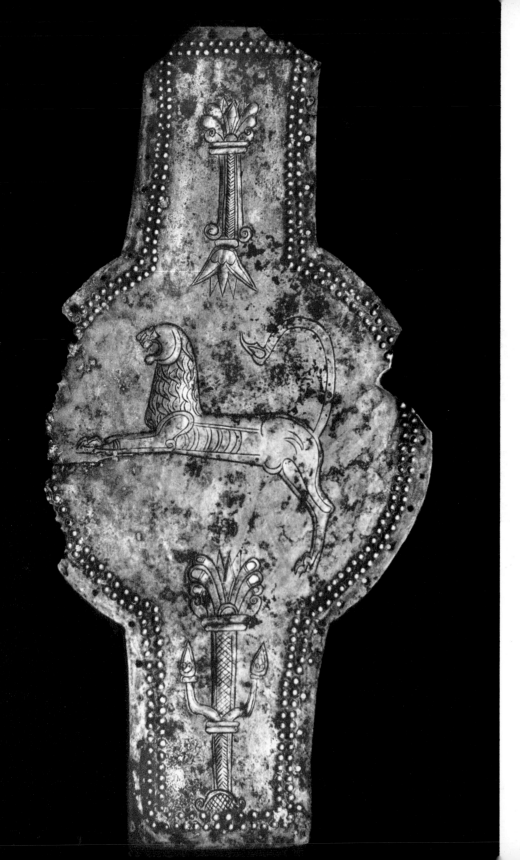

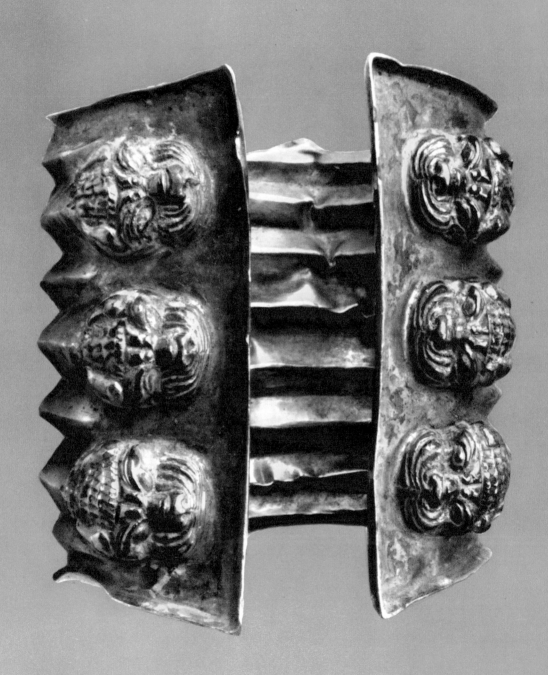

Fig. 95

Fig. 96

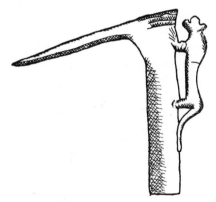

Fig. 97

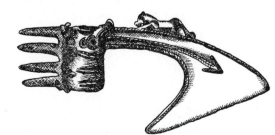

Fig. 98

made, and with more and more decoration, which we look on as the true Luristān bronzes, it has already been said that they are probably subsequent to the return of the invaders of Babylonia to their own Zagrus Mountains. In favour of this hypothesis there is the excellent reason I have adduced, namely that not a single bronze of this kind has been found in the Mesopotamian plain, although it was under Kassite domination for more than three centuries, from about 1500–1168 BC, but there is another reason which, though less striking, is just as convincing.

In all these examples we have seen how the bronze-founders of Luristān first copied the arms of their neighbours without noticeably altering them, but towards 1200 BC an event took place in western Asia which may have been the cause or one of the causes of the great changes we then find in the art of the Zagrus region.

In the ancient country of Sumer the metal-worker was not a free man: he was closely linked with the Temple-State characteristic of the civilization at the time in that part of the world. He was under the control of the religious authorities and his work was supervised by a priest who was a metal-worker. However, he was not a slave. During the reign of King Hammurabi and his successors, the ancient Sumerian economy collapsed. The various corporations dependent on the Temple became impoverished and, although they retained a certain religious prestige, seem to have gone through a difficult period which became still more difficult in the Kassite period when they were transformed into corporations of free men. The situation, therefore, was hardly favourable to expansion and innovation, in spite of secular traditions.

Towards 1200 BC the Hittite empire collapsed under the weight of the migration of peoples coming from the Balkans. The virtual monopoly of iron smelting which this state had preserved for several centuries was wiped out and the metal-workers dispersed into the neighbouring countries. Perhaps we can connect this event with the fact that Iranian art at this period includes many works in which we recognize the hand of skilful Hittite artists or their pupils, for example the lions on the gold goblet from Kalār-Dasht (coloured plate I) in Gīlān, or Hittite work pure and simple, the head, headdress, clothing and attitude of the chariot driver shown in figure 95.

In fact the abundance of Luristān bronzes seems to be due mainly to the opulence of the Kassite horse dealers who supplied the Assyrian armies. But it is possible that in addition to Kassite wealth the arrival of skilled metal-workers contributed to the speedy and extensive development of the bronze industry in the Zagrus Mountains.

We now come to something which enables us to tackle the problem of the origins of Zagrus art even more closely. Figure 96 (pl. 14) represents an axe which bears an inscription engraved in the name of King Untash-Huban. It was found at Chuga Zanbil, some twenty-five miles from Susa. It is a weapon of a very ancient type and has as head decoration a small gold animal. Here we have an animal which the Elamite bronze-workers represented in the round and at the same time we have the art of Luristān in the form we know it. The Kassites were to adopt its decorative principles, develop it into masterpieces and even carry it to extremes. I could cite a whole series of Luristān axes, consisting like this one of a weapon of an ancient type decorated with small quadrupeds, upright at first (fig. 97), then crouched (fig. 98), when they became

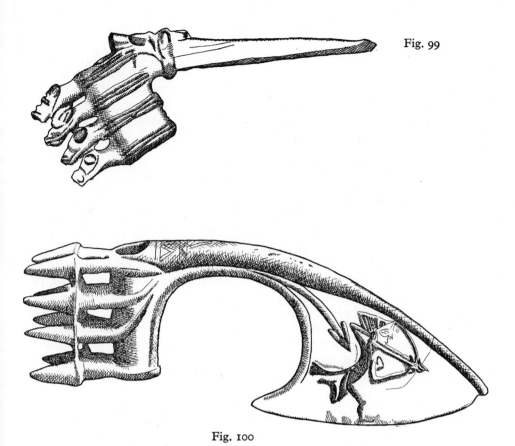

Fig. 99

Fig. 100

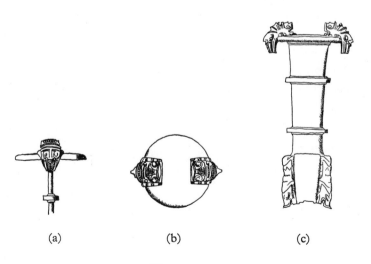

(a)   (b)   (c)

Fig. 101

more an integral part of the object. In fact if this Elamite axe from the time of Untash-Huban was not precisely identified by the name of its owner and the place where it was discovered it might appear to be one of the earliest Luristān bronzes, one of those which determined the decorative expression of the art of the Zagrus region.

Under the influence of Elamite art of the time of Untash-Huban, the weapons of former periods were covered with more and more sumptuous ornamentation—for example the adzes which illustrate this process perfectly (fig. 99). Other axes, which have turned into walking sticks or ceremonial staffs, were deformed, their cutting edge becoming almost horizontal, and they were embellished (or at least that was the idea) in various ways (fig. 100). The ancient picks from Kish[1] and Tell Ahmar curl up just as though they were coils (fig. 87). The whetstones become astonishing jewels on which the ornamentation seems to be the main feature (pl. 12). The iron swords, which come from Cappadocia according to Herzfeld, but were probably made in the Zagrus region between the years 1200 and 1000 BC,[2] became the ceremonial weapons of the army, uniformly decorated with human heads or crouched animals (fig. 101). The bit, which was so simple at first, jointed (fig. 17) or with a bar, was very specially and richly decorated when it became an offering to the dead horseman, his pillow in the tomb, a work of art with no practical use (pl. 24), and so on.

As we have been able to see in the course of this study, the range of objects made in Luristān was very extensive. Bronze, cast by the *cire perdue* method, silver, gold, then beaten or chased iron—at first more precious than gold—were the materials used by the

Fig. 102

[1] Kish, one of the most ancient cities of Sumer-Akkad, not far from the ancient sites of Babylon and Akkad, in Mesopotamia (Iraq).
[2] See note B, p. 90.

Fig. 103

Fig. 104

Kassite artists in the Zagrus Mountains to transform all the external contributions into an original art. These materials varied according to the area—north or central.

We notice traces of Hittite influence, but also something of the art of Kirkuk in Iraq on the nomads of the high plains of northern Luristān, and a strong Elamite influence on the settled peoples of central Luristān. In the extreme north, in the land of Manai,[1] the art of the Zagrus region, which had in general taken a rather different turn (fig. 102) from the art of Luristān proper owing to its contacts with the Assyrian world, was adopted by the Scythian nomads when they occupied Media and became, just as it stood, what Rostovtzeff calls archaic Scythian art. This Manaian[2] turned Scythian art, i.e. the art of the northern part of the Zagrus region was transplanted to southern Russia and almost immediately modified there by the Sarmatians who imposed on it their taste for violence, exuberance and excess. Whereas in Iran, in Manai which had now become Media and together with Urartu had become to some extent a depository[3] of Assyrian art after the fall of Nineveh, it produced the able sculptors of Persepolis. Figure 103 for example shows the pommel of a dagger which comes from the Ziwiya treasure.[4] It is a wonderful small gold object decorated with an animal typical of Zagrus art which we find reproduced on the tip of the scabbards of the Median archers' daggers at Persepolis (fig. 104). As for the art of Luristān, or at least what still remained of it, for the Kassites were literally annihilated by Sennacherib[5] the Assyrian in 691 BC, it simply merged with Achaemenid art.

[1] The land of Manai, which the Bible calls 'the land of Man', extended from the southern shore of Lake Urmiya up to Tabriz in the north and almost as far as Kirmānshāh in the south.

[2] See note C, p. 92.

[3] Urartu, the Armenia of antiquity, extended from the eastern frontier of Assyria to Lake Urmiya in one direction and from there to beyond Lake Van in the west.

[4] In my book Le Trésor de Ziwiye I explained that the treasure consisted of gold, ivory and silver objects which were found in a bronze vat once hidden at the top of one of the fortresses which defended the approaches to Izirtu, the capital of Manai. Some of the gold (figs. 102, 111, 112 a and b, and plates 29 and 33) and silver (figs. 113, 114 and plate 30) objects actually come from Manai, but they included a great number of decorative elements borrowed from neighbouring Assyria (figs. 115 and 116) and copied more or less exactly, and other less ancient elements from a different art, that of the Zagrus region. The ivories (figs. 117 and 118) were imported into Manai from Assyria. It is possible that the hiding place dates from the Median period and that the bronze vat was then filled with objects from various periods, all showing different influences, attributable to the eighth, seventh and even the sixth centuries BC.

[5] Sennacherib, King of Assyria, reigned from 705 to 681 BC.

NOTES TO PART ONE

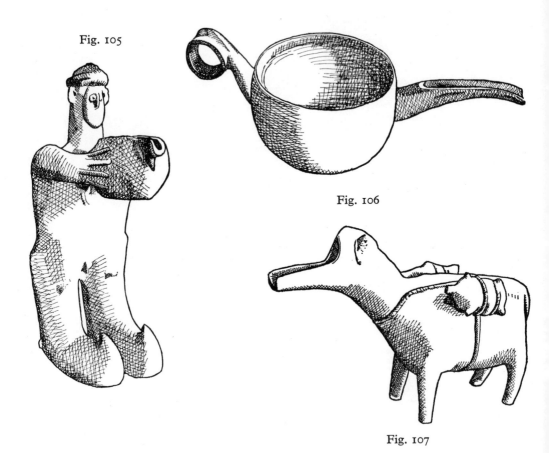

Fig. 105

Fig. 106

Fig. 107

NOTE A

THE AMLASH REGION

About sixty miles from Kalār-Dasht where a famous gold goblet was discovered by chance (coloured plate 1), various necropolises in the Amlash region at Pīr Kūh, Daylaman and elsewhere have been dug up by clandestine excavators who unfortunately have not supplied any information about the circumstances of their finds. The objects which these digs have made familiar have become popular in Europe because of their ultra-modern look. The majority of them are made of a rather fine pink clay, generally in very unsophisticated shapes (figs. 105 to 109). There are no painted ceramics in the necropolises in the Daylaman region—at least none have been found— but there are numerous gold and silver objects (fig. 110 a and b) the decoration of which is sometimes strangely close to archaic Greek or Etruscan art. They might, it seems, date from the beginning of the first millennium BC, i.e. from the same period as the gold vases of Kalār-Dasht and Hāsānlū.

Carboniferous and consequently grey ceramics do not seem to have been used by the peoples we have been considering, although they are the only ones which occur on numerous sites in Gūrgān, such as those of Tūrān Tepe, Shāh Tepe and Khurwīn, in the foot-hills of the Alburz range, though on the slope on the side of the Iranian plateau.

During the summer of 1961 Iranian archaeologists under the direction of Dr Negahban of the National Archaeological Museum in Teheran explored the intact necropolis of Marlik about twelve miles from Rūdbār in Gīlān and discovered gold beakers and pink pottery rhytons which we might attribute to the Aryanised peoples of the beginning of the first millennium.

NOTE B

IRON AND BRONZE

It might be apposite at this point to make some additional remarks concerning the attempt to date the production of Luristān bronzes by periods. As we have seen, the beginning can be placed around 1200 BC. Iron, worked by hand in Mesopotamia, Asia Minor and perhaps also in Egypt from the first half of the third millennium onwards, seems to have made its appearance, improved by tempering, in the mountains of Armenia. Its use was no longer reserved for ceremonial ornaments and weapons, but it was still rare and precious. In an inscription describing one of his hunting expeditions Tiglath-Pilasar I[1] related that he was armed with his bow and iron lance.

Towards 1000 BC the iron industry, now in full swing, made weapons and agricultural implements, but still used the shapes peculiar to bronze. The blades of axes and daggers are sometimes made of iron though with bronze decoration.

With Tukulti Nīnurta II[2] we really enter the universal iron age. The king wrote that he had received it as tribute from the inhabitants of Khabur and that he had had a mountain road built with iron picks and axes. It was probably towards this time that Luristān became in a position to undertake the manufacture of axes and halberds with iron blades, as well as pins for clothing and the long fibulae with a large disc head which we are familiar with. These can scarcely date from before the ninth century BC.

[1] Tiglath-Pilasar (Phalaser) I, king of Assyria, reigned from 1116 to 1078 BC.
[2] Tukulti Ninurta II, king of Assyria, reigned from 888 to 884 BC.

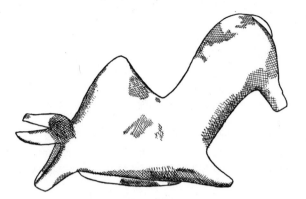

Fig. 108

Fig. 109

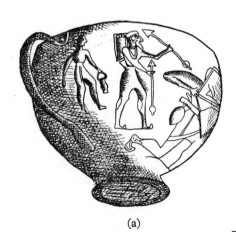 

(a)   (b)

Fig. 110

NOTE C

ZIWIYA AND HĀSĀNLŪ
FORTRESSES OF THE LAND OF MAN

The Aryan or Aryanised peoples who settled in the Zagrus Mountains during the second millennium did not consider themselves as the natural allies of the Semitic Assyrians. On the contrary they hated their cruel neighbours. The destruction of the Assyrians' military power was their constant aim.

Until recently in spite of the researches undertaken in the Van area more than a century ago by Rassam under the orders of Layard, which produced interesting objects (the ivories in the British Museum, among others), we had very little information about the population of this region. We only know, from inscriptions and the architectural decoration, such as the bronze gates at Balavat, that these peoples fought the Assyrians and that they were conquered, looted and deported by them.

The fortress of Ziwiya was revealed to us by the chance discovery of a treasure hidden before some hostile attack, possibly a Scythian invasion provoked by Cimmerian pressure, since the Cimmerians occupied Urartu and the area round Lake Van when the Scythians took Manai and Media (at the end of the eighth or beginning of the seventh century BC).

The Ziwiya treasure[1] appears to have been a collection of disparate objects (figs. 102 and 111 to 118, and pl. 29, 30 and 33), assembled by a prince or governor of the region. Another fortress has been revealed at Hāsānlū (to the south-west of Lake Urmiya), 125 miles from Ziwiya, by the Anglo-American mission which has been working on this site since 1958.

John Dyson, who led the expedition in 1958, thought that the site of Hāsānlū could be considered as that of a forward Manai fortress. A magnificent and surprising gold vase decorated with legendary scenes showing varied artistic expression was discovered there, crushed by the fall of the warrior who carried it (fig. 119 a and b). The American archaeologists put forward the hypothesis that the Hāsānlū site was made up of a group of fortified buildings.

During the summer of 1960 the find of remains of mass murder—the sacrifice of many young women—confirmed the 1958 finds and proved that Hāsānlū was indeed an important historical centre. We still have no concrete knowledge of the religion and the cults which united these peoples in a community of beliefs. The narrative on the gold vase from Hāsānlū has not yet been explained. The scenes seem to show a hero fighting to save a man whose bust rises from a hiding-place (? a tree trunk) decorated with leaf scales or perhaps primitive festoons (the symbol of mountains). The refuge is defended by a ferocious animal which has perhaps been killed by the hero, and a sort of three-headed hydra (fig. 120); then we see a nude woman, her arms extended and holding a cloak standing on a ram (fig. 121), again an eagle in full flight (fig. 122)

---

[1] See note 4, p. 86.

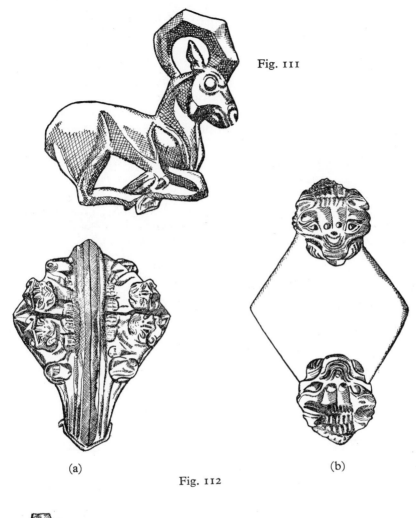

Fig. 111

(a)   (b)

Fig. 112

Fig. 113

Fig. 114

carries off a human being, only part of whose body is visible, evoking the myth of
Etana. . . .

The decoration of this vase taken as a whole calls up legends which we cannot
completely expound, myths about which it is hard to give a definite judgment.

The style of the gold vase obviously differs considerably from the one from the finds
at Ziwiya which are much closer to provincial Assyrian, Zagrus and Scythian art.

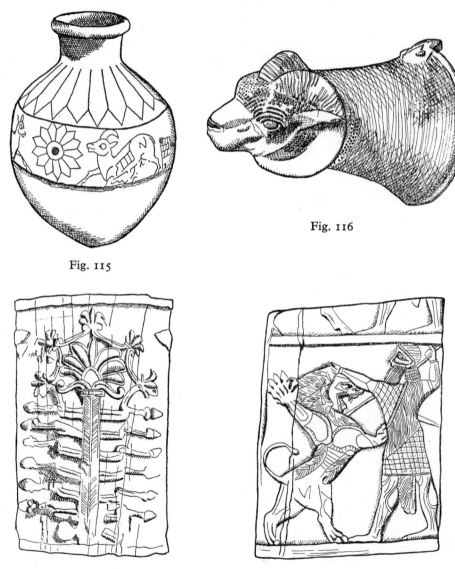

Fig. 116

Fig. 115

Fig. 117   Fig. 118

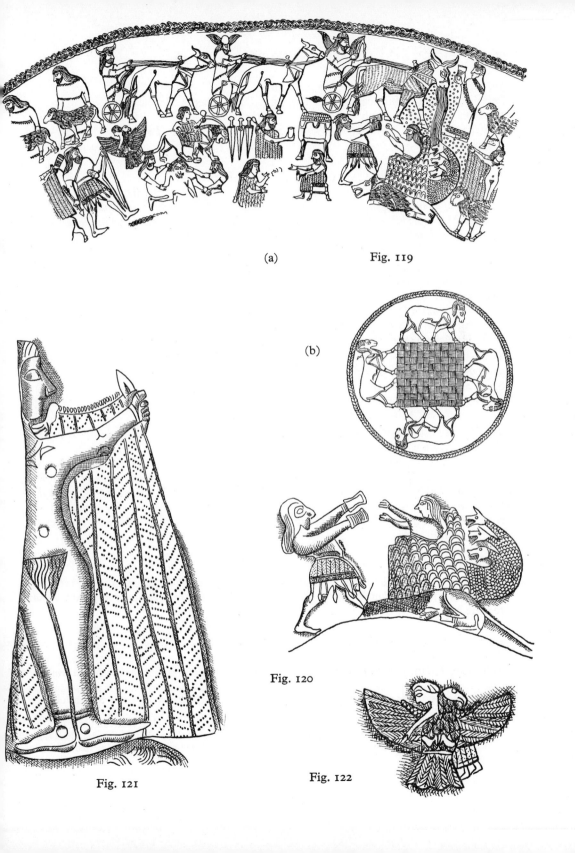

(a)

Fig. 119

(b)

Fig. 120

Fig. 121

Fig. 122

36. PROTOMA OF A LION IN LAPIS LAZULI
Persepolis. Sixth or fifth century BC. Height: 5 $\frac{11}{16}$ in. Teheran Museum.
We know how fond antiquity was of portraying the lion. Achaemenid art followed this fashion, stylizing the animal. This wild beast seems very stereotyped compared with the naturalism of the Assyrian lions.

37. TOMB OF CYRUS II (THE GREAT) AT PASARGADAE
Sixth century BC. Total height: 34 ft. 10 in. Height of the sub-structure: 17 ft. 4 in.
Materials of an imposing size were used in the construction of this tomb. It was built in Cyrus' lifetime and he was buried in it. According to R. D. Barnett, its general shape and the dimensions of its stones link it with Urartian monuments.

38. THE SO-CALLED STELE OF CYRUS AT PASARGADAE
Sixth century BC. Height: nearly 9 ft.
This bas-relief represents a guardian genius with four wings. He wears the long Elamite robe. His head is surmounted by a monumental tiara of Egyptian inspiration. An inscription, in cuneiform, Persian, Elamite and Babylonian characters, now vanished, identified the personage: 'Cyrus the King, the Achaemenid'. Obviously it can only be a portrait of Cyrus.

39. LOWER PART OF A COLUMN IN A PALACE AT PASARGADAE
Sixth century BC. Diameter: about 2 ft.
This base shows meticulously finished work.

40. BAS-RELIEF FROM A PALACE AT PASARGADAE[1]
Sixth century BC. Width: about 4 ft. 6 in.
This bas-relief, of which only fragments remain, represents a priest of Ea or Oannes, the great Mesopotamian god, father of Marduk. During the first half of the first millennium BC the priests of this cult did, in fact, wear a sort of close-fitting chasuble decorated with the image of a fish. The figure following the priest is a bull from the waist down. In its existing form, this basrelief seems to be in opposition to Mazdean orthodoxy and be in direct relation with the Mesopotamian fertility cult.

41. AERIAL VIEW OF PERSEPOLIS
This photograph published in Flights over ancient cities of Iran *by E. Schmidt shows what a good defensive site the citadel of Persepolis was built on and helps us to understand why Darius chose to move his capital which was too exposed on the plain at Pasargadae.*

42. THE TACHARA AT PERSEPOLIS
Time of Darius I (end of sixth century BC).
Temporary residence of Darius's palace; his name constantly occurs on the window surrounds.

---

[1] For the most recent work on the site the reader is directed to the reports by David Stronach in *Iran*, the journal of the British Institute of Persian studies in Teheran, for 1963 and 1964. The final report has yet to be published. Among other interesting results it has become clear that the tomb of Cyrus was used as a mosque during one of the first Islamic invasions when the citadel of Pasargadae, the Takht-i Sulaimān, seems to have been a Muhammadan settlement. It seems to have been deserted soon after AD 750.

39

43

43. DETAIL OF A PILLAR OF ONE OF THE ORDINARY DOORS OF THE HALL OF A
HUNDRED COLUMNS AT PERSEPOLIS
Time of Darius I (end of sixth century BC).
*The sovereign with a servant carrying a fly-whisk beside him is seated under a fringed baldaquin
decorated with three bands of rosettes between which there is a procession of lions and bulls. At
the top of the pillar is the winged symbol called the 'Furūhār'. The pillar in question is on the right
of one of the six ordinary doors leading into the hall of a hundred columns. Two other larger doors
give access to the hall from the courtyard of the military quarters (see figure 130 G). On the pillars
of these two large doors five rows each with ten warriors represented the army carrying the king's
throne. On the pillars of the ordinary doors fourteen throne bearers in three rows represented the
races of the various peoples of the Empire.*

44. HEAD OF DARIUS I IN PROFILE
Bas-relief from the Treasury, Persepolis. Time of Darius I (end of sixth century BC). Scale: $\frac{1}{3}$.
Archaeological Museum, Teheran.
*The hands—one holding a lotus bud—which appear in plate 58 are part of this bas-relief. They
are the hands of the son of Darius I, the future Xerxes I, hereditary prince at the time.*

45. THE CHILIARCH (?)
Bas-relief from the Treasury, Persepolis. Time of Darius I (end of sixth century BC). Scale: $\frac{1}{3}$.
Archaeological Museum, Teheran.
*Detail of the same bas-relief (plate 44). It most probably represents the chiliarch, the officer who
was in charge of the Treasury and also commander of the army. He holds his hand to his mouth as
a mark of respect on the part of an officer addressing his sovereign. It was customary for the chiliarch to be a Mede.*

46. THE DAGGER OF DARIUS
Bas-relief from the Treasury at Persepolis. Time of Darius I (end of sixth century BC.)
Length: $19\frac{1}{16}$ in. Archaeological Museum, Teheran.
*Detail of the same bas-relief (plates 44 and 45). Darius's dagger is worn by the officer responsible
for keeping the royal arms. Note the decorative motifs which continue the art of Luristān, and the
great delicacy of execution.*

COLOUR PLATE

II. DETAIL OF A BAS-RELIEF, PERSEPOLIS
Fifth century BC. Scale: $\frac{2}{3}$.
*This detail of a bas-relief decorating the stairway of the central palace at Persepolis represents the
head of a Persian archer, an excellent example of Achaemenid sculpture of the time of Xerxes I,
son and successor of Darius I. The lips of this warrior were painted red, as were the insides of the
throats of the roaring lions on the oldest capitals of the Apadanā, just as the clothes of some figures
on the Tripylon were also coloured.*

D

PART TWO

ACHAEMENID IRAN

FROM CYRUS THE GREAT TO DARIUS III CODOMANNUS

Towards the beginning of the second millennium BC large groups of nomads of Aryan origin infiltrated into the Iranian plateau via the Turkestan steppes. Some of them made for India. The others reached western Iran and, depending on the natural obstacles and local opposition they met with, either settled, temporarily as they thought, in the mountains of the western edge of the plateau or went on to install themselves in the great curve of the Euphrates and on the Anatolian plateau.

These first-comers were only the forerunners of the great mass of tribes of the same origin who came to Iran by the same route during the second half of the same millennium and among whom were the peoples known as the Medes and Persians. These two groups, whom we can call Iranians, because they inhabited Iran[1] from that time onwards, were not slow to make their power felt in the valleys of the mountainous Zagrus massif where they established themselves. They captured the native fortresses and imposed strange gods on them: Surya, the sun god; Marut, the plague god; Burya, the storm god, and taught them how to use the horse for peaceful and warlike purposes. Soon the countries in which they settled[2] became the main obstacles to the expansion of Assyrian power and there was an almost continuous succession of wars. It would take too long to give all the details of them here, on top of which the details would first have to be freed of the intolerable boasting[3] and mendacious statistics which the royal annals all too often contain. I shall only mention those which directly

[1] Iran, formerly Ariana, was originally an adjective which meant 'Aryan'.

[2] In those days the country of Parsua, or Parsuah, lay to the south of Lake Urmiya. It was the first stage on the Persians' journey to Parsumash and Parsa. The Manai country, roughly occupying the same territory as present-day Iranian Kurdistān, lay to the south-west of the lake. The land of the Māda or Medes was further east, extending right up to Mount Dimāwand. The country of the Ellipi, which the Assyrians renamed Zamma, or Mazamna, when they had conquered it, extended from the frontier of Elam to the present-day road from Baghdad to Kirmānshāh and Hamadhān, the northern approaches to which were guarded by the country of the Lullubi. The word 'Namri' was used to designate the south-western parts of the country.

[3] Here is an example. King Sargon is speaking: 'With nothing but my personal chariot and the horsemen who were by my side . . . I fell on him like an impetuous javelin, defied him and put him to rout. I made an immense slaughter of his army: I strewed the bodies of his warriors around like malt. I made the blood flow like a river over the precipices . . . and into the gulfs.' (F. Thureau-Dangin, *Une relation de la huitième campagne de Sargon*, p. 23.)

concern the Aryans' installation on the Iranian plateau. I have borrowed the facts from a book by George G. Cameron[1] on the history of ancient Iran.

In the reign of Tiglath-Pilasar II (747–727 BC), the Assyrian annals mention the Iranians as opponents. The power belonged to the Medes whose allies and vassals the Persians were, because they were apparently less numerous. Under the leadership of their chiefs the Achaemenids, the Persians abandoned Parsua to the south of Lake Urmiya in the face of Scythian pressure and later the Cimmerians who invaded the regions inhabited by the Medes.

During this time Teispes the Achaemenid settled north of Elam out of range of Scythian devastation, in the region of Anzhan and conquered the land of Persia.

Thanks to a solidly constituted and organized army, the Medes, allied to the Babylonians, took Assyria and in the Mesopotamian regions the supremacy passed to the Babylonians while the Medes consolidated their authority over Iran. A daughter of Astyages the Mede married Cambyses I and the fruit of this Medo-Persian union was Cyrus the Creat, Cyrus II the Achaemenid, who soon revolted against his grandfather and suzerain, and defeated him in the course of two successive battles in 559 BC.

In 331 BC, 230 years later, Alexander destroyed this empire which had laid down the law in the Near East for two centuries, had come very close to conquering Greece and had destroyed Lydia and all the prosperous Hellenized coastal kingdoms. Towns such as Miletus and Sardis were then governed by satraps. Darius improved the system which Cyrus had inaugurated and divided the Persian Empire into thirty satrapies which stretched as far as the Indus and included Egypt and Ethiopia.

The first Achaemenids lived a glorious warlike life of constant fighting, but the later monarchs were merely capricious sovereigns, the slaves of their own appetites and pleasures.

Fig. 123

The *Gandj Nāma*

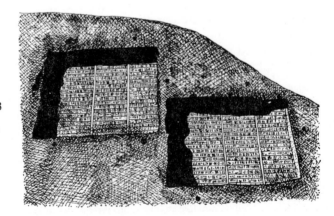

[1] See bibliography.

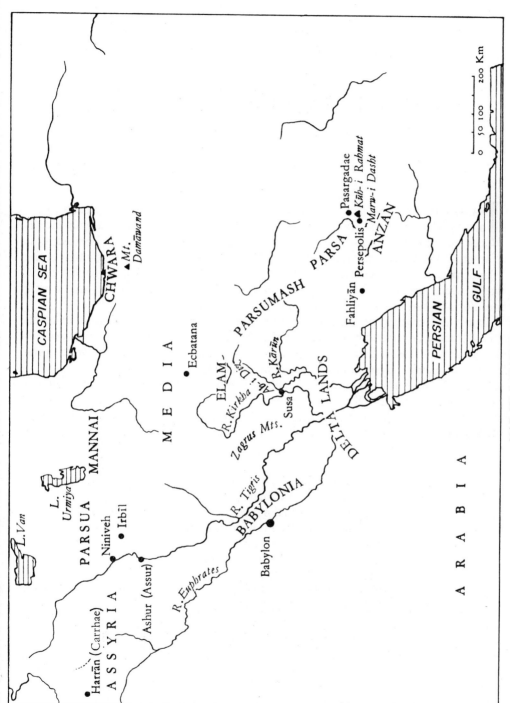

MAP II: ACHAEMENID IRAN

CHAPTER 4

ACHAEMENID IRAN

ARCHITECTURE

IRANIAN art *par excellence*, the art which bears the most convincing witness to the artistic sensibility of Iran, has always been architecture. This pre-eminence is obvious in the Achaemenid, Parthian and Sassanid periods, if only because most of what we know about them is through their monuments, but it is equally true of the Islamic period. Here, perhaps, it is the new aspect of traditional Iranian architectural works which gives the best and most precise information concerning the artistic meaning of Islam and its effects on ancient Iranian civilization.

In the last century people knew nothing, or almost nothing, even in Iran itself, about Iranian construction methods, partly because of the Persians' indifference to the remains of their ancient civilization, but also because of a fanaticism which prohibited foreigners from entering religious buildings. Because of the difficulty of travelling in the still fairly recent times of caravans and terrible roads, the few monuments described by travellers were nearly always the same, those they had found on the two routes which traverse Iran in the shape of a cross: from Tabrīz to Būshīr, via Sultānīya, Qazwīn, Qum, Isfahān and Shīrāz, and from Qasr-i Shīrīn to Mashhad (Meshed), via Kirmānshāh, Hamadhān, Qazwīn, Teheran, Dāmghān and Nīshāpūr. In addition I should point out that the hasty descriptions and drawings which came of these travellers' researches usually contradict each other.

During the reign of HM Riza Shāh Pahlawī, on the other hand, it was permissible to enter all the monuments of Iran, even the particularly sacred sanctuaries of Mashhad (Meshed) and Qum. In addition many roads were built, which facilitated the discovery of buildings hitherto unknown. For some twenty years it was possible to examine, draw, photograph and measure several hundreds of ancient monuments—in other words enough buildings for a detailed study of Iranian architecture. Obviously we are still only at the stage of monographs and hypotheses, but already many basic problems have been solved; from now on it is possible to follow the continuous thread of the history of monuments which have often been modified or restored for better or worse, from as far back as we can see until today, through the maze of influences and tendencies discernible in them.

The architecture of the peoples with whom the Medes and the Persians came into contact at the time of their massive settlement on the Iranian plateau was basically not real art at all. We know this either from remains, in the case of the Assyrians, and with the others through the Assyrian annals and the decoration of a certain number of objects, the 'Van plaque' (fig. 124) for example which belongs to the British Museum

Fig. 124

and depicts an Urartian edifice exactly reproduced by the Ka'aba Zardusht (pl. 56) at Naqsh-i Rustam, near Persepolis. We have some idea of the Manaian towns, their formidable defences, their houses 'built with art' and the palaces with lofty 'perfumed' wooden columns, the description of which corresponds pretty accurately to that of the royal castle at Ecbatana by Polybius. As for plans it seems that we know them too from the plans of the monuments of the Median period still existing in Iran: tombs hollowed out of the mountain in imitation of the peasant houses of the

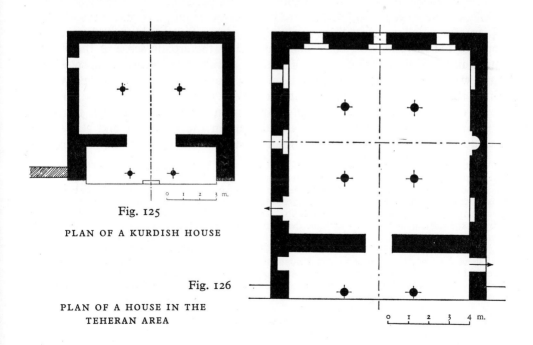

Fig. 125

PLAN OF A KURDISH HOUSE

Fig. 126

PLAN OF A HOUSE IN THE
TEHERAN AREA

type which we still see there at the present day. The house chosen as man's last habitation was the same as the one he had lived in: a vast hall with columns supporting the ceiling, with an open portico in front; the only reason for the excessively stout columns was that they were cut out of the rock. The wooden prototypes were slender. Herzfeld has published plans of similar houses discovered by him in Kurdistān (fig. 125). I have drawn them myself in the Teheran region (fig. 126). In essence both plans are the same as those of buildings at Pasargadae and Persepolis.

However, the original elements of these crude buildings were never employed on such a scale as they were in the time of the Achaemenid sovereigns. When Darius I, in the important document known as 'the Charter of the Palace of Susa',[1] declares that he built 'this palace' by the means he enumerates, indicating that involved in this affair there were himself, Darius, who gave the orders, and on the other hand the foreign workers and materials, it is to exalt his role, or more accurately the role of the all-powerful Achaemenid he was. But in reality there must certainly have been a 'master of works' between the sovereign and the workers capable of transforming so many disparate elements into the perfectly coherent and homogeneous whole of Persepolis. We perhaps know why the Great King did not mention him, but there is no doubt that he existed and that Darius, and even Cyrus, had at their disposal a corps of eminent architects and engineers, with long experience of similar difficult tasks. Pasargadae and Persepolis would be incomprehensible if we refused to admit this.

But we do not know who the skilful intelligent men were. It seems clear that there is proof of Ionian or Lydian collaboration at Pasargadae in the preoccupation with excellence, the elegance and delicacy to be observed in all parts of the construction (pl. 39). As a matter of fact those qualities, which are found subsequently in all the works of the Achaemenids, correspond so well to the artistic sense of the Persian nation, in the form we can conceive of it, that one might be tempted to acknowledge that it was an innate quality from the beginning. But there is no spontaneous generation in this field, or elsewhere. Talent is not born fully developed nor shapes completely evolved, as Athene sprang fully armed from Zeus's forehead. It is the result of many attempts and long efforts, and to explain the splendour and almost immediate perfection of Achaemenid architecture we must assume that the experi-

[1] The text is as follows: 'The decoration of this palace which I built at Susa was fetched from far away. The earth was dug down to the rock. When the digging was done—forty cubits deep in some places and twenty in others—the rubble was thrown into the pit. It was on this base that the palace was constructed. The bricks were moulded and baked in the sun by Babylonians. The cedar beams were brought from a mountain called Lebanon. The Assyrian people brought them to Babylonia. From Babylon the Carians and Ionians brought them to Susa. The wood called *yakā* was brought from Gandhāra and Karmāna. The gold was brought from Sardis and Bactria and wrought here. The magnificent stone called lapis lazuli and the cornelian were wrought here but were brought from Soghdiana. The precious turquoise was brought from Khwārizmia and wrought on the spot. The silver and ebony were brought from Egypt. The decoration for the walls was brought from Ionia. The ivory, wrought here, was transported from Kussa, Sind and Arachosia. The stone columns, which were worked here, were brought from a village called *Abiradu* in Elam. The stone dressers were Ionians and Sards. The goldsmiths who wrought the gold were Medes and Egyptians. The men who worked the sun-baked bricks, they were Egyptians. The men who decorated the walls were Medes and Egyptians.'

mental time was considerably reduced by teaching and no doubt also by the collaboration of very experienced constructors. The charter of the palace of Susa says further
that 'the stones were dressed by Ionians and Sards'. If we are tempted to deduce
from this that the last King of Lydia, Croesus, the enemy of Cyrus who became his
friend, was his adviser on architectural matters and supplied the architects who built
Pasargadae, we must remember that it was built between 559 and 550 BC, consequently before the defeat and capture of Croesus by Cyrus which took place in 546 BC.

As for the composition of the plans, since the Achaemenid palaces were nothing
more than the ordinary dwelling house enlarged to an extraordinary degree, it is likely
that the foreign constructors were not commissioned to make them; their job was
presumably to carry out the extraordinary, in execution of the king's orders. If these
constructors were Greeks, they would not have been at all surprised by the type of
plan prescribed, for the shape of the Median tombs and many buildings of the
period was that of the Mycenean megaron, the 'living and public quarters of the pre-
Hellenic habitation', so characteristic of the palace of the Achaean kings. Such was the
megaron at Tiryns[1] (fig. 127), for example, in which we recognize not only the Iranian

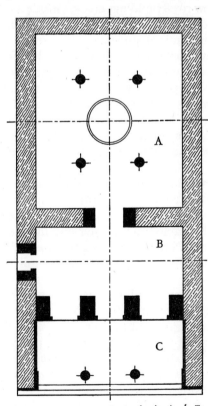

Fig. 127

PLAN OF THE MEGARON
AT TIRYNS

A. Megaron. B. Prodomos. C. Aithousa.

[1] Twelfth to eleventh centuries BC.

plan, with the exception of the *prodomos*, but Iranian construction: walls of sun-dried brick protected at the most vulnerable points, wooden columns on stone dados supporting the roof, also of wood, and an earthen terrace—which shows how true it is that the same needs and the same methods produce the same solutions.

When the Medes and Persians on their way to the west were stopped in the mountains on the western edge of Iran and settled there, the Medes, who were the first arrivals and first to get organized, dominated the Persians to begin with. Then Cyrus II, the great Cyrus, King of Anzhan like his father Cambyses, revolted against the authority of Astyages, his grandfather, who from his birth had desired his death, took Ecbatana, his capital, and assumed the title of King of Persia in 546 BC. Once he had conquered Croesus, King of Lydia, he was the undisputed master of western Asia.

An Achaemenid from a clan of the great tribe of Pasargadae, he had established his residence in their domain, at Pasargadae. When he was still only a 'petty vassal' of the king of the Medes he had built a town there, which, as a matter of fact, was not very different from a nomads' encampment in the sense that it was composed of little more than a few royal buildings erected inside a walled park and surrounded by a greater or smaller number of tents and flocks depending on the season. However, it was dominated by an artificial stone-covered terrace, the Takht-i Sulaimān, which presumably must have supported the buildings of a citadel. However, up to the present only the remains of comparatively crude constructions have been found there.

The royal edifices were excavated during 1949 and 1950. One of them, generally known as the 'Palace of the Stele', was the building through which one entered the park (pl. 38). In the past one could read this inscription on it, repeated several times: 'I, Cyrus, the King, the Achaemenid.' Another, 'the Palace of the Column', perhaps was where the sovereign held official audiences. Yet another must have been his residence.

However, it is probable that in or before 540 BC Cyrus, having conquered Astyages and overcome Asia Minor, realized that the small country village of Pasargadae in a remote valley could never become the seat of government of a great state and decided to shift his capital to a greater and more easily defended site. It was very probably he, and not Darius, who chose the site of Persepolis at the foot of the Kūh-i Rahmat, the 'Mountain of Mercy', some forty miles from Pasargadae in a very beautiful part of Fārs. He did not erect the monuments there of course, nor even start them; but he probably began to build the enormous terrace near the foot of the mountain on which the citadel of Persepolis (pl. 41) was built. No doubt he continued to inhabit his former town of Pasargadae at the same time as he cut away the rock and filled in the ravines on the site of the new city. There is no text extant enabling us to confirm or refute this, but the construction of the terrace at Persepolis represents such a considerable body of work that we cannot add the Apadanā and Tachara of Darius to it, unfinished as they were, during the thirty-six years of the sovereign's reign. No builder, even if equipped with modern technical resources, would undertake to carry out such works in such a short space of time. Consequently it is impossible to imagine Darius choosing the site of Persepolis in 518 BC, as is commonly accepted, and constructing during his reign not only the Takht-i Djamshid, i.e. the terrace at Persepolis, but also the Tachara and the greater part of the Apadanā, the immense palace for royal audiences.

When Cyrus died in 529 BC during an expedition against the Massagetae in the plains to the east of the Caspian Sea, his body was brought back to Pasargadae and placed in the tomb he had had made there. It is a small stone edifice, roughly square in plan, with a two-sided pitched roof, on a tiered pyramidal base. The only way to give an idea of its true dimensions (pl. 37) is to compare the height of the tiers with that of a human being.

After reigning for eight years, Cyrus's successor, his son Cambyses II, who conquered Egypt, died in Syria. His body was not recovered. So the tomb attributed to him at Pasargadae was not occupied by him. Incidentally it is probable that it never would have been, even if Cambyses had died in his capital or if his body had been brought back to it. And this for a reason which strongly reinforces the theory which I have just put forward about the choice of the site of Persepolis and the beginning of the construction work on the terrace by Cyrus. E. Herzfeld, who undertook the excavation of the monuments at Persepolis in 1931, spotted in their immediate neighbourhood, between the Takht and the cliff in which the tombs of Darius and his successors were hollowed out, the lower tiers of a substructure identical to that of the mausoleum of Cyrus at Pasargadae and considered that it had certainly been intended to bear the tomb of Cambyses. No one would believe it. Why should the tomb of this king have been built so far from his capital, Pasargadae? Yet if Cyrus or even Cambyses had decided that Pasargadae should be abandoned and Persepolis elevated to the rank of capital of the empire, and if the work of construction had begun, what could be more natural?

The course of events might have told us exactly what happened but, after the death of Cambyses, power passed into the hands of Darius who came from another branch of the Achaemenid family. Pasargadae, in decline because of this, was replaced by Persepolis while it was still being built. So that we could perhaps assume, as scholars have done so far, that it was only then that the site of the new capital was chosen by Darius, if it were not for the fact that this hypothesis is inconsistent with the time required to build the works I have just mentioned and the fact that the tomb of Cambyses seems to have been near Persepolis, not at Pasargadae.

The construction of the buildings on the terrace was pushed forward actively during the reigns of Darius I, Xerxes I and Artaxerxes I. Later there were nothing but a few finishing touches and additions of no great importance.

The citadel of Persepolis, resting on the Kūh-i Rahmat and facing the immense plain called Marw-i Dasht, consists of a vast group of constructions established on a substructure partly built of colossal blocks of stone and partly cut out of the mountain (pl. 41). On this gigantic base, some sixty feet high in some places, the upper platform of which has an area of no less than thirty-three acres, were crowded the reception palaces and residences of the kings, the vast storerooms of the Treasury and the military quarters, the size of which is proving greater and greater as the work on excavating the Takht (fig. 128) advances. The 'royal town' of which the historians speak lay at the foot of the terrace on the level of the plain, protected by a double wall and a moat.

But this was not how people imagined Persepolis at the beginning of this century and even more recently than that. The high platform the Iranians still call Takht-i Djamshid, the throne of Djamshid, was then considered to have been entirely occupied by the palaces of the Achaemenid sovereigns and their gardens. Until about 1930, that is to say when excavation of the site began, all that could be seen above the supporting wall of the terrace and the great stairway (fig. 128 A and pl. 53) were the following: the entrance hall (fig. 128 B), the few remaining columns of the royal reception hall, the Apadanā (fig. 128 C and pl. 60), the ruins of Darius's small residence, the Tachara (fig. 128 O and pl. 42), those of a palace of Xerxes, the Hadish (fig. 128 M), and nearby this group monuments some parts of a building which could only be, so it seemed, the Harem, the palace of the ladies of the court. A little further on could be seen the Hall of a Hundred Columns (fig. 128 G), which was a second reception hall, and facing it the 'Unfinished Gate' (fig. 128 F). It was thought that the citadel as well as the royal treasury were on the mountain, at the top of the Kūh-i Rahmat, and that the town was situated at what was later Istakhr, about four miles away. In short all that was known of Persepolis were the ruins of edifices which could pass for the residential palaces of the Achaemenid monarchs, the Harem and the two great reception halls—nothing, so it was thought, but palaces and their annexes.

But in fact the edifice called the harem would have been a very strange and uncomfortable home for the ladies of the court. It had no open space and only a double line of enormous halls with no external doors or windows which only opened on to a long central corridor. The darkness must have been almost complete, even if we assume lighting by skylights or openings in the upper part of one of the walls. We cannot really imagine the mother of Xerxes, the proud and all-powerful Princess Atossa, wife of Darius, daughter of Cyrus the Great, living in this semi-prison.

However, between the years 1934 and 1939 the excavations conducted by the Oriental Institute of Chicago at Persepolis discovered, between the supposed harem and the mountain, a whole group of halls marked out on the ground by multiple bases of stone columns and belonging to the royal treasury. Since the departure of the American expedition in 1939, the Iran Department of Antiquities, continuing their work, has revealed a series of vaulted galleries (fig. 128 L), isolated on all sides by an observation corridor which could only be entered by a small gate which was guarded by police. It was certainly the most secret and best guarded place in the treasury. From the archaeological and architectural point of view these long vaulted galleries from the Achaemenian period are obviously very interesting. What I find particularly important, however, is that in this case the Achaemenid Harem would have been inside the Treasury buildings (fig. 128 J), which is quite impossible, whereas these large dark halls, inaccessible from the outside, were so well suited to the requirements of the storerooms and deposits of the Treasury (fig. 128 K). There was no harem on the terrace at Persepolis.

It probably contained, therefore, no more than one residential palace, or at least one intended for living in, the Tachara of Darius (fig. 128 O), clearly identified by several inscriptions. This tiny building was certainly only intended to house the Achaemenid sovereign, Darius or another, temporarily in case of invasion or rebellion. The true royal palaces, vast and sumptuous, together with their gardens, were on the level of the plain in the south and south-west part of the royal town.

Now that the Hadish of Xerxes (fig. 128 M) and its surroundings have been excavated it would appear to be the very building—a large luxurious edifice next to the palace for royal audiences where the sovereign received, entertained and perhaps occasionally housed his distinguished guests—the non-existence of which would have been astonishing. Its stairways, similar to those in the Apadanā, its important guard posts, its enormous hall and the bas-reliefs representing the King of Kings entering it in great state, give it a character quite unlike that of a dwelling place.

After the departure of the Chicago expedition, the Iranian Department of Antiquities realized that the area in front of the reception buildings was divided into two parts, one of which belonged to the Apadanā and the other to the Hall of a Hundred Columns. It also discovered that a broad avenue (fig. 128 D) led from the great stairway to the courtyard of the Hall of a Hundred Columns which would probably have been entered by means of a vestibule similar to the first vestibule if that construction had ever been finished (fig. 128 F). I shall explain later why we can cons der the Hall of a Hundred Columns as having been the assembly hall, or hall of honour, of the army, i.e. the famous regiment of the 'Immortals'.

We can say, therefore, that the buildings constructed on the terrace at Persepolis formed three clear-cut groups: the military quarters, the treasury, and the third reserved for the receptions and the occasional housing of the Achaemenid kings (pl. 42).

The residential palace of Xerxes was discovered in 1952 in the royal town at the foot of the terrace, on a level with the plain. It was situated in a large garden bounded to the south and west by the town walls and included a vast ornamental lake the stone walls of which are bonded in the same way as those of the substructure of the citadel. Some column-bases, still in place in the main hall of the monument, bear an inscription indicating that it was Xerxes the King who built this Tachara. We notice that Xerxes himself says that he is 'King' and not 'King of Kings', which means that at the time of the construction of his palace he was still only Prince Xerxes, in fact the son to whom Darius entrusted the supervision of the works at Persepolis. Next to Xerxes' palace, between it and the mountain, are the remains of an even richer edifice which has not been precisely identified yet, but was perhaps one of Darius's residential palaces.

Some sondages—not enough for lack of money—suggest that the royal city stretched along the foot of the mountain for a considerable part of the way towards Naqsh-i Rustam, that is, towards the tombs of the first sovereigns of the line of Darius (pls. 56

47. A BULL AND A LION FIGHTING

Bas-relief on the northern stairway of the Apadanā, Persepolis. Time of Xerxes I (beginning of fifth century BC). Scale: $\frac{1}{8}$.

The motif of a lion and a bull fighting is a common one in Mesopotamian glyptics. Its constant repetition at Persepolis may perhaps be explained by the importance of the bull in Aryan religions. The sacrifice of the bull is bound up with the myth of Spring and renewal.

48. TRIBUTE-BEARERS

Bas-relief on the eastern stairway of the Apadanā, Persepolis. Time of Xerxes I (beginning of fifth century BC). Scale: $\frac{1}{8}$.

A frieze of tribute-bearers decorates the monumental stairways leading to the Apadanā at Persepolis. Judging by their head-dress they might be Lydians, former subjects of King Croesus, whose capital was Sardis.

49. PERSIAN OFFICERS ON THEIR WAY TO A RECEPTION GIVEN BY THE ACHAEMENID SOVEREIGN

Bas-relief on the main stairway of the Apadanā, Persepolis. Period of Xerxes I (beginning of fifth century BC). Scale: $\frac{1}{11}$.

The informality of this scene makes a welcome change from the solemnity of the usual procession of Achaemenid soldiers.

50. DETAIL OF THE FRIEZE OF TRIBUTE-BEARERS (pl. 48)

This detail enables us to appreciate the perfection of the work of the sculptors at Persepolis even more. It is interesting to compare this goldsmith's work on stone with the reproduction of a gold bracelet of the same period published by A. T. Olmstead in his History of the Persian Empire *(pl. LVIII).*

51. A PALACE SERVANT

Bas-relief from the Treasury, Persepolis. Time of Darius I (end of sixth century BC). Scale: $\frac{3}{8}$. Archaeological Museum, Teheran.

This detail is of the same bas-relief as plates 44, 45, 46 and 58. We do not know for certain what the role of this person was. He was perhaps a kind of major-domo.

52. BEARERS OF THE ROYAL THRONE

Detail of a door in the Hall of a hundred columns, Persepolis. Fourth century BC. Scale: $\frac{2}{15}$.

The figures it depicts, including one Scythian and one Sogdian, are the representatives of satrapies situated in the north-east of the Empire.

53. THE GREAT STAIRWAY LEADING TO THE TERRACE AT PERSEPOLIS

Time of Darius I (end of sixth century BC).

This double stairway has such wide and gentle steps that they can be mounted on horseback.

54. PERSIAN AND MEDIAN GUARDS

Bas-relief on the main stairway of the Apadanā, Persepolis. Time of Xerxes I (beginning of fifth century). Scale: $\frac{1}{9}$.

The Mede can be recognized by his round head-dress.

48

49

55. PERSIAN AND MEDIAN OFFICERS ON THEIR WAY TO THE RECEPTION HELD AT NAWRUZ

Decoration on the eastern stairway of the Apadanā. Time of Xerxes I (beginning of fifth century BC). Scale: ¼.

On the day of Nawruz (the New Year), the Achaemenid sovereign received the officers who happend to be in residence at Persepolis.

56. THE KAʿBA ZARDUSHT (The Cube of Zoroaster)

At Naqsh-i Rustam, near Persepolis. Time of Darius I (beginning of fifth century BC). Height: 38 ft.; width: 23 ft. 9 in.

Originally, it was probably the provisional tomb of the Achaemenid kings. Then, at a later date, it may have become the official temple in which the royal standards were kept.

57. TOMB OF DARIUS I

Naqsh-i Rustam, near Persepolis. Time of Darius I (beginning of fifth century BC). Height: about 73 ft.; width: about 24 ft.

This was the first edifice of its kind to be cut out of a cliff. It has a fine inscription in three types of cuneiform characters: Ancient Persian, Elamite and Babylonian. Two bas-reliefs, which have no connection with it, were carved below the tomb in the Sassanian period (c. AD 280). Three other tombs of Achaemenid kings were hollowed out of the rock at Naqsh-i Rustam, those of Xerxes I, Artaxerxes I and, no doubt, Xerxes II.

58. THE HANDS OF XERXES I

Detail of a bas-relief from the Treasury, Persepolis. Time of Darius I (beginning of fifth century BC). Scale: ⅓. Archaeological Museum, Teheran.

This detail belongs to the same bas-relief as plates 44, 45, 46 and 51. The hands are those of Xerxes, the son of Darius I, who is standing behind his father's throne in plate 44. Xerxes was the grandson of Cyrus the Great by his mother, Queen Atossa. Chosen by his father as heir to the throne, he was associated with the government of the empire during the lifetime of Darius. According to Herzfeld, the sculptures, which represent Xerxes touching his father's throne with his hands, date from the time when he became his associate.

E

and 57). The ordinary town was not at Istakhr, but probably in the actual plain of Persepolis outside the walls and moat which protected the royal town. Large stone constructions are still visible at some distance from the Terrace and it is quite certain that, if the trouble was taken, the remains of many other Achaemenid constructions which have been razed in the past by the local peasants but still exist below ground-level would be discovered.

So Pasargadae and Persepolis bore no resemblance. For during the short period of time separating the foundation of the two towns, the status of the Persian sovereigns had entirely changed. As Herzfeld very justly remarks, when Cyrus built Pasargadae he was still only the sovereign chief of a province of the Median Empire. When Darius undertook the construction of the monuments at Persepolis, he was the absolute master of the greatest empire which had ever existed in Asia. From this time onwards the authoritarian character of Achaemenian civilization asserted itself and the method of government became that 'solemn despotism, resting wholly on the inviolable cult of the royal person, who was god come down to earth', of which Darmesteter speaks. Art was already devoted to the glorification of the sovereign, as was the whole of Achaemenid civilization. In effect the only known Achaemenid monuments are the palaces and tombs of kings. There were few or no religious edifices—not that Persia of that period lacked religion—contemporary inscriptions witness to the contrary—but the old religion of the Aryans had no great need of temples. From remote antiquity, says Herodotus, the Persians climbed the highest mountains when they wanted to sacrifice to their gods.[1]

The Achaemenid monument *par excellence*, then, is the royal palace and more especially the vast lofty audience hall at the far end of which the sovereign, surrounded by his familiars, the great men of the kingdom and his guards, appeared as a supernatural being in the eyes of his subjects (pls. 44 and 45). This type of construction, the hypostyle hall, was known in Iran as elsewhere, in Egypt for example, but in Iran it had so far only produced works lacking grandeur and in Egypt the use of the stone lintel, which of necessity has to be kept fairly short (pl. 65), had prevented the development of this type of building. However, the use of long cedar beams, which the great king had brought from Lebanon at vast expense, made it possible to diminish the number of supporting points very considerably (pl. 61) in exchange for free spaces and consequently an increase in the monumental aspect of the constructions. Just think that the ceiling of the hall of the Apadanā, which represents an area of five-eighths of an acre, is supported by only thirty-six columns (fig. 128 C and pl. 60), that the distance between these columns measures nearly thirty feet from axis to axis and that their total area comes to only a sixth of the free space, against a little more than a quarter at Pasargadae and barely half at Karnak. Consider that these impressive dimensions were not the result of the adoption or invention of new types of ground-plan or new systems of construction. The buildings at Persepolis are neither more nor less Iranian than those at Pasargadae and the system of construction is the same. From this point of view the architecture of the age of Darius is no more cosmopolitan than that of the time of

Cyrus: one is a continuation of the other. The palaces at Persepolis owe the exceptional size of their structure to the materials, and to the long experience and skill of the constructors available to the king as the result of his conquests. It is also the result of the firm will of the monarch, what Darmesteter calls 'the caprice of an all-powerful dilettante with a taste for the grandiose'.

I have already said that there were two great hypostyle halls at Persepolis, one, the Apadanā, the construction of which was begun in the reign of Darius I and finished in that of his successor, his son Xerxes, the other, generally known as the Hall of a Hundred Columns, begun by Xerxes and finished by Artaxerxes I. Their purpose has never been much debated. However, we might well ask why the actual architecture seems to be more positive and the technique more developed in the more ancient of these edifices. But since their construction and decoration are equally skilful and well finished—the only difference being the means employed—it seems clear from the beginning that the building with the hundred columns did not try to compete with the Apadanā and consequently that the second building was not built to replace it. There is no doubt that the Apadanā remained the place for the sovereign's official receptions even after the other was put into use, but this observation does not tell us for what purpose the hall of Xerxes, even vaster than that of Darius, was intended. The writers who have mentioned it merely say that these monuments were audience halls. But why two halls and what sorts of audiences? We now know.

The excavation work on the Takht carried out by the Iranian Department of Antiquities since 1939 has shown that the vast esplanade situated in front of the two great halls was divided into two parts by a row of small rooms which formed a party wall (fig. 128 E), in such a way that each of these edifices had its own courtyard in front of it. In addition a broad avenue (fig. 128 D) led from the vestibule (fig. 128 B) situated at the top of the great stairway towards the courtyard of the Hall of a Hundred Columns, where it ended. From the entrance vestibule the visitor entered the courtyard of the Apadanā, i.e. the courtyard of the palace for the king's official receptions, via the wide gate in the side of the building, while the bay opposite the entrance gave access to the avenue which led to the other courtyard, onto which all the buildings of the military quarters opened directly or via roads and corridors (figs. 128 G and H).

So there is no doubt that the Hall of a Hundred Columns belonged to the army and was its assembly room or hall of honour. This explains why it was surrounded by a road and a wall isolating it from the treasury and the royal quarters (fig. 128 G). It also explains why the king's throne, which is carried by representatives of the nations making up the empire on all the other bas-reliefs (plates 43 and 52), is exceptionally carried by five files of warriors representing the army on the jambs of the great doors of the hall in question. It seems that this latter feature, the throne carried by the army, is particularly significant. Incidentally it was in this edifice built for the army by Xerxes I, the Achaemenid most hated by the Greeks, because he had destroyed the temples of Athens by fire, that the fire which destroyed Persepolis seems to have started and developed with most violence.

Fig. 128

PLAN OF PERSEPOLIS
A. Great stairway. B. Gate of all countries
(Xerxes). C. Apadanā. D. Avenue leading to the
military quarters. E. Wall separating the two
courtyards. F. Unfinished vestibule. G. Hall of a
Hundred Columns. H. Royal stables and chariot
house. I. East fortification. I'. North fortification.
J. Royal Treasury. K. Treasury warehouses and
stores. L. Subterranean galleries of the Treasury. M. Hadish of Xerxes. N. Palace of Artaxerxes III. O. Tachara of Darius. P. Tripylon,
the entrance hall of the central palace.

Extant sections are indicated in black; restored
sections are shaded; supporting walls are indicated
by a hairline. Unshaded areas are additions after
studies made by the Iranian Department of
Antiquities.

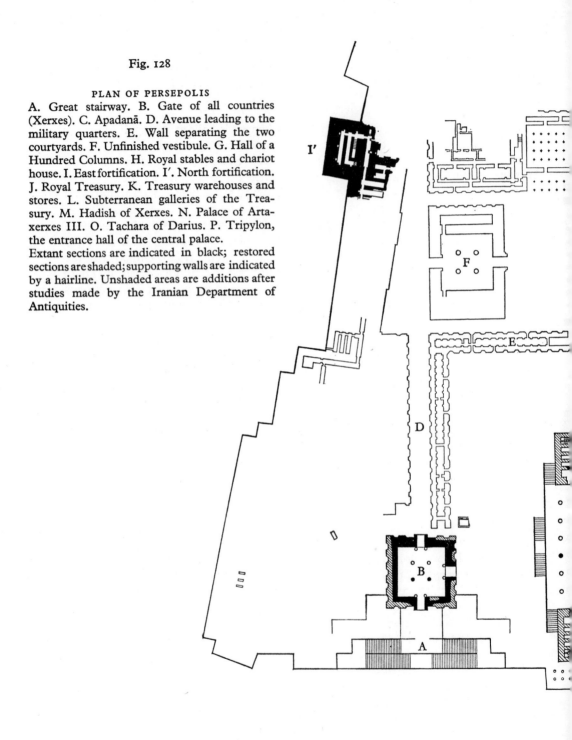

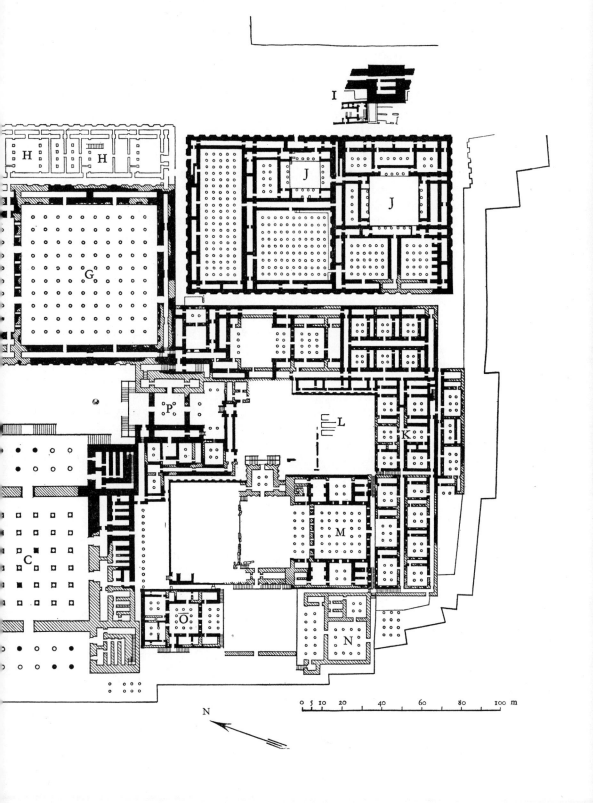

H H

J

J

I

G

P

L

K

C

M

O

N

0 5 10   20   40   60   80   100 m

N

SCULPTURE

The Apadanā, therefore, was the palace for the king's official audiences and the Hall of the Hundred Columns the army's hall of honour or assembly room. The king reached it directly from the palace by means of a door opening on to the rear of the building.

Achaemenid sculpture inherited Assyrian decorative formulae and adopted their principles. Like the Assyrians the Achaemenids used friezes carved on the bases of the walls of their palaces and in the embrasures of bays, but the gesticulations of the Assyrian figures seemed to them to lack dignity and their exaggerated realism to lack taste. They found such excess misplaced at eye level and the scrupulous reproduction of every detail irritating in the long run. The Iranian artist had already learnt that the worth of a work of art depends on making sacrifices and that decoration which is an end in itself is no longer decorative. So he simplified his technique and made it more flexible up to human height, reserving his dramatic effects for the upper parts of monuments. His base friezes have the lightness of a gently modelled drawing (col. pl. II); they do not force themselves on the observer, we feel rather than see their decorative presence, but the lions and bulls supporting the roofs have the power of the most vigorous pieces of Assyrian sculpture (fig. 135 and pls. 26, 61 and 70).

This great art has been accused of being repetitious—the files of identical warriors which decorate the base of the Apadanā for example (pls. 54 and 55). But surely it is normal for soldiers to look alike and for them to carry out the same movement simultaneously. However, if we examine another procession, that of the tribute bearers who advance behind the king's guards towards the centre of the composition (pls. 48 and 50), we shall see with what care, tact and variety, each one's character as well as his clothing and coiffure, and even the nature of his presence are indicated; but without this very shallow bas-relief striking a more emphatic note than its situation authorizes. Variety is one of the special charms of Achaemenid sculpture. It made full use of exotic shapes in its decoration, looking on them as so many souvenirs of countries which Persia had conquered, or to put it another way, as a collaboration of all those countries in the task of aggrandizing the Achaemenids. 'Look,' says Darius, 'at the image of those who bear my throne: you will recognize them. And you will learn this: that the men of Persia have fought far away from Persia.' But what could have been no more than a hotch-potch, a discordant harlequinade, obeys the taste of the constructor; it becomes harmonious and assumes a picturesque and imaginative character which only the most uncompromising and refined art would exclude (pls. 46 and 55).

In addition there is another important element of variety in the palace at Persepolis to which little attention has been paid so far: colour. The stone columns, the door jambs, the pillars, were not grey, as we see them today, the dull grey of the mountain rocks from which they come, but polished, black and brilliant, as some parts of the Tachara of Darius still are. The wooden beams and the ceilings were decorated in colour. The doors were faced with a veneer of gold or bronze, a few fragments of which can be seen in the glass show-cases of Teheran Museum. Between the outside columns of the palaces hung curtains on which, according to Athenaeus, 'were figures of animals of all kinds, very well represented'. In addition certain figures on the bas-reliefs, those of the Tripylon for example, were painted in vivid colours, some which lasted until recent years. Elsewhere, in the Tachara, the royal figures wore real gold bracelets and necklaces. The holes for attaching them can still be seen in the stone. Their head-dresses, also of gold, were covered with coloured stones. Their beards were sometimes of bronze or lapiz lazuli. If the reader feels that the extremely refined sculpture I have described was also rather barbarous when it was covered in this way with jewels and vivid colours, I shall not disagree with him. I recognize that Achaemenid art was actually both refined and barbarous, that that is how it must be presented. But this is far from unexpected since it was just the same with the Parthenon at Athens, the white marble façades of which were painted, or the delicate Korai from the Acropolis Museum, or what remains of the Hecatompedon, which dates from about the same time as the small palace of Darius.

Persepolis, decked out in this way, built in the Achaemenids' own domain, necropolis of the sovereigns of the line of Darius, was the dynastic capital of the Persian Empire. At first it was not inhabited, because it was under construction. Later it was hardly inhabited at all. Ctesias, for example, the Greek doctor, who lived at the court of Artaxerxes II for twenty years and became his historian, never saw it and does not mention it. Besides no trace of continuous or prolonged residence has been found at Persepolis. Nothing is worn—neither the steps of the stairway, not the thresholds, nor the floors. There are no graffiti, which were so numerous later. The royal plate, partly executed in Egypt, which was systematically broken by Alexander's soldiers, seems never to have been used (pl. 77). Discarded capitals (pl. 61), bases and shafts of columns still lie in the courtyard and corridors of the military quarters. The capital of Darius, the successor to Pasargadae, seems to have become fairly rapidly a sort of symbolic monument to Achaemenid grandeur, the image of its power, the Holy of Holies of the Empire, where every sovereign went, no doubt once a year at Nawruz (the New Year), to visit the tomb of his ancestors and receive the homage and tribute of the peoples who, in Darius's words, bore his throne.

When Alexander the Great set fire to Persepolis in 330 BC, he destroyed not only one of the capitals of Persia, therefore, but the very idea of Persian power.

With the Achaemenid dynasty there disappeared a whole manner of architecture. The Arsacids and the Sassanids constructed vaulted buildings and when Islamic Persia built columned palaces, she drew her inspiration from the Median tradition rather than the monuments at Persepolis.

The art of the Achaemenid period seems to have had no real influence on any subsequent ones, for its determining factors form a combination which has never occurred since. Like Assyrian art, it tried to express the wholly oriental idea of royal power, but it differs from it to the extent that an Aryan Achaemenid differs from a Semitic Sargonid. Like Greek art it had a taste for harmony, rhythm and skilful construction, but its programme was fundamentally Asiatic. However, it was not as if Persia was unacquainted with Greece: the two countries were in almost daily contact. Greeks lived at the court of the Achaemenids. The Kings of Kings probably employed Greeks on the construction of their palaces and brought back Greek works of art from their campaigns in the west: the wonderful statue, for example, which was discovered at Persepolis in 1934 and is now in the Museum at Teheran, or the gold crater by Theodorus of Samos, of which Athenaeus speaks. They were responsive to the beauty of Hellenic art but, inspired by an ideal irrevocably opposed to that which Greece pursued both in her art and her politics, they demanded that their own art depend entirely on the ancient truly oriental civilizations. When the royal power suddenly collapsed, depriving the art it had created of its support and the tremendous wealth of materials and craftsmen it had supplied, Achaemenid art disappeared with it.

COINS

The minor arts were not very much cultivated in Persia during the Achaemenid period, for the only customers who could have favoured the survival of these industries were the sovereigns themselves and the great personages, who were generally content to have their commissions executed by foreign craftsmen. The enamellers and cutters of seals were Babylonian or Phoenician. It seems that the workshops at Sardis, perhaps also those at Tarsus and Tyre, executed the darics (pl. 76) which the Achaemenids used for trade in the Mediterranean dependencies of the empire, but which Persia herself hardly used at all.

It seems certain that the first two sovereigns of the Achaemenid dynasty, Cyrus and Cambyses, did not feel the need to create a special coinage of their own and used the croeseids then current in Asia Minor, Iran itself using payment in kind or barter.

Darius I, the great organizer of the Iranian Empire, seems to have been the first to strike the pure gold coins, almost without admixture, which we know under the name of darics. However, it is believed that these coins were not put into circulation on Iranian soil, but were mainly used to pay the mercenary troops, to amass reserves in the dynastic treasuries and supply the towns on caravan routes which always were in great need of specie.

These coins (darics and shekels) have been found in Greece and Asia Minor, whereas so far as I know no treasure of darics or even shekels has ever been discovered in Iran itself. The coins which were found with the gold and silver plaques contained in the two stone chests found at the corners of the reception hall of the Apadanā at Persepolis came from Sardis and Miletus.

The foundation of the Apadanā is dated to *c.* 515 BC—conceivable if we accept that the terrace of the citadel was built before the accession of Darius, son of Hystaspes, to the throne of Persia. In any case, in 515 BC the first darics had not yet been minted and we can assume that the coinage of Darius I did not remain current even for as long as thirty years.

Xerxes minted coins in his turn. He did not try to give his darics an artistic character, any more than his father Darius. The archer (the 'melophorus')[1] figures on the obverse

---

[1] The archer is half kneeling; he wears the notched *cidaris* on his head and is clad in the *candys* which is drawn up over his left knee.

of the pieces, always in the same way. He wears the notched *cidaris* which leads us to suppose that the archer in question is indeed the Great King. The robe he wears called a 'candys' is an ample tunic sometimes drawn tight at the waist by a belt. The style of this coinage remained the same throughout the dynasty (figs. 129, 130, 131 and pl. 76). Its reverse, oval in shape, has a depression called a 'hollow square' to facilitate

Fig. 129	Fig. 130	Fig. 131

large-scale minting. Thanks to the discovery in Greece of some darics and shekels accompanied by Greek coins which can be dated, scholars have felt entitled to attribute the darics and shekels to one of the Achaemenid sovereigns, but without absolute certainty.

The clay tablets found in the archives at Persepolis, written in Aramaic and relating to accounts for the works, calculate in 'shekels', an ancient Semitic weight known in the Bible, which did not represent a payment in metal coinage but a value payable in kind: bread, wine, sheep, etc. In short, during the Achaemenid period monetary activity was virtually confined to the shores of the Mediterranean, and served for commercial exchanges between the maritime countries. But owing to the excellence of the metal in the gold daric and the silver shekel, the Achaemenid coinage was accepted everywhere.

However, the weaving industry seems to have been highly developed during the Achaemenid period. The much esteemed Persian fabrics were much exported to neighbouring nations. According to their historians, the Greeks were astonished by the richness of their Persian adversaries' costume.

In addition many bronze objects and items of metalwork continued to be produced in Iran itself (figs. 132, 133, 134 and plates 75, 77 and 78). Their shapes, the techniques and the decoration were still roughly that of the Zagrus art I mentioned earlier. For example, if we compare the plate (pl. 77), which comes from Persepolis, with another plate from Luristān, a century or two older, we can easily demonstrate their similarity. The Manaians, that is to say the inhabitants of the mountainous region situated to the south of Lake Urmiya, seem to have been particularly distinguished as goldsmiths and seem even to have been to a large extent the authors of the famous bas-reliefs at

F

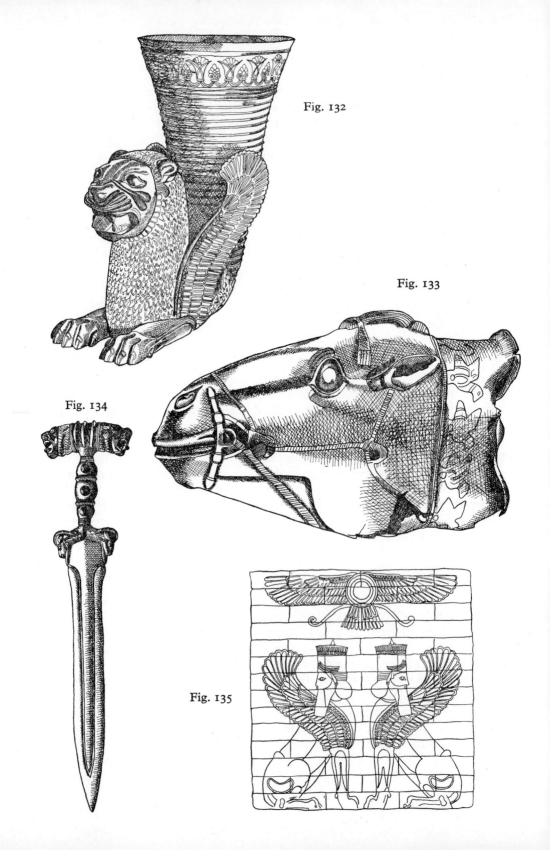

Fig. 132

Fig. 133

Fig. 134

Fig. 135

Persepolis. In fact the Achaemenid sovereigns, in order to carry out the grandiose architectural programme representative of their new grandeur, sought out the experienced artists and craftsmen they needed from all over their possessions. More or less conscripted Manaian metalworkers entered the service of Achaemenid art and, in the absence of professional sculptors, took their place, together with Egyptians. Not only does the 'Charter of the construction of the palace at Susa' state that the goldsmiths who worked the gold were Medes and Egyptians, it also says that 'the men who decorated the walls (fig. 135) were not only Egyptians but also Medes', i.e. Manaians turned Medes.

NOTE TO PART TWO

PRIMITIVE MAZDAISM

It seems clear that the Mazdean religion was, from its origins, the expression of belief in the dualism which characterized the ancient Iranian religions and led to their intransigence. Is not Zoroastrianism one of the few religions which accepts no converts?

The historian Shāhrastanī (AD 1086–1153), who was the first to take an interest in these problems and wrote in Arabic, believed that dualism existed before Zoroaster and that Mazdaism had gone past the stage corresponding to the adoration of the elements, the cult of fire and water, of which Anāhit was the protectress, a function she was supposed to combine with protection of agriculture. A kind of cult of saints, and *inter alia* of a protector (pl. 19) helping the shepherd to fight against wild beasts, rapidly became mingled with this primitive animism. The imagery of the so-called Luristān bronzes reveals an entire Sumero-Iranian pantheon which prefigures Mazdaism.

Scholars have often asked what was the religion of the Achaemenids. . . . Were they Zoroastrians or not?

Fig. 136

It seems clear that the majority of them, especially Cyrus and Darius, were eclectic enough and skilful politicians enough not to accept Ahura Mazda (fig. 136) as the sole divinity. While granting him the first place, they also admitted the power of other gods worshipped by the different peoples of the empire. In recent years archaeology has offered us an absolute proof. An expedition of the Iranian Department of Antiquities discovered at Pasargadae a bas-relief sculptured in the embrasure of a door of the entrance palace to Cyrus's capital, representing a man dressed in a costume imitating a fish (pl. 40), a kind of chasuble worn by the priests of Ea, which confirms the Babylonian and biblical evidence asserting that Cyrus practised the cult of the Babylonian god Marduk.

It seems almost certain that primitive Mazdaism was very different from Zoroastrianism, but even more so from the Mazdaism of the Sassanid period in the form revealed to us by writings collected at the end of that dynasty. There is no certain basis, no specific document enabling us to codify the scattered bits of information which we possess. Sassanid Mazdaism, on the other hand, is relatively familiar to us.

59. THE BULLS ON THE GATE KNOWN AS 'THE GATE OF ALL COUNTRIES'
Persepolis. Time of Xerxes I (beginning of fifth century BC). Scale: $\frac{1}{30}$; height of the bulls: 17 ft. 11 in.
The prophet Ezekiel (I, 4 to 12), who was taken to Mesopotamia when he was deported, saw on his way the vast winged bulls guarding the royal Assyrian residences and described these creatures which were a mixture of man, bull, eagle and lion. The Persians adopted the same guardian figures; they were responsible by their symbolical power for keeping evil spirits at bay.

60. COLUMNS OF THE APADANĀ
Persepolis. Time of Darius I (end of sixth century BC). Height: about 62 ft.
These immense shafts of stone surprise us as much by their height as by the width they stand apart. Such audacity was one of the causes of their destruction in the frequent earthquakes they have had to withstand.

61. CAPITAL WITH TWO-HEADED LION
Terrace, Persepolis. Fifth century BC. Length: about 4 ft. 7 in.
This capital was recovered intact. It had been rejected by the master builder and buried in the ground where it was discovered recently. A structural flaw in the centre was the reason for its rejection. An attempt had been made to reinforce the capital with metal cramps, but, as this precaution did not seem to be adequate, it was thought preferable to abandon it.

62. COLUMN BASE
Fahliyān, to the west of Shīrāz. Achaemenid period. Diameter: about 4 ft.
There seems to have been a stopping-place with a royal residence at this point on the route to Susa. Note the delicate decoration of the base.

63. GOLD FOUNDATION PLAQUE
From the Apadanā, Persepolis. Time of Darius I (end of sixth century BC). Length: 1 ft. $\frac{13}{16}$ in.; weight: about 11 lb. Archaeological Museum, Teheran.
This foundation document, found in a stone chest, together with a silver plaque, is written in Ancient Persian (10 lines at the top), Babylonian (7 lines in the centre) and Elamite (8 lines at the bottom) cuneiform characters.

64. COLUMN BASE
Apadanā, Persepolis. Time of Darius I (beginning of fifth century BC). Diameter: 6 ft. 6 in.
The restoration work, although carried out with great skill, is unfortunately a little too obvious, but it gives an accurate indication of the care with which the work was originally executed.

65. STONE CORNICE
Tachara, Persepolis. Time of Darius I (end of sixth century BC). Scale: $\frac{1}{34}$.
Above a row of ovolos a cornice develops, consisting of three layers of a kind of honey-comb motif. This type of cornice is known as an 'Egyptian' cornice.

66. STYLIZED FLORAL DECORATION
Eastern stairway of the Apadanā, Persepolis. Time of Xerxes I (beginning of fifth century BC). Scale: $\frac{1}{7}$.
This decorative motif, which frequently occurs at Persepolis, represents flowers in bloom. Above it, separated by a slanting line of rosettes, cypresses are depicted on terraces.

61

62

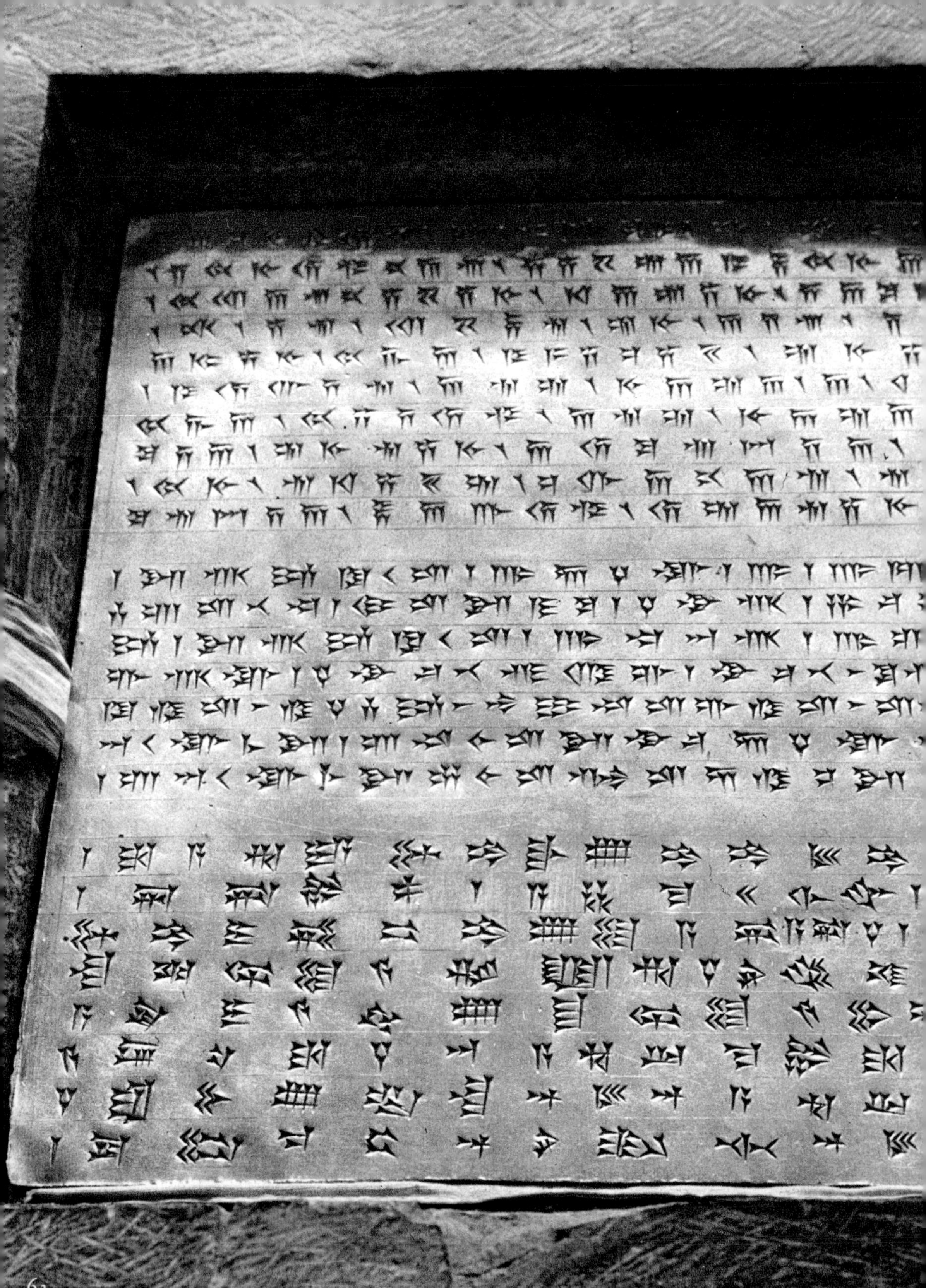

64

65

67. DETAIL OF A DOOR COLUMN IN THE HALL OF A HUNDRED COLUMNS
Terrace, Persepolis. Time of Darius I (end of sixth century BC). Scale: $\frac{1}{2}$.
Two lions and two bulls walk in single file between lines of rosettes. The whole of the baldaquin of which this is the decoration can be seen in plate 43.

68. BAS-RELIEF OF A BEARDED SPHINX
Tachara of Darius I, Persepolis. Time of Darius I (end of sixth century BC). Scale: $\frac{1}{2}$.
This sphinx with a human head, but animals' ears, represents a benevolent spirit. It frequently occurs at Persepolis.

G

PART THREE

SELEUCID AND PARTHIAN IRAN

FROM ALEXANDER THE GREAT
TO ARTABANUS V

After the burning of Persepolis, Alexander of Macedon came to the conclusion that Hellenism and Iranianism were not necessarily irreconcilable enemies; but perhaps he was also surprised at finding in the Persians a discipline, a desire to be loyal to the sovereign, a veneration of the royal person which flattered him as inheritor of the Achaemenid dynasty. He tried in consequence to make himself agreeable to the Iranians, for political reasons, to be sure, but also out of sympathy. He introduced Persian recruits into his Macedonian regiments, entrusted the administration of the provinces he had just conquered to Iranian governors, married the daughter of a Bactrian noble and encouraged his officers to do likewise. Yet Persia was the hereditary enemy of the Greeks! Such an attitude emphasizes two striking aspects of the conqueror's thought: his great desire for concord and unity, his weariness with the agitation characteristic of Greece and the esteem in which he held the Persians. Iranian legend also adopted Alexander. The great Iranian epic, the *Shāh Nāma* by Firdawsī, transformed history as follows: a king of Persia, Dārāb, sought and obtained the hand of the daughter of Philip of Macedon in marriage. The Achaemenid sovereign, dissatisfied with his wife, sent her back to her father, who was justly infuriated by this insult. On her return to Greece, the forsaken princess gave birth to a son, Alexander. Philip, according to the Iranian legend, wishing to conceal the humiliation inflicted on his daughter, announced the birth of the child as being that of his own son, so that, according to this tale, Alexander, in defeating Dārā, son of Dārāb, his step-brother, had only reconquered his heritage.

The Seleucids, heirs of the Conqueror, considered themselves in their turn as the successors of the Achaemenids. They tried to maintain the established order and to assert their authority over the Iranian satrapies. However Seleucus I, the founder of the dynasty, had to abandon the eastern satrapies and hand them over to the King of India, Chandragupta, in return for a gift of 500 elephants, the very ones which contributed so felicitously to the victory he won over Antigonus at Ipsus.[1]

---

[1] The Battle of Ipsus, in Phrygia, in the summer of 301 BC.

Seleucus had married an Iranian at the time of the famous marriage festival at Susa[1] and Antiochus I, his successor, was born of this union. But contrary to the intentions to which this alliance seemed to bear witness, the Seleucid monarchs persisted in considering themselves as Greeks in the midst of Iranians. They imposed their language and used it in the government. There was certainly no cultural aim behind this; only the will to assert Greek military and administrative authority on the Iranian world, which, the Seleucids thought, ought to be well governed, but governed by Greeks. However, Hellenism had felt the influence and even the attraction of the Orient through the intermediary of Asia Minor. Archaic Greek art used many oriental formulae and motifs. Plato, whom the Muhammadan thinkers in their turn adopted, claimed in the *Timaeus* to have come under the influence of the Persian Magi.

The Seleucids, conscious of the weakness of their establishment in Iran, tried hard to create a kind of defence network consisting of military posts which at first were placed along the main routes built by the Achaemenids and maintained by the Seleucids as a permanent system of postal communications. Sometimes colonies of retired Greeks to whom the Seleucid sovereigns had granted large or small landed properties were grouped around the military installations. These groups developed and some of them even reached the rank of 'polis', i.e. town, but obtaining this dignity and its accompanying advantages required that each new community give proof of a certain level of organization: that it could construct a stadium, a gymnasium, baths, that it had a governing body elected by the people and magistrates chosen by the governing body. The Greeks who settled in Iran seem to have been very satisfied with this régime and deeply attached to the deified King, supreme head of the state. Some of these towns were named after sovereigns: Antioch, Apamea, Laodicea, Seleucia, etc.

From the little that the archaeology of the Hellenistic period teaches us, it seems clear that there was a number of Greek cities in Iran. It is probable that one of them was at Fasā, in Fārs, where numerous fragments of Hellenistic sculptures and ceramics have been dug up. Another may have occupied the hill at Kangāwar, between Kirmānshāh and Hamadhān, where the remains of a Parthian temple dedicated to Artemis-Anāhit, according to Isidore of Charax, may still be seen. Yet another must have been around or near two solitary Seleucid columns close to a village called Khurra,

---

[1] The glorious return of Alexander to Susa and the arrival of Nearchus bringing home the fleet led the conqueror to attempt to consolidate the obedience of all the peoples which a series of prodigious victories had united under his authority. To his way of thinking nothing could better ensure the fusion of Europe and Asia than numerous mixed marriages between the élite of the Persian and Greek races. He himself had already married two Iranian women. He decided to marry two more, one the daughter of Darius III, the other of Alexander Memnon, both of whom belonged to the royal family. His companions, his officers and soldiers all followed his example, of their own free will or under compulsion. There was an enormous and sumptuous marriage feast at Susa which lasted several days. The 'Hymeneals of Susa' are famous. This attempt, which was intended to announce to the world the benefits of universal Greek domination, had, at the time that it was made, a good chance of success; perhaps the chief cause of its failure was the premature death of the hero who conceived it.

Alexander had been obeyed, but the generous ideal which had animated him was an ephemeral glow which disappeared with him. It was followed by a frightful conflict of ambitions, 'the quarrel of the diadochi', which has seemed to some historians to be a free fight between wild beasts.

not far from Dilīdjān, on the road from Qum to Isfahān. A fourth definitely existed on the site of present-day Nihāwand, not far from Malayir, and that it bore the name of 'Laodicea in Media' we know from a fine Greek inscription found there some years ago by which Antiochus III the Seleucid instituted the cult of his wife Laodicea 'in the temple of this town'.

However, the only town about which we have abundant and accurate information is the one which occupied the site of Susa in Khūzistān, where the French Government has been subsidizing archaeological excavations for some fifty years. The inscriptions from the Hellenistic period which have been found there date from the time of Antiochus III[1] to that of Ardawān the Parthian.[2] According to them, Apollo and Artemis were worshipped there as twin deities, but it appears that Artemis took the name of the Elamite goddess 'Nanaia'. A temple outside the walls was consecrated to her. At first the town was a military colony, but it contained a considerable population of Hellenized Syrians, Cappadocians, Jews and Babylonians.

In Iran custom had it that unused land and land lying fallow belonged to the king. However, the greater part of the territory was in the possession of the notables to whom these lands had belonged from time immemorial. These quasi-feudal lords lived in fortified castles and had the soil tilled by peasants who were more or less serfs. Lords great and small were surrounded in the ancient manner by a whole group of dependants and craftsmen who manufactured the objects necessary for existence in the traditional way: carpets, fabrics, furniture, pottery and various implements. The safety of these properties and the security of their inhabitants was ensured by having young men who had been born in the same domains brought up to ride on horseback, to shoot with bow and arrow and trained in ambushes by hunting. A similar state of affairs had existed since the Achaemenid period, but the Seleucids seem to have been unable to win the confidence of this quasi-feudal force.

Towards 250 BC the Parthian tribes which had long been settled in Khurāsān revolted in answer to the appeal of their chiefs. The power of this Parthian dynasty of Arsacids, which was to reign almost 500 years,[3] was already established in the period of Antiochus III, i.e. at the end of the third century BC, but it only reached the peak of its power during the second century about the time when its brilliant cavalry under Mithradates I drove the Seleucids from Babylonia. The spirit of tolerance of these new conquerors served their cause. They did not destroy the administration their predecessors had organized, they compelled no one to become a convert to the Mazdaism they practised themselves, and showed themselves generally receptive and understanding. The example of the Parthian court at Ctesiphon enjoying the performance of the tragedies of Euripides has often been quoted. The coins of their kings on which they called themselves 'philhellenes' are the formal proof of their Hellenization or their desire to become Hellenized. The Jews and members of other minorities appear to have lived happily under their government, a kind of military feudal system which

---

[1] Antiochus III (Megas), 223–187 BC.
[2] Ardawān II (Artabanus II), who died 123 BC.
[3] From 247 BC to AD 224.

MAP III: SELEUCID AND PARTHIAN IRAN

succeeded the centralized power of the Achaemenids. However, Persia, the real Persia, remained 'passive and refractory'. In her mountains she awaited the apparition of a chief of her people to reorganize the empire and link the glorious past with the future, and thus to bypass the present.

When the family of Sāssān from Fārs assumed power five and a half centuries after the fall of Persepolis and the Parthian horsemen had disappeared eastwards 'galloping away in disorder', Iranian civilization became master of its destinies again. To emphasize its purpose it linked the Sassanid dynasty with the last of the Achaemenids by a fictitious genealogical tree.

It seems clear that the Parthians were identifiable with the population of the Achaemenid satrapy of Parni. Progressive, high-minded and sincerely philhellene, they do not deserve the oblivion and contempt they meet with in the *Shāh Nāma*. They encouraged commercial traffic to the best of their ability and closely supervised the safety of the roads. During their reign, Hellenistic fashions and influences continued to spread towards the plateaux of Central Asia. The glassware found at Begram in Afghanistan a few years ago seems to confirm this. These products of Antioch or Alexandria are one of the most striking proofs of the penetration of Hellenistic art into the east of the Iranian plateau.

The caravan route city of Hatra, vassal of the Parthians until the time of its destruction by Shāpūr I the Sassanid in 250 BC, was, like Doura, one of the outposts of the east, in its combat with the Roman Empire. This dream persisted a surprisingly long time. In fact it was only very late in their ascendancy that the Parthians gave up their hope of reaching the Mediterranean. Their powerful army, composed of Iranian cavalry and Greek infantry, the remains of the Seleucid legions they had conquered, may be considered as one of the principal contributors to the decline of the empire of the West.

From the point of view of civilization, it is interesting to note that it was during he Parthian period that the cult of Mithra spread, a cult of Aryan origin the developments of which fill us with astonishment. How could this solar god have been the object of such infatuation that his cult became almost the state religion at Rome in the third century AD? Undoubtedly the Mithraic exaltation of the sentiments of duty, justice and truth profoundly influenced Roman paganism in its decline and prepared the way for Christianity, some of whose holidays, Christmas for example, have replaced the Mithraic ceremonies at the winter solstice, celebrated as the time of the birth of the 'Sun of Justice' personified by Mithra. Renan has remarked that if Christianity had been stopped in its early stages by a fatal illness the world would have been Mithraic.

CHAPTER 6

SELEUCID AND PARTHIAN IRAN

MONUMENTS

EMAINS of monuments dating from the Seleucid and Parthian period on
Iranian soil are extremely rare. They include two columns once part of a
building from the Seleucid period (pl. 88) at Khurra in the Mahallāt region,
some vestiges of a temple of the Arsacid Parthian period dedicated to the goddess
Anāhit at Kangāwar, some column-bases at Hamadhān which undoubtedly belonged
to Anāhit at another time and two bas-reliefs at Bīsūtūn in such a bad state of repair
that one can barely make out the silhouette of King Gotarzes, represented on horseback and crowned by a winged victory. The whole, in a degenerate Greek style, has
little artistic value.

Yet it was during the reign of the Arsacids that the history of the vaulted architecture
of Iran, its true architecture, begins for us. So far, in fact, we only know two monuments of this kind in the country; one of them, the palace of the first Sassanid sovereign, Ardashīr I, dates only from the last years of the Arsacid period and should rather
be classed among the monuments of the Sassanid period, while the other, the palace
of Kūh-i Khwāja in Sīstān, is as much Greco-Bactrian as Iranian, architecturally
speaking. But a number of Parthian ruins survive in Mesopotamia, among them the
remains of the palaces at Ashur and Hatra (pl. 90) where authentic works of Iranian
construction appear under a Hellenistic veneer.

The Parthians, indeed, were Iranians. Parthia was one of the Achaemenid satrapies.
When Phraates II vanquished the Seleucid Antiochus of Sidon in 129 BC he conquered the vast territories which extend from the Tigris and the Euphrates to Arachosia; it was therefore an Iranian dynasty which ruled over Mesopotamia and settled
there. Its official architecture was Hellenistic, like the Seleucids, but the Parthians,
used to the methods of construction of their own country, Khurāsān, built their
palaces and dwelling houses in their own way, although they decorated them in the
Greek mode. For, in proportion as Greek influence declined in Asia and the Greek
cities became more intimately linked with Rome, the philhellene Parthian kings,
'defenders of Hellenism against Rome', appear to have adopted an increasingly emphatic attitude of Iranian nationalism in both art and politics. It was only later under
the rule of the purely national Sassanid dynasty that the prestige of Greek art in Iran
vanished completely. However, we find a reminiscence of it in the external decoration
of the palaces at Ctesiphon (pl. 110) and Sarwistān, merely to mention architecture.

It is reasonable to assume that the Parthian town which rose on the ruins of the ancient Assyrian capital of Ashur dates from the first century AD, that it was partially destroyed by Trajan's troops in AD 116, then restored, enlarged and finally devastated in AD 198, during Septimius Severus' campaign in Mesopotamia. The palace at Ashur was probably built partly during the first period of the town and partly during the second. Hatra lies about thirty miles to the west of Ashur. Its palaces were probably built after the siege of the town by Trajan. In that case they would be contemporary with the second period of Ashur. However, the Parthian edifices in these two cities are entirely different, both in their nature and in the materials used.

The most ancient Parthian monuments of Ashur were built of sun-dried and baked brick, the latter being often employed at Babylon as we already see during the third millennium, then in the Sassanid palace at Dāmghān, in the Tārīk Khāna at Dāmghān during the Islamic period and even in our own day in alternate courses of flat bricks and bricks on edge. The largest halls of the principal palace were ceilinged and topped with a flat roof. But one of them was divided into three parts lengthwise by means of two arches resting on rectangular pillars set away from the walls and carrying transverse beams. This system of construction, so logical and so simple, seems to have been invented independently in many countries; for we can see it at Ashur where the transverse arches support vaults, as at Ctesiphon in the Tāq-i Kisrā, at Baghdād in the Khān 'Urthma, in Iran at Abarkūh, Shīrāz, Turbat-i Shaikh Djām, etc., or in France at Saint-Philibert de Tournus, Farges, the abbey of Fontenay and elsewhere, and where they bear stones or wooden beams supporting a flat roof, as in Syria, Transjordan and undoubtedly also in Iran, at Ivān-i Karkha.

At Hatra these arches were built of bonded stone with radial voussoirs (pl. 90), and consequently constructed on centering.[1] At Ashur they were constructed in this way as were the barrel vaults they supported and those which covered the numerous corridors in the palace, in vertical sections,[2] by an old process which was used everywhere in the Orient where the wood necessary for centering was lacking: in Egypt for example, where the granaries of Ramses are vaulted in this way, at Babylon in the tombs and the water channels, and in Iran at all times up to the present day.

So from the construction point of view everything is very ordinary, but here comes the peculiarity. The Parthians appear to have known only one type of vault: the barrel vault. By way of the monumental shape they invented, or took over from their predecessors in the Iranian East, the ivan (īwān). This lofty barrel vault on the façades of their buildings, which is open for its full height and generally for its full breadth, was later to become the audience hall of the Sassanid sovereigns, then in the Islamic period, the decoration of the façades and the courtyards of the madrasas, caravanserais and mosques of Iran.

This high decorative ivan which did not exist before the Arsacid period, in either

---

[1] As with the construction methods in most general use over the world, with or without a keystone, but dependent on having wood at one's disposal.

[2] i.e. by bedding a first arch only one brick thick into a section of inclined masonry, then a second, etc.

eastern or western Iran—for the most ancient example we know, at Fīrūzābād, is more than two centuries later than the palace of Ashur—is found from the Arsacid period onwards in Mesopotamia where it was probably introduced by Parthian builders.

The main body of the palace at Hatra at first consisted solely of two large ivans separated from each other by two-storey sections of small rooms (pl. 90). Later, two more large ivans were added, side by side, so that the finished monument presented a long façade with four ivans abreast facing outwards. In addition, a square barrel-vaulted ceremonial hall was built behind one of the large original ivans and communicating with it. This was the first attempt at a combination of vaulted features which became common in the Sassanid period and assumed considerable importance during the Islamic period—the combination of a square hall, vaulted with a dome with a deep, lofty ivan in front of it acting as an entrance hall (fig. 137).

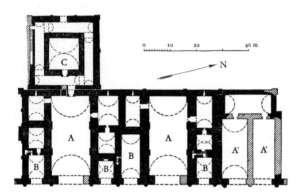

Fig. 137

PLAN OF THE PALACE AT HATRA
A. Great ivans. A′. Twin ivans.
B. Two-storey sections.
C. Square barrel-vaulted hall.

Fig. 138

PLAN OF THE PALACE AT ASHUR
A. Ivans. B. Courtyards. C. Peristyle.
D. Columned hall. E. Kitchen. F.
Baths.

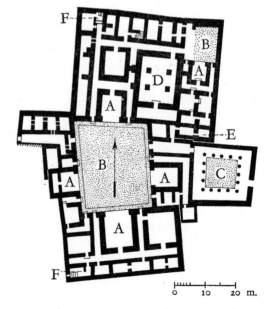

Other Parthian buildings have been discovered at Hatra: small palaces, temples and private houses. One of them consists of an ivan with its broad front open and surrounded by secondary rooms on the other three sides. In another the ivan only has lateral rooms. A third building has three ivans side by side, with the secondary rooms behind. A fourth consists of three ivans in line, preceded by a columned portico. A fifth is an ivan lined with rooms on one side only and preceded by a hall with Hellenistic columns.

The Parthian palace at Ashur already provided an example of an arrangement of ivans which was to have the most brilliant future in Islamic Iran, in addition to the ivan which served as vestibule to a square hall. It consists of four ivans in a cross around a square courtyard (fig. 138), i.e. the cruciform plan of the madrasas,[1] caravanserais and mosques of Iran. It is probable that this type of plan also came from the east of the country. Diodorus Siculus, writing in the actual Parthian period, said that the inhabitants of the region of Ghazna, in Afghanistan, from ancient times had built their houses in this shape. This plan was also that of the simplest houses at Bāmiyān during the Seljuk period, and undoubtedly had been for a very long time.

So during the reign of the Arsacids we see the appearance in Mesopotamia of the ivan, imported from Khurāsān; both the arrangement by which the ivan served as vestibule to a square hall, which was to play an important role in the history of Iranian architecture from this period onwards (at Fīrūzābād, for example), and the cruciform plan, of the houses and later of the madrasas of Khurāsān, which was to characterize the architectural course of the great madrasas of Nizām al-Mulk, the caravanserais and the furthest developed type of Iranian mosque.

As far as we can judge from the almost unique example at Hatra, the external walls of Parthian Mesopotamian palaces were faced with plaster or meticulously dressed stone ornamented with pilasters, engaged columns, acanthus leaves and grotesque masks which derive from Roman art. The audience hall of the palace at Hatra has deteriorated too much for us to be able to tell how it was decorated, but this is how a contemporary writer, Philostratus, described a similar hall in a palace of one of the last Arsacids: '. . . A hall covered with a vault spangled with sapphires, shining with celestial brilliance. In it sat the king when dispensing justice.' And here is the decoration of another hall of state: '. . . the moon, the sun and even the portrait of the king scintillated in a crystal firmament'.

The plan and construction of the royal palaces of the Parthian period appear to have remained therefore largely oriental. But the external appearance was Greek, or meant to be, a sacrifice to contemporary fashion.

At Kūh-i Khwāja, in the east of the country, the interior decoration of the palace consisted of panels of fresco painting more or less influenced by the same Hellenistic art.

Ordinary dwellings stayed much the same as the small houses of sun-dried earth and a little wood, basically composed of a columned hall preceded by an open portico, which are still found by the roadside in Iran.

[1] Madrasa, a Muslim school of theology.

As for the religious monuments of the Seleucid and Arsacid periods, they were either purely Iranian (at Badr Nishandi, Shīz, Maidān-i Naft) or the product of a slavish copy of Hellenistic monuments (at Khurka, Kangāwar and Khurra and perhaps also at Nihāwand). Others which have not yet been rediscovered were probably akin in a varying degree to these two types of monuments. In order to give an overall view of this important question I think I ought to hark back to the Achaemenid period.

'The Persians,' says Herodotus, 'are not used to erecting statues of the gods, temples or altars; far from it, they say those who do so are foolish. . . . It is their custom to climb the highest mountains to offer sacrifices to Zeus, whose name they give to all the circular extent of the sky. They have sacrificed to the sun, the moon, the earth, fire, water and the winds from the most ancient times. Those are the only gods they have sacrificed to.' According to Strabo also, 'The Persians do not erect statues or altars to their gods; they sacrifice on the high places, in the open air. . . .' On the other hand, in the inscription at Bīsutūn, Darius I prided himself on having restored the *āyadanās* which the magus Gautama had destroyed. The *āyadanā* or 'place of adoration' was 'the secret dwelling of the divine fire, the inviolable oratory where the priests maintained and prayed to the fire'.

In other words Achaemenid Persia did not possess temples in the Greek sense of the word, but open air assembly places, the 'high places' and the 'fire sanctuaries' forbidden to the common run of the congregation.

So far we do not know of any Achaemenid high place, but we do know the vestiges of several fire sanctuaries. The most ancient, probably earlier than the reign of the first Persian sovereign, is the one at the head of the Husain Kūh, at Naqsh-i Rustam, near Persepolis. This abrupt cliff in whose face Darius I and his successors had their tombs cut, was clearly a *bāgāstāna*, a 'place of the gods', like the rock of Bīsutūn at the head of the Kūh-i Parru, near Kirmānshāh. The Achaemenid tombs were hollowed out of it for the same reason which drove Darius to have his famous inscription carved at Bīsutūn. Moreover the Elamites had carved a bas-relief there a thousand years earlier, witnessing to their devotion to the gods of the place. So there was nothing surprising about a Mazdean sanctuary being situated in this sacred spot, in full view of the enormous plain of Marwdasht whose inhabitants its fires commanded to pray. In fact nothing remains of it but the well-known twin altars (pl. 35), and, a little higher up the mountain, seven other altars, four of them twins, the other three individual ones, which are probably not as ancient as the first two. But as Christensen says, 'the eternal fire required edifices in which it was protected against the ravages of time', and it is certain that there was an *āyadanā* there or nearby, on which the altars were dependent. The fire necessary for the public ceremonies was fetched from it and returned to it afterwards.

The second oldest Achaemenid fire sanctuary we know is the one which existed at Pasargadae, the capital of Cyrus. All that remains of it are two stone platforms beside the bed of a stream, the bases of fire altars which formed part of an *āyadanā* built some 300 feet away on a small hillock where one can at least still see the terraces which supported it, if not the actual edifice. At certain hours of the day the fire was carried to the altars by the priests—because the fire ceremonies had to take place in the open air —and then returned to its stronghold. This ensemble, the altar proper and the altars subsidiary to it, was surrounded by a wall of which traces exist.

However, if we wonder why the altars were situated so far from the sanctuary, we should remember that the *āyadanā* was sited on the highest point, reputedly the purest, and that the altars were preferably sited near a stream. Incidentally, it is possible that this proximity to the water so characteristic of the fire monuments ought merely to be considered as the desire to have it close at hand and not as a requirement or even a preference of the cult; however, as Strabo said, 'the Persians offer their most solemn sacrifices to fire and water'. If we were prepared to accept the latter theory, i.e. that the fire monuments were situated near water for preference because simultaneous sacrifices to fire and water were made there, we should explain immediately the twin altars which we see here for the fourth time, shall see for a fifth time and which have been so much discussed by scholars.

These two *ātash-gāhs*,[1] as Flandin points out in his *Relation du voyage en Perse*, placed side by side and to some extent twins, like those at Naqsh-i Rustam, are the second example we have come across. This observation seems to lead to this conclusion: that adoration and sacrifice on the part of the fire-worshipping Persians took place simultaneously and equally in honour of two divinities. So ought we not to conclude that the Guebres,[2] who consider that human kind lies between good and devil, found it useful to address prayers to the genius of the one, represented by Hormuzd, as well as the genius of the other, as presented by Ahriman? However, Ivan never went as far as this final consequence of dualism. The pure light, symbol of good, could not shine in honour of the god of darkness. Personally I think that the two explanations required, that of the distance separating the sanctuary at Pasargadae from its altars and the reason for the twin altars, are provided by the quotation from Strabo I have just given: 'The Persians offer their most solemn sacrifices to fire and water.'

The remains of a third fire sanctuary have been discovered by M. Dieulafoy in the plain of Susa, a few miles to the east of the ancient city (fig. 139). It is a handsome monument the composition of which clearly shows the essential part, 'the fire place', protected against any chance of profanation by a double wall. The columned porch in front of this part of the edifice with its two altars and its stair was clearly the oratory of the sanctuary, the officiating priests occupying the top of the steps and the congregation remaining in the courtyard. M. Dieulafoy attributes this monument to the reign of Artaxerxes II (424–358 BC).

In short all that remains of these three sanctuaries are the fire altars at Naqsh-i Rustam, the two platforms near Persepolis, the adjoining stepped terrace and the plan of the building near Susa. So we know hardly anything about them from the artistic

---

[1] *Ātash-gāh* means 'fire place'; secondarily it is the place where we assume the faithful assembled to pray. Only the priest approached the actual *ātash-gāh*.

[2] *Guebre: Parsi* (Parsee). The origin of the word Guebre is unknown. *Guebres* or *Parsis* is the name given to the Iranian Zoroastrians. The majority of them, about 100,000, now live in India. There are still 10,000 in Iran.

69. BAS-RELIEF OF A HORSE'S HEAD
Palace of Artaxerxes II, Persepolis. Middle of fourth century BC. Actual size.
Note that harness has hardly changed in form since the Achaemenids.

70. CAPITAL IN THE FORM OF A HUMAN HEAD
From the Tripylon of the Apadanā. Fifth century BC. Scale $\frac{1}{8}$. Archaeological Museum, Teheran.
Of a similar type to the sphinx in plate 68, it is carved in the round and painted.

71. SMALL HEAD OF LAPIS-LAZULI
Persepolis. Fifth century BC. Height: $2\frac{9}{16}$ in.; width: just under 2 in. Archaeological Museum, Teheran.
This figure, who may be Xerxes as a young man, wears a crenellated crown on top of his closely curled hair.

72. BAS-RELIEF DECORATING THE INTERIOR SURFACE OF A DOOR IN THE HALL OF A HUNDRED COLUMNS
Terrace, Persepolis. Time of Darius I (end of sixth century BC). Scale: $\frac{1}{20}$.
The hero is stabbing a winged monster which has a scorpion's tail. The creature is portrayed rampant in order to fend off the arm which is striking it.

73. CAPITAL WITH TWO-HEADED BULL
Verandah of the Hall of a hundred columns, Persepolis. Time of Artaxerxes I (465–425 BC). Length: 10 ft. 9 in., from one head to the other.
These capitals, which are in one single piece, were quarried and carved on the spot. Some of them were left unfinished.

74. DETAIL OF TOMB OF ARTAXERXES III
Mountain at Persepolis. Time of Artaxerxes III (middle fourth century BC). Scale: $\frac{1}{7}$.
Three representatives of the peoples of the Empire bear the dais on which the king is performing the sacrifice. From left to right, an Indian from Sind, an Amargian Scythian and a Scythian with a pointed cap.

75. GOLD CUP
Hamadhān region. Fourth century BC. Height: $4\frac{3}{4}$ in.; width: $8\frac{1}{8}$ in.
The cup is decorated with ovolos and coussinets in high relief.

76. GOLD DARIC OF DARIUS III
Fourth century BC. Diameter: $\frac{3}{4}$ in. Cabinet des Médailles, Bibliothèque Nationale, Paris.
This royal coin represents Darius III Codomannus (337–330 BC) who was defeated by Alexander the Great. He is running towards the right, holding a bow and a javelin.

77. SILVER PLATE AND SPOON SHAPED LIKE A LADLE
Achaemenid period. Diameter: about 8 in. Baghdad Museum.
This type of plate, decorated in the same style, was used in the most remote times. Quite a large number of them have been found at Tanit and dated c. 1500 BC. The ladle was probably made in Egypt.

71

73

74

75

76

78. HEAD AND SHOULDERS OF A WINGED IBEX

Achaemenid period. Bronze, partially gilded. Height: 10⅜ in. The Louvre, Paris.
Handle of an amphora already showing Hellenistic influence. The other handle is in the Berlin Museum.

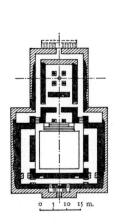

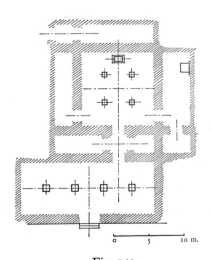

Fig. 139

PLAN OF THE
ĀYADANĀ AT SUSA

Fig. 140

PLAN OF THE FIRE TEMPLE
AT PERSEPOLIS

point of view. Perhaps there never was much to know about them. The best preserved monument, the sanctuary near Susa, of mud and wooden columns, of which Dieulafoy could still make out the lower parts, was undoubtedly not very different from the run of the mill constructions of the country such as can still be seen today by the roadsides.

Another fire monument was discovered by E. Herzfeld at the foot of the terrace at Persepolis. Its plan (fig. 140) consists of a hall with four columns preceded by a long vestibule and surrounded on the other three sides by narrow rooms; of these, the right-hand one, which is slightly larger than the others, was the place where the fire was kept. The stone slab which supported the *ātash-dān*, the fire container, is still visible *in situ*. The excavations have also revealed a certain number of Greek dedicatory inscriptions which appear to contain the most ancient identifications of Zoroastrian divinities with Greek gods, as well as the sides of a bay with sculptures of a prince and his wife. These bas-reliefs have deteriorated greatly, but Herzfeld was able to identify the male personage as one of the first princes of the small Fratadara[1] dynasty which probably began to reign over Istakhr and the surrounding country towards the end of the third century BC. He is in a praying attitude, with his right hand raised and his left hand holding the sacred wands. The queen, on the other side, wears a long garment which falls to her instep and a cloak, or perhaps a shawl. The folds of the drapery are indicated by means of crudely engraved lines. These badly drawn figures, almost without relief—their silhouettes standing out only slightly from the background—bear witness to a really primitive technique compared with the extremely elegant bas-reliefs at Persepolis.

[1] Tetradrachmae (plates 82 and 83) found in the region of Persepolis confirm Strabo's statements about the religious and material power of the princes of the Fratadara dynasty in the province of Fārs.

It is certainly curious to see how rapidly, in the course of two or three generations, the brilliance of Achaemenid sculpture faded into complete insignificance. The Achaemenid traditions became neglected and perhaps despised. Iranian sculpture lost its skill and its subsequent attempt to imitate Greek art merely resulted in the production of crude clumsy works. But we must not blame the disappearance of the Iranian artistic sense upon it, for it still remains to be seen if Achaemenid art, 'a royal fantasy', as Darmesteter has called it, really matched the actual capabilities of Iran at that period and whether it was not natural for it to disappear simultaneously with the collapse of the royal power. It also remains to be seen whether there was ever anything in common between Greek art and the Iranian artistic sense and whether one copying the other was not inevitably doomed to failure. I do not feel that it is fair to say that the disappearance of one of the expressions of the art of a people is necessarily caused by the disappearance or the decadence of the artistic sense of that people. It is rather as if one said that after the stuffiness and pomposity of nineteenth-century art was abandoned, French traditions, and with them French art, disappeared. In fact the artistic sense of a people is just as invariable in time as the very soul of the people. What changes and has to change is the appearance of its works of art. In this connection I have something to say which I feel is valid for today as well as the past and enables us to accept in the history of art the astonishing products of present-day sculpture and painting as well as the equally surprising products of Oriental ostentation which ventured to copy and claimed to assimilate a personal and sensitive art—Greek art—which was foreign to it. My brief digression will be about the 'life' of art in general.

The human race has clearly progressed from Cro-Magnon man to our days. However, a present-day artist does not draw better than a caveman, no offence to anyone intended. Animals have never been represented more wittily, or with a more expressive self-assured line than by our untutored ancestors, the hunters of bison and reindeer of Fond-de-Gaume, Altamira and Lorthet.

Art moves with a movement which is peculiar to it. It does not progress, it oscillates and under pain of stagnating in repetition, monotony and finally the sleep of death, cannot cease to oscillate between the two poles generating its energy: construction and decoration. Movement, this alternating movement, is a vital necessity to it and we can find the proofs of it in the course of our lifetimes.

Disconnected noses and feet back to front will go out of fashion; once again men will only be entitled to two eyes per head and to shock will no longer be the ultimate goal. Then we shall see slick chocolate box painting again *ad nauseam*. Then constructionism will reappear, called spherism, cylindrism or some other 'ism'. It will be welcomed as a liberator, then gradually distorted by exaggeration and be engulfed by the absurd, etc. How can it be helped?

But to return to our subject. After the impossible lengths to which Achaemenid constructive efforts had been carried came Arsacid decoration which finally became the nadir of art; then came the rough combinations of vaults in the first Sassanid palaces, their mannerism and the mathematical aridity of the first works of the Islamic period, etc. These alternatives, which the simple course of the life of art suffices to explain, have nothing to do with the so-called progress or decadence of the artistic sense of Iran.

No high places or fire sanctuaries remain from the age of the Seleucids, but at Khurra, near Mahallāt, there are some vestiges of a Hellenistic building which has no connection with fire. It is situated in a small valley wholly occupied by vineyards and was considered as having been dedicated to Dionysus for that reason. Only two columns are still upright (pl. 88), but numerous dressed stones lie about and the lower parts of the actual building could perhaps be rediscovered inside the colonnade. The columns are meant to be Ionic, but they are much too high in relation to their diameter, a reminiscence of the thin wooden columns of the country. Obviously the builders of this monument lacked the sense of proportion which really governed the art of Greece. As E. Herzfeld says, the result is a hybrid art, if indeed we can speak of an art, which is neither Greek nor Iranian, has no aesthetic value and is only of interest to history.

The religious monuments of the Arsacid period, to which we have now returned are, represented by the high places of Shāmi and Badr Nishandi, the fire temple known by the name of Masdjid-i Sulaimān, the large monument at Shīz and the Hellenistic temple at Kangāwar.

The last named edifice, which Isidore of Charax mentions as the 'famous temple of Artemis' (Anāhit), can be dated to the end of the third or the beginning of the second century BC. On the high substructure which is all that remains of the peribolus there are only a few columns left, incorporated into the houses of the little town of Kangāwar. The strangely mixed shapes of their Doric and Corinthian elements place this monument in a group of edifices which so far consists solely of it and the building at Khurra; but it will no doubt also include a temple dedicated by the Seleucid Antiochus III to his wife Laodicea, discovered recently at Nihāwand, but the excavation of which has not yet begun.

We know about it from two documents engraved on stone which were found on the borders of the town of Nihāwand and reached the Archaeological Museum at Teheran in 1946.[1] One of these documents reproduces a letter addressed by an official called

---

[1] The text of these two documents are as follows:
First document—'Menedemus to Apollodorus, the magistrates and town of Laodicea, greetings. Hereafter is attached the copy of the edict the king has written to us. So comply with what is ordered in it and take care to have the edict transcribed on a stone stele and to consecrate it in the most illustrious of the town's sanctuaries. Fare you well. In 119, the tenth of the month of Panemos.'
Second document—'King Antiochus to Menedemus, greetings. Desirous of increasing the honours of our sister the Queen Laodicea, considering this very necessary, not only because she shows her affection and her tender care in her life with us, but also because she is pious towards the divinity, we constantly and with affection perform everything which is fitting and just for her to receive from us; and especially we decree that, in the same way that the high priests in the kingdom are nominated by ourselves, there be established in the same places high priestesses of Laodicea, who shall wear gold crowns with her portrait, and whose names shall be inscribed in the deeds after those of the high priests of our ancestors and ourselves. Now since Laodicea (that is, the town here) has been named among the places under thy government, let all be done in conformity with what has been said above and let copies of the letters, transcribed onto two steles, be consecrated in the most illustrious places, so that now and in the future be manifest the excellent attitude we have . . . towards our sister. In 119, the . . . of the month of Xandikos.'

Menedemus, governor of the satrapy, to the town of Laodicea. Menedemus announces that he is passing on a royal edict and commands the magistrates of Laodicea to engrave it on a stele. The second document, engraved on a stele three feet eleven and a half inches high, reproduces the edict by King Antiochus addressed to Menedemus, prescribing the institution of the cult of his wife, Queen Laodicea, in the town's most illustrious sanctuary. These texts are dated in the Seleucid year 119, one on the tenth day of the month of Panemos, the other in the month of Xandikos. Now the Seleucid year 119, reckoned in the Macedonian style, extends from autumn 194 to autumn 193 BC. So the edict of Antiochus would be dated to March – April AD 193. Menedemus would probably have transmitted it to the town of Laodicea in Media in June–July of the same year.

Badr Nishandi lies in the largest of the oil-producing territories which used to be exploited by the Iranian Oil Co, a few miles to the north of a fire temple whose name I have already mentioned, Masdjid-i Sulaimān. In other words it is quite close by. It also resembles it, both in its general composition and the way in which it was built, and like it dates from the Arsacid period. However, the reasons for building these two monuments seem to have been quite different, even though in the end they may have been used in the same way. Masdjid-i Sulaimān, at the foot of the hills which dominate it, owes its origin to the presence of natural gas which issues from the ground there. The great majority of the faithful attending the ceremonies which took place there saw them from above. Badr Nishandi, on the contrary, is an actual height. It seems to have been precisely one of those 'high and pure' places of worship mentioned by Herodotus where the ancient Iranians were accustomed to foregather to offer their prayers to the gods.

As to the date of the construction of Badr Nishandi, we have indeed information, as a result of comparing it with the Arsacid Masdjid-i Sulaimān, reliable enough to attribute it to the Arsacid period, but whereabouts can we assign these two buildings within a period which covers two whole centuries? Undoubtedly a phenomenon

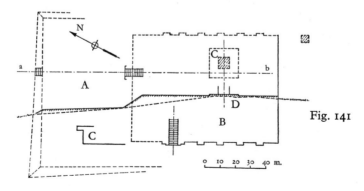

Fig. 141

PLAN AND SECTION OF BADR NISHANDI
A. Lower terrace. B. Upper terrace. C. Platforms. D. Section
along the line a–b.

as impressive as fire 'burning without fuel or ashes'[1] was considered as supernatural from the most remote antiquity and the site of Masdjid-i Sulaimān must have been reputed one of the places manifesting the divine power. The monument which was built there in the Arsacid period may equally well belong to the beginning or the end of the period. Let us say provisionally, while waiting for new finds, that because of the similarity of their architecture and the great number of coins of the same time which have been found at Masdjid-i Sulaimān, we can date our two monuments from the second half of the Arsacid period. We must realize, however, that we are speaking of the official Arsacid period, i.e. the space of time included between 250 BC and AD 226, for in fact Elymais remained a feudatory state of the Seleucids of Syria until about the year 174 of the Seleucid era, the date when the Parthian Mithradates I (170–140 BC) subdued Kamnaskires I, the indigenous dynast of Elymais. It is assumed that Kamnaskires was replaced by an Arsacid prince, but that power later returned to his family. In fact, it was only later, in the second half of the first century of the Christian era that the Kamnaskirids were definitely replaced by a dynasty of princes bearing the name of Arsacids, including the Orodes I and Orodes II to whom belonged the majority of the coins which have been found at Masdjid-i Sulaimān. So the Arsacid period in Elymais would actually only date from the middle of the first century of the Christian era to the accession to the throne of the Sassanid Ardashīr which marks the end of this principality. How long Masdjid-i Sulaimān and Badr Nishandi were in use is as uncertain as the exact date of their construction. We only know that Masdjid-i Sulaimān was used in the Sassanid period and that no trace of fire or smoke, nor any trace of construction prior to Hellenistic times, has been discovered at Badr Nishandi. However there is another platform installed on another smaller height to the north of the big terraces and about three hundred yards away. If we can judge by its supporting walls, it may date from the same time as the high place, but the ruins which cover it are less ancient. Whereas no mortar is used in the construction of the terraces, the ruined walls are made of marl reinforced with plaster, and this method of building can only be Sassanid or Islamic. It seems unlikely that they can be Islamic constructions for they could only have been farmers' houses and farmers would not have settled in such a place, without cultivable land or water. There are the remains of a broad deep ivan, occupying the whole surface of the terrace which very probably replaced an Arsacid construction. It faces towards the high place and by a wide doorway on each side which gives access to three rooms (boxes or stalls), of which the end ones at least were surrounded by walls on four sides. This unusual construction possibly indicates that in the Sassanid period there was an annexe to the neighbouring monument which had been turned into a fire temple: perhaps a priest's house, for there is nothing similar or which could take its place on the main terraces, in the sanctuary or even the place where the fire was kept.

The second of the high places so far known is also in Elymais, some twenty-five miles north-west of Masdjid-i Sulaimān as the crow flies. Splendidly situated on the top of a height dominated in its turn by the enormous Kūh-i Bilawa, it virtually

[1] That is natural gas issuing from the soil.

commands the pass giving access to the necropolis of Shāmi which I shall describe in more detail shortly. This impressive monument consists of a rectangular terrace reached by a broad stairway; on the terrace is a square platform used for prayers and sacrifices.

Since the architectural part of this high place exactly reproduces that of Badr Nishandi, it is probable that we should consider it as the typical representative of this kind of monument in the mountains of Khūzistān. Incidentally we may notice that the plan of Masdjid-i Sulaimān (fig. 142) only differs from it in that the front part of

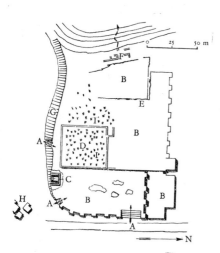

Fig. 142

PLAN OF
MASDJID-I SULAIMĀN
A. Stairways. B. Terraces. C. Monument. D. Elevated terrace. E. Remains of walls. F. Remains of buildings. G. Ramp. H. Living rooms. I. Islamic tombs.

the terrace is not the meeting place of the faithful, but the place where the fire ceremonies were held.

The monuments known as Takht-i Sulaimān and Masdjid-i Sulaimān were both built on miraculous sites. The first, situated in Azerbaidjan, is the fire sanctuary of Gandjak of the Pahlawi texts, which became the fire temple of Shīz of the Arabic geographers. It was erected during the Arsacid period, beside a 'magic' and already famous lake, whose depth 'could not be plumbed' and whose level is invariable although, according to Yāqūt, its water continually escapes by 'seven streams which run seven mills'. It profited by this notoriety and, as the number of pilgrims ever increased, rapidly added more and more altars and important annexes and was surrounded, even under the Arsacids, by a lofty wall (pl. 87). In it was preserved one of the three most famous fires of Iran, Adhur Gushnāsp, the 'fire of the warriors', or 'royal fire'. It supplied fuel to 'all the hearths of the Guebres of the East and West'.

In the Sassanid period, i.e. when Iran had transformed the Hellenistic temple into a monument where the faithful assembled and took part together in public fire ceremonies, the sanctuary at Gandjak became an immense, obviously rather exceptional fire temple, but it differs from the regular type only in some special arrangements motivated by its great age and its celebrity. Inside the Arsacid enclosure the ceremonies took place in the open air, as in the ordinary temples, but apparently they could make use of numerous altars fed by a single fire chamber, the ancient *āyadanā*.

According to Ibn Muhalkal, who wrote in 331 of the Hegira (AD 943), the divine fire was supposed to have burnt there for 700 years without interruption. Immediately after his accession to the throne each Sassanid monarch had to make his way there on foot from Ctesiphon and heap it with magnificent offerings. It was destroyed by the Byzantine emperor Heraclius in AD 628.

Masdjid-i Sulaimān, which I have already mentioned, is situated in Khūzistān, not far from Badr Nishandi. It is in a spot where the fire seems to burn miraculously, owing to natural gas escaping from the soil. During the Arsacid period a terrace was also built there; it was about 120 yards wide and 150 yards long, backing on to the mountain on one side and reached on the other by a broad stairway 12 to 15 feet high (fig. 142). It was there on the front part of the terrace that the fire miracles took place. Below, at the height of the substructure, one can still see the beginning of a small staircase which doubtless led to a lower room in which some priest regulated, activated or diminished the volume of gas. Beyond this 'esplanade' the terrace also has a raised platform, roughly 90 feet square, on which there was no doubt another square construction, as at Badr Nishandi.

The miracle, famous from the Arsacid period onwards as I have just said, was perfectly organized under the Sassanids. We can imagine at nightfall the impressive spectacle of these flames rising from the soil, first violent, then quelled, first leaping then sinking. The faithful would be massed at the foot of the terrace or assembled on the slopes and peaks of the neighbouring heights. Sometimes in certain circumstances they would be allowed to ascend the high staircase and ask the gods questions. Then the flames rose, stayed still or disappeared for an instant; each of their movements, each oscillation, had a meaning, a hidden significance which the science of the magi could explain. This curious monument, turned into a Muslim cemetery, has remained much as it was at the Sassanid period right up to the present day.

The religious monuments of the Arsacid period therefore are represented in Iran only by two high places, a fire sanctuary, a kind of open-air theatre and a Hellenistic temple. However, at the end of this period during the second century AD, the first mention is made, by Pausanias, of a temple 'in which there was a special cell, closed and covered in, where the eternal fire burns without flames on an altar covered with ashes'. In this new monument containing the home of the divine fire where the faithful participated in the ceremonies of the cult, the fire inhabited dark, firmly closed chambers, hidden among the buildings. On the other hand, in place of the cella, an open-air altar for public manifestations of the now official cult, which had no competitors, developed, both in importance and size. It was taken from the ground, placed on a high base and favoured with a canopy which was almost purely decorative, the chahār tāq, about which we shall have much to say. It was in the Sassanid period that this type of monument, its exceptions and its derivatives had their greatest vogue.

PARTHIAN SCULPTURE

Few works of Arsacid sculpture have come down to us. Moreover, they mostly have little artistic interest, being generally imitations of Hellenistic art and therefore products of a superimposed fashion having little connection with the true Iran.

However, a chance discovery in 1934 has given us information which is of particular concern to us because it introduces us to a new point in the continuous line which links the pre-Achaemenid art of the Kassites with that of the Seleucids and persisted beneath the official art of the Achaemenids, Seleucids and Arsacids. It is quite as important for the history of Iranian sculpture as the Median tombs and peasant houses the plan of which lies at the basis of Persepolis, the description of Manaian dwellings by the Assyrian annals, the construction, if not the decoration, of the Parthian palaces in Mesopotamia and the few words of Diodorus Siculus I have quoted about the cruciform plan of the house of the 'Paromisads' all are for architecture.

The site of this discovery is the region of Shāmi, some twenty-five miles north-west of Mālamīr, the ancient Idhadj. Situated consequently in what is now the Iranian province of Khūzistān, this region was, at the time of the Seleucid domination, part of the principality of Elymais, the last vestige of the Elamite kingdom. In fact, as J. de Morgan says, we do not know the boundaries of Elymais, 'but it certainly extended over the plains of the Kārūn, the Āb-i Diz and the Karkha. The finds of Elymean coins at Susa, Ahwāz and Dizfūl support the belief that the districts where those towns and ruins now are also formed part of it.' Certainly also, since the district of Shāmi, whose land lies between 3,000 and 3,600 feet, still belongs to the *garmsīrs*, i.e. the hot regions, we must assume that Elymais extended further north as far as the *sardsīrs*, the cold regions, where the flocks lived for half the year. No principality or kingdom would have been viable in this part of Iran unless it had possessed both *garmsīrs* and *sardsīrs*. Undoubtedly Elymais extended beyond the Zard-i Kūh, to the high valleys where the Bakhtiārīs of our own day take their livestock in the spring and spend the summer, like their ancestors.

In winter their black tents cover the low parts of the country, from the plain of Shūshtar and Dizfūl to the plain of Mālamir, then in April, when the harvest is in, several hundreds of thousands of sheep, goats and other animals, accompanied by a large part of the population of the tribes, including old people, women and children, make for the heights, cross the Kārūn, ascend the steep slopes of the snow-clad mountains and, after a whole month of hard travel, reach their summer encampments where they remain until autumn.

In 1934, since the former king of Iran, H.M. Rizā Shāh Pahlawī, had taken it upon himself to settle as many as possible of these eternal wanderers, some of them undertook the construction of houses in a ravine in the Shāmi region. There was a terrace there strewn with sun-dried bricks suitable for building a village on, not far from a spring and some plots of cultivable land, at the foot of a high mountain, the Kūh-i Bilawa. They dug up the ground to find more bricks and so discovered less than three feet down the remains of a considerable building and several bronze and marble statues.

The place was then visited by Sir Aurel Stein and an expedition of the Iranian Department of Antiquities. Our route, that is to say the rough track we followed from Tell Bazun, close to Maidān-i Naft, the main oil-bearing centre of Iran, rejoined the one which leads from Mālamīr to Shāmi, at the foot of the Kūh-i Piyun, in a vast verdant plain—a truly magnificent royal site to which I shall have occasion to refer again. Turning left to the north-west, we first went through this beautiful valley then, after crossing a series of increasingly wild passes, we arrived at a sort of 'Valley of the Kings', a fairly narrow fault, closed at both ends by passes, bordered on the left by the enormous Kūh-i Bilawa and on the right by a high smooth wall of strata of sloping rock. The floor of this steep ravine forms the surface of an enormous ramp consisting of debris which has fallen from the mountain since the beginning of time. There is nothing horizontal in this chaos, except the artificial terrace at the top of the slope against the mountain where the statues were found. There is nothing gracious there, except, at the time of my journey, the brilliant patch of colour made by two small gardens full of pomegranates in bloom. But it is the architectural Kūh-i Bilawa which is particularly impressive. The mountain of Bīsūtūn, which rears its 3,000 feet of rock vertically above the plain of the Pulwar Rūd, and being marvellous for that reason was called 'Bāgāstāna', the place of the gods, is a mere bagatelle beside it. It seemed clear from the first that the Kūh-i Bilawa could not have failed to be a sacred place as well and that the statues discovered at its foot bore witness to the fact. Besides, passing nomads said that there were ancient constructions on the side and summit of the mountain, as well as springs, pools and caves inhabited by dragons and djinns—all the monsters born of popular terror—and that it could only be climbed with ropes and picks—if anyone dared.

These first-night impressions, which might have been merely those of a tired traveller, were confirmed the next day by a more detailed examination of the place. There was not a single trace of a town or dwelling, except on the terrace with the statues, but below this platform the sloping ground was literally riddled with tombs. Some of the long stone slabs which served as their roofing were visible above ground. The piles of debris still covering or surrounding them seemed to indicate that they were originally surmounted by pyramids, cones and other constructions of a decorative nature. Others, whose roofing had collapsed into the ditches they covered, were marked by a depression in the ground.

Sometimes these tombs were corridors some 12 yards long or even, according to the local people, longer. That was already remarkable, although long tombs had already been reported in the cemeteries of neighbouring Luristān; but the corridors at Shāmi, instead of being very low as in Luristān, measured as much as 7 foot 6 inches high by 6 feet wide. The walls of one of these tombs consisted of stone slabs placed one on top of each other without mortar; the roofing consists of slabs nearly 6 feet long, laid flat, side by side. However, it is obvious that slabs less than 6 feet long cannot cover a room 6 feet wide. The builder solved the problem by resting the roofing slabs on similar slabs laid in the same direction as the walls, but corbelled out instead of resting fully on them. This tomb, of which only a *sondage* was carried out and inside which a well sunk some 10 yards further on sank still deeper, contained elements of markedly Hellenistic plaster mouldings.

Constructions of this kind, costly because they required the use of long ceiling slabs and others as well long enough to act as corbels, are not common. As is easy to imagine, less onerous procedures were discovered—the most generally employed being a covering in the form of a pitched two-sided roof, achieved by means of slabs leant against each other and resting on the walls of the chambers as before.

Tombs covered in this fashion are the most numerous. Their dimensions vary greatly, but they are generally narrower than the flat-ceilinged tombs and differ from them mainly in being set more deeply in the ground. Perhaps they are the most ancient. In the remains of one of them we found fragments of a bitumen cup similar to those discovered by the French archaeological delegation at Susa in large numbers and dated about 2300 BC. True nothing is more easily transported than a cup, so that this find does not prove that there were tombs at Shāmi before the Parthian period; but it would be very interesting to ascertain whether there were. In fact there is no reason why the *Bāgāstāna*—as the mountain at Shāmi was, in my view—should not date from the Parthian period. The extremity of the Husain Kūh, near Persepolis, in which the tombs of the first Achaemenids were hollowed out, was a 'home of the gods' long before the arrival of the Persians on the Iranian plateau. We can still recognize vestiges of Elamite sculpture which are not later than the middle of the second millennium BC. And the rock of Bīsūtūn was one of them long before Darius I had his famous inscription carved on it.

To emphasize the sacred character of the place, I repeat that there is a high place like the one at Badra Nishandi, but with smaller proportions, at the entrance to the ravine of Shāmi, on a small height dominating the pass and the path leading to it. It consists of a raised rectangular terrace on which a square platform, the site of communal prayers or of a small construction, as at Badr Nishandi and Masdjid-i Sulaimān, is still visible.

However, since even a sacred necropolis has to depend on a neighbouring village, I must return to the magnificent site I have already mentioned. It is about five miles from Shāmi, at the foot of the Kūh-i Piyun, at the intersection of the roads which now lead and certainly also led in the past to Mālamīr, in the south-east, to Maidān-i Naft, in the west, and to Shāmi, in the north-west. There are two modern villages there, Piyun Shaikhun and Piyun Bala. The first occupies a small section of the site of a large town which has disappeared. There is no river, but a vast sheet of underground water from which a great number of wells draw their supplies, which explains simultaneously the presence there of the large ancient town and of the modern villages.

The Iranian Department of Antiquities carried out *sondages* on the edge of the hump-backed ground which conceals the remains of the ancient city. They revealed the existence of a cemetery consisting of tombs analogous to those of the most developed type at Shāmi and dating from the same period as them; they too are covered with slab ceilings and their walls are decorated with plaster mouldings and Hellenistic ornaments. One of them, which contained numerous bones and glazed earthenware pots, is roughly 7 feet 6 inches high, 6 feet wide and 60 feet long.

After I have pointed out, in agreement with Sir Aurel Stein, that the Shāmi statues represented princely personages, we shall no doubt be able to deduce that the sacred ravine of Shāmi had become the necropolis of the kings of Elymais, the capital, or one of the capitals, of which was a few miles away, on the site of the existing villages of Piyun Shaikhun, in the same way that Naqsh-i Rustam, the necropolis of the Achaemenid sovereigns, was a few miles from Persepolis.

So we return to our bronze statues and the various objects which were discovered in 1934 by the Bakhtiārīs, then by Sir Aurel Stein and myself. I shall not say much about the building which contained these objects. This mausoleum, erected on an artificial terrace, consisted of a rectangular building about 66 feet long by 36 feet wide, preceded by a small outgrowth—a kind of vestibule—and perhaps by a columned portico as well. It had been sacked and destroyed by fire. The following objects were found among the debris: the stone pedestals of six bronze statues, six stone column-bases in a Hellenistic style, a small marble altar, fragments of two bronze ornamental candelabra, the leg of a table or seat, shaped like a lion's paw, an iron dagger, a woman's head executed in marble and certainly of Greek origin, another marble head executed locally (fig. 143) which represents a man with a pointed beard, according to

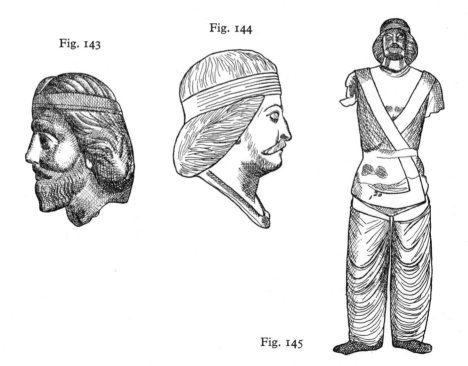

Fig. 143

Fig. 144

Fig. 145

the Parthian fashion, various bits of the mother of pearl decoration of a casket—the rest of which being perishable has disappeared—were found, together with several necklaces in the tomb of a woman adjoining the rear wall of the mausoleum.

Of the six statues it has only been possible to restore one almost completely. It only lacks the right arm, the left hand and naturally whatever was held in its hands. It is the portrait of a man in the costume of the oriental Parthians, but who is not a Parthian. His features are so exactly those of a Zagrus mountain-dweller that Bakhtiārī visitors to Teheran Museum, where this statue is exhibited (figs. 144 and 145 and plates 94 and 95), claim that they recognize it for certain as the portrait of one of their own people, whom they call Abdullah, Hasan, Husain or some other name. The Persians, says Herodotus, 'borrow the fashions of foreigners more than all other men; they dress like them and find their costumes more beautiful than their own'. This statue, 6 feet 4 inches high, consists of two parts, the head and the remainder, which were executed by different craftsmen, probably in different places. The head may have been modelled and cast in the plain, in the vicinity of Susa, by a skilful sculptor influenced by the official Hellenism. The body, the rough bronze of which is several inches thick, is so heavy that it could only have been cast on the spot, at Shami itself, by a less skilful man who certainly knew how to sculpture to judge by the excellent workmanship of the pectoral muscles, but could not provide the head with a body of the right proportions.

The man wears a short cloth tunic edged with leather, wide open over the chest but coming to a point lower down and cut square at the back. This jacket, which has no buttons or other fastening system, is kept crossed by a belt. It has long sleeves.

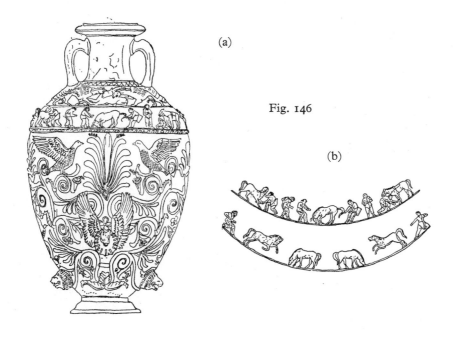

(a)

Fig. 146

(b)

There is no decorated braid. There is nothing Hellenistic, nothing of the long loose Greek-style tunics which, incidentally, the Parthians also wore, about this garment which is cut, not draped. We find it represented almost identically on the bas-reliefs at Gandhāra and by the Scythians themselves, for example on the well-known vase from Chertomlitsk (fig. 146 a and b).

The belt is represented by small rectangular medallions, with chased decoration imitated from metal originals. They were attached to a leather band which was the real belt.

A short pair of pants appears below the jacket. Between these pants and what seem to be leggings the legs are bare, from which we can deduce that our man normally walked in shorts and jacket. When he was on horseback, or needed protection against the scrub, he put his leggings on—no trousers, those trousers in which the Achaemenid sculptors dressed all the peoples of the North, including the Parthians. Doubtless a question of latitude for, as I have already said, the region of Mālamīr at an altitude of about 3,000 feet still forms part of the *garmsīr*, or hot regions.

The leggings, a kind of long pleated trouser-legs, perhaps of leather, were attached by a special belt beneath the jacket. They fall amply on the heel-less shoes whose tips are turned outwards, no doubt to hold the feet in the double straps which served as stirrups.

The weapons of this horseman on foot, at least those which attribute to him, consist solely of two daggers. Perhaps he had another in his hand, which has disappeared, but it was not a sword, the heavy sword of the Parthians and Sarmatians, for there is no fixture for attaching a weapon of this kind, sheath, cross-belt or straps, visible on the statue. Nor was it a bow, which would hardly go without a quiver. Except perhaps for a long staff, of which a kind of mace head, also found in the destroyed building, could be the tip, our man seems only to have been armed with the two daggers, one on each thigh. Attached to the inside edge of the jacket, they disappeared partly into the leggings.

Clearly we shall not be able to identify the man exactly until more extensive excavations have been made at Shāmi. However, Sir Aurel Stein, speaking of the head of another statue, of which he found fragments at this place, remarks that the diadem on the curled hair indicate that the man represented was a royal personage. I for my part wrote in 1936 that in spite of his Parthian costume the man of the Teheran statue was certainly not a Parthian, but a solid Iranian mountain-dweller clothed in the fashion of his time, perhaps lord of a small semi-independent principality, who lived in the Mālamīr valley during the first century AD. I added that he was possibly the founder of a temple situated at Shāmi, but we have since realized that the edifice in question was a tomb. So our man was presumably one of the native princes who ruled over Elymais from the middle of the second century BC, and the building which sheltered his statue was his tomb, or more accurately, in view of the number of pedestals discovered, the mausoleum of the princely dynasty to which he belonged. Moreover, a mausoleum-cum-temple, for the worship of kings, is well attested in the Near East from the reign of Alexander the Great onwards.

If we compare the statue in Teheran Museum with Seleucid and Elymean coins, it could be that of a prince who ruled a little before or a little after the beginning of our era. The statue whose head has been described by Sir Aurel Stein is probably more ancient. It represented, perhaps, Kamnaskires I.

In that case both statues would date from the Arsacid period, on the clear understanding that we are speaking of the official Arsacid period, i.e. the years between 250 BC and AD 224.

We have, therefore, a statue of the official Parthian period, a sincere portrait without regard to convention, the only Hellenistic feature of which is the craft of the sculptor who executed its face. All the rest is the real art of the country, anxious to be accurate, the work of a man ignoring the requirements of fashion, who already modelled on the same large scale as the sculptors of the Sassanid period were to do a little later and still carved the medallions of a belt in the same way that his ancestors had ornamented the disc-headed pins they intended for their temples. In fact, if we try to imagine, not the purely decorative sculpture of the palaces at Persepolis, where we continually see the same head on the shoulders of the King of Kings as on the soldiers' (col. pl. II), nor the so-called Greek sculpture of the court of the Arsacids (pl. 96), but the authentic character of the work of Iranian artists in the Achaemenid, Seleucid and Parthian periods, we shall find it gradually by such fortunate discoveries along the trail blazed by the Zagros bronzes, the Shāmi statue and Sassanid bas-reliefs and silverware. I think that as an indication and to represent provisionally unofficial Achaemenian art we can moreover place in the line of pure Iranian art a small head of lapis lazuli, carved in the round, which was found at Persepolis during the work of clearing the terrace (fig. 147 and pl. 71). Admittedly it exhibits some of the details borrowed from palace

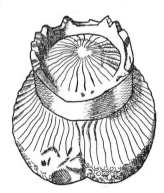

Fig. 147

sculpture, its wonderfully curled hair, for example, or the way in which the line of the eyebrows is expressed, but the face is a document which tells us more about what the Persians looked like than all the known heads of the Achaemenid sovereigns. Perhaps, with its crenellated royal crown, it represents the young Xerxes to whom his father entrusted the conduct of the work at Persepolis, as we know, and who seems to have lived there fairly continuously until the time of his accession to the throne.

79. SILVER RHYTON
Seleucid period (fourth to third century BC). Height: 8 in. The Louvre, Paris.
Compare this rhyton with the Achaemenid ibex in plate 78, already showing Greek influence. Note the two heads in particular.

80. REVERSE OF A SILVER TETRADRACHM OF SELEUCUS I
Beginning of third century BC. Diameter: $\frac{3}{4}$ in. Cabinet des Médailles, Bibliothèque Nationale, Paris.
Head of horned horse facing left. Inscription: Basileos Seleucos.

81. REVERSE OF A SILVER TETRADRACHM OF SELEUCUS I
Beginning of third century BC. Cabinet des Médailles, Bibliothèque Nationale, Paris.
Profile of elephant. Inscription: Basileos Seleucos.

82 and 83. OBVERSE AND REVERSE OF A TETRADRACHM OF OBORZA, PRINCE OF FĀRS
Beginning of third century BC. Diameter: 1 in. Cabinet des Médailles, Bibliothèque Nationale, Paris.
Oborza is reputed to have governed the regions of Istakhr and Persepolis during the reign of Seleucus I. The obverse bears a bearded head facing left, crowned with the satrap's bonnet, with its vizor and chin-piece. On the reverse the prince is represented standing at the left of a monument which could be a fire-temple. On the other side of the monument is a standard. Unlike the preceding ones, this type of coin is purely Iranian.

84. SILVER TETRADRACHM OF MITHRADATES I
170–138 BC. Diameter: 1$\frac{3}{16}$ in. Cabinet des Médailles, Bibliothèque Nationale, Paris.
The bearded sovereign, with his head encircled by a diadem, faces right. The Hellenistic influence is very obvious here.

85. SILVER TETRADRACHM ATTRIBUTED TO THE FIRST PARTHIAN ARSACID SOVEREIGNS
Second century BC. Diameter: $\frac{25}{32}$ in. Cabinet des Médailles, Bibliothèque Nationale, Paris.
Compare this purely Iranian coin with plates 82 and 83.

86. SILVER TETRADRACHM OF VOLOGASES I
First century AD. Diameter: 1$\frac{3}{16}$ in. Cabinet des Médailles, Bibliothèque Nationale, Paris.
Vologases I, who is depicted here, reigned from AD 51 to 77 and had to combat the rebellion of his own son. He was the first to inscribe his coins with Semitic characters. His reign marks the withdrawal of Hellenistic influence in Iran. One foreign influence was replaced by another.

87. THE 'MAGIC LAKE' OF SHĪZ, NOW TAKHT-I SULAIMĀN
This aerial photograph shows one of the high places of Mazdean Iran. The lake, fed by seven streams, has long been considered miraculous, for it is always full and never overflows. One of the great religious centres of the Sassanid period, the 'fire of the farmers', was situated nearby. The sparse architectural remains which exist in this spot seem to belong to the Parthian and Sassanid periods.

80

81

82

83

84

85

86

88

89

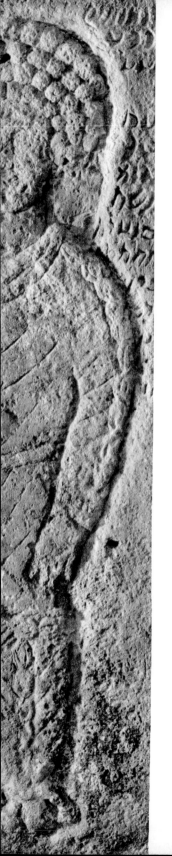

92

93

94

88. THE TWO COLUMNS AT KHURRA

Kāshān region. Seleucid period (?). Height: about 36 ft.
For a long time it was believed that these two columns formed part of a temple of the Seleucid period. The research carried out by the Iranian Department of Antiquities in 1956 has not confirmed this supposition. Not a single coin or inscription was found which would enable us to conclude that there was a large settlement there at any particular period.

89. BAS-RELIEF AT TANG-I SARWĀK

Khūzistān, Second century AD. Height of the officiating priest: a little more than 6 ft.
This bas-relief situated in the south of Iran, not far from Mālamīr, the ancient Idhadj, is on a rock twenty-one feet above ground level. This work, of no artistic merit, seems to have been executed during the Parthian period.

90. RUINS OF THE PALACE AT HATRA (IRAQ)

First to second century AD.
Here we see a part of the official, administrative and religious quarter of Hatra, which was a rectangular enclosure. The actual town, where caravans stopped, was surrounded by a strong wall with round towers at intervals and a broad ditch outside. The city was mainly inhabited by Arabs, but they owed obedience to the Parthians. In addition the architecture is Parthian. The Romans under Trajan and later under Septimius Severus unsuccessfully tried to take the town. Half a century later it was the Sassanid king, Shāpūr I (plates 101, 103, 118, etc.), who took it by storm. The 'Baals' and Syrian divinities were thrown out of their sanctuaries and the temples destroyed. Since 1950 the Iraqi Department of Antiquities has been excavating the site of the ancient town of Hatra. The objects discovered are exhibited either at Mosul or in the new Baghdad Museum.

91. PARTHIAN BAS-RELIEF REPUTEDLY OF 'ARTABANUS (ARDAWĀN) V'

Susa, in Khūzistān. Third century AD. Area: about 9 sq. ft. Teheran Museum.
This sculpture, discovered by the French archaeological expedition to Susa, is executed so perfunctorily that it would be tempting to think that artistic sense and craftsmanship had disappeared with the end of this dynasty. But Artabanus, beaten by Ardashīr, relinquished power in AD 224; the Sassanids succeeded the Parthians and once Ardashīr was king he commissioned some very beautiful sculptures (see plate 98).

92 FEMALE FIGURE ENGRAVED ON MOTHER-OF-PEARL; INTENDED AS INCRUSTATION

Tell-i Chinar at Shāmi, in Khūzistān. *c.* first century AD. Height: $5\frac{1}{16}$ in. Teheran Museum.
A female figure seen full-face and wearing a sort of tiara was the centre of a composition mainly grouping horsemen and archers.

93. ARCHER ENGRAVED ON MOTHER-OF-PEARL

Tell-i Chinar Shāmi, near Mālamīr. *c.* first century AD. Height $3\frac{7}{16}$ in. Teheran Museum.
This archer formed part of the same decoration as the woman in plate 92. He is shown drawing his bow; a bandeau keeps his curly hair in place.

H

94. BRONZE STATUE OF A PARTHIAN PRINCE

Tell-i Chinar, Shāmi, in Khūzistān. *c.* first century AD. Height: about 6 ft. 6 in. Archaeological Museum, Teheran.

This statue was found in 1933 during the construction of dwellings for settling the nomads, at the foot of the Bakhtiārī Mountains. It stood in a temple or funerary chapel, in company with other marble or bronze statues. The latter are more or less fragmentary and are on view in Teheran Museum.

95. HEAD OF THE BRONZE STATUE (shown in pl. 95)

Height: $9\frac{1}{2}$ in.

The face is beautifully executed in a style which is both sensitive and realistic. The coiffure is akin to that of the effigies on Parthian coins and leads us to believe that the prince depicted lived in the first century AD.

96. ALABASTER HEAD OF A PARTHIAN PRINCESS

Susa. End of first century AD. Actual size. Archaeological Museum, Teheran.

This princess wears a crenellated crown, insignia reserved for the Iranian monarchs. A Greek inscription on the bandeau dating from the Parthian period gives the name of the artist: 'Antiochus, son of Dryas'. According to a communication by Franz Cumont to the Académie des Inscriptions et Belles-Lettres in 1939, the alabaster head represented Queen Musa, a beautiful Roman slave, presented by Augustus to the Parthian King Phraates IV, who reigned from 37 to 2 BC.

Now, to show that the fashion of wearing Parthian costume in Elymais was not the privilege of princes, but had become general, we come to the mother-of-pearl fragments I have already mentioned found in the tomb of the woman adjoining the walls of the royal mausoleum at Shāmi (plates 92 and 93). These interesting items of a decoration which has mostly disappeared no doubt ornamented a casket, for they were found in the earth mixed up with the not particularly precious stones from numerous necklaces. The people represented are not complete, either because all the fragments of mother-of-pearl have not been recovered, or more probably because they represent the only part of decoration which was executed in mother-of-pearl, the rest having been carved on some perishable material, doubtless the wood of which the casket was made. They consist of two archers, facing to the right, a group of two horsemen, facing left, and a person full-face who must have occupied the centre of the composition between the archers and the horsemen.

One of the archers is beardless. Long wavy hair, curled around his face and held by a thin bandeau, falls to his shoulders. He wears a short jacket, exactly like the one worn by the great bronze statue of Shāmi, wide open at the chest, crossed and gathered at the waist by means of a narrow belt. It also has long sleeves. This fragment, the outline of which is perfectly limned, is almost whole. Only a tiny piece of the right elbow is missing (pl. 93).

The second archer, less well preserved, wears the same jacket with long sleeves. The right hand, which holds the bowstring and, between the second and third fingers, the feathered arrow, is very clear and extremely well drawn.

The two horsemen are bearded. They also have flowing hair, but it is not held by a bandeau. Their clothing is similar to the archers', except that their jackets are trimmed with ornamented braid. The left hand of the first horseman holds the bridle of a horse; we can see its neck and withers in front of him, but its head has disappeared.

As for the person full-face—a queen or goddess—we only see her head, wearing a sort of bonnet, her neck adorned with necklaces, and her arms (pl. 92). The rest, doubtless carved on different material, has disappeared. The hair of this queen or goddess spreads over her shoulders. Her necklaces are represented by two braids ornamented with dots. Her dress, with small pleats and decorated with rich trimming, is strikingly reminiscent of the sculptural works of Palmyra. The head, with sinuous lips and its strange headgear, is also so close to Palmyrene art that it is certainly in that direction, or more accurately in the direction in which Palmyra and Doura Europos looked, that we must seek the origin of this composition, and not in the east of Elymais. In confirmation of what our little mother-of-pearl fragments indicate, I should remark that Elymais, feudatory of the Seleucids until the middle of the first century AD, maintained much more sustained relations with the Susian plain and Mesopotamia than with the part of Persia under Parthian dominion.

In the time of the Arsacids, the minor arts, which were little cultivated in the Achaemenid period, became the object of an increasingly important trade in continuous contact with the ports of Syria and Phoenicia. The most sought-after of these export articles were the Persian tapestries already well-known in the West before the Arsacid

period and described by Philostratus as follows: ' . . . The appartments allocated to the
men and the porticoes were resplendent with gold facings, decorated as if by pictures
of gold embroidered cloths framed by silver plaques. The most common subjects of
these pictures were borrowed from Greek mythology and reproduced episodes from
the life of Andromeda, Amyone and Orpheus. Here Datis destroys the town of Naxos
with the aid of his fleet, Ataphernes besieges Eritria, Xerxes overthrows his enemies.
There one sees the taking of Athens, the battle of Thermopylae and the salient episodes of the Median wars, whole rivers drunk up by a thirsty army and disappearing
from the face of the earth, the bridge spanning the sea and the canal across the Athos
peninsula.' All this plus the Hellenistic paintings of Kūh-i Khwāja, the vaults
constellated with sapphires of the last Arsacid palates, the sun, the moon and the stars
flashing in a crystal sky, the Shāmi statues and those which have reached us from elsewhere, generally imitated from Greek statuary or Achaemenid bas-reliefs, intaglios and
terracotta statuettes, often very badly executed, coins imitated from Syrian types,
masterpieces at first (those of Mithradates I, for example (pl. 84)), but which rapidly
became debased in design and their Greek superscriptions illegible; all this, taken together, represents the art of Iran in the Arsacid period. But it is probable that when we
know it better we shall be able to distinguish a Greek Court art on the one hand,
possibly fairly pure (pl. 96), and on the other, in those regions of Iran which were not
directly subject to the influence of the central power, a more sincere art, the traditional
art of the Iranian plateau, the real art of the country (pl. 95). What we know today as
Parthian art will take its place between the two; it has been described as a 'hasty mixture without links either visible or hidden of oriental traditions and Greek forms at the
service of a thoroughly decadent technique'.

PARTHIAN COINS

Alexander of Macedon, vanquisher of Darius III, conqueror of Iran, died in 323 BC,
but coins continued to be minted in his effigy both in Iran and elsewhere, during the
reigns of several of his successors (fig. 148 a and b). The epic of the Macedonian hero
had, in fact, made such a strong impression on the minds of his contemporaries that

Fig. 148

(a)   (b)

his memory lasted and only vanished slowly. Long after his death, the Asiatic nations, desirous of unified government, reproduced on their coins the well-known image of the hero, which rapidly became traditional, thus resuming, though with a purely commercial goal, the wholly Alexandrure idea of the union of the peoples, and expressing it under the sign and, so to speak, by the intermediary of the glorious man who had tried to unite Asia with the Greek world which then represented the West (fig. 149 a and b). A certain number of coins of this type have been found, notably during the

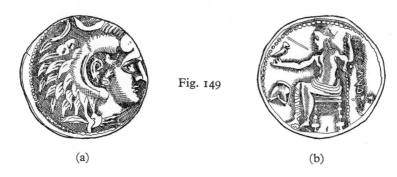

Fig. 149

(a)   (b)

excavations which the archaeological expedition of the University Museum of Philadelphia carried out at Gordion in Asia Minor. There they consisted of tetradrachmae restruck on other more ancient ones from which they differ slightly, though remaining Hellenistic works of art.

Seleucus I, one of Alexander's generals, founder in 312 BC of the Seleucid dynasty in Asia, had some tetradrachmae struck, surpassing in beauty even those of Alexander. There are some the reverse of which represents the famous elephants (pl. 81) which an Indian sovereign offered to Seleucus in exchange for his independence and the sight of which caused such panic in Antigonus's army that Seleucus doubtless owed his celebrated victory at Ipsus to them.

It was particularly during the first three centuries BC that the most beautiful portraits in numismatics were executed, both by the Hellenized Bactrians and the Seleucids, but this art, entirely dependent on Greek numismatic traditions, has little to do with the Orient. However, about twenty-five years ago finds were made at Susa, in Iran itself, of tetradrachmae with a rather bizarre appearance, in which the influence of the Orient—its taste for a certain kind of schematism—is very marked on the obverse of the coins as well as on their reverse with its Hymiaritic superscription (pl. 80). It is not impossible that these very curious pieces were minted towards the middle of the second century BC.

The Seleucids, at least up to Antiochus IV (175–164 BC), were fervent missionaries of Hellenistic art and thought in Iran, but at the end of the second and beginning of the first centuries BC, their dynasty dwindled into a series of internecine quarrels which enabled the Parthians to develop their ascendancy over Mesopotamia and drive the Hellenes back to the 'white fringe of the Mediterranean'.

The Parthians formed part of the tribes which peopled the Achaemenid satrapies of the north-west of Iran. Gradually these nomads took possession of Khurāsān—the ancient Khwārizmia Hyrcania, and Media—or perhaps only a part of that province. During the third century BC their advance had been slow, since the satraps who obeyed the Seleucid Antiochus III (227–187 BC) had slowed down their advance as much as possible.

Mithradates I (171–138 BC) appeared as the first 'King of Kings' of the Arsacid dynasty. He was also the first to declare himself a philhellene, but it should be pointed out that his intentions were political and economic rather than profound and based on sentiment. What the Parthian kings particularly wanted to preserve were the commercial relations with the towns and regions Hellenized by the Seleucids.

In 140–139 BC Mithradates won a great victory over Demetrius II, enabling him to add the rich provinces of Mesopotamia to his empire. At the same time he seized the sumptuous town of Seleucia on the Tigris, where the Seleucid dynasties minted money for over a century. Some very handsome tetradrachmae imitating the Seleucid coins appeared as a result of this conquest (pl. 84).

There has been much discussion about the Parthian coinage. Did they mint gold coins? Some numismatists, including Messrs Unvala and Aziz Beglu, have assured me that they have seen such coins minted by Mithradates II, whose reign, from 123 to 88 BC, was long and powerful (fig. 150). He it was who entered into relations with the

Fig. 150

Fig. 151

Romans to whom he had sent an embassy. He stopped a Scythian invasion and extended his power as far as Armenia.

Recently, a treasure including Seleucid and Arsacid tetradrachmae was discovered near Gūrgān in the ancient province of Hyrcania. Many of them represented Antiochus Gryphos (125–196 BC) and his sons, including Philip, who had handed over his brother Demetrius III to Mithradates II during one of those fratricidal struggles which wore out the last Seleucids.

With the passage of the years the Hellenistic veneer was wiped out. From the time of Vologases I (AD 51–77), Semitic characters appeared on that prince's drachmae, while the Greek writing still used on his tetradrachmae became more and more barbarous (pl. 86). After the first half of the first century AD therefore the decadence of Hellenistic influence became glaring (fig. 151).

While the Parthian kings, who considered themselves westernized by being termed 'philhellenes'—a term they had applied to themselves—ruled over Iran and Mesopotamia, the Iranians, at least those who believed that they represented religious and military nationalism, and thus the traditional spirit, continued to live as they had done in the Seleucid period, outside the cultural and commercial current represented by the Arsacids, their court and their main routes of communication. Apparently, one family of these feudal princes was particularly powerful and ambitious. Their domain extended in the province of Fārs over the region of Fīrūzābād and the range of mountains bordering the Persian Gulf, up to the high central plateau where they probably pastured their flocks, as the Qashqāi tribes still do. It was from this southern region of Iran that the great dynasty of the Sassanids was to emerge.

The princes of Fārs had their own coinage and one of their tetradrachmae at least is remarkable (plates 82 and 83). Indeed we must remember that some of the Seleucids, and in any case Seleucus I and his immediate successors, had minted coins at Istakhr, near Persepolis, in Fārs, that tradition conserved the memory of them and that this region belonged to the ancestors of the Sassanids.

PART FOUR

SASSANID IRAN

CHAPTER 7

FROM ARDASHIR I TO YAZDAGIRD II

ERSIA'S struggle against Greece had terminated by the defeat of the Achaemenid Darius III Codomannus and the dissolution of the Iranian state (331 BC). It was both a dynastic and a national disaster for Iran. Alexander of Macedon had just introduced Hellenism into the very heart of Asia. Later, Seleucus, conquering back his eastern heritage, founded a Greek dynasty there. Parthia, claiming to be philhellene, made itself independent. The Greco-Bactrian kingdom's frontiers were pushed forward as far as Chinese Turkestan. The Orient had apparently become a province of Hellenism. As Firdawsī says in his *Shāh Nāma*,[1] 'Centuries passed during which one would have said that there was no king upon the earth.'

However, the sacred fire was not totally extinguished and the minor princes of Fārs in particular had preserved intact the traditions of the magi of the Achaemenid period. One of them, called Papak, or more accurately Pabhagh, who was a petty king of Khīr, east of Shīrāz, and whose father, Sāssān, had fulfilled priestly functions at Istakhr, capital of the kings of Persis, had begun to increase his domains at the expense of his neighbours. One of his sons, Ardashīr, for whom he had obtained a high military post in the town of Dārābgird and who had conceived the ambitious project of recapturing the power of the Achaemenids for himself, took several towns in the province, defeating and killing the reigning princes. He put down a revolt which had broken out in the region in his charge and asserted his power by conquering the province of Kirmān. Having succeeded his father in the capacity of priest-king, master of the whole province of Fārs and Kirmān, he had a princely palace built at Gūr (present-day Fīrūzābād). It excited the jealousy of his sovereign, the Arsacid Ardawān V (Artabanus), and caused discord between the 'King of Kings' and his subjects, as a letter from Ardawān to Ardashīr testifies:

[1] The *Shāh Nāma* of Firdawsī, the 'Book of the Kings', relates the poetic and legendary history of Iran from mythical times to the Arab conquest. Its tales, of beauty and imposing nobility, greatly help our knowledge of the ancient times to which the poet's sources go back. Its influence, as vast as it is varied, still dominates Iranian literature. The thousand years which separate Firdawsī from our time have never ceased to see the birth and emergence of new audiences interested in the lofty deeds of the legendary and historical kings and heroes of Iran.

The *Shāh Nāma* has been translated into the principal European languages.

Firdawsī was born at Tūs, near Mashhad, in Khurāsān, and died there *c.* 1020. His tomb is an object of national pilgrimage.

'You wretched Kurd, how did you dare to build such a royal residence?' Ardashīr, so the story goes, revolted against his sovereign, conquered him and slew him with his own hand.

After this battle, which took place in AD 224, Gūr was called Ardashīr-Khurra, i.e. 'Glory of Ardashīr'. In AD 226 Ardashīr entered Ctesiphon,[1] the capital of the Parthian Empire, presenting himself as the Arsacids' successor. It is thought that he had himself solemnly crowned 'King of Kings of Iran' shortly after this event. We do not know where the ceremony took place, but it was probably in his family's home country, either at Istakhr, in the temple of Anāhit, whom his ancestor Sāssān had served as high priest, or at Naqsh-i Radjab, between Istakhr and Persepolis, in the shallow gorge where Ardashīr himself and his successor, Shāpūr I, both commemorated their accession to the throne with magnificent bas-reliefs carved on the rock (pl. 102).

During the next few years Ardashīr[2] conquered Media, attacked Armenia and Azerbaidjan, unsuccessfully at first, but later victoriously. He subdued Sīstān, Khurāsān, the land of Marw (Merv), Khwārizmia to the east of the Caspian Sea, and Margiana. The King of the Kūshans, who was still master of the valley of Kābul and the Punjab, sent ambassadors to him and recognized his sovereignty. His empire then comprised present-day Iran, Afghanistan and Baluchistan, the land of the oases of Marw and Khīwa as far as the Oxus in the north, and as far as Babylonia and Iraq in the west. So five and a half centuries after the fall of the Achaemenid Empire, the Persians had reconquered their Iranian domain and a new oriental empire had been created which could treat with the Roman Empire on an equal footing.

Ardashīr, a powerful politician, endowed with great military talents, but cruel and unscrupulous, posed as the protector of national traditions, especially the national religion. He linked the dynasty he had created with that of the Achaemenids[3] by a fictitious genealogy—or perhaps it was done for him.

We have seen that the dualist religion of the Medes had reached Persia during the Achaemenid period. Obviously it is not possible for us to follow the religious development which led from primitive Mazdaism to the convinced Zoroastrianism of the Sassanids. Undoubtedly the Zoroastrian magi gradually gained influence and power under the Arsacids, who were worried about it at first, then tried to take advantage of this force by acknowledging its resolute spirit and prestige. One of them, Vologases, tried to collect the fragments of the sacred texts and codify the religious literature of Iran, but he was too late. Darmesteter puts it very well: 'Magianism had found

---

[1] The building of Ctesiphon, on the Tigris near the Greek town of Seleucia, was undertaken by the Parthian Arsacids who made it their capital. Subsequently it became the capital of the Sassanid kings.

[2] Ardashīr I reigned from AD 226–AD 241.

[3] According to tradition, Ardashīr (Artakhshathra in old Persian, in Greek Artaxerxes) married an Arsacid princess, daughter or cousin of Ardawān, or niece of Farrukhān, the son of Ardawān, and thus would appear to have legitimized his dynasty by allying it to the Arsacid house; but the accounts of this marriage by Arabic and Persian authors are full of contradictions and legendary features. The story of the marriage of Ardashīr to an Arsacid woman and the birth of Shāpūr, fruit of this marriage, was probably taken from some popular legend.

an asylum and a fortress in this Persian province where it was once only a feared and suspect guest: the old rivalries between the Medes and the Persians had had time to die down beneath the long common oppression by the foreigner; in this splintered milieu Magianism was the only organized moral force around which a nationality could be rebuilt: the local kings of Persia became its champion. Ardashīr is a crowned magus' (pl. 98).

Ardashīr, the first king of the Sassanid dynasty, was cleverer than anyone else at making use of this active force. Within a few years he created a political and religious system which was to last more than 400 years (AD 226–651) and was a greater threat to Rome and Byzantium than the Romans had been to the Parthians.

Shāpūr I[1] (pl. 118), his son and successor, defeated and killed a Turanian king in Khurāsān. Then he founded the town of Naw-Shāpūr, now Nīshāpūr, on the site of the battle, afterwards assuming the title of 'King of Kings of Iran and Non-Iran' in memory of this victory. A few years later, in AD 260 when the war with Rome had flared up again, the Emperor Valerian, who commanded his troops in person, was taken prisoner (pl. 101).

Bahrām II[2] (pl. 104) initiated peace negotiations with the Romans, but because of a large-scale revolt in the east of the country hastened to conclude them ceding Armenia and Mesopotamia to his adversaries; Shāpūr II quickly reconquered them. During his reign Julian the Apostate[3] advanced as far as Ctesiphon but was halted by a strong Iranian army and died during the combats which followed. His successor, the emperor Jovian, took the Roman army back over the frontier and returned Nisibis and the disputed regions of Lesser Armenia to Iran by the peace concluded shortly afterwards. However, the Hephtalites, or White Huns, whose military power was formidable, were a serious threat to the empire. Yazdagird II[4] kept them in check. His son, Fīrūz I,[5] made a clumsy attack on them and was killed. Vologases[6] beat them and Kāwādh I[7] (pl. 116) established friendly relations with them. This great king fought successfully against Rome, reorganized the administration, restored the State's finances and checked Mazdaism. His son Khusraw (Chosroes) I Anūshīrwān,[8] Khusraw 'of the immortal soul', led the Sassanid Empire to its apogee. He took Antioch. Byzantium had to pay him tribute. He decisively crushed the Hephtalite power in the north-east. In the south his troops conquered the Yemen, which became a Persian satrapy.

A glorious reign! However, hostilities were resumed. Khusraw II Parwīz[9] (pl. 117) invaded Syria and seized the Holy Cross in Jerusalem, bringing it back to Ctesiphon.

[1] Shāpūr I (AD 241–272).
[2] Bahrām II (AD 276–293).
[3] Julian the Apostate. Roman emperor born in AD 331, died in AD 363.
[4] Yazdagird II (AD 438–457).
[5] Fīrūz I (AD 459–484).
[6] Vologases (AD 484–488). He was also called Balash, or Valash.
[7] Kāwādh I, first reign (AD 488–496); second reign (AD 499–531).
[8] Khusraw I Anūshirwān (AD 531–579).
[9] Khusraw II Parwīz (AD 590–628).

His army advanced until it was opposite Byzantium, but it had no fleet in which to cross the Bosphorus. Heraclius restored the *status quo*, cleared Asia Minor, retook Armenia and the Sassanid Empire collapsed at the battle of Nineveh in AD 627. Khusraw II was killed in prison. His son Kāwādh II Shiroes signed the peace and died assassinated or a victim of the plague six months later.

In five years twelve kings and queens succeeded each other on the throne of Iran. The empire disintegrated into dynastic squabbles and finally succumbed at Qādisīya in AD 637 and at Nihāwand in AD 642. Yazdagird III[1] tried to continue the struggle, but his strongholds were taken one after the other and Iran became a province of the Empire of the Caliphs.

Like Darius III, the last of the Achaemenids, Yazdagird III, the last of the Sassanids, died in the east from the knife of an assassin. His descendants took refuge in China where they introduced their native customs.

Unlike the Arsacid Empire, the Sassanid State was based on a powerful organization. At the summit was the king, almost a god, effective head of the army in time of war, surrounded in peacetime by a pompous ceremonial and only appearing to his people during the solemn display of his audiences. Immediately below him was the Prime Minister, a sage and sensible man, who directed the affairs of state under the control of the king and replaced him on occasion, when he was at war or travelling. Next came 'the great men and the nobles', of princely origin, with vast estates, who supplied the high officials and the senior army officers, then the clergy headed by the great *mawbad* (mobad), the great pontiff (pl. 97). This clergy, increasingly powerful, watched jealously over the strict observance of the national cult and showed itself able to quell attempts at reform like the doctrines of Mani and Mazdak. But it needed energetic skilful kings to keep the arrogance of the nobles and the encroachments of the clergy in check; it was basically for lack of such men in power and because it wore itself out in pursuit of world hegemony that the Sassanid Empire finally succumbed.

The royal chronicles, since lost, have informed later generations about its history and noble deeds; Firdawsī's *Shāh Nāma* is largely inspired by them, but the monuments of figurative art bear better witness to the grandeur of the Sassanid culture than the literary tradition; not only the imposing royal palaces and the works of rock sculpture, but also the seals (pl. 122), the silver objects (plates 120 and 121) which excavations have brought to light and the wonderful silks (coloured plate III) brought back by mediaeval pilgrims from the east which were the ornaments of our churches and are now—at least the little that remains of them—the glory of their treasuries.

A propos of these precious relics it is certainly interesting to note that the decorative repertoire of ancient Susiana was not completely wiped out by Hellenism and that in certain regions of Iran, especially the province of Fārs, the elements for a national renaissance were preserved almost intact. For example the animal art of the Zagrus Mountains, which we meet again, after the Hellenistic period, in the Sassanid period

---

[1] Yazdagird III (AD 632–651).

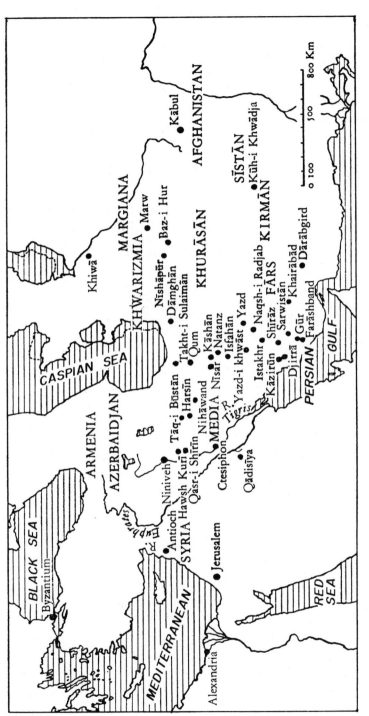

MAP IV: SASSANID IRAN

97. BAS-RELIEF OF KARTIR, THE HIGH PRIEST

Naqsh-i Radjab, near Persepolis, close to a scene of the investiture of Ardashīr I. Second quarter of third century AD.

Kartir played an important role in the religious and social life of the first Sassanids. His power increased with the years. He gradually succeeded in overcoming the influence of Mani and even managed to have him killed.

98. ROCK BAS-RELIEF. THE INVESTITURE OF ARDASHĪR I BY THE GOD AHURA MAZDA

Naqsh-i Rustam, near Persepolis. Second quarter of the third century AD.

This bas-relief which represents Ardashir I and the god Ahura Mazda face to face on horseback is one of the most beautiful examples of the rock sculpture of the Sassanid period.

99. BAS-RELIEF. BAHRĀM II ON HORSEBACK IN COMBAT WITH AN UNKNOWN OPPONENT

Naqsh-i Rustam, near Persepolis. Fourth quarter of the third century AD.

Even if history has not painted Bahrām II for us as an ardent warrior, the sculptor of this bas-relief presents him here as a sovereign who at least appreciated the qualities of the combatant.

100. BAS-RELIEF. THE INVESTITURE OF NARSĒ BY THE GODDESS ANĀHIT

Naqsh-i Rustam, near Persepolis. End of third century AD.

This bas-relief shows the goddess Anāhit on the right holding out the ring to King Narsē (AD 294–303). The hereditary prince, still a child, stands between them. In Iran and Asia Minor Anāhit was the divinity of visible and subterranean waters. She was also goddess of fertility, but instead of being represented with the coarse features of the 'Babylonian Ishtar', she is described in the Yasht 5 (§5) as a beautiful young woman.

101. BAS-RELIEF. THE TRIUMPH OF SHĀPŪR I OVER THE EMPEROR VALERIAN

Naqsh-i Rustam, near Persepolis. Third quarter of third century AD.

This bas-relief depicts the victory of Shāpūr I over the Roman Emperor Valerian, who was defeated and taken prisoner at the battle of Edessa, in AD 260.

102. PART OF A BAS-RELIEF SHOWING THE TORSO OF SHĀPŪR I ON HORSEBACK

Naqsh-i Radjab, near Persepolis. Third quarter of third century AD.

Note the suppleness of the king's torso and the elegance with which the folds of his tunic have been treated.

103. COLOSSAL STATUE OF SHĀPŪR I

Grotto near Bishāpūr. Third quarter of the third century AD. Height: 23 ft.

Shāpūr I is thought to have died at Bishāpūr. He was supposed to have been buried in a grotto close to that town where a statue representing him was carved out of a natural pillar. It collapsed, doubtless during an earthquake, then a few years ago it was re-erected and restored after a fashion by the Iranian army. It is the only statue known in Sassanid art. The face of the king, framed by ringlets, has a moustache and a beard passed through a ring, a prerogative of the reigning princes.

104. PART OF A BAS-RELIEF REPRESENTING THE VICTORY OF BAHRĀM II

Naqsh-i Rustam, near Persepolis. Fourth quarter of third century AD.

The identification is certain, so closely does his portrait resemble the one which appears on his coins. This scene is generally called 'The Arabian Triumph'. Under Shāpūr I and Bahrām II Sassanid sculpture, abandoning the static aspect it had under Ardashīr I, expressed movement down to the last detail.

98

99

102

103

105. BAS-RELIEF. INVESTITURE OF ARDASHĪR II
Tāq-i Būstān, near Kirmānshāh. Fourth quarter of fourth century AD.
The prince is receiving his investiture from the god Ahura Mazda. At their feet lies the body of a conquered enemy. Behind the king the god Mithra, with a halo of the sun's rays, holds the sabre of justice—the barsom. To the best of our knowledge it is the only representation of the solar god existing in Iran.

and right up to Seljuk art (pl. 172). The same is true of the work of the Achaemenid goldsmiths which we see again in Sassanid art without any appreciable variation in themes or techniques; and of the vaulted architecture, which existed in Fārs at the Achaemenid period, since we find it used again at Persepolis. At the end of the Arsacid period it was used to erect the most characteristic monument of so-called Sassanid architecture and later flowered to become that of Islamic Iran, whose influence can be found as far as Europe.

Whatever the survivals used by a revolution which was cultural as much as political, we see, from the beginning of the Sassanid dynasty, the appearance and reappearance of Asiatic themes and procedures completely opposed to the spirit of Greek art. A geometry conditioned by the very ancient craft of heraldry was substituted for the pliant shapes of Hellenistic art. The masterly play of light and shade in absolutely symmetrical compositions (pl. 98) was no longer concerned with mannered grace of line. The important thing was to underline the role of the deified sovereign, representative of Ahura Mazda, to depict him making war, or holding an audience, seated in state on a richly decorated throne.

As in the Achaemenid period, the king occupied the centre of the composition (pl. 105) in scenes showing investitures, campaigns and hunts; but the exuberance of a period of revival shows him accompanied by a great number of personages, of all shapes and sizes, whose masses are carefully balanced. There are as well the most unexpected animals—flying ibexes, ducks, snarling wild beasts, doves, peacock-dragons (fig. 176, pl. 121 and coloured plate III) and falcons, whose juxtaposition has no meaning except from the purely decorative point of view, and highly stylized ornaments, ribbons, pearls, palmettos, trees of life within, or without, rosettes and roundels, or running in foliated scrolls (plates 111 and 120).

One day, doubtless, scholars will succeed in determining the various origins of this highly complicated world of ornament. Perhaps they will manage to classify them in schools with the names of the various regions of this vast Iranian empire the frontiers of which were contiguous with countries of such varied civilizations. The exact chronology of Sassanid art has not yet been established. Research still goes on, but there is a difficulty, apart from the one caused by the scarcity of inscriptions; it is the absence of graves, as George Salles remarked on the occasion of the Exhibition of the Arts of Iran held in the Bibliothèque Nationale, Paris, in 1938. 'We lack,' he said, 'those reserves of documents and information which constitute the richest evidence for every other culture.'

But since then farmers have discovered necropolises containing numerous silver objects in the Sassanid tradition, for these pieces belonged to an aristocracy which had first fled the approach of the Arabs, but was gradually converted to Islam. To the south of the Caspian Sea in a region which is generally called Amlash, not far from the villages of Pīrkūh and Dailaman, necropolises have been discovered in which certain tombs contained sumptuous pieces of goldsmith's work made of electrum. These had nothing to do with the Sassanid period and were much more ancient, but the farmers also found necropolises containing many pieces of Sassanid silver.

CHAPTER 8

SASSANID IRAN

MONUMENTS

WITH the passing of the Parthians and their superficial Hellenism, the old Iranian civilization resumed the government of its empire. In the age of the Achaemenids it had deliberately confined itself to a purely oriental culture but with the advent of the Sassanids it resolved to establish relations with foreign civilizations whose prestige had attracted it and so take advantage of the benefits these contacts might bring in their train. However it was firmly determined to lose nothing of its own personality in the process: Iranian it was, Iranian it meant to remain. Not for nothing did it carve the images of its kings on the rocks at Naqsh-i Rustam, near Persepolis (plates 98, 99, 100 and 101).

The art of the Sassanid period, therefore, was at once traditional and progressive. As in the time of the Achaemenids, the principal monuments were the royal palaces; the main objective was still to present the King of Kings at the far end of his apadanā as a 'divinity come down to earth'; it was still the same programme, but the Achaemenid solution seemed too costly to the Sassanids and perhaps also impossible to develop further, because the length of wooden beams had limits which had already been reached. For the actual royal buildings they adopted vaulted architecture which was then, and no doubt was even in the Achaemenid period, the ordinary architecture of the country. They hoped to surpass the grandeur of the monuments of Darius by this popular art, and we shall see what it became in their hands; but first I would like to say a few words about the means at their disposal.

It is still generally believed that the only vaults used in the Sassanid period were barrel vaults, domes and those conical vaults which facilitated the transition from a square ground plan to the circular plan of a dome. Sassanid Iran *seems* not to have known either the groined vault[1] (fig. 152 a and b) or the cross vault[2] (fig. 153 a and b). 'From antiquity to our days,' says Choisy, 'the Persians have never accepted anything but the barrel vault[3] (fig. 154 a and b) and the dome on squinches'[4] (fig. 155).

[1] Sassanid Iran, unacquainted with interpenetrating vaults, could not have known that two barrel vaults intersecting at right angles will form a groined vault.

[2] On the contrary, the vault formed by prolonging the walls of a square hall, curving them progressively inwards over the empty space, i.e. the cross vault, was already commonly built in the Sassanid period by means of a process which appeared as early as the reign of Ardashīr I and which will be dealt with in the following pages.

[3] The barrel vault is a hemicylindrical vault built on two parallel walls.

[4] The dome on squinches which we see at Fīrūzābād in the palace which Ardashīr I had built there shows the method which the Parthians already used to cover a square hall with a dome, i.e. an edifice circular in section.

Fig. 152
(a)

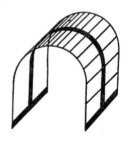

(b)

GROINED VAULT (EUROPEAN)

Fig. 153

(a)

(b)

CROSS VAULT
(RUBAT SHARAF, KHURĀSĀN)

Fig. 154
(a)

(b)

BARREL VAULT CARRIED
BY TRANSVERSE ARCHES
(EUROPEAN)

Fig. 155

INTERIOR OF THE VAULT OF THE
CHAHĀR-TĀQ AT NĪSAR

Fig. 156

CONSTRUCTION OF A VAULT WITH
THE AID OF CENTERING

'At first sight,' he goes on, 'the dome—a vault circular in section—would seem to be clearly contra-indicated for a square hall: the obvious vault would seem to be the cross vault in which the four walls of the hall are prolonged by curving progressively inwards so that they cover the building. But that would have needed centering[1] (fig. 156); the advantage of the dome is to make centering superfluous, and this precious property explains the efforts made by the Persians to combine the dome with a rectangular

---

[1] '. . . but it would have needed centering . . .' Iran lacked wood, and consequently centering, but it had been able, during the reign of Ardashīr I, to support the parts of the dome of the monument of Bāz-i Hūr corresponding to the angles of the square hall, on enormous wooden beams.

base plan.' However, the vault formed by prolonging the four walls of a square hall, 'curving them progressively inwards over the space below', is the one most frequently found in Iran, especially in the south of the country and most of all in the region of Kirmān. It is built there by means of a procedure which appeared as early as the beginning of the Sassanid period—without centering and so easily, with so little material and in such a short time that we must recognise the results of very long experience in this skilful technique. The fact that none of these vaults dating authentically from the Sassanid period has been reported is doubtless because we are still so ignorant about the architecture of the south of Iran.

Now I shall describe a small fire monument near Kāshān, the ātash kada at Nīsar which is considered by the local people as a construction of Ardashīr I, the founder of the Sassanid dynasty, and of which Houtum-Schindler also says, following the *Qum Nāma*, that it 'was one of the Sassanian Ardishīr Papakan's foundations, and had a fire-temple'. However, these verbal claims can only have any real value when confirmed by more firmly based information. Examination of the building hardly supplies us with this. In fact in the Chahār Qāpū at Qasr-i Shīrīn which was built by Khusraw II at the end of the Sassanid period we find the same crude construction of rubble and mortar that we see at Fīrūzābād, in the palace built by Ardashīr I. However the great dome of Sarwistān (pl. 107) which probably dates from the reign of Bahrām V, i.e. the middle of the Sassanid period, is built of sun-dried brick and much better executed. On the other hand, the Tāq-i Girrā, which can be considered as Sassanid, and 'not from the end of that period' according to Reuther, is built of carefully bonded and moulded dressed stone.

So we find nothing, absolutely no indication to help us on the construction side, although the shape of the arches is more suggestive. Naturally we must exclude the semi-circular arches with small and medium spans found in monuments where the builders were able to meet the cost of wood for centering. Other shapes were adopted of necessity for the large spans and the edifices which had to be built without centering for lack of wood. They are of two kinds. Builders tried to diminish the span of the arches by inclining the piers towards the interiors of bays, as is the case at Nīsar (pl. 108); or alternatively the piers remained vertical and the arch was elongated, with its springing set as high as possible, thus reducing the distance to be spanned. In appearance, the results of these two methods are rather different. The Nīsar arch seems primitive beside the other, with its curve rising in a single sweep from ground to summit. Moreover the latter arch, which belongs to the Tāq-i Kisrā at Ctesiphon (pl. 110), was probably built by Shāpūr I between AD 241 and AD 272, and then used until the end of the Sassanid period and after.

Since the purest representatives of the first type are Nīsar and Bāz-i Hūr, both traditionally attributed to the reign of the first Sassanid sovereign, there is not much risk of error in dating arches of the Nīsar type, to the beginning of the Sassanid period. This small edifice will give us valuable information about the procedure for constructing domes at the beginning of the Sassanid period. It will also confirm that Iranian masons of the time were able to build an isolated archway or a transverse arch (fig. 154a) without the aid of centering and that they were perfectly capable of making cross-vaults.

The ātash-kade at Nīsar is on a mule track which leads from Kāshān to Dilīdjān, in a very high, wild and deserted place. It was built without the aid of a single piece of wood; the only materials used were the stone found on the spot, plaster and reeds. Nīsar, 'the head of reeds', is close to a spring, at the head of a stream on whose banks reeds grew in the past; they still do today, a little lower down. Our monument was built with the help of these elements alone: stone, plaster and reeds. Its constructor did not even have scaffolding at his disposal: this is proved by the thickness of the walls of the lower part of the edifice, which seems quite excessive. It is quite clear,

Fig. 157

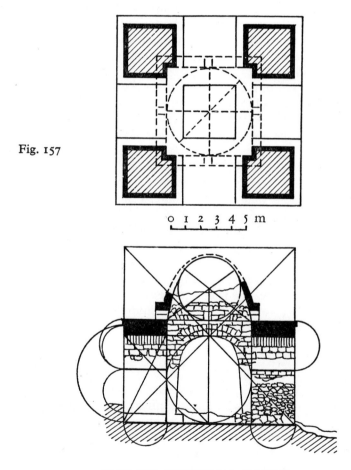

o 1 2 3 4 5 m

PLAN AND ANALYTICAL SECTION
OF THE CHAHĀR-TAQ AT NĪSAR

from the static point of view, that the thrusts of a light vault erected on top of a square hall with sides 20 feet long did not necessitate walls 9 feet thick. But before beginning his work, the mason knew that he and his workmen would have to be able to move easily and quickly round the dome under construction, without scaffolding, on the building itself. Hence the sort of service gallery, over 6 feet wide, which runs round the dome; hence also the great thickness of the walls. Nothing could be more natural.

Outside the monument looks like a mountain of cubic masonry, pierced by four wide arches surmounted by a small intermediate storey and the actual dome (fig. 157 a and b). Inside, the vault starts directly from the square base of the hall, then, by distortion, passes gradually from a square to a circular plan and ends in a dome. Here we come to the famous question of the origin of the dome on squinches. As it is difficult enough to imagine and impossible to render in an adequately explicit geometrical drawing the distortion by which this initially square vault becomes a dome, I shall compare it with those glass globes beneath which old French couples still keep their bridal wreaths. These globes are often glass domes which seem to have been forced on to a square base. They are a perfect representation of what the dome on a square base which concerns us really is.

Vaults of this type are still made daily in Iran, but mostly of mud, i.e. by a method of construction where the question of bonding the materials does not crop up. Actually, it is not very difficult, and simple village masons manage very well to execute in mud —to model one might say—the distortion in question of the lower part of the vaults. But it is more difficult, though still possible, to carry through intersections of skewed surfaces in stone or brick. Nīsar shows us how the difficulty was avoided by placing small half-cone vaults at the corners of the square; they are nothing but a simplification of the initial shape and are easily built by parallel arches (fig. 155). The Sassanid dome on squinches was originally nothing else, nothing cleverer than that. The clever thing, i.e. the transformation of this crude contrivance made by eye into a rigorous, definable and calculated construction, was introduced into Iranian architecture by the following period, the Islamic period.

So I am not in agreement with Dieulafoy and his 'pyramidal zones', nor with Choisy when he says, apropos of the transition from square to circle, that 'reconciling a dome to an octagonal plan would be a simple affair, so closely does the octagon hug the circle it envelops; the Persian solution', he says, 'consists in transforming the square plan in to an octagonal plan with the help of four squinches. . . .' The Persian solution has always been to operate by distorting the lower part of the vaults, and the octagonal plan did not appear until the Islamic period. The Sassanian dome on a square base built of mud, and in this case identical with the glass dome I mentioned, or built of brick with small squinches, is still built by Iranian villagers today. I do not know where it first appeared, but the type is probably most commonly found between Qum and Yazd.

Used for monumental architecture, this type of vault showed little development during the Sassanid period. The skewed connecting surface and the squinches still occupied the lower part of the vault itself. At the best the architect of the palace of Sarwistān thought up one slight improvement. He marked off the skewed surface at top and bottom by two thin decorated bands which divide the interior of the building into three parts: square base, intermediate zone and dome (pl. 107). He also had the idea of placing this dome on corbelling whose curved profile, comparatively flat at the axes, increases as it approaches the diagonals of the square, so that above the upper decorative band the vault is regular, i.e. horizontal sections of it are perfectly circular. However, the dome of Chahār Qāpū at Qasr-i Shīrīn, which dates from the reign of Khusraw II (AD 590–627), is still like that of Fīrūzābād, more than four centuries older.

Now let us see how the small edifice at Nīsar was built. Low down up to about half the height of the arches, it is of rubble bonded with gypsum mortar. Then squared stone up to the top of the squinches. However, the arches of the bays are built of stone dressed to the shape of large bricks. The dome, above the squinches, is of rubble and gypsum mortar.

The outline of the door-bays, characteristic of the beginning of the Sassanid period, is particularly clear here. The almost rectilinear piers[1] are inclined inwards. They curve slightly towards the top to receive the arches which are their prolongation. These very flat arches are built in vertical sections parallel to the façade courses[2] and not in convergent courses.[3] We know that it is possible to build arches in space of vertical sections without the help of centering. As Choisy has clearly shown, 'the artifice which makes it possible to build a vault without centering is summed up simply: proceeding in vertical sections and not by convergent courses. Let us accept—it is usually the case—that a barrel vault springs from a main wall. The first course of bricks is laid on edge perpendicular to the course of the wall and fixed on to the wall with mortar, thanks to the adhesion of the mortar and the thinness of the bricks, this course is made without any auxiliary support. Then the builder passes to a second layer: it is joined to the first one as it was joined to the wall, and so on. The barrel vault gradually extends. At the most it is necessary, in the absence of a main wall, to establish one arch on a frame which serves as a start, and the vault is finished without centering. But arches with radial joints cannot be built in space.'[4] In a moment I will explain how the first arch, against which the second and then the other layers were built, could have been executed without the help of wooden centering. On the arch thus built of a series of vertical sections, another arch duplicating the first but this time with radial joints was built, incidentally quite superfluous in the present case. It appears clearly in plate 108 and figure 155.

The broad walls of the square hall were built, then levelled off just above the so-called reinforcing arches, and the lower part of the dome was built, in the height of

---

[1] Pier: vertical wall or pillar supporting the beginning of a vault or arcade.

[2] See A. Choisy: *Histoire de l'architecture*, vol. 1, p. 23, fig. 4. As this figure shows, the way to build a barrel vault without centering is to proceed in vertical sections.

[3] i.e. by regular layers one on top of the other, the planes of two sections on the same level meet at the centre of the vault, inclining further as the level is higher. (Cf. fig. 154.)

[4] See A. Choisy: *Histoire de l'architecture*, vol. 1, p. 24, fig. 5 on the right. When the vault is finished, it is sometimes a barrel vault which reinforces it built quite simply previously by radial joints, this vault previously built acting as centering.

which were included the skewed surface and the squinches. Now we have reached the
moment when the masons are going to build the upper part of the dome. How are they
going to operate? This is where a method of construction comes in which possibly
characterizes Iranian constructions of the Islamic period better than any other; we
learn at Nīsar that it was already current in the Sassanid period.

Having drawn the profile of the dome and the site of the last course of squared
stone on the ground or on a flat piece of plaster, the constructor drew a line at a
certain distance from the extrados[1] and parallel to it. Thus he obtained the hatched

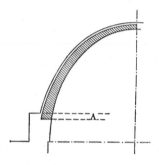

Fig. 158

DIAGRAM OF PLASTER
CENTERING REINFORCED
WITH REEDS
A. Final course of squared stone.

part of my drawing (fig. 158). Having lined it with stones or a banking of earth as is
still done today in the same case, he put reeds into this kind of mould and poured in a
gypsum mortar of medium consistency. He would make eight frames of plaster reinforced with reeds in this way, fragile in the lateral direction but fairly resistant in the
other, and whose shape was, apart from a certain thickness at the extrados, the profile
of the vault to be built increased by the height of the last course of stones. He mounted
them on the edifice under construction. He set them upright on the axes and diagonals
of the dome. They were joined at the summit with a few handfuls of plaster and pinched
between the stones of the last course at the foot. We see what remains of one of them,
like a white mark on the axis, or almost on the axis, of the arch shown in figure 155. We
see others on the axes of the squinches visible in the same figure.

So here we have our dome represented by a sort of cage consisting of eight plaster
frames a few inches thick. These eight frames demarcate triangular spaces each with a
base the eighth part of the circumference of the base and its apex the summit of the
dome. Two men, responsible for filling them in, would now hurry round the cage, on
the kind of service gallery I have mentioned, constantly supplied by assistants with
selected stones and the mortar needed for joining them. It is vital to work quickly,
because of the speed with which the mortar used sets, and in perfect agreement also,
so that the filling in of the eight panels goes on at the same rate and the thrusts exer-
cized by the weight of the masonry are automatically neutralized. In point of fact the
fragile plaster frames are only intended to guide the work of the masons; they would not

[1] The extrados is the outer curve of an arch or vault.

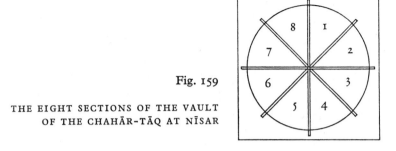

Fig. 159

THE EIGHT SECTIONS OF THE VAULT
OF THE CHAHĀR-TĀQ AT NĪSAR

be able to resist any torque or dyssymetrical stress. So long as the masonry rises an equal amount in each section, they will only be in stress in their longitudinal direction, i.e. in the direction of their greatest resistance. Moreover they will only undergo a slight lateral thrust, neutralized progressively as the work advances. With this in mind one of the masons takes up position opposite one of the panels to be filled in, No. 1, for example, and the other one faces him, in front of No. 5 (fig. 159). In the same time they do the same amount of filling in, i.e. to the same height, then move on simultaneously to panels 2 and 6, then 3 and 7, etc. Thus they keep on turning in the same direction, as if in pursuit of each other, but always four panels apart, and arrive together at the top of the dome. Since the height of the plaster frames only represents, as I have said, a part of the thickness of the dome, their upper surface is thus inside the vaulting and uniformly distant from its extrados. It only remains to cover the whole, inside and out, with a protective coating.

Now let us return to the construction of the arches of the bays at Nīsar, which we had provisionally left to one side. How was it possible to build the first layer of these arches in space without a wooden frame? Here again a flimsy frame of plaster reinforced with reeds plays its part. We notice on the façades of the building that the first section of these arches is not flush with the exposed part of the walls, but set back a few inches (pl. 108). This slight discrepancy was the site of a plaster arch which has disappeared. It could have been removed after the constructi n was finished, or even as soon as it became superfluous, i.e. after the first two or three sections of the stone arch had been placed in position, but it was left in place and covered with the general coating. Time destroyed it, but some significant fragments of it remain. When the work was done, it would also have been possible to replace the plaster arch by a layer of dressed stone similar to the ordinary sections, and it is probable that that was quite often done, but not at Nīsar. Thanks to this monument we learn that both isolated arches, and the crowns of barrel vaults, of small buildings at least, were commonly and easily built without wooden centering, from the beginning of the Sassanid period onwards.

This is how they went about it. Once the piers were built, the springers were prepared, that is to say the oblique surfaces on which the connecting arches were to rest, then the shape of these arches was drawn on the ground. It was lined with stones or banked earth, the reeds were placed in this sort of mould and the mixed mortar poured in. When four arches had been built in this way, they were installed on the four ex-posed faces of the building on the springers. They were joined to the construction by a few handfuls of gypsum mortar, then the masons coated their inside surface with mortar and rapidly applied the stones of the first layer. They attached the second layer to the first in the same way, the third to the second, and so on.

Such was the ingenious, cheap, yet adequate expedient which, as from the Sassanid epoch and doubtless even before, made it possible to build vaults without wood and erect in space, without scaffolding, or perfectly regular, light and economical domes, ready for any further treatment the constructor or decorator might have in mind. I have mentioned this particular procedure first because it virtually dominates the whole future of Iranian architecture; but Iran was familiar with others of equal interest which I shall mention when the occasion arises.

We know, therefore, that Sassanid Iran built massive vaults as well as light ribbed vaults and that in both cases the constructor's main preoccupation, which determined all the procedures of his craft, was his permanent predicament of having to build without, or virtually without, the help of wood for frames. The panelling of the surface he had to cover was only used so that he could work without centering. The ribs he used had nothing to support but their own weight when the vault was finished. In-corporated into the masonry after having borne it for an instant, part by part, their sole function, in the case of light vaults made of flat bricks, was to prevent its de-formation. In the case of stouter constructions they no longer had any part to play: brick arches, which had become integral parts of the vault, worked more or less in the same way. Plaster arches, like those in the dome at Nīsar, even have a weakening effect on the construction. From the static point of view it would be better if they did not exist. So there is nothing in common here with Gothic architecture, the ends and means of which were quite different.

I shall dwell a little on this question of oriental and western ribbed vaults, which were common both to Iran and the French Middle Ages, but which were totally un-connected. Besides I am tired of reading and hearing that 'it was during the Seljuk period that Gothic architecture, of Iranian origin, was introduced into Europe'. I hope that the reader will believe that I am solely preoccupied with archaeology here.

The story of the origins of French mediaeval architecture is a very old one. 'Forty years ago,' wrote Melchior de Vogüé in 1860, 'it was generally accepted that Gothic architecture came from the Arabs and had been introduced to France as a result of the Crusades; this opinion suited the romanticism of the age. It was later abandoned by almost all serious thinkers; it disappeared in the face of the innumerable works which revealed the true character of our architecture and explained its metamorphoses with-out having recourse to the Orient. For some time now, as the result of an increase in travel, this opinion appears to be reviving: those who visit the Holy Land nearly always adopt it owing to a certain tendency on the part of travellers to ascribe every-thing to what has charmed them. Except that to conform to the taste of the day, this system has abandoned its poetic aspect and assumed a scientific aspect well suited to dazzle and seduce at first sight.'

Thanks to the works of de Vogüé, Vilolet le Duc, Verneihl, Anthyme de Saint Paul, Lassus, Gense, Mérimée, Lèfevre-Pontalis, etc., it seemed to have been proved once and for all that Gothic architecture derives naturally from Romanesque architecture by a slow transformation in the science of building and that it was in the Ile de France, in the royal domain, during the second half of the twelfth century, that the complete transformation was effected.

Now, once again, 'owing to a certain tendency on the part of travellers to ascribe everything to what has charmed them', the origins of Gothic art are called in question. I do not think we need revert to the fierce disputes of the past, for the matter has been seriously discussed and no fact of importance has turned up to invalidate the conclusions of the inquiry, but all the same brilliant words have been uttered in support of less brilliant arguments and we ought to examine their importance, for they are just the sort mentioned by de Vogüé, which have 'assumed a scientific aspect well suited to dazzle and seduce at first sight'.

The history of Iranian vaults is the history of how they could be built directly in space. Choisy said as much in almost those terms. As for the history of Gothic vaults, it is generally admitted that it is just the history of how to give the central nave of a church direct lighting. So the ideal of the Iranian architect was to construct without centering, and that of the French architect to make a clerestory. Nothing, not a single shape or feature of Iranian architecture, exhibits the least desire to obtain more light, which was always excessive—which, on the contrary, was carefully guarded against, to such an extent that many buildings, the mosques in central Iran for example, are only illuminated by thick sheets of alabaster. Nor is there anything, not a shape nor an active element in Gothic architecture, which shows any desire to do without centering. In these circumstances how could the Frenchman, who thought solely of diminishing the screening effect of his walls, have borrowed anything from the Iranian, for whom the problem never arose? How could French constructors have borrowed from Iran a technique which it did not possess? However, if scholars want to find the origins of Gothic architecture in Iran, they must discover in it examples of the systematized localization of stresses and the resultant architectural arrangements. Yet we find nothing of the kind, either in fact or intention.

Possibly, some people will doubtless say, but the Iranian ribs, although not performing the same function as the Gothic ones, could have given French constructors the idea: the ways of the mind are secret. It is thus, by the terms of the same axiom of pseudo-archaeology: 'This resembles that, therefore this comes from that', that Chateaubriand once explained the upsurge of the pillars of our churches and the ramifications of the ribs of their vaults as reminiscent of the forests of Germany.

The oldest known Iranian dome is that of the palace of Ardashīr at Fīrūzābād. Built on excessively thick walls, so inaccurate that several feet above its original base plan its horizontal section is still not circular, it is probably one of the first monumental realizations of the type of vault which the peasants of Fārs had long known how to construct of marl or mud. The most ancient examples of it have disappeared. This vault was not much improved during the Sassanid period. Moreover, the connecting zone between the square plan of the space to be covered and the circular plan of the dome was still made by eye until the Islamic period, but nevertheless it became the favourite vault, the monumental vault of the Iranian constructors of the Sassanid period. Some thirty examples, more or less ruined, are still visible in the west of the country, as opposed to only a handful in the east, at Dāmghān, Bāz-i Hūr and Kūh-i Khwāja. The west also saw the continuation of the most interesting of the first types of Iranian mosques, the kiosk-mosque, whose essential feature is the Sassanid chahār tāq, a dome on four pillars enclosing arches. From this we are entitled to conclude not that the Iranian dome was definitely born in the west of Iran, in Fārs to be precise, but that it first appeared there in its monumental form and also had its greatest vogue there. Admittedly Assyria had built domes long before these, if we believe the bas-reliefs of Kuyundjik, not to mention Egypt, Mycenean Greece, and Rome, but by different techniques, which only proves that many parts of the world undertook to cover square or circular halls with domes and that in all these places they found a way of doing it.

The Iranian architecture of the Sassanid period, therefore, commonly built barrel vaults and domes of dressed or undressed stone, and burnt or sun-dried bricks. It was able to build light ribbed domes, as we have seen at Nīsar, and cross vaults, doubtless by the same methods. It did not know how to make vaults intersect and consequently was unaware of the principle of the groined vault. When it juxtaposed an ivan and a dome, for example, the ivan rested against the wall of the square hall, below the origin of the vault, or stopped before reaching the dome, as at Sarwistān. When the secondary ivans opened into a principal ivan, their barrel vaults were set, as at Fīrūzābād, in the side walls of the great ivan, below the springing of its vault.

Now let us look at the actual works. In fact the most representative monument of Sassanid architecture, the palace of Fīrūzābād, was built by Ardashīr, son of Papak, before his victory over the last Arsacid, Ardawān (Artabanus) V, i.e. still in the Parthian period. So strictly speaking we ought not to call architecture Sassanid when its most typical monument dates from the Parthian period and received all its architectural elements from that period; nor ought we to call it Parthian since the great majority of its monuments date from the Sassanid period. Perhaps we could speak of the architecture of Fārs, for it is in this region that the art of the palaces of Fīrūzābād was developed and where the remains of the most numerous of the monuments of this kind still are, at Fīrūzābād itself, at Girrā, Farashbānd, Kāzarūn, Yazd-i khwāst, Sarwistān, etc.; but the historical divisions, Achaemenid, Seleucid, Parthian, Sassanid, and later Seljuk and Mongol periods, etc., although arbitrary from the artistic point of view are convenient in the sense that our minds easily place them in time—on condition that we always remember that the architecture of a period is not born of winning a battle, that it existed before and continues to exist after another battle has put the political power in the hands of another dynasty.

The palace at Fīrūzābād, the most ancient known monument of the type we shall continue to call Sassanid, is also the one with the most complete plan and clearest composition (fig. 160). Built next to an abundant spring rising in the centre of a pool

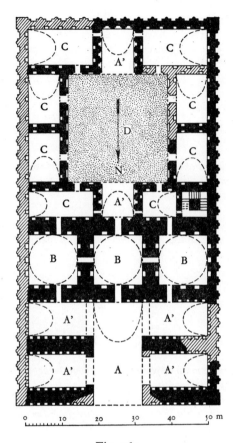

Fig. 160

PLAN OF THE PALACE AT FĪRŪZĀBĀD
A. Main ivan. A'. Secondary ivans. B.
Square domed hall. C. Barrel-vaulted hall.
D. Courtyard.

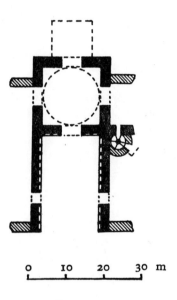

Fig. 161

PLAN OF THE
QALʻA-I DUKHTAR
AT FĪRŪZĀBĀD

the shape and dimensions of which are still visible in aerial photographs, the palace
covers a rectangular area measuring approximately 338 by 179 feet, divided into two
almost equal parts, one of which contains the reception buildings, the other the living
quarters.

The first group consists of the entrance ivan, with its opening in the centre of the
main façade. It is flanked by four smaller ivans and gives access to three vast domed
halls side by side.

The harem, whose buildings are lower than those of the first group, consists of
narrow barrel-vaulted halls, arranged symmetrically around an internal courtyard
with two ivans opening on to it.

106. ROCK BAS-RELIEF DEPICTING ROMAN PRISONERS
Bīshāpūr. Third quarter of third century AD.
The Sassanid kings—especially Shāpūr I—were very proud of their success over the Romans and Shāpūr celebrated the event several times: at Naqsh-i Rustam, Naqsh-i Radjab, Bīshāpūr, etc. This bas-relief consisting of several rows of figures was possibly inspired by the decoration of Roman triumphal columns. In fact many Roman prisoners worked at Bīshāpūr on constructing the town and the execution of the rock decoration of the gorge.

107. DETAIL OF THE PALACE OF SARWISTĀN
Fifth century AD.
The highly developed technique of this dome bears witness to the progress of Sassanid architecture since the construction of the Palace of Fīrūzābād, in the third century of our era.

108. FIRE MONUMENT
Nīsar. Beginning of the Sassanid period. Width: 37 ft. 5 in.
The type of edifice called 'Chahār Tāq', i.e. 'four arches', consists of a dome resting on four pillars and housing the traditional fire at the hours of prayer.

109. WALL OF THE PALACE OF SHĀPŪR
Bīshāpūr. Third quarter of third century AD.
Detail of the base wall of the central building.

110. RUINS OF THE PALACE OF CTESIPHON IN IRAQ
Sixth century AD.
Ctesiphon, founded by the Parthians, appears to have been an important town from the beginning of the Christian era. Sometimes the construction of the great palace is attributed to Khusraw Anūshīrwān (AD 531–578), but it is more likely that it was the work of Shāpūr I (AD 241–272). The part we see here is called the Tāq-i Kisrā; to the right we see the immense hall for royal audiences.

111. THE GROTTO, TĀQ-I BŪSTĀN: CARVED PILASTER
Sixth century AD.
Detail of a scroll of flowers and acanthus leaves carved on the façade of the largest grotto at Tāq-i Būstān.

112. THE GROTTO, TĀQ-I-BŪSTĀN: BACK WALL
Sixth century AD.
Three figures are seen full face. Khusraw II is receiving his investiture from Ahura Mazda and the other personage is a woman, no doubt the goddess Anāhit, who played an important role as goddess of waters and springs under the name of Ardwi Anāhit. On the lower level Khusraw II on horseback, wearing helmet and coat of mail, is preparing to fight an enemy.

113. GROTTO, TĀQ-I-BŪSTĀN. GENERAL VIEW
Sixth century AD.
The side walls, below the springing of the vault, are decorated with scenes of Khusraw II hunting: right, stag-hunting, left, boar-hunting. Two victories holding a crown surmount the semi-circular arch on the façade; in the centre, a crescent surrounded by ribbons.

107

108

III. THE PEACOCK-DRAGON

Sixth–seventh century AD. Diameter of the outside circle: 14¾ in. Musée des Arts décoratifs, Paris.

The motif of the peacock-dragon, with threatening jaws and claws ready to rend, frequently appeared in Sassanid art, decorating fabrics or engraved on the costume of Khusraw II Parwiz at Tāq-i Būstān* (fig. 176). We also see it on the base of the silver bottle shown in plates 120 and 121, and even on the surrounding wall of the palace at Mshattā, where it might be seen as the signature of the sculptor.

* See F. Sarre, *L'art de la Perse ancienne*, French translation, plate 94.

I

A single entrance at the far end and on the axis of the principal ivan serves the reception and dwelling halls.

The Qal'a-i Dukhtar is a fortified palace which dominates the mouth of the ravine by which the river Buraza and the road which follows its course penetrate into the plain of Fīrūzābād. It is situated on a rocky height whose summit was once surrounded by walls and acted as the fortress's courtyard. From this courtyard staircases built inside two enormous square towers led to an upper platform on which still rise the ruins of the castle proper, an ivan of 45 feet 6 inches wide, the vestibule of a square domed hall whose sides have the same measurements (fig. 161). This combination, which we have observed in the palace on the plain, is isolated here and all the more characteristic as a result. More skilfully and even too audaciously built, with its vaults resting on excessively thin walls which have been forced apart, this small group of buildings is obviously some years later than Ardashīr's other palace.

Fig. 162

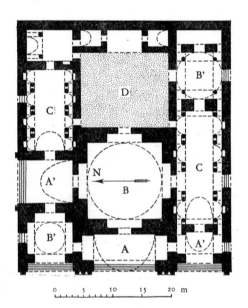

PLAN OF THE PALACE AT SARWISTĀN
A. Main ivan. A'. Secondary ivans. B.
Square domed hall. B'. Secondary domes.
C. Barrel-vaulted hall. D. Courtyard.

In the palace of Sarwistān, which scholars agree in dating to the reign of Bahrām Gūr (AD 420–438), an entrance ivan, not very deep but combined with a square, domed hall, also forms the essential part of the composition. Behind the hall with the main dome is a courtyard surrounded by living quarters, as at Fīrūzābād, but the rigid symmetry of the arrangement has disappeared and the variously shaped rooms succeed each other haphazardly. The composition of Sarwistān is like that of Fīrūzābād in principle, therefore, but much freer and more varied in its details (fig. 162). In fact, a reception there would have been really cramped if we imagine it confined to the central hall; yet the other halls are too vast, too few and too sumptuous, with too

many doors opening externally for them to have been living quarters. It is probable
that this edifice, the area of which is four times less than that of the Fīrūzābād monument, was purely a reception palace, perhaps one of those castles, which, according to
Ṭabarī, the ostentatious minister of Bahrām Gūr, Mīr Narsā, had built on his estates
in Fārs.

I have already said, speaking of the vaults which the Sassanid period handed on to
the architecture of the Islamic period, that the main dome of this palace, built of baked
brick and no longer solely of rubble, rests on corbelling and that in consequence the
dome is perfectly accurate, i.e. circular from its start, but I purposely omitted to
mention a curious vaulting arrangement. It has been said that this represents 'the first
attempt at the system of construction of which Gothic architecture is the supreme
realization', but it is in fact the product of an interest in decorative effect rather than
the solution of a constructional problem. A. Choisy has given an excellent drawing of it
in axonometric perspective[1] in his *Histoire de l'architecture*. This is what he says: 'We
here show a second example of the combinations of equilibrium in Persian archi-

Fig. 163

AXONOMETRIC SECTION OF THE PALACE AT
SARWISTĀN

[1] Fig. 163 shows the axonometric general section of the palace of Sarwistān after O. Reuther.

tecture: a barrel vault, the abutments[1] of which are massifs reduced by hollowing out niche-shaped spaces with half-domes *on* squinches (*Survey of Persian Art*, Vol. I, fig. 132, p. 505). These niches rest on groups of twin columns and are arranged so as to bear against the central barrel vault.'

On the long sides of the lateral halls of the Sarwistān palace we can still see groups of short columns, both free and coupled, connected by slabs of stone which form their capitals and joined to the wall by means of small arches. These groups support rectangular pillars between which semi-domes on squinches were built. So along the walls of these halls there is a whole series of large vaulted niches, the top of whose arches support the barrel vault. Contrary to what one might believe the point was not to increase the width of the halls, for they only measure 25 feet 9 inches from one wall to another, disregarding the columns and what they supported, and Iranian constructors had long since known how to build vaults with a span of over 45 feet, as at Fīrūzābād, and even almost 84 feet as at Ctesiphon. So the Sarwistān masons could easily have vaulted their halls with a span of 25 feet 9 inches; there was nothing to force them to reduce, as they did, the span of the barrel vault to the rather ridiculous one of 16 feet 7 inches. Their reasons for doing so had nothing to do with constructional problems. The minor arrangement they invented so that the long, narrow state halls did not look like corridors was purely decorative. It happens that this decoration—perfectly successful, incidentally—seems to us like a *system* of construction, but it is clear that it was nothing of the sort in the eyes of the Sassanid constructors. The proof is that they did nothing and deduced nothing from this combination of vaults and arches, so full of possibilities, and that it is never found again in their architecture.

The art of grouping and localizing the thrusts exercised by the pressure of vaults and arches did not exist in the Sassanid period, when experience was the constructor's only guide. The thickness of the walls which support the main dome of the Sarwistān palace is right, not because it was accurately calculated but because the walls of the palace at Fīrūzābād were too thick and those of the Qal'a-i Dukhtar were not thick enough. Step by step, mistake by mistake, the builders reached the truth and it was thus that Sassanid architecture made some progress between the beginning of the Sassanid period and the reign of Bahrām Gūr. However, the method of properly placing a dome on a square base had not been discovered at this time.

The palace of Dāmghān, of which only a part has been excavated, is an edifice the essential monumental feature of which was represented by a large entrance ivan combined with a square, domed hall. But whereas the ivan and the square hall at Fīrūzābād and Sarwistān only communicate by means of narrow doors, the domed hall at Dāmghān is a genuine chahār tāq, i.e. a dome on four pillars, which communicates with its surroundings by wide bays. The vault of the ivan rests on rows of columns along the side walls (fig. 164).

This very open composition, the programme of which no longer has much connec-

---

[1] Abutment: massif of masonry responsible for neutralizing the thrusts exercised on a part of a building.

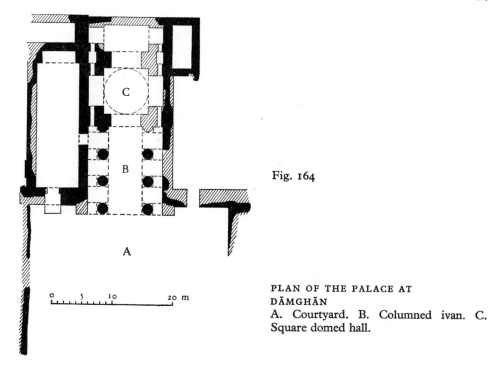

Fig. 164

PLAN OF THE PALACE AT
DĀMGHĀN
A. Courtyard. B. Columned ivan. C.
Square domed hall.

tion with that of the ivan-vestibule of a square, domed hall, seems to post-date the
palace of Sarwistān, i.e. the reign of Bahrām Gūr.

The palaces of Qasr-i Shīrīn and Hawsh-Kurī, built by King Khusraw II Parwīz
(AD 590–628), are even more recent.

The great complex of ruins which bears the name of Shīrīn (*the Sweet*), the beloved
of Khusraw II, is next to the modern town of Qasr-i Shīrīn, on the edge of the age-old
route which is still the main means of access from the Mesopotamian plain to the
Iranian plateau. According to Arab historians, the constructions represented today by
a chaos of rubble and broken down walls were surrounded by a park of nearly 300
acres, gardens, pavilions, fresh-water pools, menageries and reserves in which the
rarest animals lived at liberty. The water of the river Hulwān was piped there in
abundance and distributed by an aquaduct which formed the actual surrounding wall.

The palace which is still called 'Imārat-i Khusraw' included the official and private
apartments of the king. It rose in the centre of this celebrated *firdaws*, on a terrace
which was reached by double ramps similar to the great stairways at Persepolis. It was
an enormous construction, 1,209 feet long by 617 feet wide, and resembled in its
general composition the palaces at Fīrūzābād and Sarwistān. A vast columned ivan,
like the one at Dāmghān, led to a square hall covered with a dome 48 feet in diameter
and flanked by long barrel-vaulted halls. Beyond this comparatively small complex, a
sort of fore-part of the palace, there was a courtyard giving access to the private apartments and the servants' quarters. It still retained therefore the plan of the old

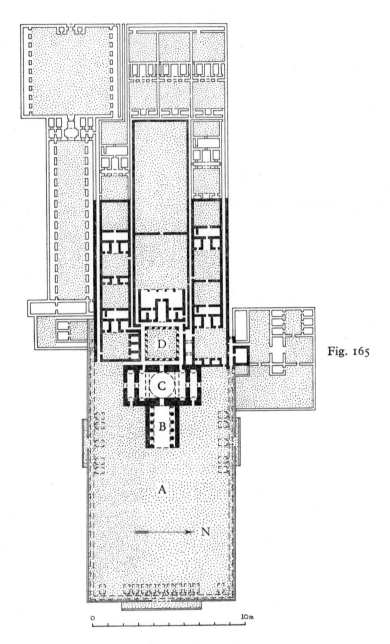

Fig. 165

PLAN OF THE IMĀRAT-I KHUSRAW PALACE AT
QASR-I SHĪRĪN
A. Courtyard. B. Great columned ivan. C. Square domed hall.
D. Interior courtyard.

Iranian palace, but here, in this enormous monument, the residential buildings surrounded more than one courtyard. From the main courtyard, decked out with a portico and an ivan, one penetrated into two other courtyards in succession, on the principal axis, then via long corridors to another eight courtyards, four to the right and four to the left, on to which the residential buildings opened (fig. 165).

There are other important ruins of the same period a few miles away to the north. The Kurds of the region call them Hawsh-Kurī, the *house of horses*, because they claim to recognize them as Khusraw's stables, but there is no doubt that they really formed a palace, a royal or noble residence, with gardens, secondary buildings and various dependencies, the composition of which is roughly like that of Qasr-i Shīrīn.

The whole thing, 'one of the wonders of the world', says Yāqūt, did not last long. Some twelve years after the death of Khusraw II, the power of the Sassanids disappeared in the Moslem whirlwind and the palaces of Qasr-i Shīrīn became deserted. Hastily and badly constructed, they quickly fell into ruins.

All that remains, in the southern corner of the park of Qasr-i Shīrīn, surrounded by crumbling buildings, is an enormous domed hall. Scholars still disagree as to whether it was a fire monument or a royal audience hall. This isolated square hall, with inside measurements of just under 54 feet, is undoubtedly the vastest built in the Sassanid period. It is made of coarse rubble, except for the arches of the bays which are of baked brick, and is not much better constructed than the halls at Fīrūzābād, almost four centuries older. It is a strange phenomenon that, at the moment when Islam was to transform the empirical procedures of the Sassanids into a planned and skilful technique, Sassanid architecture reverted to the rough and ready methods of its origins.

The ruins of the palace of Ctesiphon, the most gigantic of the royal Sassanid residences, cover an area of almost twenty-nine acres, including the edifice we know by the name of Tāq-i Kisrā, 'the arch of Khusraw', or Īwān-i Kisrā, 'the ivan of Khusraw', as well as some remnants of an edifice situated to the east of the latter, at a distance of about a hundred yards, another called Harim-i Kisrā to the south, and to the north various ruins hidden underneath a modern cemetery.

The Tāq-i Kisrā, the only part of this complex with a few coherent elements above ground, was the building for royal audiences, In spite of a tradition attributing it to Khusraw I, it seems clear that it was built by Shāpūr I, son and successor of Ardashīr.

This monument, which some regard as the most beautiful product of Sassanid architecture and others as 'a Persian building masquerading as European ... a monument of artistic dishonesty', was constructed on a terrace, like the majority of Mesopotamian palaces and like those at Persepolis and the Imārat-i Khusraw of Qasr-i Shīrīn. On this base, at the centre of a façade similar to that of Fīrūzābād, but ornamented with six storeys of blind arcades which give it a fantastic scale, an elliptical arch 82 feet 8 inches wide and 110 feet 6 inches high, the forward arch of an ivan 139 feet 8 inches deep, springs in a single sweep from ground to apex. This immense nave which covers a larger area than the palace of Darius at Persepolis was the Sassanid king's hall for public audiences. A simple door in the wall at the far end gave access to a line of small rooms which were traversed to reach a hall as wide as the ivan, and 49 feet 8¾ inches long, probably covered with a barrel vault (pl. 110).

To the left of this group a long gallery, with transverse arches and barrel-vaults, served two halls 55 feet 3 inches wide by 112 feet 6 inches and 136 feet 6 inches long respectively, covered with barrel vaults and separated from each other by a square hall of the same width, which may have been domed. We may assume that the right-hand side of the building, which was not cleared during the excavations of 1928-9, was similar to the left side. In short a badly composed monument which would be of little interest if it did not include that masterpiece the Tāq, witness to the greatest effort made in Iran to equal and even surpass the grandeur of the Achaemenid palaces.

It is quite interesting to note also that in the Tāq-i Kisrā, as in the Mesopotamian monuments of the Parthian period, the only type of vault used was the barrel vault. However, as I have had occasion to remark, it is possible that the two square halls on the sides of the Tāq were domed—though it would still be true that the constructors of this monument did not attach the importance to the dome that we find in Iran proper. In fact from Fīrūzābād to the Imārat-i Khusraw at Qasr-i Shīrīn, a domed hall preceded by an ivan acting as its vestibule was always both the main reception room of the palace and the essential feature of its architectural composition.

Of course there were other Sassanid palaces, but they have disappeared completely; the one to which the Tāq-i Būstān belonged, for example, near Kirmānshāh, and the one at Harsīn, formerly Shāpūr Khwāst.[1] The only remains of the latter palace, close to an even more abundant spring than the one at Tāq-i Būstān and an immense vertical panel carved in the rock like those at Bīsūtūn, are a pool and some channels also cut out of the rock, as well as the scattered elements of a vast stone construction.

Nothing remains of the palace called Tāq-i Būstān. The capitals of columns which have been found there no doubt belonged to a small kiosk near the spring, not to a large building. Of the grottoes, hollowed out in the shape of barrel vaults, one dates from the reign of Shāpūr III (AD 383-88), the other, larger one, from the reign of Khusraw II Parwīz (AD 590-628) (pl. 113).

In the same region, just beyond Sarpul-i Suhab, the road which leads to Kirmānshāh begins to climb a steep slope which is sometimes known as 'the gateway to the Zagrus Mountains'. For the most part it follows the course of an ancient track and en route passes a small edifice,[1] the Tāq-i Girrā, a sort of barrel-vaulted grotto, but actually built of large blocks of dressed stone. There is no clue either in its lay-out or the ancient texts enabling us to imagine what its purpose was. Various explanations have been put forward: a dedicatory chapel commemorating the completion of the road, a royal resting-place, etc., but it seems preferable to link the construction of this edifice with the fact that at this point the high road crossed the frontier of the Parthian province of Media. This supposition would date the Tāq from the time of the Arsacids, but today there is a tendency to attribute it to the Sassanid period, some scholars saying from the end, others 'not from the end' of that period.

In addition to the Sassanid palaces which are fairly numerous, as we have just seen,

[1] Shāpūr Khwāst (now Harsīn) is supposed to have been founded by Shāpūr I.

at least in relation to those which have come down to us from the Achaemenid, Hellenistic and even Islamic periods, we now have visual evidence for some forty religious monuments in Iran authentically dating to the Sassanid period: fire sanctuaries, fire temples and the inevitable exceptions, i.e. exceptional arrangements of the main types.

The Arsacid āyadanā of Takht-i Sulaimān, which I have mentioned previously, occurs again in the same shape, but on a smaller scale, in two small edifices which were reported for the first time by E. Herzfeld, one near Shāpūr, in Fārs, under the name of Imāmzāda Sayyid Husain, the other near Djīrra, in the same area (fig. 166). The first was undoubtedly a fire sanctuary, the second seems to have been a church, but its plan scarcely differs from that of the Imāmzāda near Bīshāpūr. Both of them, like the āvadanā of Takht-i Sulaimān, consisted of a domed hall surrounded by a band-vaulted corridor preceded by annexes roofed in the same way.

Among the fire sanctuaries we must undoubtedly include the small edifice forming part of the palace of Kūh-i Khwāja, in which a fire altar has been found and which consisted of a square hall surrounded by the usual corridor. This monument was discovered and described by H. de Bouillane de Lacoste. Kūh-i Khwāja is a name which comes from a saint 'Khwāja Sara Sarir', reputed to be a direct descendant of Abraham; his tomb is at the northern tip of the hill where the whole of Sīstān assembles at Nawruz. Herzfeld, who excavated it himself, says that it is Parthian and gives it a dome on squinches in his reconstruction, but the monumental dome, still so primitive at Fīrūzābād two centuries later, probably did not exist in the first century AD, the date to which Herzfeld attributes the construction of the palace. In the second century the square hall of Hatra was still barrel-vaulted. Moreover the palace and sanctuary of Kūh-i Khwāja are not parts of a single composition, but two buildings built on to each other. It is probable that the sanctuary was constructed as an adjunct to the Parthian palace at the time of its restoration and re-arrangement, which Herzfeld himself dates during the third century.

So we are fairly well informed about the Iranian fire sanctuaries. In the Achaemenid period we see a clearly defined type of āyadanā, that of Susa (fig. 139) which we rediscover almost unchanged in the Arsacid period at Takht-i Sulaimān, then in the

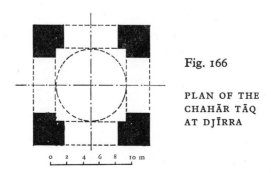

Fig. 166

PLAN OF THE
CHAHĀR TĀQ
AT DJĪRRA

0   2   4   6   8   10 m

Sassanid period in the Imāmzāda Sayyid Husain, near Shāpūr, and in the small monument in the valley of Djīrra (fig. 166). In addition we know of a pre-Achaemenid
sanctuary, the one at the tip of the Husain Kūh, which incidentally has no architectural
interest, a monument of the Seleucid period at the foot of the terrace of Persepolis
and a small sanctuary in the palace at Kūh-i Khwāja.

Perhaps the ātash-gāh at Isfahān at the top of an isolated hill, of which only the
supporting walls of a platform remain, was also a fire sanctuary. Perhaps it controlled
the fires of the plain of Isfahān as the āyadanā at Husain Kūh controlled the fires of
the plain of Persepolis. This is only a supposition.

The fire temple, the place for public fire ceremonies, is mentioned for the first time
by Pausanias[1] during the second century AD. There were fire sanctuaries in Iran at
that time, as we have just seen, and on the other hand religious edifices which were
actual temples, but had nothing in common with the fire cult. The temple at Kangāwār
was one of them. It was consecrated to the goddess Anāhit. These edifices which
were independent of the fire monuments lasted as such until the end of the Arsacids'
reign, until about the time when Pausanias spoke of a temple 'in which there is a
special cell, closed and covered in where the eternal fire burns without flames on an
altar heaped with ashes'. I have already said that in this new type of monument, the
home of the divine fire where the faithful took part in the ceremonies of the cult, the
fire was kept in a dark, firmly closed room, in one of the outbuildings. The altar, on
the contrary, in the centre of the courtyard, developed in importance and size. It
stood on a high substructure, the chahār tāq, which enabled the assembled crowd to
see it from afar and boasted a dais which was mainly there for decoration.[2]

Some of these chahār tāqs in varying stages of ruin still exist, at Natānz, Kāzarūn
and Fīrūzābād (fig. 167), but the buildings which surrounded them have disappeared.
We do not possess a single complete plan of an Arsacid or Sassanid fire temple; all we
know are a few natural sites arranged as temples and some modern edifices.

However, the celebrated Fire Temple at Fīrūzābād, built, like the palace and the

Fig. 167

PLAN OF THE
CHAHĀR TĀQ OF THE
FIRE TEMPLE AT FĪRŪZĀBĀD

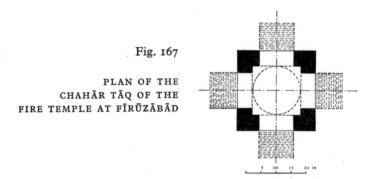

---

[1] Pausanias. Greek geographer and historian of the second century AD, author of a celebrated *Itinerary of Greece*.
[2] Chahār tāq, literally 'Four arches'.

Qal'a-i Dukhtar, by the first Sassanid king, Ardashīr, has been so often mentioned, if not described, by Ibn-al Balkhī, Istakhrī, Firdawsī, Ibn Fakīh, Mas'ūdī and Tabarī, that with the help of what remains of it on the spot we can imagine it fairly accurately. It was vast. Firdawsī says of it that it was: 'an enormous establishment, comprising a rectangular platform raised 6 feet above the ground outside, sheltered by shady trees. In the centre of this was a high substructure (the ruins of which still exist) which bore a chahār tāq housing the altar for the fire ceremonies. Around this platform were the gardens and outbuildings of the temple, the various storehouses and living quarters of the personnel. To the east of the monument there was a pool which collected water brought from the mountain by an aqueduct four to five miles long and to the south in the exact geometrical centre of the surrounding wall of the ancient town, a high tower, a kind of ziggurat, on the top of which the divine fire appeared at the hours of prayer.'

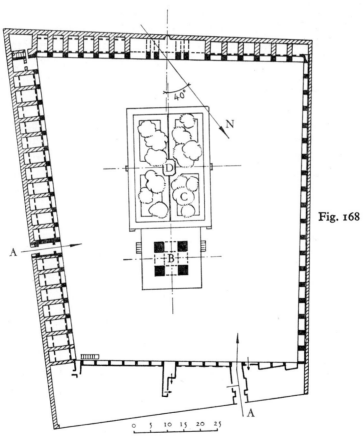

Fig. 168

PLAN OF THE ATIK MUSALLĀ AT YAZD
A. Entrances. B. Chahār tāq. C. Courtyard. D. Pool.

Such a complex of buildings, accompanied by gardens, an aqueduct, a small lake and a signal tower obviously did not represent the monument, the current type of which was established during the reign of the last Arsacid kings. The only edifices still standing which have retained such an appearance are an eighteenth-century temple at Bākū and an Islamic monument, the Musallā at Yazd. At Bākū the place for the public fire ceremonies, underneath a monumental dais, is in the open air in the centre of the vast courtyard of the temple, which is the place for prayer reserved for the congregation of the faithful. Around the courtyard are the outbuildings, storehouses and living quarters. The Musallā at Yazd is arranged on the same principle (fig. 168).

Naturally there are exceptions to the regular type of fire temple, Takht-i Sulaimān in Azerbaidjan, which I have already mentioned, Masdjid-i Sulaimān in Khūzistān, which I have also mentioned and Takht-i Rustam in the district of Shāriyar (Shāhruyāz), not far from Teheran.

Takht-i Rustam consists of two platforms, one a third of the way up and the other on the summit of a rocky peak isolated in the middle of a vast plain. The one on the summit was the site of a fire, a sort of signal visible from Teheran itself some twenty-five miles away and beyond. The lower one was the place for the fire ceremonies which, judging by the considerable dimensions of the terrace, must have been public. The home of the fire was very near, in a small edifice with a Sassanid dome. It supplied the fire necessary for the ceremonies on the terrace and the signal on the summit (fig. 169).

With the advent of Islam in the seventh century, all life disappeared from the majority of the sanctuaries and temples. The monuments constructed were destroyed or gradually disintegrated, falling to bits for lack of use. As Georges Perrot says: 'The

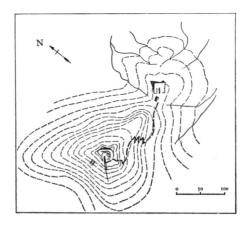

Fig. 169

OVERALL PLAN OF TAKHT-I RUSTAM

ātash-gāh had to diminish in size, return to ground level, hide in a courtyard strictly forbidden to the eyes and footsteps of unbelievers.' And indeed that is how we finally find the largest of fire temples at Yazd—after many detours and not without difficulty, among the various buildings of a school where your guide is surly and unhelpful.

The fire is traditionally preserved there in a large metal vase, the ātash-dān, placed on a stone base, the indispensable adusht which raises it from the ground, in the centre of a room which is lit by a large arch with a grille which looks out on to the meeting hall of the faithful. Two doors lead from this hall to a gallery which surrounds the fire chamber. Here, therefore, we have sanctuary and temple united and reduced to a minimum, and the ātash-gāh proper, once so jealously hidden from the public, is only the thickness of a grating away. There is no longer any question of the thirty yards which once had to separate the Sacred Fire from the believer in a state of impurity, as there is no longer any question of the open air, the fire brilliant and clear beneath the vault of the sky, nor incidentally of the several categories of fire which purify one another. Now the ritual ceremonies unfold in the fire chamber before the crowd assembled on the other side of the grating. One temple at Yazd, a small white villa without much interest, reproduces roughly the same arrangements. The one at Teheran, a small columned pavilion in a garden, also consists of a fire chamber adjacent to a hall for public prayer.

I have already said that we still only know a very small number of chahār tāqs which belonged to temples, the ones at Fīrūzābād, Kāzarūn and Natānz, and the one at Bākū which is comparatively recent. There are others, the 'signals', which are more numerous, doubtless because they were isolated, far from towns and because monuments have always suffered more from men than from centuries. These signals were described in the *Annales du Service archéologique de l'Iran*, 'Athār-é Īrān'. Those at Farashbānd, Djirra, Tūn-i Sabz, all three in the valley of Djirra, those at Atashkūh, near Dilīdjān, and Nīsar, between Kāshān and Dilīdjān, are pure chahār tāqs, that is to say they consist solely of a dome on four pillars. Another, the Qal'a-i Dukhtar, not

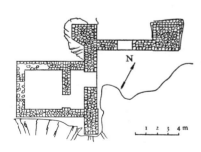

Fig. 170

PLAN OF THE
QAL'A-I DUKHTAR
AT QUM

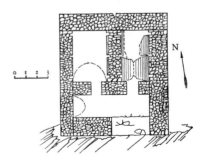

Fig. 171

PLAN OF THE
QAL'A-I DUKHTAR
AT SHĀHRISTĀNAK

far from Qum, adjoined a small fire chamber served by a corridor (fig. 172). Yet
another signal at a height of more than 9,000 feet, also called Qal'a-i Dukhtar, above
Shāhristānak in the Alburz mountains, was not a chahār tāq but a small rectangular
building containing two rooms, one for the fire, the other for its attendants, reached
by a corridor. The rooms and the corridor were barrel-vaulted. M. Siroux, its dis-
coverer who drew the plan, says that the Sacred Fire, carefully maintained in one of
the cells, was doubtless exposed at nightfall in front of or on the edifice, in view of the
mountain villages and the scattered shepherds on the neighbouring heights (fig. 171).

These monuments, situated on heights which were visible from afar, generally
built beside important routes, and often marking passes, were illuminated at the
hours of prayer, and at the same time showed travellers the way.

Today we can add three still extant chahār tāqs to this list, at Yazd-i Khwāst in
Fārs, at Khairābād in Khūzistān, and at Burzu in the region of Qum. The one at
Yazd-i Khwāst, once isolated on a hill with almost vertical sides which projects into a
fairly rich and populous valley, was gradually surrounded by houses, then became
the mosque of a new suburb. In 1887 E. G. Browne saw it still in activity, but about
thirty years ago, so it is said, an earthquake shook the hill, its houses overhanging the
precipice and its mosque, in the floor of which then opened a fissure twenty inches
wide, and the village was abandoned. Since then during the last war the fissure enlarged and the dome of the monument collapsed. It is certain that at least half of what
remains will not be long in toppling into the valley with the part of the hill which
bears it.

The chahār-tāq at Khairābād, a little above and some hundred yards from the ruins
of a Sassanid bridge, told travellers where to cross a river long before they reached it.

The one at Burzu is about seven miles from Radgird, on the road from Qum to
Sultānābād.

So now we know a dozen signals. They are all Sassanid and all situated in the west of
Iran, with one exception, the edifice at Bāz-i Hūr in Khurāsān, on the road from
Mashhad to Turbat-i Haidarī (fig. 172). However, with its aisles it is not exactly a

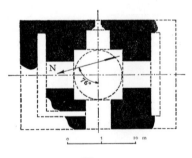

Fig. 172

PLAN OF THE EDIFICE AT BĀZ-I HŪR

chahār tāq nor perhaps a religious monument at all, but a simple outbuilding of two fortresses, Qalʻa-i Pisar and Qalʻa-i Dukhtar, which once defended the entrance of a gorge.

As we shall see later, these small edifices, the chahār tāqs, these simple kiosks, played an important part in the history of the Iranian mosque.

SCULPTURE

At the same time as this new genuinely aboriginal architecture, free of any compromise with the Hellenism of the Seleucids and Parthians, with the first Sassanid kings there appeared a new form of Iranian sculpture in Iran. It appeared simultaneously with him, as if this lord of Fārs, whose family were guardians of the Sacred Fire of Istakhr, had also been, in the absence of a national power, the depository of the traditions of Iran. In fact, vaulted architecture, the true architecture of the country, had not yet produced any work of importance, whereas we know antique works of Iranian sculpture; but it existed and we may say that one and the other, architecture and sculpture, had disappeared beneath the Hellenistic surface of the Arsacid civilization and that it was the anti-Hellenism of the end of the Parthian period which made it possible for them to express themselves freely.

I have already said that the palace of Ardashīr, at Fīrūzābād, the most ancient known monument of Sassanid architecture, was also the most representative. After it there was little technical progress and no better plan appeared. As for sculpture, after a short period of time during which the Iranian craftsmen tried their hands at vast rock-sculptures intended to put the prestige of the new dynasty on an equal footing with that of the glorious Achaemenids, we suddenly see the appearance of the magnificent bas-reliefs of Naqsh-i Radjab and Naqsh-i Rustam in the names of Ardashīr and Shāpūr I (plates 98, 101 and 102).

It has been claimed that Sassanid sculpture was greatly influenced by Roman art, by Greco-Bactrian painting and even that Roman sculptors collaborated with the Iranians to some extent, but it is as well to know what we are talking about. Doubtless we can talk of foreign influences in connection with the two winged victories which decorate the main façade of the larger of the two grottoes at Tāq-i Būstān (pl. 113), perhaps also in connection with the hunting scenes carved on the side walls of the same grotto (plates 113 and 114); but these works belong to the seventh century, i.e. the end of the Sassanid period and not to the great period of its art, the third century. Faced with the sculptures of the third century, we ought not to think of painting, whatever others may have said, but of Verrocchio, Benvenuto Cellini—of the great sculptors of the Italian Renaissance who were also goldsmiths. The *Horse of Shāpūr*, for example, with its powerful truly sculptural rounded shapes, as sharp as bronze and ornamented with elegant chiselling (pl. 102), which so reminds one of Colleone's horse in Venice, is definitely the work of an Iranian; it is a descendant of those craftsmen who were so skilled in decorating the votive pins and the weapons still found today in the tombs and temples of Luristān. There is no point in seeking an alien

114. GROTTO, TĀQ-I-BŪSTĀN: STAG-HUNTING
Sixth century AD.
Khusraw II pursues stags at full gallop. He is also visible motionless on the upper part of the bas-relief listening to the female harp players who are doing their best to charm him.

115. HORSE'S HEAD OF SILVER: PARCEL GILT
Iran. *c.* sixth century AD. Height: $5\frac{1}{2}$ in.; length: $7\frac{7}{8}$ in. Louvre.
This beautiful head with its elaborate mane has a finely chased blaze on its forehead.

116. DETAIL OF THE FAMOUS CUP KNOWN AS 'THE CUP OF SOLOMON'
Iran. Sixth century AD. Diameter: *c.* 11 in. Cabinet des Médailles, Bibliothèque Nationale, Paris.
For a long time this cup belonged to the Treasury of Saint Denis. This carving on rock crystal, photographed and enlarged, has the sharpness, purity and precision of a work on metal. The sovereign, represented in majesty, wearing the head-dress with the double crescent, is no doubt King Kawadh I (AD 488–531), although for a long time he was thought to be Khusraw II.

117. SILVER DISH
Iran. Sixth century. Diameter: $12\frac{3}{16}$ in. Cabinet des Médailles, Bibliothèque Nationale, Paris.
This piece of cast and chased silver-gilt represents the monarch, doubtless Khusraw II, hunting. He wears the head-dress with a crescent of the last Sassanids. Among the beasts he is pursuing we can make out two elk (one is dead), wild boars, gazelles, wild sheep and young rodents. Note the beauty of the horse; its head is similar to the one in plate 115.

118. GOLD COIN OF SHĀPŪR I
Third quarter of third century AD. Diameter: $\frac{13}{16}$ in. Cabinet des Médailles, Bibliothèque Nationale, Paris.
King Shāpūr I wears the crown with a triple crenellation topped by a globe.

119. REVERSE OF THE ABOVE COIN
Two men guard the fire altar. They are clearly the king and his son, the hereditary prince. The inscription is in Pahlavi characters.

120. GILDED SILVER BOTTLE WITH REPOUSSE DECORATION
Iran. Fifth to sixth centuries AD. Height: $10\frac{7}{16}$ in. Archaeological Museum, Teheran.
This very beautiful piece of silver may have been used for tasting the first wine of the vintage, the new wine. The motifs are inspired by the cult of Dionysus, but the treatment of the subject is Iranian and very characteristic of the Sassanid period. The sides of the bottle are decorated with four female figures reminiscent of Bacchantes.

121. THE BASE OF THE ABOVE BOTTLE
The peacock-dragon is one of the most frequently found motifs in Sassanid art (see figure 170 and coloured plate III). The openings on the garlands formed by the mouths of the lions doubtless served to collect the must of the new wine.

122. CORNELIAN SEAL BELONGING TO A HIGH PRIEST

Fifth century AD. Height: $1\frac{1}{2}$ in.; width: $1\frac{7}{16}$ in. Cabinet des Médailles, Bibliothèque Nationale, Paris.

Iranian royal personalities rarely wore the mitre. In order to give more relief to the details the photograph was taken of the bottom of the seal. That is why the profile is facing left, whereas in reality it faces right, so the writing is seen in reverse in this plate. There is a similar piece in Berlin.

origin for this art, it is the art of old Iran, its monumental expression. It is even—but I must explain myself—the natural outcome of Persepolitan sculpture.

I have also said of this latter art that it was entirely subordinated to architecture, and depended on its requirements: we have on the one hand powerful work in the round, on the heights close to the roof of the Apadanā, but on the other, on the wall of the stairways of the same building, relief reduced to drawing almost without modelling—to a procession of silhouettes without depth. The danger of this extreme simplification, perfectly satisfactory from the overall point of view, was obviously the impoverishment of sculpture *qua* sculpture. These people, beneath whose clothing we do not imagine a body, whose very lively representation is nevertheless rudimentary, would have looked like mere sketches if, from time to time, some details, the sheath of a dagger (pl. 46), the heads of the tribute bearers (pl. 50), the heads of the animals and the jewels (pl. 50) they are presenting to the sovereign, did not give the whole, without modifying its simplicity, a finished air, the impression of completion necessary to accompany the architecture. These details are wonders, but wonders of metal-work rather than sculpture. In them we rediscover the talent, skill and wit of the bronze founders of old. We feel that the Iranian artist was at home in this art and that if the tribute bearers at Persepolis offer the king so many necklaces, bracelets, vases and carefully wrought weapons, it is, as I have already said and want to repeat, much less because the regions of the empire they represented were specialized in metal-working than because the authors of the bas-reliefs themselves were goldsmiths.

Under the Hellenism of the Seleucids and the Parthians, the art of Luristān continued under cover for a long time, to reappear one day in the sculpture and gold-smith's work of the Sassanids. As has been very justly said, the Iranian element in Iranian art has always been of capital importance. In adverse circumstances it was difficult to identify, but whenever circumstances were favourable, it sprang triumphantly to the fore. It triumphed in Sassanid sculpture for some three quarters of a century, then disappeared for a time for lack of 'favourable circumstances'. According to Focillon's metaphor, it is 'what happens when a river disappears. Its course suddenly seems to be interrupted, it disappears underground and then we see it reappear in the light of day farther on. It is not a new river nor a fresh source. History too has its subterranean routes.' For it is the drama of all the arts that being the visible expression of the civilizations with which they are associated, they shine with great brilliance in the glorious periods of those civilizations and disappear with them. Compare, for example, the architecture of Darius and Xerxes with that of their successors. Look at the first Sassanid coins and the last, or the coins from the beginning of the reign of Parthians and those from the end. It was the same story with Sassanid sculpture.

All the great Sassanid bas-reliefs lie in the dynasty's country of origin, Fārs, with the exception of the one near Salmas, to the west of Lake Rizaiya, and those at Tāq-i Būstān, near Kirmānshāh. Save for a single sculpture at Naqsh-i Rustam, which does not represent a king of the dynasty, all these monuments are exactly dated by inscriptions or the kings' crowns. Thus we know that they belonged to the third century, with the exception of those at Tāq-i Būstān, i.e. two bas-reliefs executed c. AD 380 (pl. 105) and the sculptures in the grotto of Khusraw II (plates 111, 112, 113 and 114), which date from c. AD 600.

They split up into three groups, the first of which includes:

Four reliefs of Ardashīr I (AD 226–241) (two at Fīrūzābād, one at Naqsh-i Rustam, one at Naqsh-i Radjab). Eight reliefs of Shāpūr I (AD 241–272) (two at Naqsh-i Radjab, two at Naqsh-i Rustam, four at Bīshāpūr). One relief of Bahrām I (AD 273–276) (at Bīshāpūr). Five reliefs of Bahrām II (AD 276–293) (two at Naqsh-i Rustam, one at Naqsh-i Bahrām, one at Bīshāpūr, one at Sar Mashhad). One relief of Narsē (AD 293–303) (at Naqsh-i Rustam). One relief of Hormuzd II (AD 303–310) (at Naqsh-i Rustam).

The second group includes:

A relief of Ardashīr II (AD 379–383) (at Tāq-i Būstān). The tympanum of the small grotto at Tāq-i Būstān representing Shāpūr II (AD 310–379) and his son Shāpūr III (AD 383–388).

The third group includes the sculptures in the grotto of Khusraw II (AD 590–628), at Tāq-i Būstān.

Two of the four reliefs of Ardashīr I were sculptured on the rocky banks of the river Buraza, which flows into the plain where the future king founded the town of Ardashīr Khurra, today Fīrūzābād, even before his victory over the last Arsacid. One of the bas-reliefs recalls this victory, and the other, like those of Naqsh-i Radjab and Naqsh-i Rustam, Ardashīr's investiture by Hormuzd. The first three of these four reliefs can be considered as representing the formative period of Sassanid sculptural art and the fourth as its first masterpiece (pl. 98). In none of them do we find anything alien to Iran, nor anything Achaemenid, either, except, according to E. Herzfeld, 'the passivity of the personages, their lack of participation in the action represented, the fact that these figures never express an emotion'. However, these imperfections, common to every nascent art, may only be the result of the clumsiness of extempore sculptors. On the other hand we find a preoccupation with a strictly symmetrical composition which is quite characteristic and was already observed by F. Sarre in the *Investiture at Naqsh-i Rustam* (pl. 98). Every time the sculptor can, he says, 'he aims at exact symmetry. For example, the two horses and the lower part of the body of king and god. In other respects he aims as far as possible for harmony. To the figure stretched out beneath the god's horse, which probably personifies Ahriman, the principal of evil, corresponds the figure of Ardawān, the last of the Arsacids, who lies under the king's horse. The fly-whisk held by the eunuch matches the god's flowing cloak, the gesture of adoration of the king's arm the sceptre of Ahura Mazda . . .' This type of symmetry is even more marked in the investiture scene in the ravine at Fīrūzābād, probably the most ancient of all Sassanid bas-reliefs.

King and god, both on foot, face to face, with one foot forward, hold the beribboned crown placed exactly on the main axis of the composition with the same gesture. And then, since the king had to have a retinue, it was represented behind him as best the sculptor could. It is the work of men who knew exactly how to vary and arrange the projections of a small scene in relief and compose it symmetrically according to the ancient Iranian tradition, but who were still clumsy carvers of stone. There is nothing Achaemenid about it, for the Achaemenids composed differently, that is to say their conception of symmetry, dominated by architecture, was different. Here are two examples:

On each side of the stairways which are the central feature of the Apadanā at Persepolis, long files of soldiers one on top of the other (pl. 49) and tribute bearers (pl. 48) advance towards the axis of the building. This is absolutely rigid symmetry. But in these files the figures follow one another, one by one or in small groups, carrying vases, jewels, the king's throne, his weapons, leading his war chariot, rams, horses, camels, etc. No symmetry here but, on the contrary, an astonishing search for variety, in the masses and lines as well as the details. On the other hand, consider a panel of Achaemenid sculpture the shape of which is roughly that of Sassanid reliefs. King Darius is seated on a throne (pl. 44), with the hereditary prince behind him (pl. 58). Behind the prince stand the majordomo and the officer who carries the royal weapons (pl. 46). In front of the king is the sacred fire, then a man who bows in a gesture of salutation (pl. 45). Unsymmetrical, but this is how and where symmetry comes in: the scene is delimited to right and left by columns supporting a dais. Beyond these columns two guards on each side present their arms. The whole has the appearance of a solid frame inside which the scene represented enjoys complete freedom.

The stairways of the Apadanā, and this freely composed but perfectly framed bas-relief, are excellent examples of Achaemenid symmetry. The symmetry of the first Sassanid reliefs, where the elements of the composition which are sometimes the same ones, confront or balance each other independently of the surroundings, is that of the scenes done in repoussé with which the ancient Caspi already ornamented the discs of the pins they offered to their temples. Only the ancestral practice of the craft of the goldsmith enabled extempore sculptors to compose the first Sassanid reliefs so knowledgeably and execute them, even if clumsily. The demanding symmetry of shapes and masses, acceptable only in the restricted composition of small subjects, soon disappeared from the vast rock reliefs. As early as the *Investiture of Shāpūr I* at Naqsh-i Radjab, the horses move further apart from each other, the king's hand stretches towards the ring held by the god but does not reach it, the ribbons stream, the wind swells the clothes (pl. 102). In the *Triumph of Shāpūr over Valerian* at Naqsh-i Rustam, there is nothing left of the original symmetrical arrangements (pl. 101). Henceforth the arrangement of bas-reliefs was extremely varied, the subject represented remaining the glorification of royalty, as in Achaemenid sculpture. Sometimes, at Naqsh-i Radjab, Shāpūr I on horseback is followed by a group of personages on foot; sometimes, at Naqsh-i Rustam, the king is on horseback and the Emperor Valerian on his knees before him. At Bīshāpūr where the same scene is represented several times, the triumph of the Sassanid occupies the centre of the scene, flanked in the Achaemenid manner by rows of figures, one on top of the other. On the left, one of the reliefs shows the Iranian nobility on horseback and on the right people on foot carrying unspecified objects which are probably trophies; while in another relief there is a triumphal procession where the booty won is carried by Roman prisoners (pl. 106) and Iranian soldiers. A similar bas-relief close to the preceding one, the *Indian Triumph*, apparently commemorates a victorious expedition of Shāpūr to India. In the centre is the king on his throne. To the left, the Iranian cavalry, and to the right, the triumphal procession, a jumble of men, animals and objects among which we can make out an elephant and people bearing severed heads. This relief remained unfinished; it probably dates from the end of the reign of Shāpūr.

These bas-reliefs of the time of Shāpūr I represent the mature period of Sassanid sculpture. More experienced artists succeeded the artisans of Fīrūzābād, Achaemenid elements appeared in the composition and the drawing of certain details, but, as Herzfeld very justly says, 'we have no right to introduce the hypothesis of a workforce of foreign artists, Romans for example, except possibly in the great representation of the *Triumph of Shāpūr over Valerian at* Bīshāpūr'.

A statue in the round, the great statue of Shāpūr I, was also sculptured at the same period. It was found broken and lying on the ground in a natural cave in the ravine of Bīshāpūr which is probably the tomb of a king (pl. 103). This statue, which is more than three times the height of a man, was carved out of a freestanding natural pillar of rock in a hollowed-out part of the cave, not far from the entrance. It represented the king standing, one hand on his hip, the other on the pommel of his sword, his feet on the ground and the globe which surmounted his head touching the roof. It has been said that it was knocked down by iconoclastic Muslim inhabitants of the region, but nothing on the spot supports this idea. It is probable that it collapsed under its own weight, perhaps during a minor earthquake, because the natural pillar, which the sculptor had made exaggeratedly thin, had become too weak at ankle level.[1]

It is generally thought that Sassanid sculptural art reached its zenith in the *Investiture of Bahrām I by the God Hormuzd* at Bīshāpūr. The virtuosity of the relief which exhibits all the transitions from work in the round to the most delicate bas-relief, the deliberate balance of great smooth masses and very detailed sections are indeed admirable, but this relief is a copy of the *Investiture of Shāpūr I* at Naqsh-i Rajab and I think that we may prefer the original to the copy; it is on a larger, more sculptural scale in which the relative proportions of horsemen and horses are more accurate. The only thing against it, as compared with the relief of Bahrām, is that it has reached us in an even worse state of preservation.

After the reign of Bahrām I, Sassanid art produced well composed and sculptured bas-reliefs, the *Triumph of Bahrām II over an Arab Tribe*, at Bīshāpūr; the *Combat of Bahrām II with two lions*, at Sar Mashhad, the *Investiture of Narsē by the Goddess Anāhit*, at Naqsh-i Rustam (pl. 100), for example, and some fine portraits, the one of Bahrām II in the *Arabian Triumph* (pl. 104), those of the king's attendants in the bas-relief at Naqsh-i Bahrām and in the unfinished scene of homage at Naqsh-i Rustam. But, more and more details are repeated, flowing draperies are no more

---

[1] This extremely beautiful statue of Shāpūr I, who died at Bīshāpūr in AD 272, was re-erected after the last war, but extraordinarily ineptly.

than a handy way of filling in the gaps of a composition, the design becomes heavy, the source of invention seems exhausted.

After a combat on horseback executed in the reign of Bahrām II (AD 276–83) at Naqsh-i Rustam, we have to wait for the end of the fourth century, then the beginning of the seventh, to find the last works of monumental Sassanid sculpture, not far from Kirmānshāh. There, next to an abundant spring, there are an open air bas-relief on the site of an ancient royal 'firdaws', at Tāq-i Būstān from the time of Ardashīr II (AD 379–83) (pl. 105), a small grotto ornamented with figures of Shāpūr III (AD 383–8) and his father, Shāpūr II, as well as a larger grotto (pl. 113), decorated with the well-known hunting scenes (plates 113 and 114) and the famous equestrian statue of Khusraw II (AD 590–628) (pl. 112) on the back wall.

After the two bas-reliefs which represent the second period of Sassanid sculpture were executed, two centuries elapsed before the larger of the two grottoes at Tāq-i Būstān was hollowed out of the rock. But whereas the art of sculpture in stone had almost completely disappeared between the first and the second period, the grotto of Khusraw II is evidence of a renaissance of this kind of decoration. There are several reasons for this; as I have already mentioned, the arts shine with great brilliance in the glorious period of the civilizations they are associated with and disappear with them. Now the reign of Khusraw II was a great reign and Khusraw himself was a great king, powerful, loving pomp, and a serious protector and patron of the arts. Moreover, at the moment when the work of Sassanid metal workers had reached its greatest skill and its greatest vogue, it was quite natural for a technique like that of the relief at Naqsh-i Radjab, which represented Shāpūr I on horseback followed by people on foot, i.e. a goldsmith's rather than a sculptor's art, to appear in the grotto of Khusraw. For my part I see no difference, either in its workmanship or in the effect obtained, between the *Wild Boar Hunt* at Tāq-i Būstān (pl. 114) and the one which decorates the famous cup in the Cabinet des Médailles in the Bibliothèque Nationale in Paris (pl. 117). As for the colossal *Khusraw on Horseback* (pl. 112), nothing of him is visible beyond an ample garment, a coat of mail which covers his body and head up to his helmet, his decorated belt, his quiver full of arrows and his buckler. For the artist who had to execute it, this statue doubtless represented, rather than a portrait of the king, a chance to carve with scrupulous care the designs on his clothing, the chain-mail of his armour and all the details of a horseman's armament and a horse's trappings. It is not the work of a sculptor, but neither is it the work of a painter. The grotto of Khusraw II at Tāq-i Būstān seems to me to mark the triumph of the art of the metalworker.

METALWORK

One of the most representative pieces of this art, the silver bottle shown in plates 120 and 121, has belonged to the Archaeological Museum of Teheran since 1937. It is ovoid in shape and its decoration, in relief on a gilded background, consists of four arcs elegantly decorated with grapes and vine leaves beneath which dance women comparable to those on certain vases in the Hermitage Museum. Below two of these female figures are the heads of lions with mouths which are orifices of the vase. From the very reduced size of these openings and their situation on the lower part of the object we can assume that it was used to collect the first wine of the year when plunged up to the neck in the vat where the first grapes of the harvest had just been pressed. At the base of the vase is the peacock-dragon, the signature of Sassanid Iran.

The dancer in pl. 120, with elegant clothes and coiffure, holds a thyrse-head in her right hand and in her left a cup which seems to contain fruit. To her right we see a small fox, the robber of grapes, and to her left a bird with a long tail. One of the two lion's heads is below the woman's feet. In a spandrel we note a little musician playing a sort of guitar.

In *The Treasure of the Oxus* O. M. Dalton reproduces a vase, also published by Smirnov, the base of which is pierced like a sieve and says that this object was used to filter wine. Since our bottle is also pierced underneath and its decoration is quite similar to that described by Dalton, it seems that it may also have been used in connection with wine.

The women who look like bacchantes, the animals accompanying them, the thyrses and the musicians doubtless evoke those Dyonisiac processions the vogue for which spread as far as India after Alexander's conquest.

The inclusion of the Sassanid peacock-dragon and the similarity between the shape and decoration on the silver bottle in Teheran Museum, and the many other pieces of Sassanid silverware we know, lead me to suggest that our vase could have been executed in a region which was under both Iranian and Hellenistic influences, perhaps on the shores or in the neighbourhood of the Black Sea, during the fifth or sixth century AD.

The very beautiful silver horse's head shown in pl. 115 is also Sassanid, but considerably more ancient than the silver bottle. It has the ample contours of rock sculpture and is quite unconnected with Hellenism. It is purely Iranian. I do not know where or for what purpose it may have been executed.

FABRICS

At the approach of winter, when the Mesopotamian plain became even bleaker than it normally was under the summer sun, Khusraw Parwīz, according to the writer Bal'amī, installed himself on his famous 'winter carpet' and virtually lived there, even eating his meals on it, because it gave him the illusion of springtime. We know that this carpet sixty cubits square, also called Bahār-i Khusraw, the *Springtime of Khusraw*, represented a garden with its walks, streams, lawns and trees the branches and flowers of which were of gold, silver and differently coloured precious stones.

Nowadays still, Iranians leave the town as often as they can and put down a new carpet and a samovar beside some familiar stream in the vast beige expanse which serves as their countryside. Seated on their woollen garden, the only touch of colour for miles around, next to their gleaming fountain of hot water, they recite the poems of Hāfiz and would not change places with the king.

This is a modern reminder of the origin of the carpet: the flowering garden, so frequent in Iranian literature but so rare in reality, and the oriental love of colour— a natural reaction against the depressing monotony of the landscape.

The *Springtime of Khusraw* incidentally is neither the only nor the most ancient garden-carpet of which we have a record. Carpets are depicted in a Sassanid bas-relief at Tāq-i Būstān. Ta'alibī describes the Takht-i Tāqdis, the *Dome-shaped Throne*, which was at Gandjak, in the royal palace next to the sacred fire of Adhur Gushnāsp, and was destroyed by the Emperor Heraclius in AD 628. This throne, surmounted by a gold and lapis-lazuli baldachin on which were represented the sky and the stars, the signs of the Zodiac and the seven climes, was entirely covered with four brocade carpets embroidered with gold and ornamented with pearls and rubies. Each of these carpets depicted one of the four seasons.

The garden-carpet became the favourite type of Iranian carpet, so magnificent that gardens imitated it in their turn and became carpet-gardens. Not only did flower-beds copy their designs and the arrangement of their colours, but also in places where it was impossible to make real gardens for lack of water, imitation gardens were actually composed of different coloured stones.

For this same reason, Iranian architecture adorned itself more and more with a clothing of colour reacting against the poverty of materials at its disposal. In France, with its varied landscapes, buildings did not seek the attraction of colour. Take the slate roofs of Loches, one of the most purely French landscapes that I know. A single panel of new tiles would be unbearable among the subtle greys of the objects and atmosphere which compose it. On the other hand we know how charming Finnish houses painted green, red and bright blue are in the snow-clad northern landscapes, or again the splendour of the golden domes of Kazimain and Sāmarrā appearing above the Mesopotamian plain.

The Orient, which had little but its own earth to build with, built with sun-dried or burnt brick, mostly with sun-dried brick. Hence the need to protect the walls against shocks, rain and sun, and the use of durable facing materials for this purpose. Hence too the choice of more or less sumptuous facing materials, metal, stone, glazed ceramics and stucco in contrast to the interior poverty of the buildings. The Sassanids, who built vaulted edifices of brick by a rather crude technique, nevertheless tried to give them the grandeur of the Achaemenid monuments by carrying the breadth of their composition and the richness of the decoration to extremes. The great Ivan of the palace of Ctesiphon, the Tāq-i Kisrā, the hall for official royal residences, is almost 85 feet wide by 132 feet deep. Its façade, 94 feet high, was covered with painted stucco, according to some authorities, and gilded or silvered copper plaques according to others. The inner walls of the immense hall were covered with silk hangings and mosaic panels representing the siege of Antioch by Khusraw I and the battles which took place outside that town. On audience days, the floor was covered with silk brocade carpets picked out with silver and gold, including, at the time of Khusraw II, the famous 'Bahār' itself. The throne was surmounted by a gold crown ornamented with pearls, rubies and emeralds, which was hung from the vault by a gold chain. The king, seated on a gold brocade cushion, his hands resting on his sword, was even more richly adorned. St John Chrysostom says that his beard was gilded and that he had the air of a mythical being. Hormuzd II, according to Theophylactes, wore a gold tiara ornamented with emeralds surrounded by pearls. His garment was 'bedizened with gold, hand-woven and of great value'. Khusraw II, covered with pearls and jewels from head to foot, wore 'a rose-pink tunic, sky-blue trousers and a red crown', according to *The Album of Portraits of the Sassanian Kings.*

Most of this luxury was paid for by the silk trade. In fact Iran itself did not produce the silk it wove, at least until the reign of the Emperor Justinian (AD 527–565). It got it from China in the form of thread, raw silks not yet prepared for weaving and dyeing, and of silk fabrics which it unravelled, i.e. unwove, so as to use the thread thus recovered over again. It was only towards the middle of the sixth century that sericulture, the art of raising silk worms, and reeling off a continuous thread from their cocoons was introduced into Iran. We know the story of the two monks who went to collect silk worm's eggs in China in AD 552 on Justinian's orders. They found them in Khotan and took them back to Constantinople with the knowledge necessary for raising caterpillars. From the reign of Justin II, Justinian's successor, onwards the new industry was in full swing.

Before then the silk which the West wove came by two main routes both of which started from Tashkurgan (the Stone Tower) in the vicinity of Khotan, the point where the land routes of Chinese trade destined for the interior of Asia met. One of these routes reached the Indus valley and Barbaricon, near the mouth of that river, from where the bales of silk were sent by sea to the Persian Gulf and the Egyptian ports on the Red Sea. The other route went via Balkh, Hecatompylos, the Caspian Gates, Media, the valley of the Euphrates and the Mediterranean.

When Iran, like Egypt, Syria and Byzantium, itself produced the raw silk material it needed, the silk trade between the Far East and the West was not affected, for the vogue for silk materials had meantime become such a craze that the demand was always greater than the supply. The raising of silk worms in Iran was most active in Gīlān, Māzandarān and Khūzistān. However, we do not yet know where the first factories were nor when they were set up. It has been said that Shāpūr I founded the Iranian silk industry by transporting the weavers of Antioch to Shūshtar in AD 260. However, if it seems established that until the third century BC China allowed no knowledge of her silk or silk goods outside her territory, we nevertheless find traces of the subsequent migration which gradually brought to western Asia first spun silk and silk fabrics, and finally the art of spinning and weaving the precious thread. We do not know at what point this migration reached Iran. Examination of the actual fabrics does not tell us much. Cloths from Byzantium and Iran exhibit such a striking family likeness that mostly we cannot guarantee their origin or fix the dates of manufacture.

These same subjects, hunting and battle scenes, people and animals, nearly always in decorative roundels facing each other or back to back, which we know already from

Iranian sculpture and metalwork, decorate both the reputedly Byzantine and the reputedly Iranian silks. The symmetrical compositions which the Byzantine weavers made on looms specially arranged for this type of work, i.e. by reversing the pattern, was also used by the Iranians. The colours were the same. How then can we find our bearings? Sometimes, it is true, when the Byzantines took it into their heads to replace traditional subjects by circus scenes (for example, the pieces in the Cluny Museum, Paris, and the Museum in the Parc du Cinquantenaire, Brussels, in which medallions with blue, violet or purple backgrounds enclose circus performers driving four-horse chariots) or Christian subjects (for example, the *Annunciation* in the Vatican), discrimination is easy, but we must still hesitate to say whether the silk fabric in the Treasury of the Church of Notre Dame de la Couture at Le Mans is Sassanid or post-Sassanid (fig. 173). 'Should we classify it as Islamic?', asks G. Migeon. 'Falke thinks as follows: the two green lions on a red background, confronting one another on either side of a fire altar, are clearly a Sassanid representation, but according to him the animals are more reminiscent of the lions sculptured on the walls of Diyarbekir. I am not so sure.'

'The cheetahs facing each other on the beautiful Chinon silk,' says E. Mâle, 'which were believed Sassanid, are Islamic, as a long unnoticed inscription has proved.'

Fig. 173   Fig. 174

Of a silk in Saint Ursula at Cologne representing two horsemen facing each other, mounted on winged griffins, seizing a winged plumed quadruped by the throat, and another silk belonging to the Berlin Museum, ornamented with two personages who face each other on winged horses carrying a lion cub in their arms, G. Wiet recently wrote as follows: 'Watelin seems to have been the first person to ask himself whether the Berlin piece was not Byzantine. A. U. Pope considered that they were both Sassanid at the time of the London exhibition (of 1931) which, after the Munich one (of 1911), also hailed as Sassanid the fabric from Saint Cunibert at Cologne with a very different style which must be re-attributed to Byzantium. Recently Mrs Phyllis Ackerman refused to accept them as Sassanid. It seems to me only fair to re-attribute the Berlin and Saint Ursula silks to Sassanid workmanship.'

Incidentally a great number of ancient pieces are dated by the best experts to the 'sixth to the eighth centuries', which means that they may be Sassanid, Byzantine or Islamic, and we are none the wiser.

Admittedly we have the assistance of some dozens of fabric designs carved in relief on the clothes of the personages figuring in the hunting scenes at Tāq-i Būstān to help us solve this tricky problem. But there again the criterion is not very certain, for the winged griffin itself, so typically Sassanid, which ornaments the king's clothes (fig. 174) is found almost identically on a tenth-century Byzantine silk.[1] It follows that the number of authentically Sassanid silks may be very much reduced. It becomes more and more so in proportion as further studies are pursued and it is by no means certain that 'a good number of objects catalogued as Coptic, Byzantine, Islamic or even Romanesque may one day return to Sassanid art'.

Besides it was not yesterday but as much as fifty years ago that Ch. Diehl, having noted the marked influence Sassanid fabrics had on Byzantine materials, wrote this passage:[2] 'A whole series of valuable monuments attests the imitation of these models: they are in particular the silks with hunting subjects and representations of horsemen (fig. 175). Fine examples are the pallium in San Ambrogio, Milan, which shows a Persian prince on horseback, with bow taut, shooting at a wounded lion which is pulling down a wild ass, the whole enclosed by large medallions with a green background, the silk in St Cunibert at Cologne and the fabric in the Victoria and Albert Museum, where the identical motif is repeated on a blue ground, while a sacred tree separates the two horsemen, who face each other. Lessing[3] dates this fabric, a Byzantine imitation of a Persian original, to between the sixth and the eighth centuries.' Elsewhere the same lion hunters on horseback appear in medallions with a red ground on yellowish silk (Kaiser Friedrich Museum, Berlin, from Akhmīn), Treasury of St Servais at Maestricht (Lessing, Book 7) and Treasury of St Ursula, Cologne (Louvre, Marteau collection. Lessing, Book 8), all from the sixth to seventh centuries; or else they are on foot in Persian costume fighting lions with swords (Kaiser Friedrich Museum, treasure of the Sancta Sanctorum, fifth or sixth century). Elsewhere we see horsemen, singly or facing one another, sceptre in hand, a bird flying above their horse's head, while in the row below a man on foot armed with a lance stands beside a stork (Kaiser Friedrich Museum, c. sixth century. Lessing, Book 11).

'The palmetto decoration which is often combined with the figures on the last-

---

[1] The peacock-dragon is found in many versions, on silks (coloured plate III), carved on stone (fig. 174), on the base of the silver bottle in Teheran Museum (pl. 121), etc. It is even found, if I am not mistaken, among the sculptured ornaments which decorate the façade of Mshattā in Transjordan, thus giving evidence for the sculptor's nationality. . . .

[2] Ch. Diehl: Manuel d'Art Byzantin, Paris, 1925, Vol. 1, p. 272.

[3] J. Lessing: Die Gewebesammlung des Königlichen Kunstgewerbe Museums, Berlin 1900–1913, 4 vols.

Fig. 175

named fabrics and the sacred tree which the horsemen face once again bear witness to a Sassanid model, but the Greek inscriptions woven into the cloth proclaim a Byzantine manufacture.'

Since the time when Ch. Diehl wrote those lines, many other fabrics of the same kind which had been thought Sassanid have been reattributed to Byzantine art. Now they are called 'Byzantine imitations of Sassanid models', but no one has ever seen these models, i.e. the fabrics imitated, and we may well ask whether the Byzantine fabrics in question were not imitated from Sassanid sculpture and especially metalwork rather than cloths. In fact the works of Smirnov and Orbeli have made us familiar with a large number of cups and dishes on which horsemen hunt the wild ass, the wild boar and the ibex, attack wild beasts and are attacked by them. There was no lack of that type of model and we may concede that the Byzantine craftsmen were able to fit the subjects thus supplied into an Iranian arrangement of circles, lozenges and other geometrical shapes. Moreover the Byzantine workshops, which employed Greek, Coptic and Syrian workmen with long experience of tapestry-making, 'painting with the needle', could have executed the delicate work needed to represent the people-scenes we are talking about long before the Iranian ones. The writers of the Byzantine period frequently mention the beautiful fabrics which were used to decorate the churches in the form of curtains, hangings and tapestries. One of these curtains, which hung between the columns of the ciborium above the altar of Santa Sophia, was des-cribed at length by Paul the Silentiary. In the centre could be seen Christ, standing beneath a golden dome, clad in purple and gold, holding the Gospels; by his sides, the apostles Peter and Paul clothed in white completed the well-known scene of Our Saviour proclaiming the law. On the edges Christ's miracles were recounted; to them the artist had added buildings, hospitals and churches, recalling the good works of Justinian and Theodora. On the other curtains of the ciborium were depicted the images of kings, standing in front of the Virgin or bowing below Christ's hand as He blessed them. In this precious fabric, 'the work of skilful technique', the silk threads of various colours were woven with gold threads to produce a wonderful harmony.

Asterios of Amasia compared those of his contemporaries who wore garments covered with sacred or profane scenes to 'walking murals'. Bishop Theodoretus of Cyrene reports that it was not uncommon in his time to find the whole history of Christ woven or embroidered on the toga of a Christian senator.

In its fabrics, therefore, Byzantium tried to compete with painting, whereas Sassanid art was satisfied to use the elements of its traditional decoration, lions, griffins, winged horses, wild boars, goats and wild sheep (capridae) and birds of all sorts, highly stylized plants, trees of life, fruit trees, palmettos, etc. Its drawing is simpler than the Byzan-tine, but more expressive and stronger, often even of extraordinary power. The scale of its motifs is larger. Certain compartments in the pattern, called 'roundels', occupied by a single bird, could contain all the characters of a Byzantine crucifixion. It makes absolutely no attempt at prettiness or preciosity as Byzantine art does, and as it un-doubtedly would have done by contagion if the reign of the Sassanids had lasted longer. The Sassanid artist is interested in the decorative arrangement of familiar masses and shapes which he draws from his most ordinary repertoire and which please him be-cause they satisfy his traditionalist thinking and decorative sense at the same time.

However, the Sassanids and the Byzantines used the same colours, but not in the same way. The Byzantine colour is that of the mosaics in San Vitale, Ravenna, where women in Theodora's train appear clothed in fabrics in striking colours brocaded with gold, and the empress's cloak has a trimming representing the Adoration of the Magi picked out in gold on a violet background. Sassanid colouring is much soberer, less sumptuous and more artistically distributed, and only uses a few hues which match the design in simplicity. A great number of pieces, including some of the best we know, only used one colour, those for example which Vol. IV of the *Survey of Persian Art* shows in plates 201 a, 202 a and 202 b. The wild boar, the ram and the winged horse which are their principal subjects, as well as the circles with white dots and the palmettos which fill up the gaps, stand out in dark blue against the once white, now yellowish ground of natural silk. The bird and the lotus blossom which decorate No. 198 a retain the colour of the natural silk and are on a red ground. Others, Nos. 198 b, 199 a, 200 (coloured plate III), 201 c and 202 c, from the same work use only two colours apart from the white ground: red and black, dark blue and green, two tones of green, red and blue, green and black respectively. Those which use three, Nos. 199 b (dark blue, green, violet) and 201 b (dark red, green, pink), are rare. So there is no real polychromy; nor are small subjects executed in minute detail. As Mrs Phyllis Ackerman has quite rightly observed: 'They are the most masculine of all known silks.' In point of fact they are virile, and even a little barbarous, if we accept that barbarous is the opposite of finicky; but they are no more so than Achaemenid art with its black columns and its painted bas-reliefs the figures in which were adorned with coloured stones, real necklaces and real gold bracelets; no more so than any art which seeks its own mode of expression, Greek art of the sixth century BC, for example, and even that of the Parthenon which coloured its wonderful marble, or the painting of our own day in pursuit of its definition of Beauty.

The use of traditional elements of the decoration of ancient Iran, simple, well-executed compositions in which the decorative importance of the masses counts more than the symbolical significance of the subjects represented, sober powerful drawing and colours: this sums up the art of Sassanid fabrics. Naturally it does not follow that we may not come across a Sassanid silk representing a hunting or battle scene, for we know that Byzantine craftsmen worked in the Sassanid workshops, notably those who were transported from Antioch to Shūshtar by Shāpūr I, and that they must have brought with them their decorative formulas as well as their methods of manufacture. And since the Sassanid Empire extended from the Euphrates to Balkh, its artistic tendencies must have been as varied as the actual population. The fabrics of Bactriana and Khurāsān must have been very different from those of Fārs and Mesopotamia. However, since we do not necessarily look on political frontiers as the frontiers of art, the Sassanid fabrics as far as we are concerned are the ones which were made in the western part of the empire. All things considered, even if the designs of the Tāq-i Būstān fabrics do not give the right impression for lack of colours, they still clearly exhibit the essential characteristics all the more because they date from the time of Khusraw II, i.e. from the end of the reign of the Sassanids, and are to some extent its ultimate expression. Would we find the old winged griffin on the king's tunic if the art of Iranian fabric had already adopted or invented the fashion of scenes crowded with characters?

Silk fabrics were not the only ones decorated in the Sassanid period. Woollen cloths were also used, but because wool does not last as long as silk, our knowledge of them is still rudimentary. An Egyptian site supplied our first information about this industry.

Fairly numerous fragments of woollen fabrics woven in Gobelins stitch and decorated with Sassanid motifs were in fact found between 1896 and 1910 in the necropolis of an Egyptian town, Antinoe, which was founded in AD 130 by the Emperor Hadrian and developed rapidly. In the fifth century it was the civil capital of the Lower Thebes and in the sixth century the residence of the military head of the whole of Thebes. But as early as the beginning of the fourth century the civil and military officials on duty there had introduced the taste for Sassanid fashions.[1] According to A. Gayet, who has written about the excavations of Antinoe, Persian costume became the ceremonial costume there, as at Byzantium. Feminine fashion followed the same movement, the numerous 'funerary cushions' found were adorned with Sassanid designs and it is quite clear that the fabrics woven to make these cushions could not have been manufactured in Zoroastrian Iran. In the same way, the leggings ornamented with the image of a Sassanid king seated on his throne could not have been imitated from a Persian original as has been said, for even if it was possible to depict Christ and the emperor on clothes at Byzantium, it is extremely doubtful that Iranian artists would ever have risked representing one of their kings on leggings. The 'Sassanid Gobelins' of Antinoe, found in the company of Hellenistic fabrics the ornamentation of which is merely a crude interpretation of Sassanid decoration, were probably made in Egypt itself or Syria.

Since the time of the discovery of these, much better, authentically Sassanid objects have appeared, including the cock in the Hermitage, the eagles in the Robert Woods Bliss collection, the post-Sassanid but still magnificent cocks which have been published by R. Pfister and even, in tapestry, the ibex in the collection of Mrs William H. Moore. On them we recognize, decked out in more brilliant colours, for wool dyes much better and more easily than silk, the animals we have met on the silks, but freer and mostly liberated from the constraint imposed on them, as I have mentioned, by the generalized use of looms specially fitted to obtain the heraldic effect of confronted men or animals.

COINS

Although the Sassanid period produced many valuable works of art, carpets, fabrics, sculpture, etc., its coinage has no obvious artistic interest. On the other hand, the historical and other information furnished by its coins is of the highest importance. Thanks to the variety of the royal crowns it is often possible for us to attribute works of art, and even architectural monuments, to their authors. For example, consider the famous rock crystal cup described as 'from the Treasury of Saint-Denis', now in the Cabinet des Médailles in the Bibliothèque Nationale in Paris, but known in the Middle Ages as the 'cup of Solomon' (pl. 116). For a long time it was attributed to Khusraw II, but it is now thought that the central medallion does not represent that

[1] Le costume en Egypte du 3e au 13e siècle d'après les fouilles de M. Al. Gayet (Exposition universelle de 1900. Palais de costume), Paris 1900.
Al. Gayet: Notices relatives aux objets recueillis à Antinoë, Paris, 1901, 1902, 1903 and 1907.

123. THE TOMB OF QĀBŪS IBN WASHMGĪR KNOWN AS THE 'GUNBAD-I QĀBŪS'
Gūrgān. AD 997. Height: *c*. 165 ft.
Not so long ago this brick tower with a conical brick roof once stood in the middle of a steppe where the Turcomans grazed their horses. Today a hurriedly built town has replaced the ancient Gūrgān. Near to it, some twenty years ago, finds were made of large numbers of Iranian ceramics in excellent condition which had been buried by their owners at the coming of the Mongol hordes. According to a legend which has not been disproved so far, the body of Qābūs who was a Ziyarid prince of Gūrgān notorious for his cruelty and who died in AD 1012, was suspended from the summit of the tower in a glass coffin. Note that the tower has no staircase, exterior or interior. The only decoration apart from the beauty of the ten brick flanges of the monument is two very fine Kūfic inscriptions.

124. DETAIL OF A CORNER PILASTER OF THE RED TOMB (GUNBAD-I SURKH)
Marāgha. Twelfth century.
The Red Tower is the most ancient of the five mausoleums of Marāgha. It was completed in 542 H (AD 1147–1148). The corners of the edifice are reinforced by stout engaged pilasters, soberly decorated with geometrical patterns in brick the dark red colour of which is set off with dots of blue glazed brick.

125. COLUMN FROM THE MOSQUE KNOWN AS THE TĀRĪK KHĀNA
Dāmghān. Eighth century.
The mosque at Dāmghān which is known as the Tārīk Knāna, 'The House of God', is the most ancient mosque of the Arabian type preserved in Iran. Typical Sassanid techniques were employed in its construction.

126. THE MASDJID-I DJUM'Ā AT NĀYIN
Tenth century.
The remarkable stucco decoration of this mosque suggests that at this time groups of craftsmen circulated through the Muslim world, unifying techniques in the process.

127. THE HAIDARĪYA MADRASA AT QAZWĪN
Eleventh and twelfth centuries.
This Seljuk building was incorporated into the buildings of a madrasa built in the Qādjār period, during the nineteenth century. The decoration consists entirely in the varying patterns of the baked brick facing—and in a very delicate stucco inscription frieze in floreated Kūfic.

128. EXTERIOR OF THE BLUE TOMB (THE GUNBAD-I QABŪD)
Marāgha. Twelfth century.
This tomb, built a quarter of a century before the Mongol invasion of Iran, is a polygonal monument each facet of which is filled by a niche with a pointed arch. It was completed in 593 H (AD 1196–1197).

129. MIHRAB OF THE HAIDARĪYA MADRASA AT QAZWĪN
Qazwīn.
The mihrab of the Haidarīya madrasa (compare plate 127) is of carved stucco, once painted blue. It represents one of the high points of Iranian stucco work and is remarkable for the high relief of stylized pomegranates and pinecones which frame the mihrab and fill the arch of the dome above it.

123

124

125

131

130. COLONNADE IN THE FRIDAY MOSQUE AT ISFAHĀN
Fourteenth century.
The Masdjid-i Djum'ā or Friday Mosque is one of the most interesting monuments of Isfahān. It has undergone many transformations since it was first built in the Seljuk period (eleventh century AD). The round columns and the pointed arches with their traditional Sassanian style of construction which we see here date from the Muzaffarid period.

131. MIHRAB OF THE FRIDAY MOSQUE AT ISFAHĀN
Fourteenth century.
This extremely beautiful mihrab decorated in carved stucco was made on the orders of Uldjāitū Khudābanda the Mongol Il-Khān of the beginning of the fourteenth century.

132. MINARET OF THE 'ALĪ MOSQUE AT ISFAHĀN
Eleventh or twelfth century.
The 'Alī minaret is still 156 ft. high; as the topmost section has disappeared, we may assume that its total height exceeded 160 ft. It is decorated with a sober geometrical pattern executed entirely in brick. The 'Alī mosque adjoining the minaret is totally independent of it and dates from the Safawid period: 928 H (AD 1521).

133. FAÇADE OF THE CIRCULAR TOMB AT MARĀGHA
Twelfth century.
The Kūfic inscription at the base of the tympanum gives the date 563 H, that is AD 1167–1168. The inscriptions, the polygon-and-star decoration of the tympanum and the jumbled swastikas on the architrave are all in turquoise glazed brick.

134. FRAGMENT OF A KŪFIC INSCRIPTION
Khargird (Khurāsān). Eleventh century.
This decoration in terra-cotta, from the Seljuk period, belonged to a madrasa built by Nizām al-Mulk, the celebrated minister of Malik Shāh. Note how the inscription appears in high relief on a background of low relief foliage scroll.

COLOUR PLATE

IV. PART OF A HUNTING CARPET
Sixteenth century AD. Width: 9 ft. A strip at one end is missing but it must have been about 11 ft. 6 in. in length. Musée des Arts décoratifs, Paris (donated by J. Maciet).
The most beautiful carpets adorning museum collections are known to belong to the period of Shāh Tahmāsp. (AD 1524–1576). This king, who was himself a painter and calligrapher, saw to it that his craftsmen always had guaranteed commissions. A letter from this prince, to the Sultan of Turkey, Süleyman the Magnificent, which we still have, suggests that they should make carpets for the Süleymaniye Mosque which had just been completed. The carpet, a detail of which we reproduce here, represents a hunting scene in which the Simurgh, a mythical Islamic bird, is depicted.

king but more probably King Fīrūz or King Kawādh, for the crowns with two crescents which they wear on their coins are identical with the one worn by the central figure on the cup (pl. 116). Although this crystal bowl is particularly beautiful and well made, certain Sassanid intaglios, those, for example, which represent a high personage of the empire, a king according to some, a high priest according to others (pl. 122), are of a quality perhaps even more admirable from both the point of view of workmanship and design.

The Sassanids only minted a few gold pieces, but they struck many wide thin silver pieces which were more easily stacked. From the reign of the first sovereign of the dynasty, Ardashīr, son of Papak, the sacerdotal tiara worn by the Parthian sovereigns disappeared, to be replaced by a crenellated crown surmounted by a sort of globe (pl. 118). The reverse showed the fire altar between the king and the hereditary prince. The barely legible inscriptions are in 'Pahlawī', the written and spoken language of Middle Persia (pl. 119). Towards the middle of the fifth century AD the Sassanids added a crescent to the front of the crowns on their coins.

NOTE TO PART FOUR

ZOROASTRIANISM; SASSANID MAZDAISM; MANICHAEISM AND MAZDAKISM

The Zoroastrian religion is a reformed version of primitive Mazdaism, which was already dualist. The biography of Zoroaster or Zarathustra is still in the field of legend. However, in certain episodes it may be compared with the life of Buddha, who may have been his contemporary (sixth century BC).

However, whereas Buddhism led the believer to Nirvana, i.e. total dissolution, Zoroastrianism is an optimistic religion which does not propagate any form of renunciation and doubtless developed at the favourable moment when the great Achaemenid Empire had achieved its victory.

The good Zoroastrian, as Zoroaster conceives him, is healthy and simple; his guide is the Spirit of Wisdom (Vahu Manah), comparable to the Holy Ghost. He must shun asceticism, fight against evil and never abandon the idea of the necessary victory of good. Ideally he is the head of a large family and busies himself with agriculture, especially the raising of cattle, which share in his agricultural work, horses, the warrior's mount, and dogs, guardians of flocks and the house.

Blood-sacrifice, characteristic of all the ancient religions, became purely spiritual in the doctrine of Zoroaster. He recommended prayer before the fire of Mazda, evoking Vahu-Manah. Physical and moral balance, benevolence and the desire to aid his fellows are the ideals of his cult.

Zoroaster perhaps believed that he was the saviour of the world, he who would lead mankind to a relative state of perfection. However, the Magi, a Median priestly class corresponding more or less to that of the Indian Brahmins, took possession of the Iranian religious world and contrary to Zoroaster's wishes, we believe, strangely complicated the Mazdean religion by the addition of meticulous and exacting rites. This opinion, which is Herodotus's, does not agree with Pliny's, who asserts that the Magi were essentially disciples of Zoroaster.

Kartir, the celebrated high priest, the chief of the Magi and high pontiff, whose portrait can still be seen sculptured on the rock at Naqsh-i Rustam, near Persepolis (pl. 97), was a sort of minister of religion to several Sassanid kings for some thirty years—Shāpūr I, Hormuzd I, Bahrām I, Bahrām II—and, at the same time as he reorganized religion, did his best to expel the representatives and propagandists of foreign cults from the empire. We are informed about this in a long personal inscription which was discovered at Naqsh-i Rustam in 1939 by the Archaeological Expedition of the Oriental Institute in Chicago, which was working at the time in the region of Persepolis.

'The Mazdean religion,' he says, 'was consolidated by me, and wise men became powerful in the empire. The heretics and those of the Magi who did not observe the established rules received their punishment from me; they mended their ways and again became acceptable. Many sacred fires were established by me, Magi were appointed and this was provided for by the gods, the king and myself. Those who followed the doctrines of demons abandoned them because of me and recognized the gods. . . . The religion grew in every way, the work of the gods was multiplied. . . .'

Kartir adds that fire temples were founded everywhere that the armies of the King of Kings had passed.

During the reign of the Sassanid dynasty the fire cult remained dominant, more sacred than that of the other elements. The earth had to be respected, preserved from all defilement, particularly from contact with corpses which had to be exposed to beasts of prey. Waters were beneficent; they played a very important role, as yet insufficiently emphasized, in this cult, and included prayers at certain times of the day as well as in certain circumstances in life. The king, all the members of the royal family and many officials were required to make sizeable offerings to the clergy.

Such an administration required a vast and powerful organization whose personnel, made up of magi, often of very noble origin, were initiated into their role in establishments like seminaries. We know that the main one was situated not far from Rayy, near Teheran.

There were charters of pious foundations to establish and manage, accounts to keep and consequently a whole complicated bureaucracy which could not do without writing. For a long time oral tradition seems to have been adequate, but it was necessary to seek out, regroup and study the sacred texts, and note down the hymns, prayers and legal codes very accurately. These numerous documents were not all as ancient as each other, nor were they all of Iranian origin. The oldest, written in a language which had long since been obsolete, had to be translated into Pahlawī, i.e. 'Middle Persian'. A whole literature appeared which transmitted both the old myths and the new ideas.

The dualism of Zoroaster's *Gathas*[1] became a much more rigid dualism which divided all the beings in the universe into good and bad. The old conflict which opposed Ahura Mazda to Ahriman was finally given a solution. Ahriman, envying the beauty of Hormuzd's world, created beings to attack it. Hormuzd the omniscient, who knew in advance that victory would be his, accepted the battle. The two sides confronted each other. Ahriman triumphed for a time, which was our time, but was to end in the purification announced by Hormuzd. This is the idea of the Last Judgment in the form Catholicism received it from Zoroastrianism. After the victory of Hormuzd, the demons would destroy each other. Ahriman would be reduced to total impotence. The souls of the just would rediscover their bodies which they had been waiting for since the day of their death. As for the impious, they were already in hell, but not for eternity. Sassanid Mazdaism awaited universal salvation and 'a beatitude which would be life in the light of God'.

How was the world to reach this goal? It could only happen by the government of those kings mentioned in the ancient myths, who were of divine race and to whom was owed an almost religious obedience.

However, religion was not confined to the temple and the court. Side by side with the sacred fire of the priests and the sacred fire of the kings, there was the sacred fire of the farmers and, in addition to the high-ranking clergy, a whole group of Magi

---

[1] The *Gathas* are the hymns of the Zoroastrian religion which appear to have been composed at the beginning of the sixth century BC and were added to the *Avesta*.

ministering to the religious life of the most humble subjects of the King of Kings. Not only was a Magus necessary for grace before meals, but he also intervened in everyday life—funerals for example.

Actually, exposure of the corpse was never Zoroastrian, but exclusively a Magian custom which did not replace the original method of burial until after the beginning of the Christian era, when the reaction against Zoroaster's teaching was given concrete form by the final establishment of the Iranian church, Zoroastrian in name, but Magian in fact. The only real tombs we know—both royal and private—date from the Achaemenid period. The *ostothekai*, the ossuaries, clear proof of exposure, did not appear before the Arsacid period and did not become really common until the time of the Sassanids.

The Manichaean doctrine or heresy is connected with Mazdaism by its belief in dualism, that essential feature of all Iranian religions. Mani lived in the third century AD. Kartir, the head of the Magi, persuaded Bahrām I to arrest, try and execute him in AD 277. Previously, especially under the reign of Shāpūr I, Mani seems to have enjoyed the favour of the Sassanid kings. He wrote and had scribes write down his religious precepts, hoping to perpetuate his teachings.

However, the various religions which dominated the hearts of men in the West as well as the East, Christians, Moslems or even the Chinese, although of a benevolent nature, all tried to stamp out the vestiges of Manichaean thought. Saint Augustine was affiliated to the sect for more than ten years, which enabled him to supply us with a great deal of information showing that Manichaeism believed that it possessed a perfect knowledge of nature and the divine attributes.

At every moment the Manichaean was exposed to the power of evil, whose power seemed to dominate the world, while the divine presence showed itself modestly, without display. Its pacific and gentle light was often attacked by the warning dark powers of evil, which could spring up at any moment.

Manichaeism created a whole hierarchy among men, making their duties more difficult to practise as their rank was higher. The Elect, or Perfect Ones, had to withdraw from the world and abstain from all activity: they could not own worldly goods, procreate, cultivate or kill; consequently they could neither fight nor defend themselves. The Hearers had fewer obligations, but they had to believe in dualism and seek perfection in asceticism.

The pontificate of the Manichaean church was in Babylon, then in Samarkand. The belief lasted longest in eastern Iran and among the Uigur Turks.

Manichaeism was considered harmful by all authorities, both political and religious, because of its tenets of total abstinence and detachment.

Mazdak, while preserving dualism, the real basis of Iranian religions, added principles totally opposed to Zoroastrianism.

Mazdakism believed in the triumph of good over evil, but this ideal could only be realized by sacrifices offered by the human community united in a social order renouncing every kind of war and organized as a communist society. Renunciation and withdrawal from material things were the goals of Mazdakism. The prophet Mazdak was executed during the reign of Kawādh I (pl. 116) towards AD 529.

PART V

ISLAMIC IRAN

CHAPTER 9

THE MOSLEM ERA

THE invasion of Iran by the Arabs, 'those locust eaters', came as a crippling blow to the great Iranian nation which had been so proud of its ancient and brilliant civilization, and its successes against Byzantium and Rome. But in reality Iran had been exhausted by excessive wars, and the country was in anarchy as a result of incessant dynastic quarrels and court intrigues. Ctesiphon, the capital of the Sassanid Empire, was taken in AD 637, after the battle of Qādisīya. Less than twenty years later, in AD 656, before the death of the third Caliph, 'Uthmān, the Arab invasion had reached every region of the Iranian plateau as far as Balkh, except Makrān and the lands which lay beyond it. This invasion was too rapid to be considered an occupation or a definitive conquest. However, the installation of strong garrisons in towns such as Shīrāz, Nihāwand and Ahwāz enabled the Arabs to keep a foothold while waiting until the settlement of the revolts caused by their intrusion allowed them to consolidate their position. For it is quite clear that the immediate and complete acceptance of Islam was very rare: if intellectual opposition was not overt at first owing to stupor or terror, it was not slow to assert itself and turn into open revolt.

The Zoroastrians, although outwardly accepting Islam, continued to practise their religion, especially in Fārs and Azerbaidjan. Others found refuge in the various mountain massifs of the plateau, where they lived under the authority of small local dynasties. The first emigration of Zoroastrians to India took place in AD 700. Armed resistance was particularly tenacious on the shores of the Caspian Sea, where coins were still minted in the image of the Sassanid kings. The hereditary chiefs of this region remained independent, although numerous expeditions were sent to subdue them. Not until the middle of the ninth century was an Ispahbād,[1] Kārin ibn Shahriyār, converted to Islam: moreover he became a Shī'a, not a Sunnite (or orthodox Muslim).[2] In the eleventh century, Pahlawī writing was still used in the inscriptions on the monuments of the north slope of the Alburz, several of which still exist.

On the other hand whole groups of Yazdagird III's army apparently went over to the Arabs of their own accord and many Persians were converted so as to avoid paying the heavy tax imposed on non-Muslims, or simply to be on 'the side' of the conquerors.

---

[1] The word *ispahbād* means head of the army. Later it became the title of high-ranking officers, then that of great governors.
[2] See note, page 337.

Moreover the conquest brought Muslim Arabs to Iran—tradesmen, craftsmen and other workers—in ever-increasing numbers during the Umayyad Caliphate, but Iranian opposition still formed an obstacle for some time to the conversion of the country to Islam. The delegates of the governors of Basra and Kūfa, who administered the eastern regions of Iran, had a hard time performing their functions. Khurāsān rebelled and their manifold troubles continued until a large garrison had been installed at Marw and, shortly afterwards, 50,000 Arab settlers, so it is said, had been settled with their families in Khurāsān.

We know that the Prophet Muhammad,[1] who did not want the leadership of the Islamic world to be hereditary, had decided that the Caliphs would be elected by the Moslem community and chosen as being the most worthy to occupy the post. His first successors, Abū Bakr, Umar, 'Uthmān and 'Alī,[2] i.e. the four orthodox Caliphs, were elected in this way. But on the occasion of a dispute between the fourth Caliph, 'Alī, and the powerful governor of Damascus, Mu'āwiya, the latter, supported by his family and his friends, forced an ambiguous judgment which enabled him to proclaim himself Caliph.[3] In this way, less than thirty years after the Prophet's death, his instructions were disobeyed and the Caliphate had become a hereditary monarchy based on the Umayyad dynasty at Damascus. The theocratic period of the history of Islam was over.

We have seen that the Islamic conquest had left large groups of Iranians antagonistic to Muslim doctrine. For one thing the Arabs did not treat the new converts as equals and they in turn were dissatisfied on finding that they were under the yoke of people they looked on as intruders and upstarts. Highly sensitive to the contempt of the Arabs whom they despised, they supported, as did the non-converts, the political and religious claims of the Abbāsid family, descendants of an uncle of the Prophet, Abbās ibn 'Abd al-Mutalib,[4] from the union of the supporters of 'Alī and the Abbāsids. A force which was violently opposed to the Umayyads was born. Khurāsān joined the faction and after a series of battles which took place during the seventh century the Abbāsid dynasty replaced the Umayyad dynasty.

The situation of the Persians, not only in the Islamic world but also in Persia itself, was suddenly entirely transformed. Whereas they had been excluded from high office by the Umayyads, they were nominated to the most important posts in the new court of the Caliph, which was transferred from Damascus in a Semitic country to Baghdād,

[1] Muhammad (or Mahomet), born in AD 570, had to leave Mecca and took refuge in Madina in AD 622. This emigration, known as the Hegira, marks the beginning of the Muslim era. On the death of Muhammad in AD 632, Arabia was united by the first Caliph, Abū Bakr, father of Ayesha, the Prophet's second wife.

[2] Abū Bakr, first Caliph (AD 632–634). Umar, second Caliph (AD 634–644). 'Uthmān, third Caliph (AD 644–656). 'Alī, fourth Caliph (AD 656–661).

[3] Ali was stabbed to death at the door of the mosque in Kūfa. Of his two sons, the elder, Hasān, abandoned his rights in favour of Mu'āwiya, was proclaimed Caliph in AD 661 and founder of the Umayyad dynasty; the second, Husain, died in AD 680 on the battlefield of Karbalā while fighting the army of the new Caliph Yazīd (AD 680–683), son of Mu'āwiya.

[4] Abbās ibn 'Abd al-Mutalib, uncle of the Prophet Muhammad, died at Madina in 32 H (or 33 H) (AD 652–653), aged 88. The Abbāsid Caliphs were descended from his son 'Abd-Allāh.

a stone's-throw from the site of Ctesiphon, the capital of the Sassanid Empire. The Persian tradition and way of life assumed considerable importance in the new centre of political power. The Caliphs chose their ministers and councillors from the great families of Persian origin. One of these families, the Barmakids,[1] actually had a predominant role in running affairs of state for several decades.

Hārūn al-Rashīd,[2] the fifth Caliph, put an end to this lengthy favouritism of one family, but Persian influence continued to predominate at the Abbāsid court, especially during the Caliphate of his son, al Ma'mūn,[3] whose mother and wife were Persian. But for this very reason, because of an almost offensive use of Persian customs, fashions and splendour, a change or rather an attempt at a change took place. The tenth Caliph, al-Mutawakkil,[4] planned to make Damascus the capital of the Arabian Empire once more so as to avoid living in the Iranian atmosphere of Baghdād which he considered corrupt. Later he undertook the construction of an entirely new capital, north of Baghdād, at Sāmarrā on the Tigris, where al-Mu'tasim[5] and al-Wāthiq[6] had both built palaces. But he found the atmosphere polluted there as well. During his reign, the Shī'ites, whom he detested, the Christians and the Jews were forced to wear yellow garments and the only steeds they were allowed to own were donkeys and mules. His reign was also marked by the appearance of the growing power of the Turkish, Berber and Slav mercenaries, former slaves whom the Caliph al-Mu'tasim had used as his guard, now an army which became increasingly arrogant. Finally they were so much out of control that in AD 296 of the Hegira (AD 908) a thirteen-year-old Caliph, al-Muqtadir,[7] was forced to grant its leader the title of Amīr al-Umarā,[8] 'the Amir of amirs', thus handing over to him what was virtually absolute power.

During this period of anarchy the governors of the Iranian provinces which had been converted to Islam gradually broke away from the Abbāsid Caliphate, founded minor national dynasties and in so doing prepared the way for the political and cultural renaissance of Persia in the ninth and tenth centuries. We have the Tāhirids,[9] descended from a general of the Caliph Ma'mūn, Tāhir ibn al-Husain,[10] who ruled Khurāsān during the ninth century. Also the Saffārids,[11] natives of Sīstān, who for some time were masters of Khurāsān, the Kābul area, Kirmān and Fārs. But these ephemeral

[1] The Barmakids (the 'Barmecides'), a Persian family from which came the first Persian ministers of the empire of the Caliphs.

[2] Hārūn al-Rashīd, the fifth Abbāsid Caliph of Baghdad (AD 786–809).

[3] Al-Ma'mūn (AD 813–833).

[4] Al-Mutawakkil (AD 847–861).

[5] Al-Mu'tasim (AD 833–842).

[6] Al-Wāthiq (AD 842–847).

[7] Al-Muqtadir (AD 908–932).

[8] Amir al-Umarā: head of the *amirs* (or emirs) or 'general in chief'. Because of the weakness of the Caliphs, the personages who bore the title of Amir al-Umarā became the real sovereigns of Iran as well as of the regions ruled by the Caliphate.

[9] Tāhirid dynasty (AD 820–873).

[10] Tāhir ibn al-Husain, Persian general of Caliph Ma'mūn, founder of the Tāhirid dynasty in AD 820. Died in AD 822.

[11] The Saffārid dynasty, founded by Ya'qūb ibn Layth al-Saffār who ruled Persia for 33 years. Died at Djundai-Shāpūr in AD 879. His successor was his brother 'Amr, whose descendants remained in power until 1163.

powers, and yet others, in Media and Azerbaidjan, were considerably inferior in prestige and authority to the Sāmānid family.[1] These were natives of Balkh, who had at first been in the service of the Tāhirids and held high office in Transoxiana when disturbances in Khurāsān and the fall of the Tāhirids gave them the chance to establish their power under the nominal sovereignty of Baghdād in Khurāsān. They gained control over various areas, Transoxiana, Khurāsān, Sīstān, Kirmān, Gūrgān, Rayy and Tabaristān. Their very great importance, from the cultural point of view, lies in the fact that, during their reign and owing to their activities, a Persian form of Islamic culture developed in Khurāsān, and later still further afield.

In western Iran the new national Persian spirit showed itself in the form of small local powers, such as the Ziyārids[2] who dominated a part of the Iranian plateau for a certain time and were later confined within the boundaries of Tabaristān and Gūrgān. At almost the same time as this the Būyid dynasty[3] appeared. They were descended from that Abū Shudjā Būya[4] who, at the head of a warrior horde composed mainly of Daylamites,[5] had already played an important part in the quarrels between Alids and Sāmānids. The real founders of this dynasty were his three sons, 'Alī, Hasan and Ahmad. In order to conform to Daylamite *mores* they professed to be Shī'as, but religious questions were not of primary importance to these barbarian warriors. The Būyids, who had entered the service of Mardāwidj ibn Ziyār,[6] declared their independence in AD 935, then took over successively Khūzistān, the province of Shīrāz, Iraq and Kirmān.

In AD 945, Ahmad ibn Būya[7] made his entry into Baghdād, where the Caliph al-Mustaqfī[8] hastened to name him Amīr al-Umarā,[9] with the title of Mu'izz al-Dawla, by which he is more generally known. Alī received the title of Imād al-Dawla[10] and Hasan that of Rukn al-Dawla.[11] Then the Caliphate experienced a period of complete abasement during which the Commander of the Faithful was a mere toy in the hands of the Būyid amirs. But discord soon divided the descendants of Būya and finally was fatal to them. The most brilliant of their reigns was that of Azud al-Dawla,[12] son of Rukn al-Dawla, who was master of Baghdād in his turn in AD 978 and reigned until

[1] The Sāmānids, an Iranian dynasty from Transoxiana (AD 874–999, approximately).

[2] The Ziyārids, an Alid dynasty of Iran, who ruled over western Persia and Tabaristān, and later Gūrgān, from 316 H to 470 H (AD 928–1077).

[3] The Būyids (Būwaihids), an Iranian dynasty of western Persia (AD 933–1055).

[4] The founder of the Būyid dynasty was Abū Shudjā Būya.

[5] Daylamān is the name of the mountainous part of Gīlān. The Daylamites supplied large numbers of mercenaries to the army of the Abbāsid Caliphs.

[6] Mardāwidj ibn Ziyār, founder of the Ziyārid dynasty, died at Isfahān in 323 H (AD 995).

[7] Ahmad ibn Būya, the third son of Abū Shadjā Būya.

[8] A Būyid sultan, born in 326 (AD 948–949) at Ishahān, died at Baghdād in 372 H (AD 983).

[9] Mu'izz al-Dawla: title granted by the Caliph to Admad, the first of the Būyids to be named Amir al-Umarā.

[10] Imād al-Dawla Ali, the eldest son of Abū Shudjā Būya, was head of the Būyids in Iran for 18 years.

[11] Rukn al-Dawla Hasan, succeeded his brother Imād al-Dawla in Iran and kept in power for nearly 30 years.

[12] Azud al-Dawla ruled simultaneously in Iran and Baghdād. He was called Shāhinshāh, i.e. 'King of kings' or, in Arabic, malik al-mulūk.

AD 983. His son, Bahā al-Dawla,[1] continued to govern Iraq. In AD 1005 the arrival of the Seljuk Sultan Toghrul Begh[2] in Baghdād put an end to the Būyid dynasty.

They had been able to devote little time to peaceful tasks, with the exception of Azud al-Dawla who worked hard to increase the internal prosperity of his empire. He protected scholars and research, and built mosques, hospitals and other establishments for the public good. He also had canals and sanded-up wells cleared, and distributed aid to the poor and sick on a generous scale. But this beneficent administration was of short duration.

In the middle of the tenth century power in Persia was divided as follows: the Sāmānids held the north-east of the country, the Ziyārids the Caspian region, the Būyids a large part of the Iranian plateau, Fārs, Kirmān and Iraq as well as unofficially ruling over Baghdād. Towards the year AD 1000, then, Persia was only attached to the Arab world by very tenuous bonds. Besides, the serious disturbances which had troubled western Iran had been settled. Persian had become the literary language of the country and imposing groups of poets and scholars were seen in the entourage of the Būyid courts and other cultural centres. At the same time the multiple religious currents of the period spread through the various classes of the Muslim population and led western Persia, caught between eastern Sunnite Persia and Mesopotamia which was also Sunnite, to lean towards the Shī'ite creed.

The tenth century was also the period when the Turks made progress in Persia. Until then they had only been soldiers and military leaders in the service of provincial governors and local princes. With the Sāmānids many of them had held high military and administrative office, but with the weakening of the dynasty they served, the Turkish commanders strove to become political leaders. This was how a certain Subuktigīn[3] made himself independent in the region of Ghazna and Kābul, in Afghanistan. After his death his son Mahmūd, generally known by the name of Mahmūd of Ghazna,[4] founded an independent principality in Khurāsān and chose first Balkh, then Ghazna as his capital. He extended his empire to Sīstān, as far as western Iraq, and consolidated his possessions by conquests in India and Transoxiana. However, the last Būyids managed to retain their power in the west of Iran.

Like the court of the Sāmānids, Mahmūd's became the rendezvous of poets and for a period was one of the poles of attraction of the Islamic world. All that remains of Ghazna itself are some pathetic ruins, a few tombs, including Mahmūd's, and two triumphal towers. There is also a literary monument from the same period which it is rather difficult to associate with the name of Mahmūd the Turk—the national Iranian epic, the work of the poet Firdawsī,[5] who spent some time at Ghazna.

The prodigious wealth amassed by Mahmūd of Ghazna in the course of sixteen

---

[1] Bahā al-Dawla, son of Azud al-Dawla, won power but his fratricidal struggles with the son of Azud al-Dawla prepared the way for the advent of the Turks.

[2] Toghrul Begh, the Seljuk prince, was the first of this Turkish dynasty to rule over Iran—Isfahān became his capital.

[3] Subuktigin (Sabuktekin), founder of the Ghaznawid dynasty (AD 976–997).

[4] Mahmūd of Ghazna (AD 997–1030).

[5] Firdawsī, the epic poet (AD 933–1021?).

looting expeditions he organized in India was not a fairytale. However, when Firdawsī
came to present him with his epic, the *Shāh Nāma*, which had cost him thirty-three
years of labour, Mahmūd gave him such a derisory sum in reward for his gesture that
the disappointed poet gave it away as tips to the attendants of some public baths. This
lack of generosity, which the sovereign subsequently regretted, may be imputed to
several causes—though primarily, according to the chroniclers, to his immoderate
love of money. Furthermore Mahmūd was a Turk and a Sunnite, whereas Firdawsī
was Persian and a Shī'ite. Nevertheless Sūfī poetry[1] has made this Turk into a hero of
Iranian culture. A certain liking for the arts and even some poems were attributed to
him. His rise and that of the Ghaznawid dynasty,[2] however, were nothing but a
prelude to the Turkish invasion by which the Seljuk power was asserted in Persia and
beyond.

From the beginning of the eleventh century the Turks had begun to emigrate to
eastern Persia in spite of the measures which the Sāmānids and the Ghaznawids had
taken to prevent them. Very soon after their first appearance in Khūrāsān, their chief,
Toghrul Begh, had invaded the north of Persia and entered Baghdād. When the power
of the last Ziyārids and Būyids was destroyed and the Iranian possessions of the
Ghaznawids greatly diminished, Persia was once again united under the Turkish
dynasty of the Seljuks.[3]

Toghrul, who had proclaimed himself king at Marw and in an official audience with
the Caliph at Baghdād was hailed with the title of King of the East and West, settled
at Rayy. His nephew and successor, Alp Arslān,[4] took the Byzantine monarch Dio-
genes Romanus prisoner at the battle of Manzikert (Malazgird) in AD 1071; he
treated him generously, sparing his life and merely imposing on him the payment of an
annual tribute. He had as his prime minister one of the greatest minds the Orient has
produced, Nizām al-Mulk[5] (pl. 134), the minister also of his son Malik Shāh,[6] whose
long career of fifty-five years was providential for Persia. Under his government the
Seljuk Empire extended from the borders of China to Syria, from Transoxiana to
Arabia. A number of remarkable men lived in Iran at this time, three of whom are
world-famous. The first, whom I have just mentioned, was the great Nizām al-Mulk,

[1] Sūfism, a vast philosophical and religious system, the doctrine of the Islamic mystics.

[2] The Ghaznawid dynasty, a Turkish dynasty in Afghanistan (AD 962–1040) and the Punjab (AD 1026–
1187).

[3] The Seljuk Turks formed part of the nomadic Ghuzz (Oghuz) tribes of the Aral Sea. Towards
AD 1040 their chief, Toghrul Begh, won Khurāsān from the Ghaznawids, then captured SW Persia and
Mesopotamia from the Persian dynasty of Būyids. In AD 1051 he took Isfahān, in AD 1055 Baghdād. The
Abbāsid Caliph recognized him as 'temporal head of Islam' although he had made his submission to the
Sunnite creed.

[4] Alp Arslān, Seljuk sultan, nephew and successor of Toghrul Begh (AD 1063–1072).

[5] Nizām al-Mulk. Persian writer and statesman (AD 1020–1092). He created a sort of Church state, a
'fortress of theologians', the madrasa, which 'aimed to put an end to religious and philosophical dissen-
sions'. New programmes, uniquely inspired by Sunnite thought, definitively confirmed orthodoxy. The
madrasa, which was first conceived in Iran, was to spread throughout the Islamic universe. In establishments of this kind were formed the minds which contributed to the resistance to the Crusaders and the
Mongols. One might see the madrasa as the political saviour of Islam.

[6] Malik Shāh. The Seljuk sultan 405–486 (AD 1072–1092).

an administrator of genius, the founder of the *Nizāmīya*, a genuine school of government at the same time as an establishment for higher religious studies. In addition the Nizām composed a remarkable work for the use of princes, the *Siyāsat Nāma* or 'book of government'. However, in spite of his devotion to the Seljuk family and the constant aid he gave it for so many years, the Nizām had many enemies in the actual court. They centred round the person of Terken Khātūn, wife of Malik Shāh, and her favourite, Tādj al-Mulk, who managed to have him dismissed some years before his assassination. The second was the great poet Omar Khayyām,[1] certainly one of the greatest poets and in many people's opinion the very greatest poet of Iran.

The third is Hasan-i Sabāh,[2] whom Marco Polo and the chroniclers of the Crusades have made known under the name of 'The old man of the mountains'. Many important personages, including Nizām al-Mulk himself and the Abbāsid Caliph al-Rashīd Bi'llah, were assassinated by his 'fidaïs' or 'devoted ones', the former near Sahna, on the road from Hamadhān to Kirmānshāh, the latter at Shāhristān near Isfahān.

The last of the great Seljuks, Sandjar,[3] although ruler of this immense domain was really only master of Khurāsān, which he had governed for a long time. He had to cope with difficulties which after his death led to a disintegration of the empire which was only halted by the Mongol conquest.

From the religious point of view the Seljuks conformed to the tradition of the Sāmānids and Ghaznawids by becoming champions of the Sunnite creed. Western Persia, however, proclaimed itself non-Sunnite owing to Ismāʿili propaganda which resulted in the capture of the fortress of Alamūt, near Qazwīn, by Hasan-i Sabāh, in AD 1091. This propaganda had its sources in the east and west, but its political effects made themselves felt in Persia in Djibāl, that is 'the mountains', the name given to the area comprised by central and north-western Iran, in Fārs, Khūzistān and to a lesser extent in Kūhistān. Hasan-i Sabāh created a political power in western Persia which Malik Shāh and his successors tried unsuccessfully to break.

The Seljuks had organized a system of non-hereditary military fiefs in their empire which was intended to create a group of armies commanded by leaders devoted to their cause which would be constantly at their disposal. But in fact the chief consequence was the relaxation of the central authority which gradually passed into the hands of individual military governors known as *atabegs*; the main dynasties of these were those of Azerbaidjān, Luristān, the province of Yazd, and Fārs, which annexed Kirmān. After the death of Sultan Sandjar, the Seljuks were supplanted in Khurāsān by the Khwārizm Shāhs[4] who established an enormous empire with surprising rapidity.

---

[1] Omar Khayyām, Persian poet, astronomer and mathematician. Died in AD 1124. The date of his birth is still unknown.

[2] Al-Hasan, ibn al-Sabāh (or, in Persian, Hasan-i Sabāh), head of the Persian Ismāʿilites. First Grand Master of the Hashishin, or Assassins (AD 1056–1124). The Ismāʿilis are Muslim Shiʿites supporting Ismāʿil, the seventh imam and his descendants.

[3] Sultan Sandjar. Governor of Khurāsān in AD 1096 and Sultan of the Seljuk dynasty in AD 1117. Died in AD 1157.

[4] Khwārizm Shāh, title of the princes of Khwārizm, already in use at the time of the Arab conquest.

They were descended from a Turk, a royal cup-bearer, to whom Malik Shāh, the Seljuk, had given the realm of Khwārizm, the region of the oasis of Khīwa on the lower course of the Amū Daryā (the Djayhūn or Oxus). His family became more and more important and the best known of its representatives, 'Ala al-Dīn Muhammad,[1] was for some years ruler of an enormous area. At the moment of the Mongol invasion which he provoked by his presumption and conceited folly he represented the greatest Islamic power of the time.

In the meantime the Ghurid dynasty[2] had appeared. They were natives of the mountainous massif of Ghur (or Ghor) in Afghanistan. It was they who destroyed the Ghaznawid power in Persia by the capture of Ghazna in AD 1149. They made themselves masters of Sīstān, Bāmiyān and eastern Khurāsān, then they too abandoned most of their possessions to the Khwārizm Shāhs. Sometimes they allied themselves with the nomadic Ghuzz,[3] or Oghuz and it can be safely said that their devastations mark the beginning of the decline of culture in the north-west of Persia.

This decline was accelerated by the Mongol invasions. After the Khwārizm Shāh 'Ala al-Dan Muhammad had been defeated by Djinghiz Khān[4] in AD 1218, the Mongols took the territories they possessed in Transoxiana. They penetrated and conquered Khurāsān, as well as the north of Persia as far as Azerbaidjan, and pursued 'Ala al-Dīn who took refuge on a small island in the Caspian Sea where he died. His son, Djalāl al-Dīn,[5] fled to India. The great towns of Khurāsān were devastated and the population massacred.

Southern Persia was spared for the time being, but soon afterwards Djalāl al-Dīn left India, where he had taken refuge, and made for Azerbaidjan and Armenia, so provoking a second Mongol invasion in AD 1256. It was directed both against the Ismā'ilis and the Baghdād Caliphate. This expedition, which subdued the whole of Persia and abolished the Caliphate in AD 1258, was led by Hūlāgū,[6] grandson of Djinghiz Khān.

---

[1] 'Ala al-Din Muhammad, Khwārizm Shāh AD 1200–1220.

[2] The Ghurids, a Turkish dynasty of Afghanistan and North India (AD 1155–1213).

[3] At one time the main settlement of the Ghuzz tribes was on the lower course of the Sir Daryā (Jaxartes). Towards the end of the fourth century (AD tenth) they began to emigrate to Muslim territory. At first they settled in the region of Bukhārā. In the eleventh they crossed all the civilized regions of western Asia as far as the Mediterranean and devastated the Balkan peninsula as far as Greece but soon afterwards were wiped out by the Bulgars. Those who survived entered the service of Byzantium and later seem to have merged with peoples of the Byzantine Empire.

The Seljuks who were Ghuzz by origin gradually subdued all the area from Chinese Turkestan to the frontiers of Egypt and the Byzantine Empire. The Seljuks seem to have preferred to establish their turbulent relations on the western frontier of the State and that is how Asia Minor and the northern provinces of Iran received their Turkish population. In the East only one great movement by the Ghuzz is subsequently reported. In 548 H (AD 1153) the tribes established near Balkh revolted against Sultan Sandjar, resulting in the capture of the Sultan and the devastation of Khurāsān, but these events only influenced the political situation for a short time and had little influence on the ethnographic situation. The territories abandoned by the Ghuzz along the Sir Daryā as well as to the north of the Caspian and Aral Seas were occupied by the Qipchaks.

[4] Djinghiz Khān, born in AD 1155 (549–550 H), died in AD 1227. Founder of the Mongol Empire.

[5] Djalāl al-Din Mangubirti, the last of the Khwārizm Shāhs, eldest son of Muhammad. Died in 628 H (AD 1231).

[6] Hūlāgū Khān, Mongol Khan of Persia (AD 1217–1265).

He settled in the north of Persia, at Marāgha, which was first of all favourable to the Nestorian Christians and Buddhists, who were numerous in his entourage. He was a Buddhist himself and his wife, Doqūz-Khātūn, was a Christian. 'The princess Doqūz-Khātūn,' observes Rashīd al-Dīn, the author of *The History of the Mongols in Persia*, 'born a Christian, constantly protected her co-religionists. Out of affection for her Hūlāgū favoured the Christians who took advantage of this time of prosperity to build churches in all the provinces under his dominion. There was always a church where the sound of bells rang at the entrance to the ōrdū[1] of Doqūz-Khātūn.' Islam was not privileged at the beginning of the Mongol period and Christianity, which had lost all hope since the religious persecutions of the Sassanid age, took heart, but at the end of the thirteenth century, Sultān Ghazān,[2] great-grandson of Hūlāgū, was converted to Islam and Christians, as well as Buddhists, were persecuted once more.

Before him, Abāqā[3] had been favourable to the Christians, like his father Hūlāgū. During his reign, converted Jews, for example the doctor Sā'd al-Dīn[4], had often won high posts at court. He became an all-powerful Prime Minister but having virtually declared war on Islam urged Arghūn,[5] son of Abāqā, to stop entrusting important posts to Muslims. When Arghūn was stricken with a serious illness of which he died, Sa'd al-Dīn was put to death, together with his most prominent co-religionists. The accession of Ghāzān Khān, son of Arghūn, in AD 1293, marked the triumph of Islam. His conversion was celebrated with great pomp and his death deeply regretted by his Persian subjects who at last felt safe under the authority of a Muslim sovereign with Shī'ite tendencies.

His son Uldjāitū[6] proclaimed himself a Shī'ite Muslim. He sent ambassadors to several foreign monarchs to inform them that he was prepared to establish relations with the whole world. As a result of these initiatives he was in correspondence with the King of Egypt, the Pope, Edward III of England and Philippe le Bel. He died while still young and was buried at Sultānīya in the sumptuous monument which was to be first his tomb (plates 136 and 137) and secondly was intended to be the tomb of the early Imams who died in Mesopotamia. However, it became his tomb again when the Arabs of Nadjat and Karbalā refused to return the remains of their saints to Persia. His son, Abū Sa'īd,[7] was only a child when he succeeded him in AD 1317 and he let jealousy and intrigue work against the great doctor and historian Rashīd al-Dīn[8] and his son who were assassinated on suspicion of having killed Sultan Uldjāitū.

At the same period the destruction of the Ismā'ili power and the lengthy un-

[1] Ordū (or Urdu) is a Turkish word meaning army and hence, as here, the place where the army is stationed, i.e. camp.
[2] Ghāzān Khān, Mongol Khān of Persia (AD 1295–1304).
[3] Abāqā, Mongol Khān of Persia, son and successor of Hūlāgū (AD 1265–1281).
[4] Sā'd al-Din al Sawī, Wazir (Minister) of Ghāzān Khān.
[5] Arghūn, Mongol Khān of Persia (AD 1281–1292).
[6] Uldjāitū Khudābanda, eighth Ilkhān of Persia, reigned from AD 1304 to 1316.
[7] Abū Sa'id, 717–736 (AD 1316–1335), son and successor of Uldjāitū Khodābanda.
[8] Rashid al-Din, historian (AD 1247–1318).

certainty of the Ilkhāns'[1] attitude to the Moslem religion had brought Persian Islam to a state of profound crisis. Nevertheless Sheikh Safī al-Dīn,[2] the ancestor of the Safawid dynasty, was then living at Ardabīl (pl. 135).

The age of the Mongol dynasties in Persia was particularly rich in historians. Their cruel deeds on their arrival perhaps inspired a wish to recount them. At the same time, the Mongol sovereigns wanted their own and their predecessors' noble deeds to be celebrated in a way acceptable to them and preserved for posterity. Djuwainī,[3] the first, wrote a history of the Mongols and their conquests up to the defeat of the Ismā'ilis with observations about their sect mainly borrowed from works found at Alamūt. Then the *Djamī'al-Tawārīkh* was composed by the celebrated Prime Minister of Sultans Ghāzān and Uldjāitū, Rashīd al-Dīn, who had at his disposal the State archives, the chronicles of previous reigns and some Chinese documents. Another remarkable Persian historian is Hamd Allāh Mustawfī Qazwīnī,[4] who published a general history of the eastern world, the *Tarīkh-i Guzīda*, and a great historical poem, the *Zafar Nāma*, a continuation of Firdawsī's *Shāh Nāma*.

It was also during this period that Iranian painting seems to have freed itself from the hitherto predominant influence of Christian and Chinese art. The numerous manuscripts with miniatures which Rashīd al-Dīn had made for his *Djamī'al-Tawārīkh* contributed greatly to artistic development in Persia.

After the death of Sultan Abū Sa'īd, who had already had great difficulty in preserving the unity of his states, the Ilkhān dynasty ceased to exist. Powerful chiefs then tried to take advantage of the troubles which followed to make themselves politically independent. The most successful were the Muzaffarids in Fārs and Kirmān who maintained their power in the south of Persia from about AD 1340 until their defeat by Tīmūr (Tamerlane) in AD 1392, and, for some time, as far as western Persia (Iraq-i Adjam) and Azerbaidjan. Azerbaidjan then passed into the hands of the Khān of the Golden Horde[5] and later to the Djalā'irid dynasty of Baghdād.[6] The east of Persia was divided between the dynasty which ruled at Herāt, the only large town in Khūrāsān which had escaped Mongol devastation, and the Sarbadār clan, a 'genuine republic of brigands', whose capital was Sabzawār. Then the end of the fourteenth century saw the advent of fresh Mongol hordes led by Tīmūr the Lame,[7] who claimed authority over Persia, basing his claim on the fact that he was a descendant of Djinghiz Khān. By about AD 1370 he had conquered Balkh. In AD 1380 he subjugated Khurāsān,

[1] The Ilkhāns, the Mongol dynasty established in Persia after the first Mongol invasion in the seventh-eighth centuries H (thirteenth-fourteenth centuries AD).

[2] Sheikh Safī al-Dīn, ancestor of the Safawids, born at Ardabīl in 650 H (1252–1253) and died in 735 H (AD 1334).

[3] Djuwainī, Persian official and historian, died at Isfahān in 651 H (AD 1253).

[4] Hamd Allāh Mustawfī Qazwīnī. Persian historian and geographer, born in 680 H (AD 1281–1282). We do not know the year of his death.

[5] The Golden Horde: a kingdom founded by the Mongols; it extended over southern Siberia and the south of Russia. It came to an end in the fifteenth century.

[6] The Djalā'irid Dynasty. A Mongol dynasty which was founded at Baghdād by Hasan Djalā'ir in 736 H (AD 1335) on the death of Sultan Abū Sa'id and dispersed in AD 1411 by the Qara-Qoyunlu dynasty.

[7] Tīmūr (Tamerlane), the Mongol Khān, founder of the second Mongol Empire (AD 1336–1405), born in 736 H. Died in 807 H.

Sīstān and Māzandēran. In AD 1383 he took western Persia, Azerbaidjan and Fārs. The greatest atrocity in this cruel campaign was the sack of Isfahān in the course of which he is reputed to have had 70,000 people beheaded. He also had all the Muzaffarid princes killed.

The well-known meeting between Tīmūr and the poet Hāfiz[1] is supposed to have taken place at Shīrāz. Hāfiz had written: 'If that cruel Turkish girl from Shīrāz agreed to take my heart in her hand, I would give Bukhārā and Samarqand for the beauty spot which adorns her cheek.' On hearing about this, Tīmūr sent for the poet: 'With my glorious sabre,' he is reputed to have said, 'I have conquered a large part of the world and destroyed thousands of towns to embellish my chief cities. And thou, thou wouldst give them away for a beauty spot?' To which Hāfiz immediately replied: 'Lord, it is because of such liberalities that Your Highness sees me in such misery.' Tīmūr was delighted by this reply and offered the poet a handsome reward, as was the custom.

Tīmūr did not reside in Persia for long, but entrusted its government to several of his sons, principally Shāh Rukh,[2] who became King of Khurāsān and Sīstān in AD 1397. Mīrān Shāh[3] reigned in Azerbaidjan. After the death of Tīmūr in AD 1405, Shāh Rukh, who reigned until AD 1447, managed to safeguard the political unity of the empire conquered by his father and tried hard to repair the damage caused by his campaigns. After him, various descendants of Tīmūr, the Timurids,[4] wrangled over the regions of Persia. The most important of them, Sultān Husain Baiqarā,[5] ruled at Herāt, his capital, over Khurāsān, Sīstān and Djurdjān (Gūrgān).

However, painters and writers had been able to work even during the desperate days of Tīmūr's reign. Some of their works have survived that troubled period, including the *Shāh Nāma* now in Cairo, which dates from AD 1393–1394, the *Kalila and Dimna* in the Bibliothèque Nationale at Paris and some manuscripts of works by Khwādju Kirmānī,[6] among them the collection of poems which was copied at Baghdād

---

[1] Hāfiz, Persian lyric poet. Born at Shīrāz c. AD 1320, died in 791 H (AD 1389), but possibly not until 792 H.

[2] Shāh Rukh, Mongol Khān, son of Tīmūr (AD 1377–1447).

[3] Mīrān Shāh, died in 810 H (AD 1414–1415).

[4] The Timurid dynasty. The history of the Timurids comprises two quite distinct periods. In the first, the empire, divided between the sons and grandsons, was soon reduced to two large States, in the west that of Mīrān Shāh, in the east that of Shāh Rukh which was at first confined to Khurāsān with the addition of Transoxiana, but after a few years included almost the whole of the domain of Timur. It was a brilliant period. Shāh Rukh tried hard to repair the ruins left by his father and encouraged intellectuals as much as possible.

In the second period, beginning with the death of Shāh Rukh, the empire disintegrated a little more each day. Every prince wanted his own kingdom. But by a bizarre contrast the renaissance which had marked the reign of Shāh Rukh continued just as brilliantly under his successors. The whole of the fifteenth century was the golden age of writers, artists and scholars. The court of Husain Baiqarā, the penultimate Timurid, was quite the equal of Shāh Rukh's.

[5] Sultan Husain Baiqarā (878–912 H) reigned at Herāt for 37 years. He conquered Khurāsān, Tukharistān, Sīstān and Māzandaran, always triumphing over his rivals, but the last eight or nine years of his life were sad. He was ill and had to fight his sons who had rebelled against him. He died going to fight the Shaiban. His son and successor, Badī al-Zāmān, was the last of the Persian Timurids.

[6] Khwādju Kirmāni, Persian poet, born at Shīrāz in 679 H (AD 1281), died at Shīrāz, probably in 753 H (AD 1352). He lived a peaceful life and was able to write for his various protectors, going to Yazd and Shīrāz, where the Muzaffarids reigned, and to Baghdād, to the court of a Djalā'irid.

in 798 H (AD 1396) by the great calligrapher Mīr 'Alī of Tabrīz and is now in the British Museum. This magnificent work was illustrated by the painter Djuna'id, a pupil of Shams al-Dīn, the same Djuna'id who also decorated the *Miscellany* in the British Museum dated 813–814 H. The works of this artist, who seems to have worked mainly for Sultan Ahmad Djalā'ir, are a magnificent introduction to Timurid art. They already possess all its essentials: harmonious composition, a satisfying balance between the actors in the scenes depicted and the framework within which they move, meticulous attention to detail, increase of the space available by raising the horizon, and so on. Although the majority of these miniatures were painted at Shīrāz, they are much less related to that town's school of painting than to the style which was established at the Djalā'irid court of Baghdād towards the end of the fifteenth century, which enabled the eminent painter and writer Dust Muhammad to declare that in fact 'modern' painting, i.e. that of his age, had its origin 'at the court of the Djalā'irids'.

The most remarkable thing about this Djalā'irid style incidentally is not the acquisition of the new qualities I have just mentioned, but the fact that it manifests the later developments of pictorial art. The Djalā'irid artists had already determined the main conventions of the Timurid miniature.

And so a school of painting appeared at the end of the fourteenth century which showed its talent in combining newly acquired formulas and creating illustrations in which the human figures still preserved a hieratic attitude but in which the landscapes escaped convention to penetrate the world of visualized dreams. The earth rises towards the sky which is studded with gold dots evoking the stars. Men and women still do not emphasize their presence.

In the relatively calm and productive post-Timurid period, artists were able to develop their talents more amply, encouraged by the sovereigns and great personages of the age. There was a flourishing production of masterpieces which illustrated many epic or episodic poems, such as the tales of famous loves, of Humāy and Humayūn, of Lailā and Madjnūn, and so on.

So it is only during the second part of the fourteenth century therefore that we can recognize Iranian tendencies in painting in Iran. Then, after a period of consolidation there came the triumphal period of the predecessors of Bihzād and of Bihzād himself. Then tradition, the taste for dreams and the movement of life combined in an atmosphere of refinement where the arid soil of the deserts of Central Asia was enamelled with delicate flowers and had silver streams meandering through it. The hunter appeared among the rocks in pursuit of some frightened gazelle. Horses galloped freely in the steppe, while noble horsemen paraded and fought as if in a tourney.

The sixteenth century was a period of intensive activity. Artists, grouped in workshops, calligraphers, painters, bookbinders and gilders, produced manuscripts the splendour of which we still admire, for example the *Būstān* of Sa'dī, illustrated by Bihzād which is preserved in the Cairo Museum, the *Shāh Nāma* of Firdawsī which belongs to the Gūlistān Palace at Teheran, the *Humāy and Humāyūn* by Khwādju Kirmānī, which is now in Vienna, and many other works scattered throughout the world (coloured plate VI).

During the latter half of the sixteenth century, skilful artists had become so numerous that miniaturists emigrated to Kābul, then to India where they settled in the courts of the Great Moguls, at first under the direction of authentically Iranian painters, 'Abd al-Samad of Shīrāz, Mīr Sayyid 'Alī of Tabrīz, Aghā Rizā of Herāt, etc. This court—Indian yet completely impregnated with the Iranian spirit—gave birth to a truer, sincerer and in any case more naturalistic art than Iranian art. It concentrated mainly on portrait studies, flower and animal studies and the interpretation of landscape.

Later, during the seventeenth century, Iranian artists tried to give painting greater and greater preciosity. The languor of their sitters' attitudes and the softness of their colours then gives their productions an air of mannered deliquescence which takes much of the original interest away from this art form.

Architecture, architectural décor and the minor arts in general particularly flourished in Iran in the Timurid period (plates 142, 143 and 144). Persian cultural influence was considerable then in the Caucasian regions and Moslem India, but not in Khurāsān where the Turkish Djaghātai literature developed in the intellectual centre of Herāt. It was propagated by Alī Shīr Nawā'i[1] at the court of Husain Baiqarā. It was at this point culturally speaking that eastern Persia began to be separated from the western half.

The events which prepared the way for the advent of the Safawid dynasty, generally considered as the national Persian dynasty *par excellence*, mainly took place in Azerbaidjan. It was in this province that the Turkoman Qara-Qoyūnlū[2] dynasty, or the Black Sheep, first settled, with Tabrīz as their capital. Under the most illustrious of its sovereigns, Djahān Shāh,[3] the great builder (plates 145, 146 and 147), its power extended over most of western Persia and as far as Herāt in the east. Then Uzūn Hasan,[4] of the Aq-Qoyūnlū,[5] or White Sheep, penetrated into Azerbaidjan after his victory over Djahān Shāh in AD 1467. He took western Persia inaugurating a series of wars with the Ottoman Turks which was to last three centuries. His successors quarrelled with the Safawid chiefs, Sheikh Haidar[6] and Sultān 'Alī, who were their close kinsmen and had acquired very great influence in Azerbaidjan by this time.

The Safawid movement originated among various Turkish tribes in which Shī'ite doctrine had been widely spread by Sūfī propaganda. The political importance they

---

[1] Mir 'Alī Shīr Nawā'i, the creator of Turki literature, one of the circle of Sultān Husain Baiqarā. *Turki* is the name given to the dialect spoken by the inhabitants of Azerbaidjan and Khurāsān who are of Turkic extraction.

[2] The Qara-Qoyūnlū dynasty. A Turkoman dynasty which ruled in western Asia from 777 to 873 H (AD1275–1468).

[3] Djahān Shāh. Third sovereign of the Qara-Qoyūnlū dynasty, died in 872 H (AD 1467).

[4] Uzūn Hasan, king of the Aq-Qoyūnlū dynasty, 857 H (AD 1454), died at Tabrīz in 882 H (AD 1478).

[5] The Aq-Qoyūnlū dynasty, founded in 838 H (AD 1434–1435). Its possessions were united with those of the Safawids in 920 H (AD 1514).

[6] Sheikh Haidar, died in 898 H (AD 1488), was the son of Sheikh Djuna'id of Ardabil, grandfather of Shāh Ismā'il, the founder of the Safawid dynasty. Sheikh Haidar married Halima Begum, daughter of Uzūn Hasan, who became the mother of Sultān 'Alī, Sayyid Ibrāhim and Shāh Ismā'il.

acquired under the founder of the Safawid dynasty,[1] Shāh Ismā'īl,[2] could be seen as a reaction against the official Sunnite doctrine of the Aq and Qara Qoyūnlūs, a reaction which was not unwelcome to the peoples of western Persia who were always ready to show their opposition to a foreign power. Hence the national Persian character of the Safawid dynasty, although its leaders were Turks. Shāh Abbās the Great had not a drop of Persian blood in his veins.

Shāh Ismā'īl was a sixth-generation descendant of Sheikh Safī al-Dīn of Ardabīl and a spiritual leader like his predecessors. There were no omens to foretell his extraordinary future. There were three brothers whose father Sheikh Haidar had been killed in fighting the army of the Shīrwān Shāh, Sultān Ya'qūb,[3] son of Uzūn Hasan of the Aq-Qoyūnlū dynasty; their uncle wanted to get rid of them, but they were his sister's sons, which might have caused some complications. He had them incarcerated and guarded in the fortress of Istakhr according to some authorities and on an island in Lake Van in what is now Turkish Armenia according to others, but they survived and were able to take refuge at Lahidjān in Gīlān where they had many supporters.

At the age of thirteen Ismā'īl left this town where he appears to have lived incognito. He only had an escort of eleven men with him, but as he advanced—even before he reached Ardabīl which had always been the town of the Sūfīs—many supporters had joined him. He stayed on the shores of the Caspian Sea for some time, hunting and fishing, while groups of men from all parts came to offer him their services. When he had collected a small band, supported by his father's disciples and the Turkish tribes which had embraced his cause, he threw his men against the king of Shīrwān who had killed his grandfather, Sheikh Djuna'id.[4] His rallying cry, 'Allah! Allah! 'Alī is the friend of Allah!' spurred them on. The Shīrwān Shāh was killed and all the members of his family.

A Venetian merchant who happened to be in Gīlān at the time wrote: 'The Sūfī is loved and revered by his people like a god, and especially by his soldiers, many of whom came forward to fight without weapons, believing that their master Ismā'īl would know how to protect them in battle . . .'. The same merchant added: 'In Persia the name of god is forgotten and only that of Ismā'īl is pronounced.'

Ismā'īl had always professed the strictest form of the Shi'ite doctrine. As soon as he was crowned in Tabrīz in AD 1502 he had this doctrine proclaimed as the state religion. He abandoned his title of 'Sheikh of the Sūfīs of Ardabīl' and, in his capacity as Shāh of Persia, made Tabrīz his capital. He conquered Shīrwān (i.e. the area of which Baku in Soviet Azerbaidjan is now the capital), Azerbaidjan and western Persia. In AD 1508 his power extended as far as Herāt to the east and to the west as far as Baghdād, where he seized the holy tombs of Nadjat and Karbalā.

Shāh Ismā'īl maintained good relations with Sultān Husain Baiqarā whose court at Herāt remained an artistic and cultural centre until his death. But two powerful

---

[1] The last sovereign of the Safawid dynasty was Abbās III. The dynasty ended with the accession of Nadir Shāh in AD 1737.

[2] Shāh Ismā'il assumed the title of Shāh in 908 H (AD 1502). He died in 930 H (AD 1524), at Ardabīl.

[3] Sultan Ya'qūb, son of Uzūn Hasan the Aq-Qoyūnlū.

[4] Sheikh Djuna'id, father of Sultān Haidar, was killed in 860 H (AD 1456).

enemies were watching him, ever ready to take advantage of a favourable opportunity to attack him: the Uzbeks[1] and the Turks. Shāh Ismāʿīl defeated the Uzbeks at Marw in a battle during which their chief, Shaibanī Khān,[2] was killed, but he suffered a reverse at the hands of the Turks, who took possession of Tabrīz as well as Mesopotamia and western Armenia as far as Mōsul. However, the conquest of Georgia somewhat relieved his chagrin. He died in AD 1524 at Ardabīl where the tombs of his family were.

The Safawid dynasty lasted until AD 1736, i.e. until the death of Abbās III,[3] grandson of Shāh Sultān Husain.[4] Its religious and cultural traditions gave it the character of a national dynasty, although its leaders, as I have already mentioned, were Turks. Moreover its long duration and the country's isolation in religious matters considerably aided the emergence of a genuine Persian nation, capable of surviving, as it did, the troubled period of the eighteenth century, and asserting itself more and more afterwards. However, throughout their dynasty the Safawid monarchs had to reckon with the existence of virtually independent governors and the tribes from which the nobles and high officials of the country came. The civil and military administration never acquired the cohesion and continuity which would have been desirable. Government authority could only be maintained in the interior by extreme severity of the kind practised by Abbās Shāh I. For the same reason the Safawid frontiers to east and west were never very stable. The eastern part of Khurāsān and the regions situated further south, long detached from western Persia culturally speaking, did not become Safawid again. Balkh and Marw came under almost continuous Uzbek domination. Only the west of Khurāsān as far as Herāt, the Sanctuary of Mashhad and a part of Sīstān, belonged to Safawid Persia.

To the west the Ottoman Turks and the Persians were in almost perpetual strife over the possession of a strip of territory which ran from the Persian Gulf to Georgia. In the sixteenth century the Turks had the advantage and occupied Mesopotamia, Iraq and Azerbaidjan. Under Shāh Abbās the majority of this territory was reconquered, but the recapture of Baghdād by Murād IV[5] in AD 1628 put an end to Persian supremacy in the Tigris valley; however, Iran retained power over Azerbaidjan and parts of Armenia and Georgia.

The majority of the Safawid sovereigns had very long reigns. Shāh Tahmāsp I ruled

---

[1] Abū'l-Khair, sovereign of the Uzbeks and the originator of their empire, was a descendant of the youngest son of Djushi, the Shaiban, and was born in 816 H (AD 1412). He was proclaimed Khān in 832 H. In 834 H he took Urgandj (Djurdjāniya), in 850 H Sighnat and Uzkand, in Khwārizm, but was defeated by the Kalmuks in 861 H. Towards 870 H (AD 1465–1466) the split reputedly took place by which the inhabitants of the steppes in the real sense of the word, afterwards called Kazakhs, separated from the rest of the people. The year of the death of Abū'l-Khair is given as AD 1468. The empire he created was re-established after a brief interruption by his grandson Muhammad Shaibanī and attained unexpected grandeur.

[2] The Shaibanī Khān Abū'l-Fath Muhammad (also called Shāhī Begh) was born in 885 H (AD 1451). He conquered Transoxiana, over which he reigned from 906 H to 915 H (AD 1509–1510). He died in 915 H (AD 1510).

[3] Shāh Abbās III, a Safawid prince, born in 1145 H (AD 1732), died at Isfahān in 1149 H (AD 1736).

[4] Shāh Sultān Husain, Shāh of Persia (AD 1694–1722).

[5] Murad IV the Ottoman Sultān reigned from AD 1623 to AD 1640.

for fifty-two years, from AD 1524 to AD 1576. Personally this fanatically cruel monarch was not very attractive, but it was during his reign that the art of Muslim Persia seems to have reached its apogee. The famous painter Bihzād,[1] who had worked at the court of the Timurid Husain Baiqarā, then at Tabrīz, for Shāh Ismā'īl, directed his studies of calligraphy, painting and binding until his death in AD 1537 and trained artists such as Qāsim 'Alī, Aghā Mīrak and Muzaffar 'Alī. The reign of Shāh Tahmāsp also saw the production in the north of the country of the carpets with hunting scenes (coloured pl. IV) of which one of the most magnificent, perhaps the most famous, is preserved in the Poldi Pezzoli Museum, Milan. As a result of a lengthy visit to his court by the Emperor of India, Humāyūn,[2] a new school of painting, directly inspired by Iranian art, came into being at the court of the Grand Moguls.

However, the most brilliant reign of the Safawid period was that of Shāh Abbās I,[3] grandson of Tahmāsp I. He inflicted a bloody defeat 'from which few escaped' on the Uzbeks who had seized Mashhad. He defeated the Ottomans near Tabrīz, then signed a treaty with them in which he guaranteed to send an annual tribute of a hundred loads of silk. A few years later he captured Mosūl from them. He occupied Georgia and wrested the islands of the Persian Gulf, including Hormuz, from the Portuguese. Transferring his capital from Qazwīn to Isfahān, he built superb monuments there, created vast avenues, planted gardens and turned it into a splendid royal town (pl. 155). He assembled skilled artists and craftsmen, and actually removed the whole population of Djulfa on the Araxes and had a town built for it in a suburb of Isfahān which is still called Djulfa. He built roads, bridges, palaces and caravanserais throughout Persia and ensured security of communications by the pursuit and destruction of brigands. He encouraged foreign establishments, both religious and commercial, and maintained close relations with the European powers.

The first, second and fifth sovereigns of the Safawid dynasty, Ismā'īl, Tahmāsp and Abbās, were really princes of great stature. The others were merely cruel and fanatical.

Towards AD 1709 a rebel Sunnite movement came into being at Kandahār in Afghanistan. Shāh Sultān Husain was unable to crush it and it thus became the origin of the Afghan State. In AD 1722 the army of Mīr Mahmūd the Afghan[4] captured Isfahān and was subsequently master of Persia for some eight years. The Safawid princes were all massacred, except one son of Shāh Sultān Husain, Tahmāsp[5] (pl. 179),

---

[1] Bihzād, the famous Persian miniaturist, in whose work we find a perfect sense of composition and colour, as well as remarkable realism. He died in 942 H (AD 1536–1537) and was buried at Tabrīz.

[2] Nāsir al-Dīn Humāyūn, eldest son of Sultān Bābur, was born in AD 1508 in the citadel of Kābul, became Emperor of India in AD 1530 and died at Delhi in AD 1556 as the result of falling from the roof of his library.

[3] Shāh Abbās I, called the Great, a King of Persia of the Safawid dynasty, son and successor of Muhammad Khudābanda, was born in 965 H (AD 1557), and died at Farahābād, in Māzandarān, in 1038 H (AD 1628) after a reign of 43 years.

[4] During the reign of Shāh Sultān Husain, the Afghan Mahmūd, son of Mīr Wais, seeing the weakness into which the Safawid monarchy had fallen, invaded Persia and took Isfahān. The Shāhinshāh abdicated and crowned Mahmūd with his own hands. Thus it was that the chieftain of an Afghan tribe became Shāh of Persia.

[5] Tahmāsp II, the third son of Shāh Sultān Husain, was proclaimed hereditary prince during the siege of Isfahān by the Afghans 1135 (AD 1772), but escaped at the head of 600 men and tried un-

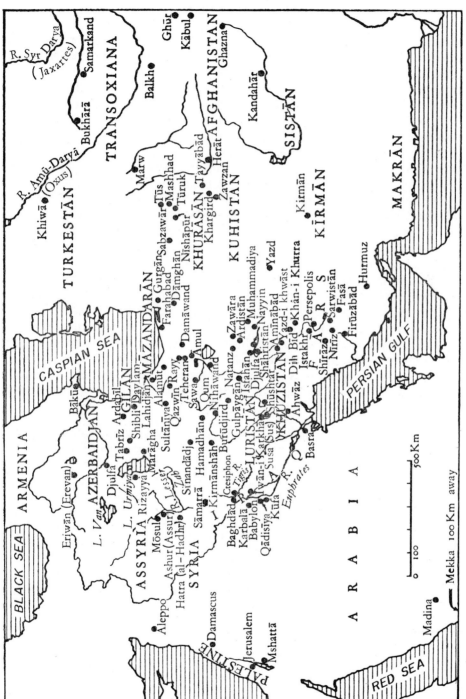

MAP V: ISLAMIC IRAN

who managed to flee and took refuge on the shores of the Caspian Sea where a tribal chieftain of Khurāsān, Nādir Qulī, the future Nādir Shāh,[1] came to offer him his services.

At this time Peter the Great of Russia concluded an agreement with the Turks with a view to an eventual partition of Persia. While waiting for this programme to be realized, each of the two confederates took what they especially coveted. For the Turks, this was Eriwān, in Transcaucasia, and Hamadhān. Peter the Great took Dārband and Bākū on the western shore of the Caspian Sea.

Nādir Khān, crowned in AD 1736 after deposing the last Safawid, Husain II, led his armies from Baghdād to Bukhārā and Delhi, in India. He was assassinated in AD 1747.

While his son Shāh Rukh[2] ruled over Khurāsān, an honourable man, Qarīm Khān Zand[3] who modestly called himself the *Waqil*, or representative (deputy), succeeded him in AD 1750, re-united Persia and gave it some twenty years of peace. He built largely and well, although architecture and the arts of his period in general (plates 163 and 167) had nothing very original about them (plates 164, 165 and 166).

His death in 1779 was followed by a period of troubles and dynastic squabbles between the Zand family, that of Karīm Khān, and the important Qādjār tribe which came from Māzandarān. One of the Qādjār chiefs, Agha Muhammad Khān, took advantage of these troubles to bring the entire empire under his authority. Enthroned at Teheran in 1796, he was assassinated during the following year. He was the first of the Qādjār dynasty which lasted until 1925.[4]

The founder of the national dynasty which now rules Iran was crowned with the name of Riza Shāh Pahlawī on August 25, 1926. His farsighted but severe government

---

successfully to raise troops in Qazwīn. He kept a footing in Māzandarān with the support of Fath 'Alī Khān, chief of the Qādjārs, and was rejoined there by the future Nādir Shāh who brought him 5,000 men. After the assassination of Fath 'Alī by Nādir, the latter was appointed commander in chief of the Persian troops, took Mashhad, Mihmān Dust and Mūrcha Khurt and entered Isfahān where Tahmāsp followed him and rewarded him for his services by granting him the provinces of Khurāsān, Sīstān, Kirmān and Māzandarān with the title of Sultān. Encouraged by the victories of his lieutenant, Tahmāsp decided to take command of the army, but was defeated by the Turks near Hamadhān in 1144 H (AD 1731). In the following year he made peace in return for ceding Transcaucasia, with the exception of Tabrīz and the region to the south-east of that town. Nādir protested against the conclusion of this treaty. He marched on Isfahān, seized Tahmāsp and sent him as a prisoner to Khurāsān, putting on the throne a son of the Shāh aged eight months, under the name of Shāh Abbās III. When this son died, Nādir had himself proclaimed King of Persia in 1148 H (AD 1736). But in 1160 H (AD 1747) he was in turn assassinated in his camp, near Fathābād, by the Qādjār and Afshār chiefs aided and abetted by his bodyguards.
[1] Nādir Qulī, the future Nādir Shāh, belonged to the Turkoman tribe of the Afshārs, a part of which had settled in northern Khurāsān. He was born in 1100 H (AD 1688). On entering the service of Tahmāsp II, he was surnamed Tahmāsp Qulī Khān.
The Safawids succumbed to the force of an Afghan invasion in AD 1722. This new domination lasted barely fifteen years. It was replaced by that of Nādir Shāh who made the whole of Asia tremble.
[2] Shāh Rukh the Afshārid. 1161 H. He was deposed and blinded in 1163 H. His second accession (djūlūs) was in 1163 H and his third in 1168 H. He was finally deposed in 1210 H.
[3] Muhammad Karim Khān Zand, of a Lur family, had himself called Wakīl, i.e. the deputy, i.e. the Regent, but was in reality King of Persia. He reigned from 1163 H to 1193 H.
[4] Qādjār dynasty (1876–1925). The last sovereign of the dynasty, Ahmad Shāh, was dethroned in 1342 H.

favoured the modernization of the country, to which his energy contributed a remarkable impetus. The present Shāhinshāh is his son, H.M. Muhammad Riza Shāh.
Matured by the difficulties which Iran underwent as a result of the war and the
deposition of H.M. Riza Shāh by the Allies in 1941, he may justifiably hope to
realize the great projects he has conceived to ensure the advancement of his country
along the path of progress and happiness or, at least, social justice.

CHAPTER 10

ISLAMIC IRAN

IRST of all one must explain how a pre-Islamic Iranian monument differs from other Iranian monuments of the Islamic period. It must be clearly understood that it is not a question of comparing a Sassanid palace with a mosque on the Arabian plan, in other words with an imported type of edifice imposed on Iran which disappeared after a few centuries of use, but with monuments of purely Iranian origin —for example comparing the palace of Fīrūzābād or Sarwistān with the Masdjid-i Djum'ā at Isfahān or the Timurid madrasa[1] of Khargird. Each of these four buildings is an arrangement of ivans and domes on a square plan, the same sort of ivans and the same domes. What is different is not the construction nor the forms, nor even the plan, for there is not really much difference between that of the palace of Fīrūzābād and that of the Timurid madrasa of Khargird, but the appearance, the dress in which Islam clothed the Sassanid monuments, the spirit with which it attempted to imbue Iranian architecture, as with all the peoples it dominated.

Muslim architecture has long passed for a simple aggregate of constructional procedures and decorative formulae adapted by Islam from the techniques of the peoples under its domination. The undeniable originality of its productions seemed to be the result of the unification of these various techniques and the unification itself the result of their adaptation to the special needs of the Moslem world. If this were so the history of the origins of Islamic architecture would be no more than the enumeration of the various origins of pre-existing elements, the observation of the successive stages of the automatic process of assimilation. The whole point for the historian would then be to weigh up definitively the contribution of each civilization in order to deduce, as has been done, that Muslim architecture was mainly Iranian, or Egyptian, or Byzantine, or even Roman, or more simply still that it was Coptic in Egypt, Byzantine in Syria, Iranian in Iran, etc., which, when all is said and done, would reduce it to nothing.

But today the notion of the study of an art merely from the material point of view is no longer accepted. Art is not stone, brick, words or tricks of the trade; it is above all the reflection of the artist's soul, the visible expression of the forces which drive him, and architectural technique, like language, is only a means of expression, an instru-

---

[1] 'Madrasa' is a form of the Arabic verb 'darasa' which means to read, to study. At the beginning of the fourth century it merely meant a private school for religious studies, but became a powerful instrument of political and religious propaganda under the official control of the State.

ment in the service of the mind. In the same way that what first matters in literature is the writer, what counts in architecture is the architect. What counts in the architecture of a people is the collective soul of that people. To us Greek architecture is not so much a certain way of building as the visible expression of the harmonious soul of Greece; the origin and development of Roman architecture lie completely, in the qualities of order and power, in the massive force and utilitarianism which characterize the Roman mind; Byzantine architecture is the complex reflection of the Helleno-Asiatic soul of Byzantium; that of our great European cathedrals is an elevation, a prayer.

This was equally true of Muslim architecture. The spirit which governed the use of decorative formulae and the methods of construction peculiar to them characterizes it better than its borrowings, all the more so as we have to do here with an art which never felt a great love for the professional side of its work. In effect Islam was not a great constructional force both in the sense that frequently it constructed deplorably and in the sense that it did not invent or appreciably improve many architectural forms or systems of construction. From this point of view no Muslim monument is comparable with the Parthenon, the Pantheon at Rome or the cathedral at Amiens. The mosque itself is no more than a complex of borrowings. Plan, minaret, mihrab and minbar are found in the contemporary architectures of the Arab conquest, as are the features of its decoration, polychromy, the use of polygons and the decoration of monuments with inscriptions.

This was only to be expected. Completely lacking architectural knowledge and traditions, coming to this art with empty hands so to speak, Islam, when it had to take over the administration of its vast empire, meet its needs and build in its turn, willy nilly, took over haphazardly whatever of the scanty architectural methods around it came into its hands and used them arbitrarily, without even being in a position to choose or wanting to choose. At first it used all types of vault, Syrian, Roman, Byzantine and Persian, the flat arch, the column, the pilaster, brick, stone, marble, mosaic, painting and sculpture, every method of construction, every method of decoration in use in western Asia and showed no preferences. It ordered, it 'gave commissions' and did not interfere but it soon educated itself and rapidly eliminated from its borrowings those which proved in practice foreign to its nature or too inflexible to bend to the exigencies of its taste. It became an architect but remained not much of a constructor. The ideal of the true technician, to build skilfully, for eternity, was always foreign to it: it was not interested in the duration of its monuments. Even more, it always felt a kind of sacred horror of the idea of duration: 'The proof of God,' it said, 'is in the perishable nature of that which is not Him.' In a certain sense no art has been more independent of its technique, none was more purely and deliberately intellectual. Consequently it is pointless to suppose that its nature can be explained purely by seeking its origins in the imitation of foreign styles of architecture. Its true origins lie all heart and soul in Islam; they emanate from a certain conception of the universe which is peculiar to it and which we find at the back of all the manifestations of its thought.

Some of the weaker, less courageous Arabs let themselves be seduced by the hope

135. THE TOMB OF SHEIKH SAFĪ AL-DĪN
Ardabīl. Middle of fourteenth century.
This tower, built over the tomb of Sheikh Safī al-Dīn, the founder of the Safawid dynasty, was probably built by his son Sadr al-Dīn. The motif which is the basis of the decoration of the drum comes from the Arabic way of writing Allah. This angular script, which recalls archaic Chinese seals, first occurs as a decorative motif on the monuments of the first Il-khans and thus may well be a case of Far Eastern influence.

136. THE MAUSOLEUM OF THE MONGOL SULTĀN ULDJĀITŪ KHUDĀBANDA
Sultānīya. Beginning of fourteenth century.
This building, which is an octagon on a square base and is entirely of brick, is surmounted by a magnificent dome. It was built during the reign of Sultān Uldjāitū between 703 H and 716 H (i.e. between AD 1304 and 1316) and was intended to receive the remains of the first Shī'ite imams; in fact it became the tomb of Uldjāitū. Round the base of the drum of the dome we again see an inscription frieze in this angular Chinoiserie style.

137. DETAIL OF THE DECORATION OF THE ABOVE MAUSOLEUM
This geometrical decoration is executed in a mosaic of glazed dressed bricks coloured turquoise blue, cobalt, black and white. The bands of geometric decoration which frame the doorway here play the same role as the bands of moulding round the doors of Hellenistic temples.

138. FUNERARY TOWER OF ALA'AL-DĪN AT WARĀMĪN
End of thirteenth century.
This monument was finished in the year 688 of the Hegira (i.e. in AD 1289). The goffered drum is a development of the principle which we see in the flanges of the Gunbad-i Qābūs (pl. 123) and occurs also in tomb towers at Radqān and Rayy.

139. THE FRIDAY MOSQUE AT WARĀMĪN
Fourteenth century.
Detail of the porch. The decoration, like that of Sultānīya, consisted of a combination of bricks and glazed faience mosaics. This mosque, which was begun in the reign of Sultān Uldjāitū Khudā-banda, was finished in the reign of his son and successor Abū Said in 722 H (AD 1322). However, the great inscription on the base of the dome bears the date 726 H (AD 1325–1326). The mosque was restored in 815 H (AD 1412). The ruinous state of the stalactite moulding in the vault of the porch casts an interesting light on the development of the stalactite from the Sassanian squinch arch.

140. REMAINS OF A CARAVANSERAI AT SARCHIM
First half of fourteenth century.
Remains of the porch of a Mongol caravanserai erected between Tabrīz and Sultānīya dated to 733 H (AD 1332–1333).

141. DOME OF THE FRIDAY MOSQUE AT WĀRAMĪN
Fourteenth century.
This dome, which has lost or never had its facing of glazed faience, belongs to the mosque shown in plate 139.

136

137

139

140

141

143

144

145

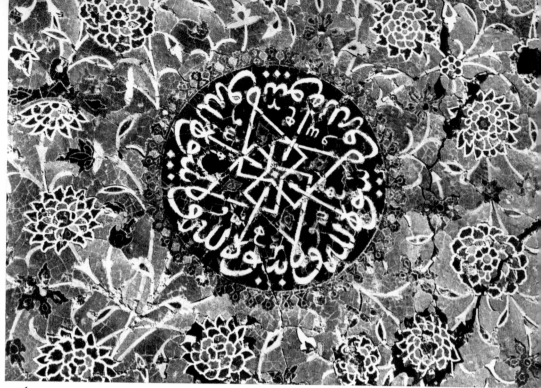

146

147

142. DETAIL OF GLAZED FAIENCE DECORATION IN BRICK AND STONE
Tīmūrid period.
Alternating geometrical and floral motifs.

143. DECORATIVE MOTIF AT ARDABĪL
Tīmūrid period.
Decorative motif placed after its completion on the mausoleum of Sheikh Safī al-Dīn (Cf. Pl. 135).

144. EXTERNAL DECORATION OF THE DO DAR MADRASA (THE MADRASA OF THE TWO GATES) AT MASHHAD
Tīmūrid period.
This decoration is dated to 843 H (AD 1439–1440).

145. INTERIOR DECORATION OF THE BLUE MOSQUE AT TABRĪZ
Fifteenth century.
This monument was built by the Tīmūrid Sultān Djahān Shāh and bears the date 870 H (fifteenth century AD). The plate shows in an interesting way the different uses of decorative script: firstly, on the right an elaborate naskhī inscription frieze (Cf. pl. 147); secondly the rows of medallions in the decoration of the side wall of the ivan, which contain inscriptions which suggest the development of nastalīq; and thirdly, the stylized pseudo-Kūfic of the lozenges which lie between those medallions to which allusion has already been made.

146. DETAIL OF DECORATION IN THE BLUE MOSQUE AT TABRĪZ
Fifteenth century.
Floral decoration around a mosaic medallion of glazed faience.

147. DECORATIVE INSCRIPTION FROM THE BLUE MOSQUE AT TABRĪZ
Fifteenth century.
The floral decoration is carved on a block of crystal brought from Lake Urmiya.

148. THE PALACE OF THE ʿALĪ QAPŪ AT ISFAHĀN
Tīmūrid and Safawid periods.
Isfahān, which had long been the capital of Iran, was abandoned by the Safawid dynasty. However, Shāh Abbās decided to re-establish his capital there and installed himself in the palace of the ʿAlī Qapū. Subsequently he completely transformed this residence; he retained only the Tīmūrid foundations and had the various storeys built and decorated, as we see in plate 149.

L

of an easier existence in one of the richer more fertile countries; they became Syrians or Iranians, but the majority remained faithful to the old ideal of Bedouin life. These, whose way of life had remained unchanged, constituted the conquering armies, and later, as military leaders, governors of provinces and caliphs were the first patrons of Muslim architecture and thus are especially important to our enquiry. How and why these 'people from the age of ignorance', as their converted Muslim descendants contemptuously termed them, these primitive shepherds, the poorest of men, these 'illiterates', these Bedouins, were able to exert such a strong influence on an art which up to that time had been completely foreign to them, is a problem which presses for a solution. Let me suggest an answer. . . .

The Bedouin is a shepherd and a nomad. Depending on the season he leads his camels and his sheep from the heart of the desert to the edge of the rich populous countries where his tenacious love of liberty prevents him from settling, where only extreme poverty induces him to stay permanently. When the spring rains have covered the earth with a mantle of new grass, he makes his way via a succession of pastures to arid solitudes where his flocks, sated with sappy plants, can live far from watering places and where he himself feeds on the milk of his camels. It is the season of abundance, but the sun very soon dries up all vegetation and the black tents once more approach inhabited regions. The sheep are then sold, exchanged for cereals, fabrics, weapons and jewels for the women. Sometimes, however, the desert experiences periods of absolute aridity which may last for several consecutive years or again particularly violent rains suddenly transform the valleys into broad rivers which carry away encampments and livestock. Sometimes the sun is prematurely fierce, sometimes raiders and epidemics decimate the flocks. Then comes destitution, misery. Then, the weakest go to the wall. There are frequent murders, and interminable vendettas go on which are sometimes ended only by the annihilation of one of the adversaries or the disappearance of whole tribes. There is little charm and friendliness in this life, whatever Renan[1] may have said, but no lack of privations, suffering, brigandage and bloody quarrels.

As regards morals the Bedouin is the end-product of the harsh conditions of his existence. He is an anarchist, in the strict sense of a man without a master, undisciplined, fiercely individualist, as we still see today, as he always was, except during the early heroic period of Islam, during which an ardent fanaticism managed to bring together, if not to unite completely, the ungovernable sons of the desert.

The Bedouin is a villain, let us face it, but his way of life, by forcing him to live in isolation, also forces him to have indefatigable energy. His individualism, while exaggerating his pride in freedom, develops his native gifts of courage, generosity and hospitality. He is generous to the degree of prodigality, of improvidence, of absurdity. But his most remarkable quality, the one which served him best in his struggles against Byzantium, and Iran, and enabled him to defeat better armed and organized enemies, is his *sabr*, his 'patience'. This indomitable tenacity developed in him in his daily

---

[1] 'In the whole history of ancient civilization, I do not think there can be a more charming, likeable and more animated picture than that of Arab life before Islam.'

fight against hostile nature—the glacial cold of the nights, fatigue, hunger, the suffo-
cating south wind—the wild beasts of the desert and other men. This impassioned
resistance, the pre-condition of his liberty, has fashioned him 'a temperament of steel,
at once supple and resistant, which enables him to live and prosper in a climate where
everything except the Bedouin and his camel wilts and is endangered'. To confirm this,
one must re-read the marvellous Bedouin poems of the pre-Islamic period, the two
hamāsa or 'collections of bravery', by Abū Tāmman and al-Buhturī, the Mu'allaqāt,
and especially the incomparable poem by al-Shanfarā, the celebrated *Lāmīyat al-'Arab*:
'... How many times, have I not crossed on my two legs these desert plains, bare as the
back of a buckler, where the caravans do not pass ... How many times, on one of those
cold nights during which the hunter burns his bow and arrows to warm himself, how
many times have I not set off through the gloom and the rain, with hunger, cold and
terror for company ... How many times, on one of those days ... when the air,
turned liquid, forms visible waves on the ground, when the vipers wriggle on the sand
like glowing coals, how many times then have I not exposed my head to the sun with
no other protection save a ragged cloak ... I set off in the morning ... like a wolf with
lean flanks and grey hair whom one solitude leads to another solitude. He starts at
break of day, wrapping up his hunger in the folds of his entrails, trotting against the
wind, leaping into the bottom of ravines and trotting harder than ever ... If you see
me, O devouring cares, exposed like the sand snake to the burning sun, my body
scarcely covered and my feet bare, know that I am the lieutenant of patience, that I
wear his cloak without shedding my hyena's heart and that steadfastness takes the
place of sandals for me....'

    The knowledge which these men sought to acquire was almost entirely confined to
genealogy, which they had not learned to distinguish from the history of their race,
knowledge of the stars which guided them during their nocturnal marches and to
which they attributed an influence on the rains, i.e. on the state of the pastures, and
consequently on their material living conditions, but especially and above all knowledge
of the grammatical structure and rich vocabulary of their language. They had a passion
for eloquence and poetry; they raised to the zenith the subtle taste for elegant con-
cision as well as rhythm and the musical arrangement of words.

    From the artistic point of view there was very little to show before Islam, and even
if we limit our definition of the word 'art' to its plastic expressions, it is clear that there
was no such thing as Bedouin art.

    It was not, as Ibn Khaldūn has unfairly said, that the men of the desert have always
had 'a great aversion to the arts': they loved beautiful weapons, jewels and fine fabrics
which they bartered for the products of their pastoral industry at the frontiers of Syria
and Iran. When the period during which they scrupulously observed the rules of
simplicity which the prophet and his immediate successors had prescribed had passed
and when the possession of vast empires with luxurious habits began to have its
natural influence upon them, the leaders of Islam began to construct towns and buildings as sumptuous as those of their predecessors and showed a striking taste for architecture. As soon as they were placed in favourable circumstances, their open minds and

receptive intelligence enabled them to assimilate with ease the cultural developments of the most advanced civilizations. But before Islam, in their deserts, their way of life did not include the practice of the arts. They were neither sculptors, nor painters, nor architects. There is nothing artistic about their weaving. Their *wasm* or signs of ownership which they engraved on the boundary stones marking the limits of their grazing land have extremely rudimentary designs and their only known temple, the Ka'ba[1] at Mekka, was no more than an enclosure with low walls covered by a light roof of palms.

However, these clumsy draughtsmen, ineffective builders and inartistic weavers were able to raise their own kind of monuments to the memory of their heroes and their exploits—noble and sumptuous poems which throw enough light on the artistic ideal of the Arab soul to make a glance at pre-Islamic Bedouin poetry not out of place in this work.

As a matter of fact this poetry differs so much from our own, both in its ends and its means, that it is quite difficult for us to appreciate it at its true worth. To us poetry is primarily the expression of a poetic sentiment; moreover this poetic sentiment is expressed in rhythmic language. But the second condition, the rhythm, has become of minor importance. We admit without blinking that prose poems can exist. With us, poetry is no more than a state of mind, so to speak, or even a habit of mind. The word 'poet' no longer has the sense of composer of poems; it has become roughly synonymous with lover of poetic sentiments.

Arabic poetry is something quite different. It puts rhythm in the front rank of a poem's qualities. Then come ingenuity and subtlety of form, and only lastly the subject and originality of thought which please us so much. It never forgets that it is born of the camel-driver's chant, which is its most ancient form. Later on when Arabic poetry discovered the *hidjā* (satire), which played an important role in the public life of the Arabs and was considered as a dangerous, magical weapon (when it was directed against an enemy it was reputed to paralyse his ability to act), when it discovered the battle-song, love and sorrow, the description of nature, the praise of heroes, it preserved the essential characteristics of its origins, rhythm and the musical arrangement of words.

We come across it again in the *qasīda* which finally absorbed all the other modes. Its general schema is so strict and the dominance of form carried so far that people have felt able to criticize its rigid framework and say that 'in this form, poetry, which was already far from overflowing with ideas, became still emptier'. But this is to judge an art which is not to our taste by our own taste.

The *qasīda*, like the poetic modes which preceded it, thus places the rhythm, sonority and beauty of diction before all other qualities. But, in this it was both more skilful and more precious than they—since it added ingenuity and subtlety of mind which the Arabs had always considered as particularly pleasing, to become a poetry of courtliness and ostentation. It was for this reason, and not out of incapacity or insensitivity, that they arrived at a conception of poetry the quintessence of which is constant renewal

---

[1] The Ka'aba, situated approximately in the middle of the Great Mosque at Mekka, is a sort of international sanctuary and the centre of a great annual pilgrimage.

within a restricted framework, gradually reduced to the dimensions of a few subjects which have become traditional. To find a new way of depicting the sadness of abandoned encampments, the joys of vengeance or the charms of the beloved, to juxtapose these vignettes without even bothering to find a connection between them, to make of a poem an iridiscent collection of decorative panels with as studied, ingenious, varied and colourful a technique as possible; this was what art meant to the pre-Islamic Arab poets, a pure intellectual pastime.

This is the point I have been trying to make. Is it not the case that the highly particular direction of this aim, which incidentally we find in even more accentuated form in Arabic music, exactly characterize the works of Muslim art? They both manifest the same decorative bias, one might say, and lead to the same result: to the extent that a poet was able to adorn traditional subjects with new images and the attraction of fine language, he had done the work of an artist in Arabia; to the extent that an architect could adorn the traditional shapes of a mosque in a new and sumptuous way, he did the work of an artist in Islam. But how on earth could there be 'traditional' shapes for mosques before Muhammadan art began?

We frequently—much too frequently—hear about 'the origin of the mosque', as if only a single type of this kind of building had existed. On the contrary it would be possible to cite a fairly large number of different kinds, beginning of course with the Arabian mosque, a development of the court of the typical house of the Hidjāz,[1] that of the Prophet Muhammad at Madīna, for example. It was nothing more than an area of ground enclosed by walls, one of which had an arcade along it roofed with palm-leaves. The idea was so crude and primitive that one cannot imagine the proud Arabs faced with old and brilliant civilizations which they had conquered imposing or even suggesting a temple of this kind. It is, moreover, clear that at the time of the conquest the ritual prayers were generally said in the open air or in already existing buildings which may or may not have been modified for the purpose.

As for the buildings later used as mosques, the majority of them belonged to the contemporary architecture of the conquered countries. In Iran for example they were (a) the chahār-tāq, i.e. the dome on four pillars which covered the fire altar in the Zoroastrian temples (figs. 155, 157 a and b, 166, 167 and plate 106); (b) the ivan of Khurāsān, the high, deep porch introduced by the Parthians into the west of Iran where it had become the audience hall of the Sassanid palace (figs. 137, 138, 160, 162, 164, 165 and plates 90 and 110); and (c) the square, domed hall preceded by an ivan which is found in Fārs from the first years of the Sassanid period, and the gallery with a dome in its centre, as still partially exists in the palace of Shāpūr II at ivan-i Karkha, in Khūzistān.

These monuments, therefore, which all existed in the Sassanid period, had such a long past by the time they were used as mosques and a fortiori when they became models of mosques that one could have spoken of their traditional shapes long before the appearance of Islam. It is possible that the chahār-tāq of Yazd-i-khwāst was con-

---

[1] The Hidjāz is an Arabian province, on the Red Sea. The Yemen, formerly a province, is now nominally an Imamate, in the south-west of the Arabian peninsula. The Hadhramaut, a province of Arabia, is situated to the east of the Yemen and to the north-east of Aden.

verted into a mosque even before there was any question of the Arabian type of mosque in Iran.

Not until much later did 'the infection of the foreigner' and the normal development of luxury enrich the initial formula of the Arabic mosque. It was perhaps the conscious imitation of Christian basilicas which gave more splendour to the primitive shelter turned hypostyle hall. It was not until nearly a century after the Hegira that someone had the idea of indicating the direction of Mekka by means of a niche, the mihrāb, perhaps a reminiscence of the apse of the basilica. Even in the middle of the second century of the Hegira when the Abbāsid sovereigns undertook the construction of large mosques of the Arabian type in Iran they could only supply a schematic plan. The architectural details and methods of construction had to be left to the initiative of Iranian builders.

The first mosques founded by the Arabs were built in towns which at first were no more than fortified camps for the armies of Islam: Basra and Kūfa in Mesopotamia, Fustāt in Egypt.

In fact the first caliphs were forced to maintain the governments of conquered countries for lack of administrators and to use existing buildings for lack of constructors. Gradually, however, the conquered adapted their edifices to the needs of the conquerors, and this was when an Islamic element began to appear in the art of the Middle East. It seems that it first occurred to Palestine and Syria. In any case the first known works of Muslim architecture, though still marginally Muslim, are in Jerusalem and Damascus for political reasons which I must mention here.

According to the rules laid down by the Prophet Muhammad, his first successors, Abū Bakr, 'Umar, 'Uthmān and 'Alī, were elected by the Muslim community. However, quarrels between pretenders to the caliphate subsequently conferred the supreme power on a pure Arab, Mu'āwiya, son of Abū Sufyān, who was born in Mekka but had governed Syria as undisputed master for some twenty years and had the majority of his partisans there. On becoming the head of Islam, he continued to live at Damascus as before. He was not the upholder of the *sunna* (or Revelation) of the Prophet, steadfast in the observance of what one might call the 'Imitation of Muhammad', as his predecessors had been, but a real king. Breaking with the plebiscitary system of election which had determined the succession of caliphs since the death of the Prophet, he had his son Yazīd elected in his lifetime. Yazīd had his own son Mu'āwiya II elected in the same way. So came 'the equivocation which lasted ninety years', as long as the sovereignty remained in the Umayyad family, until the victory of the concept of legitimism and the accession to power of the descendent of the Prophet's uncle, al Abbās ibn 'Abd al-Mutalib ibn Hāshim.

During these ninety years the members of the Umayyad family gradually shedding the rusticity of the old Arabs and the simplicity of manners suitable to religious leaders, surrounded the Caliphate with a pomp which was purely profane. The Caliph became a Syrian monarch, a sort of *basileus* like the one he had replaced in one of his provinces. Damascus became the political capital of the empire instead of Madīna, and attempts were even made to confer on Jerusalem the religious prestige with which

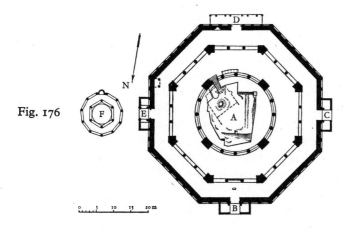

PLAN OF THE QUBBAT AL-SAKHRA
(THE DOME OF THE ROCK) AT JERUSALEM
A. Al-Sakhra (i.e. the rock itself). B. Bāb al-Djanna. C.
Bāb al-Gharb. D. Bāb al-Qibla. E. Bāb al-Silsila. F.
Qubbat al-Silsila.

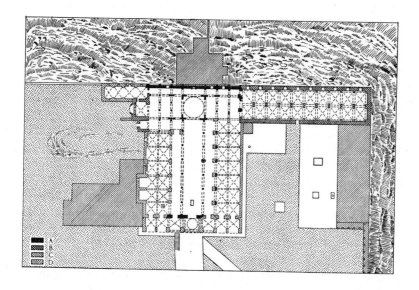

Fig. 177   PLAN OF THE AL-ʿAQSĀ MOSQUE
AT JERUSALEM
A. Basilica of Justinian. B. Construction by the Templars. C. Original Arab
additions. D. Modern Arab building.

Mekka had hitherto been surrounded. It was in these two towns, Jerusalem and Damascus, that the first great Islamic sanctuaries were built: the Qubbat al-Sakhrā (The Dome of the Rock), the al-'Aqsā mosque and the Great Mosque of Damascus.

The Qubbat al-Sakhrā, 'the Mosque of 'Umar' (though it has nothing to do with Umar), is more generally known as the Dome of the Rock. It was built by the Umayyad 'Abd al-Malik[1] and is dated to AD 691. Basically it consists of a lofty domed building built above a rock which Jews, Christians and Muslims all revered and which the Arabs called the 'navel of the world'. Two concentric ambulatories surround this edifice the general design of which resembles the circular Christian churches like the cathedral at Busrā (Bosra in Syria). It was certainly built by Christian workmen, and Byzantine artists, sculptors and mosaicists decorated its walls (fig. 176).

The al-'Aqsā Mosque, like the Qubbat al-Sakhrā, rises from the esplanade of the Haram al-Sharīf at Jerusalem. 'Abd al-Malik probably built it, too, towards AD 690, but it was damaged by an earthquake, then restored and considerably modified by the Abbāsid Caliph al-Mahdī[2] in AD 774–775. This basilical mosque now has seven aisles, of which only the three in the middle can have been built in the Umayyad period. The central nave, which is particularly wide and high, intersects with a transept of the same height and is domed at their crossing (fig. 177).

The Great Mosque of the Umayyads at Damascus was built by the son of al-Malik, al-Walīd,[3] on the site of the sanctuary of the Syrian god Hadad, to which succeeded a temple of Jupiter Damascenus and then a basilica dedicated to John the Baptist. It consists of a hall with three naves running east-west and to the north opens on to an enormous arcaded court. The three naves are crossed in the centre by a sort of north-south transept in the middle of which is the celebrated Dome of the Eagle. Mosaics, made by Byzantine craftsmen, embellished the walls. The mosaics in the hall of prayer have disappeared during the frequent fires which have ravaged the edifice, but those in the court have partially survived. Recently freed of the coating which covered them, they enable us to form an idea of the ancient and sumptuous decoration of this Umayyad monument (fig. 178).

The strongly Christian character of the three great Muslim monuments at Jerusalem and Damascus—the Dome of the Rock, the al-'Aqsā Mosque and the Great Mosque of the Umayyads—stands out therefore. But this is not true of the buildings in Transjordan, the most remarkable of which are at Mshattā and Qusair 'Amra.

There have been and still are endless discussions about whether the first is Muslim or pre-Islamic. Should it be dated to the fourth, sixth or seventh centuries? However, the hypothesis of an Umayyad foundation certainly seems to be the best. Walīd II[4] probably commissioned this building. The main building, in the form of a three-aisled basilica ending in a triple apse, recalls Syrian churches, but the brick walls of the other buildings and the enclosure wall the upper part of which is decorated with triangles

---

[1] 'Abd al-Malik ibn Marwān, 64–86 H (AD 685–705).
[2] Al-Mahdi, 158–168 H (AD 775–785).
[3] Al-Walīd I, 88–98 H (AD 705–715).
[4] Al-Walīd II, 743–744 H.

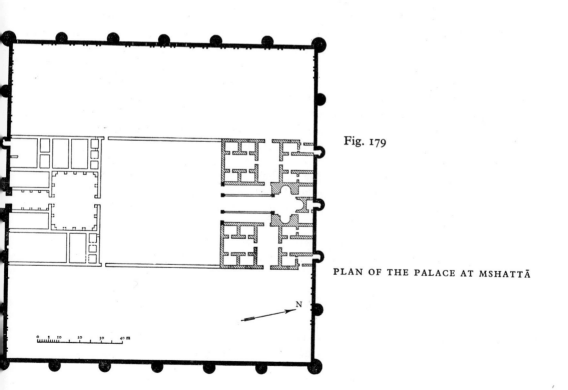

Fig. 178

PLAN OF THE
GREAT MOSQUE
OF THE UMMAYADS
AT DAMASCUS
A. Bāb Djairun.
B. Bāb al-Farādis.
C. Bāb al-Barīd.
D. Ma'dhanat
al-'Arus.
E. Ma'dhanat
al-Gharbīya.
F. Ma'dhanat 'Isa.
G. Bayt al-Māl.
K. Ablution fountain.
I. Shrine of John the
Baptist's head.
J. Dome of the
Eagle. L. Mihrāb.
M. Library.

Fig. 179

PLAN OF THE PALACE AT MSHATTĀ

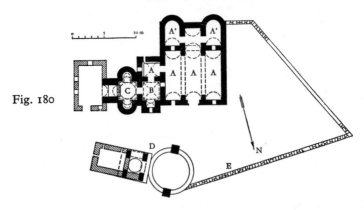

Fig. 180

PLAN OF THE PAVILION AT QUSAIR 'AMRA
A. Barrel-vaulted halls. A'. Barrel-vaulted rooms,
absidal in form. B. Square hall with cross vaults.
C. Square domed hall. D. Well. E. Fortification.

adorned with vine-trails, animals and large rosettes in relief belong to Hellenistic and
Sassanid art (fig. 179). We even find the peacock-dragon, so characteristic of Iran (fig.
174, pl. 121 and coloured plate III).

However, there is no doubt at all about the origin of the little palace of Qusair 'Amra.
It is a hunting lodge of the type we know the Umayyad princes, who were great
hunters, to have possessed on the edge of the desert. The six barrel-vaulted halls of
which it consists were entirely covered with paintings (fig. 180). The majority of them
clearly belong to the Hellenistic or Byzantine tradition, but some hunting scenes and
various female figures seem more closely connected with Sassanid art.

So we see the marked dualism the art of early Islam. Iranian influence made itself
felt on the borders of Syria and continued to assert itself even after the triumph of the
Baghdād Caliphate. In fact in the middle of the eighth century, in AD 750 (132 H) to be
precise, an event took place which was to have a considerable influence on the destiny
of the Islamic world, in particular the fate of Muslim culture and consequently of
Muslim art. This was the overthrow of the Umayyad Empire by the Abbāsids, which
meant in essence the transfer of the political centre from Syria to Mesopotamia and
the substitution of Sassanid and Iranian influences for Byzantine traditions.

Under the thrusts of the armies of Khurāsān, organized by Abū Muslim, and the
partisans of the Abbāsid pretender, Abū'l Abbās 'Abd Allāh, who had proclaimed
himself Caliph at Kūfa, the troops of the last Umayyad sovereign Marwān,[1] son of
Muhammad, son of Marwān, were beaten in Mesopotamia and Syria, and what
remained of them in Egypt where Marwān was killed by his own companions in AD 750
(132 H). The Umayyads were tracked down and exterminated everywhere. Their
bodies were disinterred and their remains scattered abroad. Their palaces and other
buildings were destroyed so that henceforth nothing would recall their memory.

[1] Marwān II, the last Umayyad Caliph, died in AD 750.

The Abbāsid dynasty, descended from Abbās, the Prophet's uncle, survived five centuries, but its power only remained intact for about 150 years.

After this period, now that the problems of Muslim art had been posed, and the solution found which Islam then tried to impose on the peoples it had subdued, the Islamic Empire began to disintegrate. For three centuries it had been the most civilized part of the world. It had created a wealth of splendid towns . . . but the spirit of faction which had always been the defect of the Arab race did not disappear with its adhesion to Islam. From the death of the Prophet onwards rival clans disputed the leadership of the community and their disputes degenerated into bloody quarrels. By the time of the Rashīdin Caliphs[1] the 'theocratic democracy' of the Muslim world had become a hereditary monarchy and the seat of government had passed from Madīna to Damascus. However it was still an Arab government. The Umayyads were pure Quraishites.[2]

With the advent of the Abbāsids came the preponderance of Iranian influence. The seat of State was transported to Baghdād where the Arabs were only a tiny minority in the midst of a turbulent multitude of converts of various races. 'Political unity could not exist. Everywhere ethnic and separatist tendencies which had seemed to be dead began to reappear. . . . The first real split took place with the advent of the Abbāsids. A member of the disappointed Umayyad family fled to Spain where he established a rival Caliphate at Cordoba, a Caliphate recognized as legitimate not only by the Spanish Muslims, but also by the Berbers of North Africa. Subsequently another Caliphate, the Fatimid Caliphate, was established in Egypt. As for the Abbāsid Caliphs of Baghdād, their power gradually declined until the moment when they became mere puppets in the hands of the Turks.'

During the Abbāsid period the various artistic techniques, which Islam had borrowed from all parts of its empire and used haphazardly at first, began to be organized. A unified Islamic art was established, but this great effort, the effects of which were still felt several centuries after the disappearance of the Abbāsids, ceased with the breaking of the political unity of the Muslim Empire. Various States appeared or reappeared, among which the spirit of Islam perpetuated the unity of spirit of Muslim art. But henceforth, for lack of contacts and of a unified leadership and exchanges of workmen, and for lack of those sets of formularies[3] which had hitherto done so much to organize the artistic techniques of Islam, the tendencies particular to each people were once

[1] The Rashīdin, i.e. 'legitimate' Caliphs chosen without any reference to heredity were the first four successors of the Prophet: 'Abu Bakr, 'Umar, 'Uthmān and 'Ali.

[2] Nothing is obscurer than the very modest beginnings of the imperial tribe of Quraish. The groups of nomads who lived and travelled in the outskirts of Mekka have always counted among the most uncouth of western Asia. The primitive clan of Quraishites, though small in numbers and composed of shepherds and robbers, became in turn the auxiliaries and the scourge of Mekkan trade and led a precarious existence 'in the depths of wild gorges' among the bare mountains encircling the sacred territory. An adventurer from Qusaiy, of foreign extraction, from the northern steppes near Syria, united the scattered groups of the tribe and succeeded in installing them in the heart of Mekka by a surprise attack. They rapidly secured political supremacy which they consolidated by their possession of the sanctuary of the Ka'aba. This revolution took place during the last quarter of our fifth century, barely a century after their ancestors had ceased to be nomads.

[3] F. Sarre and E. Herzfeld: Archäologische Reise im Euphrat- und Tigris-Gebiet. vol. 3, plates XIV–XVI.

more freely expressed. Ancient traditions reappeared, provoking the rise not of different Muslim arts but of different schools of Muslim art.

Nothing much remains of the sumptuous Baghdād of the beginning of the Abbāsid period, but there are, on the banks of the Tigris and the Euphrates, the ruins of palaces, fortresses and mosques of the eighth and ninth centuries which suffice to acquaint us with the architecture of the time. The following quotation from the *Muqaddimah* (the introduction to his history) of Ibn Khaldūn is perhaps specially applicable to this moment in the history of Islamic art: 'When the Arabs had ceased to observe the strict precepts of their religion and acquired the taste for a luxurious life, they learnt the arts of architecture from their Persian subjects.'

At Raqqa, on the right bank of the Euphrates, 125 miles east of Aleppo, the ancient Raqqa, founded by the second Abbāsid Caliph, al-Mansūr,[1] was surrounded by its high walls which still stand. It contains the ruins of a Great Mosque, a palace and a very fine gate, south-east of the town. Their brick architecture, their lines of arcades and decorative niches similar to those of the Taq-i Kisrā at Ctesiphon recall the constructions of the Sassanid period. However, the arches of the great bays, instead of being semi-circular or elliptical, are pointed and show the remains of cusps.

Samarrā, on the left bank of the Tigris, about 55 miles north of Baghdād, was, as I have already mentioned, founded by al-Mu'tasim, the eighth Abbāsid Caliph. Alarmed by the frequent revolts of his Turkish and Berber troops, he had a palace built there and took up residence in it in AD 838. His immediate successor, al-Wāthiq, built another palace for himself, then al-Mutawakkil built many more, including the vast and magnificent complex of buildings and gardens called al-Balkuwāra and the mosque which bears his name. He even undertook the construction of a new town, further north, al-Mutawakkilīya, feeling that residence in Samarrā was none too safe. He moved into it in AD 860, then was killed there the following year by his son al-Muntasir[2] who returned to Samarrā. In AD 889 al-Mu'tamid[3] returned to Baghdād where his security in fact was no more threatened than anywhere else, 'abandoning the beautiful residences which seven Caliphs had inhabited and which were gradually going to fall into decay'. Today all that remains of them is a vast area of ruins from which rise only the three entrance ivans of the great palace, the walls and the minaret of the Great Mosque of al-Mutawakkil.

The Great Mosque of Sāmarrā and that of Abū Dulaf, some seven miles to the north, give us a fairly accurate idea of religious architecture in the age of the Abbāsids. The first of these two monuments is now no more than an enormous rectangle of high walls of burnt brick, reinforced externally by bastions in the form of almost semi-circular towers. Inside, the Haram, or hall of prayer, which runs along the south wall of the buildings and contains the main mihrāb, consisted of twenty-five aisles perpendicular to the south wall ten rows of columns deep. The arcades built on to the east and west walls were five rows of columns deep and those on the north side four.

[1] Al-Mansūr, Abbāsid Caliph of Baghdād, 136–158 H (AD 754–775).
[2] Al-Muntasir Bi'llāh, Abbāsid Caliph, died in 248 H (AD 862).
[3] Al-Mu'tamid, the Abbāsid Caliph, 256–279 H (AD 870–892).

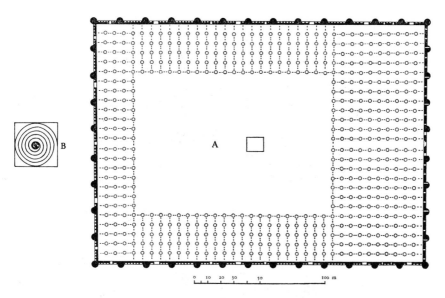

Fig. 181   PLAN OF THE GREAT MOSQUE
                                      AT SĀMARRĀ
                                 A. Mosque. B. Spiral Minaret.

The enormous court, thus surrounded on all sides, was adorned in the centre with a
rich fountain for the ablutions of the faithful (fig. 181). The Abū Dulaf Mosque was
built to the same type of plan, but its area was smaller, just as its walls and minarets
were lower. It also had brick pillars instead of columns.

The three entrance ivans, which are still standing, of the great palace of al-Mutawakkil, al-Balkuwārā, formed the central architectural motif of a façade which was at
least five-eighths of a mile long. These ivans, which faced on to a broad terrace overlooking the valley of the Tigris, as well as the vast stairs and gardens with fountains
which led up to it, were no doubt the sovereign's outer reception halls, like those of the
Sassanid palaces. Behind them, arranged in the rough shape of a T, were the inner
reception rooms, the Caliph's private appartments, the various houses of the harem,
esplanades, gardens, pools, the barracks of the Caliph's guard and their annexes, stores,
and so on. Around this palace were grouped large seignorial residences as well as more
modest dwellings, but generally all arranged in the same way, as a series of courtyards
on to which the rooms opened.

Generally speaking the main rooms of the palaces and the dwelling houses at
Sāmarrā were decorated with high dadoes made of carved stucco, sometimes surmounted by decorative niches. The embrasures of the bays, doors and windows were
decorated in the same way. These compositions and their execution varied considerably; they could be restrained or complicated, in light bas-relief or semi-sculpture in
the round, finely chased or roughly carved. The decoration most frequently employed

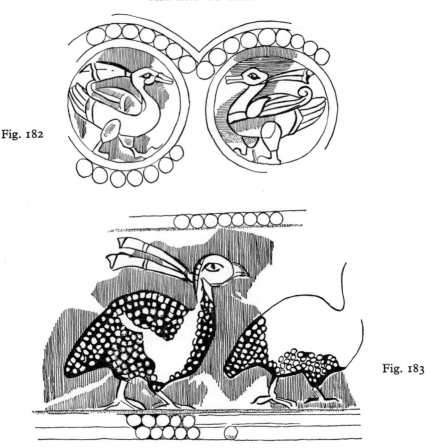

Fig. 182

Fig. 183

was of the simplest, almost severe, kind, with straight lines predominating. Others were richer and even had a rather heavy opulence, flowers in the centre of geometrical figures entwined with ribbons and pearls, as the Sassanid roundels were, bunches of grapes and coiled vine shoots. Both these stucco dadoes and the ceilings were sometimes touched up with painting in which animals and even human beings appeared. Sassanid tradition is clearly predominant, but traces of Hellenistic influence can be observed.[1]

[1] I would ask the reader to take special note of Plates XLVIII and XLIX of E. Herzfeld's work, *Die Malereien von Sāmarrā*, showing fragments of painted stucco found in the palace of Djawsaq at Sāmarrā, during the excavations made in 1911–1913. They depict the duck (fig. 182) and guinea-fowl (fig. 183), two birds, which are among the favourite Sassanid decorative motifs, and even bear the Sassanid *kushti* (that is, the fringed ribbon or sash which is so much associated with Sassanid depictions of royalty). Another plate (LXIX) in the same work represents a female figure which seems to be doubly Sassanid (fig. 184), firstly because it depicts Shīrīn carrying a calf on her shoulders, thus illustrating the well-known Iranian legend and also because the character, the decoration of her costume and the colours are typically Sassanid. Sāmarrā, being Islamic, tells us these paintings are also Islamic. Found elsewhere, however, they would perhaps be called Sassanid.

Fig. 184

The same influences are noticeable in the glass and ceramic objects found at Sāmarrā. Excavations have produced enamelled, engraved and coloured glasses, bottles, goblets, lamps and small pieces of glass which were clearly used in mosaic. As later at Rayy, in Iran, pottery with a carved or scratched design (i.e. *sgraffiato* ware) under a transparent glaze existed at Sāmarrā, as did lustre ware, which was also used to decorate the walls. At Sāmarrā it is remarkably advanced in technique, but gives absolutely no clue to the origin of its manufacture.

Having examined and compared monuments and objects of which I have not been able to present enough examples for lack of space, I hope I have done enough nevertheless to demonstrate that Muslim Mesopotamia remained Sassanid artistically

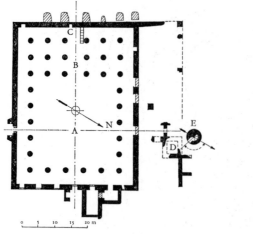

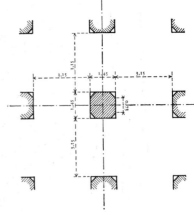

Fig. 185

PLAN OF THE TĀRĪK KHĀNA
AT DĀMGHĀN
A. Square courtyard lined with
colonnades. B. domed quincunx.
C. Mihrāb. D. Disused minaret.
E. Seljuk minaret.

Fig. 186

PROPORTIONAL ANALYSIS
OF COLUMNS IN THE
MASDJID-I DJĀMIʿ AT SHŪSHTAR

speaking. Even when it imitated the shape of the minarets of the Sāmarrā mosques
from Assyrian and Babylonian sources. But what do we find in Iran itself?

As a matter of fact, up to now we know very little about Iranian architecture of the
earliest Islamic period in the flesh; only a few of its monuments have come down to us.
On the other hand, as we have seen, we know the monuments of the Sassanid period
well, and also those of the Seljuk period. Since the latter only differ from the former by
their lack of Islamic accretions, we can fairly easily hypothesize a restoration of the
edifices of the intermediate period. Later we shall see how Sassanid monuments which
were turned into mosques were enlarged by the addition of architectural features
which follow the Sassanid model. We shall recognize that love of scrupulously executed
decoration and that taste for constant novelty within a rigid framework which characterizes the artistic sense of the Arabs in the pre-Islamic period. We shall rediscover the
same lack of constructional skill which we already observe in the Semites of Akkad
and also in the productive but unimaginative building of Babylon and Assyria.

The Iranian mosques can be classified quite naturally in two groups, one comprising
a small number of buildings with the plan of the primitive Arab mosque, the other
consisting of purely Iranian monuments. As I have already said, the history of the
first group is brilliant but short. We can imagine the Arabs of the conquering and
later the occupying armies building religious monuments of their own type in Iran
and we know from their historians that the first Caliphs erected great mosques in the

main towns of the country, built according to the Arabian plan. One of them is undoubtedly the Tārīk Khāna at Dāmghān which possibly dates from the middle of the
second century of the Hegira (eighth century AD) (pl. 125 and fig. 185). Others, ruined,
modified or transformed in varying degrees have been found at Yazd, Rayy,[1] Susa,[2]
Shūshtar and Ardistan. The Masdjid-i Djāmiʿ at Shūshtar is one of the constructions
which were built by the Abbāsid Caliphs. In 254 H, the Caliph al-Muʿtazz Biʾllāh
Abbāsī[3] ordered it to be built, but since his Caliphate only lasted a short time, it was
not finished until the reign of al-Mustārshīd.[4] Basically it consisted of a large rectangular prayer hall the plan of which we see only a detail in fig. 186, contained a quincunx
of pillars supporting a flat roof. It was thirteen bays wide and eight bays of wooden
columns in depth parallel to the qibla wall;[5] incidentally there are only six today, as
the first two rows of columns have disappeared. In its modern reconstruction it appears
as a complex of small domes on enormous pillars of masonry. The beautiful minaret of
this monument was built by the Djalaʿirid Sultān Sheikh Uways.[6] We probably ought
to include in this group the mosque which was built at Istakhr with columns, pillars
and stone slabs brought from Persepolis.

These mosques had few successors; they include the Masdjid-i Djāmiʿ at Nāyīn
(fig. 187 and pl. 126), from the fourth century of the Hegira, the one at Dimāwand,
from the next century, and much later the Masdjid-i Wakīl at Shīrāz (pl. 167), a
builder's folly of the Zend period. There were others, of course, some parts of which
will perhaps be found one day among the buildings of more modern edifices, and still
others the existence of which is known to us only from the accounts of Muslim
historians. For example we know that Abū Muslim,[7] the famous propagandist of the
Abbāsids, erected mosques of this type at Marw and Nīshāpūr, that in 548 of the
Hegira (AD 1153–1154) the Ghuzz tribe destroyed the Mutarris Mosque at Nīshāpūr,
which could hold 2,000 people. But the methods of construction remained Iranian
and the schematic plan to which the Arab contribution was almost solely confined
is found at Nāyīn as at Damāwand, already so whittled down and so debased that
it seems clear that this pattern met with little success in Iran. Powerful kings, such
as the Abbāsids were, were able to build as they wished; what they could not do was to
chain the future and impose the spirit of a foreign architecture on the 'land of continuity'. So mosques built according to the Arabian plan rapidly disappeared from the

[1] In 1935 E. Schmidt excavated the foundations of the Great Mosque which was built there by the
Caliph al-Mahdi.
[2] In 1948 R. Ghirshman found the brick bases of columns of a mosque of the Arabian type there; it
lacked the right-hand riwāq (that is a colonnaded or arcaded portico) and the bay of the oratory
facing it.
[3] Al-Muʿtazz Biʾllāh, the Abbāsid Caliph, proclaimed king in 252 H (AD 866) and deposed in 225 H
(AD 869).
[4] Al-Mustārshīd Biʾllāh, Abbāsid Caliph, 515–529 H (AD 1118–1135).
[5] The qibla wall in a mosque is the wall perpendicular to the direction of Mekka, and is generally
perpendicular to the main axis of the mosque as well.
[6] Sheikh Uways, 756–776 H (AD 1355–1374).
[7] Abū Muslim, Iranian head of the religious and political movement in Khurāsān which overthrew the
Umayyads and put the Abbāsids on the throne. Assassinated in 137 H (AD 755).

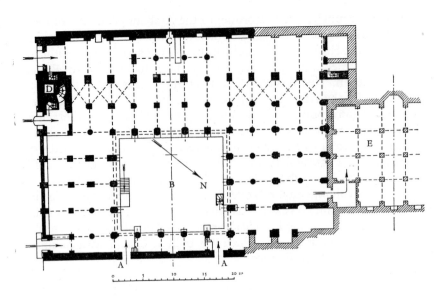

Fig. 187   PLAN OF THE MASDJID-I DJUMʿĀ AT NĀYĪN
                  A. Entrance porches. B. Courtyard. C. Mihrāb.
                  D. Minaret. E. New mosque.

living architecture of Iran. And after the fifth century of the Hegira, it seems clear that
the mosque became completely Iranian in both plan and construction.

    The first mosques of this second group, the Iranian group, are no less ancient than
the others. In fact it was normal for meeting places of the pre-Islamic period, whether
religious or not, to become first of all the places of assembly of the new religion; and
this was all the more natural since Islam, as we know, had never felt a great need for
specially built places of worship, nor indeed necessity for any building at all. The
musallās, where the great prayers were said communally, during the feasts of Fitr and
Kurban, in times of epidemics or excessive drought, were often no more than vast
expanses of bare ground in the neighbourhood of the towns, 'open air oratories' as
G. Marçais said. The ancient mosques of Khurāsān were sometimes no more than a
bit of cleared desert, with or without a low wall as enclosure, at the far end of which
stood a simple niche which served as the mihrāb (fig. 199). Even today, says E. Diez,
speaking of the mosques of Bukhārā, which possess great ivans but have no courtyards,
'the crowd assembles in front of these mosques. This is very much the rule in Turkestan. As the ivans and the niches were only niches of monumental proportions, there
was no need for anything else.' In effect the word 'masdjid', which we translate by
'mosque', means no more than 'the place of prostration', or more accurately, 'the place
where one throws oneself on the ground'. 'Wherever thou art at the hour for prayer,'
said the Prophet Muhammad, 'thou shalt perform the *salat*:[1] that place is a masdjid

    [1] i.e. the prayer.

According to Islamic custom, 'all places are equal in the eyes of God and the humiliation before Him expressed by the ritual prayer can take place anywhere'. In other
words any building can become a place for prayer. The Great Mosque of Constantinople was a Byzantine church, the famous Santa Sophia built by the emperor Justinian.
The mosque at Salonika was originally the Byzantine church of the Apostles. That at
Istakhr was originally a fire temple.

Consequently it is not surprising that when Islam conquered Iran, it first installed
its cult in existing monuments, with or without special modification. As a matter of
fact, up to the present we only know of one, the Sassanid chahār-tāq at Yazd-iKhwā st[1]
(fig. 188), but it was certainly not the only one.[2] Incidentally it was the chahār-tāq, a
dome on four pillars with arches between, i.e. the most common type of Sassanid
architecture, the canopy of all those fires which had glowed on the hill sides or mountain tops in pre-Islamic Iran, the form of the altars situated in the centre of the courtyard of Zoroastrian temples, which became the principal feature of the great Iranian
mosques, at first by itself then in conjunction with other features of the contemporary
architecture. This is how it most probably occurred.

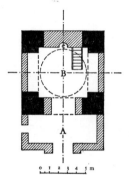

Fig. 188

PLAN OF THE
CHAHĀR-TĀQ AT
YAZD-I KHWĀST
A. Courtyard. B. Dome.
C. Mihrāb.

I have mentioned that the Abbāsid Caliphs built mosques on the Arabian plan in the
main towns of Iran. Perhaps the Iranians themselves were forced to build some too,
but nothing of the kind has come down to us. Doubtless people preferred, since Islam
did not oppose it, to use existing buildings as mosques just as they were or slightly
altered by the addition of a mihrāb. Then they built others, in imitation of the main
types of buildings in use in the various regions of the country. So it came about quite
naturally that in the west, the land of domes and vaults, they used the chahār-tāq, and
this became the kiosk-mosque. In the east, the source of the ivan, they built ivan-
mosques for preference and in the south edifices of the Iwān-i Karkhā type, i.e.
barrel-vaulted galleries with a dome in the centre. However, there were no frontiers
which delimited the use of the various types, merely zones of preference. For example,

[1] The archway which corresponded best in orientation to the wall facing Mekka was blocked up and
thus became the qibla wall. This wall contained the mihrāb niche.
[2] The Masdjid-i Sang would seem to have been another of this type, though we have no confirmation
that it was a church in Sassanid times.

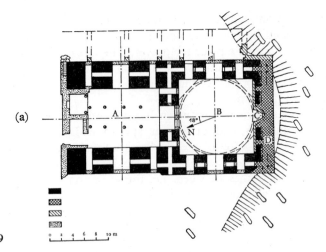

(a)

Fig. 189

PLAN AND SECTION OF THE
MASDJID-I DJUMʿĀ AT ARDABĪL
A. Ivan. B. Square domed hall. C. Mihrāb. D. Qibla wall.

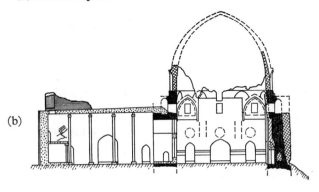

(b)

there is an ivan-mosque at Nīrīz in Fārs (fig. 201 b) and two mosques in the form of a
gallery with a central dome at Muhammadīya, east of Isfahān[1] (fig. 202). To the three
types of buildings which were used by the first builders of Iranian mosques, perhaps
we ought to add a fourth, the complex of ivan and domed square hall, that of the
Sassanid fortress at Fīrūzābād, exactly reproduced by the Masdjid-i Djumʿā at Ardabīl,
in Azerbaidjān (figs. 189 a and b).

The two most important types are certainly the chahār-tāq and the ivan. They were
at first employed independently of each other, one in the west and the other in the east
of the country, but later joined forces, as we shall see, to form the Iranian Great
Mosque with a central courtyard and four ivans of the Seljuk period.

[1] Several domes on squinches made their appearance in the Sassanid period in the palace at Kūh-i
Khwādja.

THE KIOSK-MOSQUE

The Sassanid fire temple basically consisted of a vast courtyard in the centre of which was the altar, generally raised and topped by the dome of a chahār-tāq. In our own day it is still the plan of the fire temple at Bākū. Western Iran adopted it when it started to build mosques of its own, but slight modifications were necessary in order to adapt it exactly to meet its new requirements. It retained the great rectangular courtyard and tried to make its main axis coincide with the qibla of the mosque, i.e. with the direction of Mekka. It pushed the chahār-tāq back against the southern wall of this courtyard, that is the qibla wall, and substituted a mihrāb for the fire altar. This edifice (fig. 190), wide open on three sides, bearing on the qibla wall and sheltering the main mihrāb,[1] is the characteristic feature of this type of mosque. The faithful assembled in front of it in the courtyard at the hours for communal prayer. It is possible that this sort of mosque, the kiosk-mosque, had at a very early date, a minaret, built on or against the monument's enclosing wall, near the entrance door; one example, from as early as the middle of the second century of the Hegira, is the Tārīk Khāna at Dāmghān (fig. 185), and later the Masdjid-i Djum'ā at Sawa (fig. 191) which is dated to 504 H (AD 1110–1111). The minarets of the ancient mosques of Ardistān (fig. 190) and Nīrīz (fig. 202 a) are similarly placed, and, no doubt because tradition preserved it, the minaret of the earliest-known mosque with a central courtyard and four ivans, the Masdjid-i Djum'ā at Zawāra (fig. 205), dating from the year 530 H (AD 1135–1136).

However, two of the kiosks we know, at Gūlpāygān and Barsiyān, were not built against the wall of a courtyard, but were isolated from it—or more probably stood on unenclosed ground where the faithful prayed like the oratories of some musallās, that at Tūruk (fig. 192), near Mashhad (fig. 193), for example, or many mosques in Turkestan according to Diez's remark I quoted above. What goes to prove this is that the minarets of the ancient kiosk-mosques were most often based on or against the enclosing wall of these monuments, as I remarked, whereas those at Gulpāygān and Barsiyān are one with the kiosks, built into the south-west pillar, in the first case (fig. 194), and at the back of the building in the second (fig. 195).

The following are the main kiosk-mosques known to me at the present time:

Ardistān: Masdjid-i Djum'ā (fig. 190); Barsiyān: Masdjid-i Djum'ā (fig. 195); Burūdjird: Masdjid-i Djāmi'; Gūlpāygān: Masdjid-i Djāmi' (fig. 194); Isfahān: Masdjid-i Djum'ā (plates 130 and 131 and fig. 198 a); Qazwīn: Masdjid-i Djum'ā; Qazwīn: Haydarīya Madrasa (plates 127 and 129 and fig. 197); Qum: Masdjid-i Djum'ā; Natanz: Masdjid-i Djum'ā; Rizaiya (Urmiya): Masdjid-i Djāmi' (fig. 198); Sawa: Masdjid-i Djum'ā (fig. 191).

These kiosk-mosques were all enlarged at various periods; some, the Masdjid-i Djum'ā at Isfahān for example, soon after they were built, others, such as the one at Gūlpāygān and the Haydarīya Madrasa at Qazwīn (fig. 197), not until the Qādjār period. The majority of them became mosques with a central courtyard and four ivans.

---

[1] Depending on the importance of the mosque, it might or might not have secondary mihrābs on either side of the chahār-tāq, in the qibla wall.

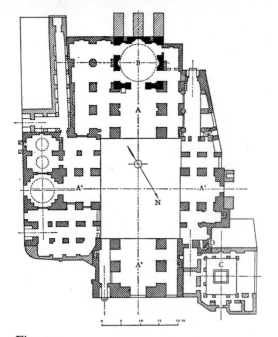

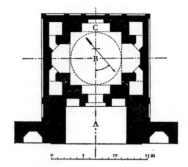

Fig. 192

PLAN OF THE
MUSALLĀ AT TŪRUK
A. Ivan. B. Square domed
hall. C. Mihrāb.

Fig. 190

PLAN OF THE MASDJID-I DJUMʿĀ
AT ARDISTĀN
A. Ivans. B. Hall with the main mihrāb.
C. Madrasa. D. Minaret.

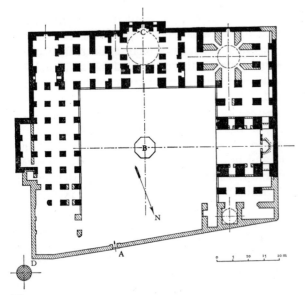

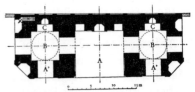

Fig. 193

PLAN OF THE MUSALLĀ
AT MASHHAD
A. Main ivan. A'. Secondary
ivans. B. Square domed rooms.
C. Mihrābs.

Fig. 191

PLAN OF THE MASDJID-I DJUMʿĀ
AT SAWA
A. Entrance. B. Ablution fountain.
C. Mihrāb. D. Minaret.

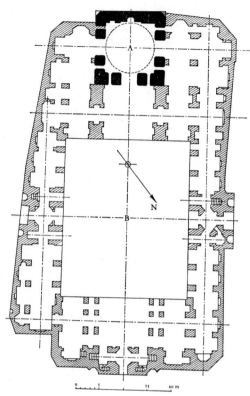

Fig. 194

PLAN OF THE MASDJID-I
DJĀMI' AT GŪLPĀYGĀN
A. Seljuk building (in black).
B. Qādjār building (hatched).

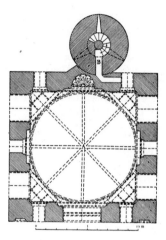

Fig. 195

PLAN OF THE MOSQUE
AT BARSIYĀN
A. Square domed hall.
B. Minaret.

However, there is still one building, the Atik Masdjid-i Musallā at Yazd which has retained the arrangement of the Zoroastrian temple: a chahār-tāq in the centre of a courtyard, open on all sides, without a fire altar, naturally, but also without a mihrāb (fig. 168), because of the four arches which have been left open.

THE IVAN-MOSQUE

The ivan, originally from Khurāsān, became a mosque, or the main feature of a mosque, in the east of Iran, even more simply than did the chahār-tāq in the west of the country. For example, on the site of the towns of Bāmiyān destroyed by Djinghiz Khan in 618 H (AD 1221) I have observed the ruins of small mosques which were no more than a correctly orientated ivan, containing a mihrāb and with a courtyard in

PLAN OF THE MASDJID-I DJUMʿĀ
AT ISFAHĀN
A. Building known as the Mosque
of Malik Shāh. B. Gunbad-i-Khākī.
C. Madrasa. D. Mihrāb of Sulṭān
Uldjāitu Khudābanda. E. Winter hall.
F.–Fʾ. Quincunx-dome and hall of
Shāh Abbās I. G. Ablutions.
H. Latrines. I. Mortuary. J. Oratory
of Madjlisi. K. Hall with modern
dome. L. Door dated 515 H. M. Door
dated 768 H. N. Door with an
inscription of the Muzaffarid Qubt
al-Dīn Shāh Mahmūd. O. Door
dated 999 H. P. Porch dated 1218 H.
Q. Door dated 1301 H.

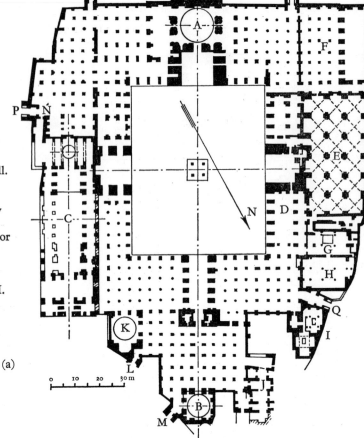

(a)

Fig. 196

PLAN OF THE BUILDING
OF MALIK SHĀH
A. Entrance. B. Dome.
C. Mihrāb. D. Qibla wall.

(b)

PLAN OF THE GUNBAD-I
KHĀKĪ

(c)

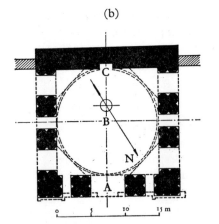

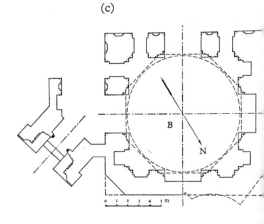

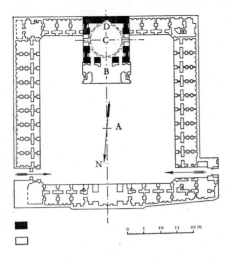

Fig. 197

PLAN OF THE HAIDARĪYA MADRASA
AT QASWĪN
A. Courtyard. B. Ivan. C. Square
domed hall. D. Mihrāb.

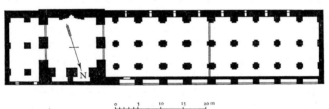

Fig. 198

PLAN OF THE MASDJID-I DJĀMIʿ AT RIZAIYA

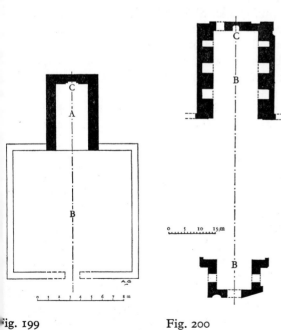

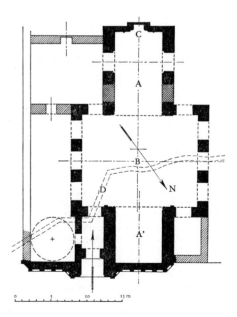

Fig. 199

PLAN OF THE MOSQUE
AT BĀMIYĀN
A. Ivan. B. Courtyard.
C. Mihrāb

Fig. 200

PLAN OF THE MOSQUE
AT ZAWZAN
A. Plan at tribune level.
B. Ivans.

Fig. 201

PLAN OF THE MOSQUE
AT FURŪMAD
A. Main ivan. A'. Secondary ivan.
B. Courtyard. C. Mihrāb. D. Culvert.

front enclosed by a low wall. In fact, this type of construction, about 9 feet wide and less than 18 feet deep, was scarcely more than a mihrāb, but as E. Diez has said, 'there was no need for anything else' (fig. 199). However, the style grew rapidly until in 616 H (AD 1219–1220) we have the enormous building at Zawzan[1] (fig. 200) in Khurāsān. It gave birth to the great mosque typical of this region of Iran, made up of two ivans facing each other on either side of a courtyard lined to west and east by buildings of lesser importance. Such are the mosque at Furūmad (fig. 201) and those at Zawzan, Sabzawār, Nīshāpūr, etc. It also became, in contrast to the tradition in the west where the dome was the dominant feature, the immense and magnificent ivan which proclaims from afar the funerary mosques and the musallā mosques of Khurāsān, at Tāyyābād (fig. 208), Turbat-i Shaikh-i Djām, Tūruk and elsewhere. As we shall see later this original plan of a central courtyard and four ivans became a classic and was employed in Iranian madrasas, caravanserais and mosques.

I have said that the Parthians probably brought the ivan to Mesopotamia in their migration from Khurāsān. We find it at Ashur and Hatra (pl. 90) from where it crossed into Fārs. At Fīrūzābād, still in the Parthian period, for the palace of Ardashīr was built before the fall of the Arsacid dynasty, it is the monumental hall in the centre of the main façade, which gives access to all the other parts of the building (fig. 160). In the Sassanid period, Ardashīr, who became king after conquering Ardawān V, built, also at Fīrūzābād, an edifice on the fortified height which commands the spot where the ravine of the river Burāza enters the plain. The building consists essentially of a square domed hall, preceded by a colossal ivan which opens on to a courtyard from which he could see all the surrounding countryside. Shāpūr I, his son, erected the enormous Tāq-i Kisrā, the public audience hall of the palace of Ctesiphon, an ivan with an internal width of 72 feet 7 inches and a depth of 139 feet 6 inches (pl. 110). As we know, he founded the town which bears his name, Bishāpūr, or Shāpūr in Fārs, and built a palace there (pl. 109) with a square courtyard, probably the main one, decorated with four ivans in a cruciform plan.[2]

Other Sassanid palaces, that at Sarwistān (pl. 107) built by Mīr Narsī, that at Qasr-i Shīrīn, the work of Khusraw II Parwīz, and that at Dāmghān, in short all the ones we

[1] The interior of the main ivan of the mosque of Zawzan is roughly 44 feet wide and 91 feet deep.

[2] According to R. Ghirshman, who excavated the greater part of this courtyard and its ivans, it was not a courtyard and ivans, but a completely covered hall. According to him, 'the hall is 120 feet 3 inches wide from one door to the other, but the projecting parts which form the walls at each entrance are about 24 feet 6 inches deep, which reduces the central space to a square of only 71 feet 6 inches. This was probably domed, whereas the four narrow parts at the entrances were roofed with a vault.' These four narrow sections, i.e. the ivans, must have been barrel-vaulted as ivans usually are. As for the dome with a diameter of 71 feet 4 inches, built of rubble bound with plaster, I find it impossible to believe that it ever existed. Of the thirty or so Sassanid domes now known, the largest, those of the chahār-tāq of the fire temple at Fīrūzābād and the isolated chahār-tāq of Qasr-i Shīrīn, which incidentally have collapsed, have diameters of 54 feet 4 inches and 54 feet 6 inches respectively. Those of the palace at Fīrūzābād measure 44 feet 2 inches and that of the palace at Sarwistān 41 feet 8 inches. The biggest Seljuk domes, those of the Masdjid-i Djum'a at Isfahan and the Masdjid-i Djum'a at Qazwīn, both measure 49 feet 5 inches. It seems to me beyond question that the 'square of 22 metres' at Shāpūr was a courtyard flanked by an ivan on each side. It is the plan of the Parthian palace at Ashur, and that of the private house in Khurāsān, which was taken to Mesopotamia and from there reached Fārs.

know today, used the ivan as the principal entrance feature and most frequently as the hall for public audiences.

Then came Islam.

I have already said that when the Iranian mosque was established in the west of Iran it for the most part used the architectural feature most commonly found there, the chahār-tāq. The ivan, although the Sassanid palaces had attached great importance to it, does not appear to have interested the first mosque builders very much, either because this native Khurāsānian shape had not yet been adopted by the current architecture of the west or more probably because the spirit of continuity which characterizes the Iranians in general led them to plan their new religious buildings on

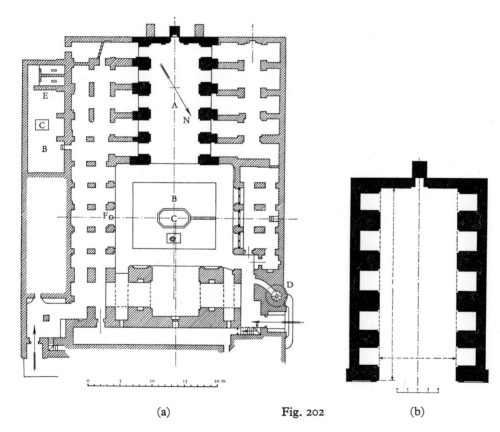

(a)

Fig. 202

(b)

PLAN OF THE MASDJID-I DJUMʿĀ AT NĪRĪZ
(PRESENT STATE)
A. Ivan. B. Courtyards. C. Ablution fountains.
D. Minaret. E. Latrines. F. Well.

PLAN OF THE MASDJID-I
DJUMʿĀ AT NĪRĪZ
(ORIGINAL STATE)

traditional lines. This continuity explains why we find at the end of the Husain Kūh near Persepolis an Elamite bas-relief representing a god seated on a coiled snake which serves as a throne, an Achaemenid, and later Sassanid fire sanctuary (pl. 35), and an *imām-zāda*,[1] the Imām-Zāda Ismā'īl, which incidentally is only a rock on which the local peasants go to pray and sacrifice sheep on certain occasions. The tomb of Cyrus at Pasargadae (pl. 37) has become a Muslim chapel where candles burn. The nomads on their journeys up to the cool heights or down to the hot regions smear its walls with the butter or milk of their ewes. Some fifteen years ago at Tūs, near Mashhad, on the occasion of the construction of Firdawsī's tomb, the poet of the ancient kings of Persia, small fires which were going out were found every morning in the corners of the funerary room. Near Teheran there is an isolated hill, the Takht-i Rustam, which once bore a Zoroastrian 'signal fire' and at the foot of which there is now an īmām-zāda, the Imām-Zāda Qāsim.

However, up to the present we only know of a single ivan-mosque in the west, the Masdjid-i Djum'ā at Nīrīz, not far from Shīrāz. Like the ordinary kiosk-mosque, it consists of a building which this time is an ivan attached to the southern wall of a rectangular courtyard and containing the mihrāb (fig. 202 a and b). According to the historian Muqaddasī, it is supposed to have been built in 340 H (AD 951), though like other ancient mosques it has been subsequently considerably enlarged.

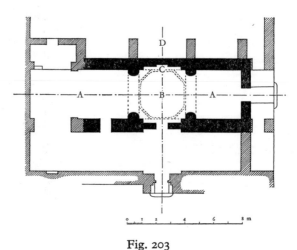

Fig. 203

PLAN OF THE MOSQUE AT MUHAMMADĪYA
A. Gallery B. Dome. C. Mihrāb. D. Courtyard.

---

[1] Imām-Zāda, a Persian title given to the descendants of the Imāms, and, by derivation, to their tombs.

THE MOSQUE OF THE IVAN-I KARKHĀ TYPE

The third type of Iranian mosque consists of a barrel-vaulted gallery, with a dome in the centre, i.e. an edifice which occurs in Khūzistān in the Sassanid period, at Ivān-i Karkhā. The faithful assembled for prayer in front of this gallery, as they did in front of the chahār-tāq and the ivan of the kiosk-mosque. At present we only know two other small mosques of this type, both situated at Muhammadīya, near Nāyīn (fig. 203). They can be dated to the fourth and fifth century of the Hegira.[1]

THE IRANIAN GREAT MOSQUE WITH A CENTRAL
COURTYARD AND FOUR IVANS

By the time of the Seljuks, therefore, Iran was in possession of all the constituent elements of the Iranian Great Mosque with a central courtyard and four ivans. It had the chahār-tāq, i.e. the square hall vaulted with a dome and open on all four sides, the ivan, the combination of an ivan with a chahār-tāq and even the courtyard with four ivans. And on the other hand, Iran, rejecting mosques built on the Arabian plan, sought to perfect its own religious edifices and make them rival the spaciously luxurious Abbāsid mosques. The Great Mosque in Iran seems to have been born quite naturally from a happy rearrangement of familiar elements. But it was not so simple. It required the intervention of the four-ivan madrasa native to the East, and this leads me to retrace my steps and follow the madrasa from its origin in Khurāsān up to the moment when its encounter with the kiosk-mosque produced the monument which has been very justly called the 'madrasa-mosque'.[2] As scholars have long sought the origin of the madrasa of four ivans in Syria and Egypt, for lack of adequate knowledge of the architecture of eastern Iran, I shall first of all consider the question of its origin.

'Appearing first in Khurāsān towards the beginning of the fourth century of the Hegira, the madrasa was initially no more than a private school for the study of Sunnite theology, i.e. the study and exposition of religious tradition (hadīth), exegesis of the Qur'an and law.' Van Berchem adds: 'It is a curious thing that the madrasa seems to have been established in the midst of Shī'ite peoples of eastern Iran, where there flourished from the second century of the Hegira onwards a very prosperous centre of Sunnite studies connected with the Shāfi'ī rite. The professor at this time taught in his own home.'[3] These primitive madrasas are known at Nīshāpūr, Marw, Bukhārā, Tūs and Tabarān, as far afield as Baghdād and in other town of Iran and Mesopotamia.

However, the madrasa gradually assumed a more clearcut character. It was still only a simple house, but it was now arranged for teaching and was often built by the professor himself, near a mosque or his own residence. Whereas official instruction was generally given in the mosque, the teaching there was independent and personal.

---

[1] The mosque of Kūhpa on the road from Isfahān to Nāyīn may possibly be another, but it was so much altered, especially in the Mongol period, that it would be very difficult to assert this positively, without making an intensive study.

[2] In contrast to the mosque as temple, i.e. the Arab mosque.

[3] The word 'madrasa' originally only meant a place for study in general.

Towards the middle of the fifth century the madrasa abandoned its modest role and developed considerably for reasons which have been admirably analysed by van Berchem: the decadence of the Caliphate, orthodox reaction and later the coming of the Mongol dynasties. The school of theology then left the private sphere to become a political institution under the official control of the State and its products learned as they were in laws and theology became the civil servants of the dynasty. But as early as the middle of the eleventh century Nizām al-Mulk, the vizir of the Seljuk Sultan Alp Arslān, and his successor Malik Shāh founded one of these madrasas in Baghdād for the celebrated jurist Shīrāzī.[1] Some years later he set one up at Nīshāpūr for another jurist, the famous Djuwainī, then others at Basra, Isfahān, Balkh, Herāt, Mōsul, Khargird Tūs and elsewhere. His successors imitated his example and the madrasa spread throughout the empire of the Seljuks.

It was in this form, that of a powerful instrument of religious and political propaganda, that the madrasa was introduced into Syria during the sixth century of the Hegira by the Sunnite Atabegs,[2] notably by Nūr al-Dīn,[3] then in Egypt by Salāh al-Dīn.[4] When it appeared in the latter country, its plan was already fixed: a small square courtyard open to the sky, surrounded by four high walls, with four halls opening on to the courtyard by means of a lofty arcade, and at the corners of the edifice, the annexes for the personnel and the domestic offices. This symmetrical quadruple composition corresponded perfectly to the needs of the four-sect madrasa, i.e. the school intended for the four main Sunnite sects, Hanafī, Shāfi'ī, Malikī and Hanbalī,[5] which explains why this type was adopted, but we must beware of linking the question of its origin with that of the reunion of four sects in the same building. From that point of view the place of the four-sect madrasa in relation to the four-ivan madrasa is exactly the same as I am in relation to the house I live in. I chose it because it suited my way of life.

The plans of the first-known four-sect madrasas, the Mustansirīya at Baghdād[6] and

[1] Nizām al-Mulk ordered the beginning of the building of this madrasa, the first Nizāmīya, in 457 H and inaugurated the courses two years later, on Saturday 10 Dhu'l Kada 459 H (AD 1067).

[2] Atabeg (from *Ata*, father, and *Beg*, lord) was originally the name given to the tutors and preceptors of the Turkish princes of the Seljuk dynasty who when quite young were put in the charge of respected amirs who acted *in loco parentis*. Later this title became permanent and was conferred on important amirs.

[3] Nūr al-Dīn, Atabeg of Halab (Aleppo) and Damascus. He was born in 511 H (AD 1118) and died in 569 H (AD 1174) at Damascus.

[4] Salāh al-Dīn, Kurdish Sultan of Egypt and Syria, better known under the western corruption of his name Saladin, founder of the Ayyubid dynasty, was born at Takrīt in 532 H (AD 1132) and died at Damascus in 589 H (AD 1193).

[5] The four main Sunnite sects: Hanafī, Shāfi'ī, Malikī and Hanbali founded in the ninth century of the Hegira still share the government of the orthodox Muhammadan world. The Hanafī sect founded by the Imām Abū Hanifāh (died in 767 H) is the least strict of Islam. It was adopted by the Turks and has remained dominant in Central Asia and India. The Shāfi'ī sect, the school of Muhammad Ibn Idris, who was born at Baghdād and died in 820 H, was the official religion of the Abbāsid Caliphate. The Maliki rite, originated by the Imām Malik Ibn Anas (died in 795 H), predominates in the Maghreb, i.e. the western half of the Islamic world (Tunisia, Algeria, Morocco) and Central Africa.

The Hanbali sect, founded by Ahmad ibn Hanbal (died in 855 H), has only a small number of adherents in Central Arabia and on the shores of the Persian Gulf. It is the strictest of the orthodox sects.

[6] The Caliph al-Mustansir Bi'llāh had it built in 631 H (AD 1234).

the Sālahīya at Cairo,[1] are, however, not cruciform. The former included six ivans assymmetrically arranged around a rectangular courtyard, about 84 feet by 205 feet. The latter had two pairs of ivans each separated by a corridor. Moreover the bringing together of the four Sunnite sects in a single building is a later development even in Egypt than the cruciform madrasa. The Nāsirīya, the first four-ivan quadruple madrasa in Egypt, was completed in 703 H (AD 1303–1304), whereas the first Egyptian madrasa with four ivans, the Zahīrīya, was finished at the beginning of 662 H and inaugurated on 5 Safar of the same year, i.e. December 9, 1265. In an account of the origin of the cruciform madrasa, published in 1922,[2] K. A. C. Cresswell, having shown that the generally accepted hypothesis of a Syrian origin proposed by van Berchem is untenable, concludes that it is Egyptian:[3] 'The result of our investigation therefore is that, although the first four-rite madrasa is found at Baghdād, the first madrasa of cruciform plan is found in Cairo; that the cruciform plan was Egyptian in origin and that it is practically unknown outside Egypt.' However, being better informed than scholars were forty years ago, we now know a certain number, I may even say a great number, of buildings in eastern Iran with a central courtyard and four courtyards sometimes as much as several centuries prior to the Zahīrīya at Cairo. We may quote, for example, the palace which Daniel Schlumberger discovered at Lashkarī Bāzār, in Afghanistan, which dates from the time of Sultān Mahmūd of Ghazna.[4]

Among others we have the Nizāmīya madrasa at Khargird, in Khurāsān, which is decisively identified by the inscription in the name of its founder, Nizām al-Mulk, which decorates the wall of the qibla ivan.[5] It is not dated, but Nizām is described as Ghazi al-Amīr al-mu'minīn (that is The Champion of the Commander of the Faithful) on it, a title which was not granted him until shortly after 480 H. So we may assume that it was completed c. 480 H (AD 1087).

It is no longer even a ruin, but a heap of debris, in which Diez, Herzfeld and myself could for a long time only make out a courtyard and an ivan at the far end of which was the mihrāb of the building. However, a few years ago, I decided to verify once and for all whether the courtyard of the Nizāmīya at Khargird originally possessed one, two or four ivans, in other words whether this monument could or could not be considered as the oldest specimen known of the large madrasa with a central courtyard and four ivans. I looked therefore through the chaos of sun-dried brick which today represents both the original constructions and the ruins of the additions made to it over the centuries for the remains of the original walls which it was possible to place by relation to the ivan still standing. I obtained some important and exact dimensions, those which appear on the plan (fig. 204) and made measurements which confirm these.

From these observations we can deduce that there were, around a square courtyard,

---

[1] The construction of this madrasa was begun in 640 H (AD 1242).

[2] In *Bulletin de l'Institut français d'archéologie orientale du Caire*, Vol. 21, 1922.

[3] The only problem at the time was whether the origin was Syrian or Egyptian. Iran was so little known as not to enter the question.

[4] Sultan Mahmūd of Ghazna, 388–421 H (AD 998–1030).

[5] The mud walls of this ivan were so close to collapsing that the Antiquities Department of Iran decided to remove the precious inscription and transport it to Teheran Museum, where it is now.

149. THE ROOM KNOWN AS THE 'CHINĪ-KHĀNA' (OR PORCELAIN ROOM) ON THE THIRD STOREY OF THE PALACE OF THE 'ALĪ QAPŪ

Safawid period.

This decoration of cut-out painted wood was intended to hold real or imitation flagons of wines and liqueurs. Several palaces of the time of Shāh Abbās had similar rooms, for example his palace at Ardabīl.

150. MIHRAB OF THE MOSQUE OF SHAIKH LUTFULLAH AT ISFAHĀN

Seventeenth century.

The hall of the mihrāb is square in shape and is connected to the drum which bears the dome by pendentives. The glazed decoration which is particularly magnificent here recalls the sumptuous carpets woven by Iranian craftsmen.

151. DETAIL OF THE PORCH OF THE MOSQUE OF THE SHĀH AT ISFAHĀN

Seventeenth century.

The porch of the mosque is covered by a half-dome faced on its inner surface with stalactites decorated with glazed faience mosaics. The porch situated alongside the royal palace must have had a mainly decorative function and it is somewhat hastily built. It was finished in 1025 H (AD 1615), three years after the work had been begun. The mosque itself was not completed until some twenty years later.

152. THE MAUSOLEUM OF SHĀH ZAID ON THE OUTSKIRTS OF ISFAHĀN

Safawid period.

This mausoleum, which was most probably built at the beginning of the Safawid period, was restored under Shāh Sulaimān (AD 1666–1694). The dome, or at least its facing of yellow and blue faience, is modern. We should note in the interior of this monument frescoes representing the martyrdom of the Shī'ite Imāms, for it is rare to find religious paintings in Iranian monuments of this date. (More recently and especially in modern times religious painting, which is often very spontaneous and charming, is of frequent occurrence in Shī'ite monuments.)

153. THE TOMB OF BĀBĀ RUKN AL-DĪN AT ISFAHĀN

Safawid period.

Bābā Rukn al-Din was a theologian who died in AD 1367. The tomb has a pentagonal base and is surmounted by a decagonal drum and roof.

154. THE INTERIOR OF THE MOSQUE OF THE SHĀH (THE MASDJID-I SHĀH) AT ISFAHĀN

In the background can be seen the south ivan and the top of the dome of the main sanctuary. Begun in AD 1612 under Shāh Abbās, it does not seem to have been finished until after his death, in AD 1628.

155. AERIAL VIEW OF PART OF ISFAHĀN

In the foreground is the Mosque of the Shāh, to the left, the Great Square. This photograph is taken from E. Schmidt's Flights over Ancient Cities of Iran.

149

152

153

154

157

158

160

156. DOME AND MINARET OF THE MOSQUE OF THE SHĀH AT ISFAHĀN
Safawid period.
The three most important domes in Isfahān faced with glazed ceramics are those of the Masdjid-i Shāh, the Masdjid-i Shaikh Lutfullah and the madrasa on the Chahār Bāgh. All three date from the Safawid period.

157. DECORATION OF THE FAÇADE OF THE MADRASA ON THE CHAHĀR BĀGH (that is, the imposing avenue built by Shāh Abbās as part of the amenities of his capital)
Beginning of seventeenth century.
The decoration is of brick and glazed faience mosaics on the façade; part of the dome and the minaret of the madrasa appear in plate 162.

158. PART OF THE DECORATION OF THE INTERIOR OF THE MOSQUE OF THE SHĀH AT ISFAHĀN
Safawid period.
These floral scrolls are executed in small squares of kāshī, i.e. patterned glazed tiles, which is a more rapid process than faience mosaics. It was the sovereign, Shāh Abbās, who carried out a remarkable building programme and who generalized this technique.

159. PART OF THE 'BRIDGE OF THE THIRTY-THREE ARCHES' OR 'ALLAHWARDI KHĀN BRIDGE'
This bridge with thirty-three arches, the work of Allah-wardi Khān, general of Shāh Abbās I, is c. 45 ft. wide and 959 ft. long.

160. GENERAL VIEW OF THE ALLAHWARDI KHĀN BRIDGE AT ISFAHĀN
End of sixteenth century.
Above the arches is a storey of arcades, two per arch, which forms a parapet.

161. THE BRIDGE-DAM AT ISFAHĀN (OR BRIDGE OF KHĀDJŪ)
Seventeenth century.
This is one of the constructions of Shāh Abbās II on a more ancient dam. It is a bridge with twenty-four arches of stone and brick erected on sturdy masonry piers of dressed stone. A system of sluices made it possible to use the bridge as a dam. Small pavilions were built at the way on, in the centre and at the way off the bridge.

162. PART OF THE DOME AND A MINARET OF THE MADRASA ON THE CHAHĀR BĀGH
End of the Safawid period.
The Madrasa on the Chahār Bāgh was built between AD 1670 and 1714 to house theological students. Here we see a detail of the lofty drum which bears the main dome and which is pierced by a clerestory. On the left we have one of the two minarets of the south ivan.

M

V. PART OF THE DOME OF THE SHĀH SULTĀN HUSAIN MADRASA AT ISFAHĀN
Beginning of eighteenth century AD.
*This madrasa (the building is often attributed to the 'mother of the Shāh', hence its name of the Madar-i Shāh Madrasa) is in reality the work of Shāh Sultān Husain, as is shown by the inscription in the entrance porch which begins thus: 'This imposing madrasa was ordered to be built by the Prince of the Sultāns of the world . . . the Sultān of Sultāns, Khāqān of Khāqāns, Abūl'l-Muzaffar Khān, Sultān Husain al-Safawī, al-Musawī, al-Husainī, Bahādur Khān. . . .'
On the outside, at the end of the great circular inscription which we see on the drum of the dome, is the date of the completion of the monument and the name of the writer of the inscription: 'It is 'Abd al-Rahīm al-Djazairī who wrote this in 1122' (AD 1710). This plate represents part of the dome of the madrasa, the facing of which consists of glazed briquettes one and a half to two inches thick, which are thus quite strong enough to resist the destructive effects of the weather and the pigeons' claws.*

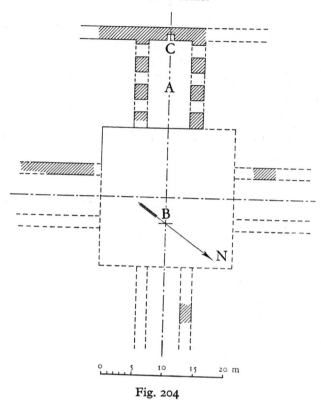

Fig. 204

PLAN OF THE NIZĀMĪYA MADRASA AT KHARGIRD
A. Ivan. B. Courtyard. C. Mihrāb.

a large ivan, against the qibla wall, two other slightly narrower ivans in the centre of
the other sides and opposite the qibla a fourth, still narrower, ivan which must have
been the entrance hall to the madrasa. The Nizāmīya at Khargird therefore consisted
of a square courtyard, four ivans arranged in a cross on the longitudinal and transverse
axes of this courtyard, with living rooms and domestic offices at the corners of the
building so defined. In this monument we certainly have the earliest of the great
madrasas with four ivans now known.

We know nothing about the plan of other Nizāmīyas, except perhaps by deduction
from the plan of the one at Isfahān which must also have had four ivans. In fact we
know through Ibn al-Athīr[1] that in 515 H (AD 1121–1122) the Djāmiʿ at Isfahān was
'burnt by the Batinians'.[2] It consisted at the time of a vast courtyard to the south, out

[1] Ibn al-Athir, the Arab historian (AD 1160–1234).
[2] The Batinians from the Arabic *batin*, esoteric, interior, hidden, are 'those who seek the inner or
hidden meaning of the scriptures'. The name Batinians was applied by Arab authors to several sects
which all played an important political role. One of the largest of these sects, the one referred to here, is
the Ismāʿīlī sect, a Shīʿite sect so named because it considers that the Imāms end with Ismāʿīl, so that
Ismāʿīl, son of Djaʿfar al-Sādik, the sixth Imām, is the seventh Imām for them.

of which rose the domed building, the Nizāmīya. In other words nothing which could burn. At that period the courtyard was still lined with monasteries, hostelries, the library, the various annexes of the original mosque, the Abbāsid mosque which the historian al-Māfarrūkhī[1] described. It was these annexes which were burnt. The decision to undertake the partial reconstruction in front of these ruins, which have come down to us, as well as the transformation of the building from kiosk-mosque to madrasa-mosque, was probably taken then. An inscription in Kufic characters, still partly legible, on one of the doors of the north side of the monument, tells us that 'this construction was renewed after the fire during the months of the year 515', the actual year of the disaster. In this case, obviously, it was only the reconstruction of a door, but we are entitled to think that the construction of the courtyard with four ivans was undertaken about the same time, firstly because this courtyard is completely Seljuk[2] and between the date of the fire, during the reign of the last Seljuk, Sultān Sandjar, and his death, there was scarcely more than the time necessary to construct the buildings in question; secondly because between the date of the decoration of the door of 515 H, and the decoration of the eastern ivan, obviously so little water had flowed under the bridges of the Zand-i Rūd that we can surely consider the ivans and the door as contemporary.

Now when the construction of the four-ivan courtyard of the mosque at Isfahān was decided on and then undertaken, in or about 515 H, this type of edifice was already well developed and must have been copied from a similar edifice nearby which at the time could only be the brand-new Nizāmīya, which had such prestige.

The success of the madrasa mosque, made up of the addition of a madrasa courtyard to the kiosk of the ancient Iranian mosques, was so great and so swift that in 530 H, only fifteen years after the burning of the Masdjid-i Djum'a at Isfahān, we see a four-ivan mosque as a single composition at Zawara (fig. 205).

However, it took this new type of edifice, which as we have just seen, first occurred in the west of Iran, three centuries to reach Khurāsān. The most ancient madrasa-mosque that I know in that area, without going outside the boundaries of present-day Iran, is the mosque of Gawhar Shad at Mashhad.[3] It dates from 821 H (AD 1418). Further east, at Samarqand, there is another, slightly older one, generally called the Mosque of Bībī Shānim or Bībī Khānum, but which is actually a madrasa built in imitation of the mosque with a central courtyard and four ivans. It dates from 801 and 808 H (AD 1398 and AD 1405) and served as a model for all the great madrasas of Turkestan.

[1] Al-Māfarrūkhī, the Arab historian, author of a *History of Isfahān* dated 421 H (AD 1030).

[2] The façade of the eastern ivan, which is classically Seljuk, has not been modified since the time of its construction, That of the southern ivan, rediscovered beneath the facing of glazed tiles of Uzūn Hasan, is also clearly Seljuk. Moreover we now know from an end pillar found in 1938 inside one of the piles which support the hall of the mihrāb of Uldjāitū Khudābanda that the façades facing the court, between the ivans, were also Seljuk.

[3] The Iranian Great Mosque with a central courtyard and four ivans was introduced to Khurāsān by Iranian constructors, especially from Isfahān and Shīrāz, employed by the Timurid sovereigns, mainly Timūr himself. His tomb, the Gūr-i Mīr, was built at Samarqand by the craftsman Muhammad Mahmūd of Isfahān. It is dated 807 H (AD 1404).

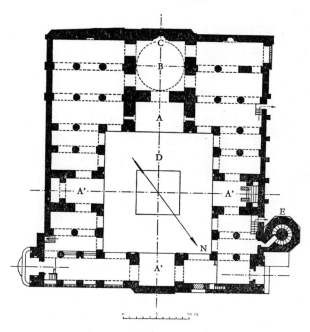

Fig. 205

PLAN OF THE MASDJID-I DJĀMI'
AT ZAWARA
A. Main ivan. A'. Secondary ivans.
B. Dome. C. Mihrāb. D. Courtyard.
E. Minaret.

So it really did take a matter of three centuries. The reason it took so long was that eastern Iran, the land of the ivan, had a type of mosque which was peculiar to it and to which it was strongly attached, the two-ivan mosque, those at Zawzan (fig. 200), Furūmad (fig. 201), and so on. It was not until the all-powerful Timurid lords acquired a taste for the architecture of western Iran that the madrasa-mosque penetrated into their domain.

In Khurāsān we find yet another type of religious construction, consisting of a square hall vaulted with a dome, generally rather low, with a very high ivan in front of it, which was used as a funerary mosque, at Tāyyābād (fig. 206), for example (the Masdjid-i Mawlānā), at Turbat-i Shaīkh Djām (the Masdjid-i Qalī) or as a musallā like the mosque at Tūruk (fig. 194). These monuments have no counterparts in the west of the country. Incidentally I do not know a single genuine musallā mosque from that part of Iran. As for the funerary mosques, if we may so call the tomb of Sultan Uldjāitū Khudābanda at Sultānīya (pl. 136), the Imām-Zāda Dawāzda Imām at Yazd, or the Masdjid-i Alawīyān at Hamadhān, for example, they have a quite different character. In them the dome is pre-eminent. They are in the direct and normal line of descent from the kiosk of the ancient Iranian mosques.

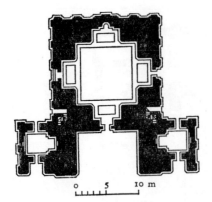

Fig. 206

PLAN OF THE
MAUSOLEUM OF ZAYN
AL-DĪN AT TĀYYĀBĀD

The madrasas and caravanserais[1] evolved, as I have said, from the Khurāsān house, but did not change much over the centuries. They differ only slightly from the Seljuk madrasa at Khargird (fig. 204). In the madrasa, when the principal axis of the edifice coincides with the qibla, one of the ivans, the qibla ivan with a mihrāb most often serves as the place for prayer, whereas one of the other four ivans is used as the entrance vestibule. As a result one of the ivans, the qibla ivan, is generally higher, wider and deeper than the others, but there are exceptions, either because the monument, the Tīmūrid madrasa at Khargird, for example, already has a mosque and in consequence the four ivans are equal in size, or because the main ivan is only, as in a great number of mosques, the vestibule of a domed hall containing the mihrāb. That is the case of the madrasa built by Shāh Sultān Husain at Isfahān (fig. 207, pl. 162 and coloured pl. V). Very simple madrasas also exist consisting merely of nondescript buildings around a central courtyard, and even simpler ones, which are ordinary dwelling houses.

In addition to the detail of their often very ingenious and varied plans, the caravanserais have preserved as carefully as the madrasa the essential feature of their original composition, the central four-ivan courtyard. However, some of them are octagonal, as at Dihbīd (fig. 208), Amīnābād (fig. 209) and Khān-i Khurra,[2] all three on the road from Isfahān to Shīrāz, but their external form which repeats the form of the courtyard within does not prevent the presence of ivans on the normal axes. Others in particularly cold regions of the country, the caravanserai at Shibli, for example, on the road from Qazwīn to Tabrīz, at the foot of the pass whose name it bears, are completely roofed in. But it remains true that the majority of the great Iranian

---

[1] The rubāt or *ribat* (cf. *ribat* in the Encyclopedia of Islam) was firstly a kind of fortress or garrison at exposed points on the Muslim frontier. Since the frontier war was at this time considered primarily as a struggle for the faith, these buildings had a character which was both religious and military; then it gradually became a post station, a caravanserai and a place of refuge for the population in case of danger.

[2] The caravanserai of Khān-i Khurra. This building is one of three caravanserais (Dihbīd, Amīnābād, Khān-i Khurra) to be found between Isfahān and Shīrāz, in the same area of Iran and probably attributable to the talents of the same builder. The caravanserai at Dihbīd no longer exists but we know it from a fine drawing by Texier which Siroux has reproduced in his work *Caravansérails d'Iran* (No 30, p. 74).

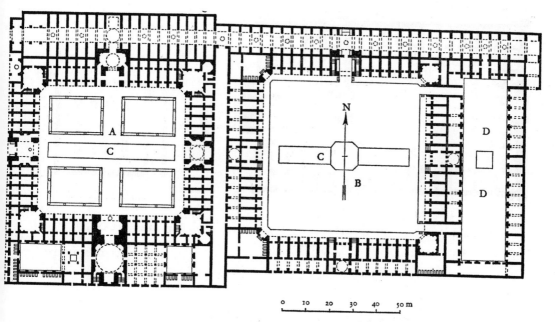

Fig. 207   PLAN OF THE MADRASA OF SHĀH SULTĀN HUSAIN AT ISFAHĀN
A. Madrasa. B. Caravanserai. C. Ornamental canal. D. Stables.

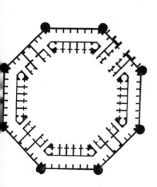

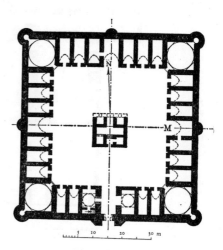

Fig. 208

PLAN OF
THE CARAVANSERAI
AT DIHBĪD

Fig. 209

PLAN OF
THE CARAVANSERAI
AT AMĪNĀBĀD

Fig. 210

PLAN OF
THE RIBAT KARĪM

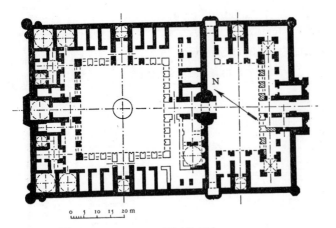

Fig. 211   PLAN OF
THE RIBAT SHARAF

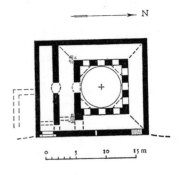

Fig. 212   PLAN OF
THE CARAVANSERAI
AT GAMBUCHT

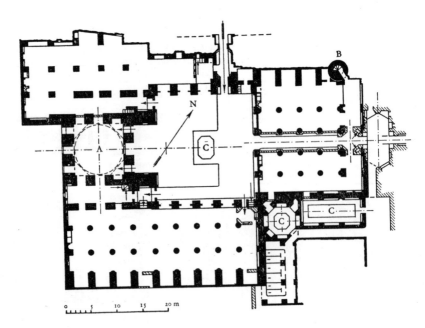

Fig. 213   PLAN OF THE MASDJID-I
DJUM'Ā AT SAMNĀN
A. Domed hall. B. Seljuk
minaret. C. Pools.

caravanserais consist essentially of a central four-ivan courtyard, lined with one or two storeys with galleries[1] or cells,[2] or both,[3] or sometimes a dome over one ivan to mark the entrance to the building.

I have only mentioned monumental caravanserais here, just as I have only cited the great madrasas, but there are many caravanserais in Iran which are merely open courtyards lined with undistinctive buildings, usually two-storeyed, and other caravanserais in the mountains which are completely roofed in, vaulted and sometimes half buried in the earth. Siroux has published the plans of four of these buildings[4] which are situated on the road from Damāwand to Amul, between the Imām-Zāda Hasham, at a height of about 9,000 feet, and Pilur, a few miles away.

In these monuments, the kiosk-mosque, the ivan-mosque, the Khurāsān two-ivan mosque, or the Ivān-i Kharkā type, the four-ivan mosque, the caravanserais and madrasas, to which should be added minor constructions like tombs which are extremely numerous in Iran and are often no more than more or less developed domed structures on a four-pillar base, we note the pre-Islamic forms which we have seen to be the native Iranian style. The cruciform Iranian Great Mosque of more modern times[5] is no different in principle from what it was when it was invented, c. 530 H (AD 1135); however, over the centuries, Islam introduced some improvements and, as I have already mentioned, this has given the mosque a totally different aspect.

I have already referred to the greater accuracy in the transition from a square base to the circular plan of the domes, as the result of which we see the vault resting on a regular octagonal base most frequently obtained by means of squinches,[6] but there were other improvements.

Large masonry vaults are usually thinner at the top than at the bottom. Until the Mongol period, a vault three bricks thick at the bottom passed successively to two-and-a-half bricks, then to two bricks, then to one-and-a-half bricks. In the case of large buildings, mosques, tombs and others, this produced on the extrados of vaults—since the intrados, visible from the interior of the monuments, had to be smooth—a series of abrupt steps with a rather unfortunate effect which had to be hidden beneath a decoration of dressed or glazed bricks. At Sultānīya this decoration was carried by blind arcades built subsequently[7] (pl. 136). Then another feature

[1] The Pasangān caravanserai, for example.

[2] The Rubāt Karīm, for example, which probably dates from the twelfth century AD (fig. 210), as its four equal and well-built ivans show (beginning of the sixth century H).

[3] The Rubāt Sharaf, for example, on the ancient road from Nīshāpūr to Marw (fig. 211), the construction of which was probably finished in 508 H (AD 1114–1115).

[4] Among them the Gambucht caravanserai (plan reproduced in fig. 212) (in: Caravansérails d'Iran, Mémoires publiées par les membres de l'Institut francais d'archéologie orientale du Caire, Vol. 81, pp. 40–42).

[5] Those of the time of Fath Ali Shāh Qādjār, for example at Teheran, 1212–1250 H (AD 1797–1834), and others at Qazwīn, Samnān (fig. 213), Burūdjird, etc.

[6] Or even with its eight sides doubled, i.e. on a base the interior perimeter of which is a sixteen-sided polygon which hugged the inscribed circle more closely even than the octagon could.

[7] In the Masdjid-i Djum'ā at Warāmin (pl. 139), in the Imām-Zāda Husain ibn Mūsā al-Qāzim near Tabas, in the tomb which Diez calls 'Hadshimasiah' near Djādjarm and elsewhere, the decoration and its support have totally disappeared, leaving visible the steps produced on the extrados of the vault by the abrupt diminutions of thickness.

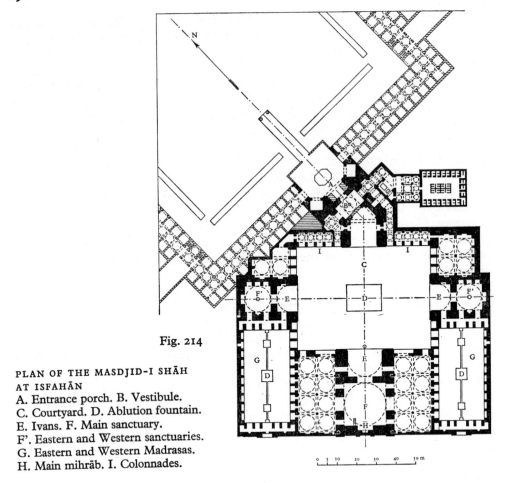

Fig. 214

PLAN OF THE MASDJID-I SHĀH
AT ISFAHĀN
A. Entrance porch. B. Vestibule.
C. Courtyard. D. Ablution fountain.
E. Ivans. F. Main sanctuary.
F'. Eastern and Western sanctuaries.
G. Eastern and Western Madrasas.
H. Main mihrāb. I. Colonnades.

was invented. Since monumental religious buildings, from the Mongol period
onwards, tended to rise to an enormous height against the sky and the interior
height of these buildings was not under any compulsion to copy this movement,
they conceived the idea of topping large domed halls with two vaults instead of
one; the height above ground level of the first was dictated by the interior decoration of
the building, while the second outlined the monument in space. From then onwards it
was no longer necessary to hide the stepping of the lower vault—it was now situated
between the two domes. Similarly, when it was decided to vary the thickness of this
upper vault in the same way as the lower one, as in the case of the Masdjid-i Shāh at
Isfahān, for example (fig. 214 and plates 155 and 156), the stepping could be placed
between the two vaults and thus was invisible.

    Moreover, the system of constructing light vaults, those of small buildings at least,
by means of light arches (i.e. a kind of ribbing, which made it possible as early as the

Sassanid period to build in space, without the aid of wooden centering or scaffolding), was sometimes applied to the large simple vaults of the Seljuk period and during the Mongol period, to the upper vaults of these double domes, in order to guide the work of the masons. The lower vault of the Khānaqā of Alā'al-Dawla Samnāni for example, thick and heavy and the real covering of the building, was built without auxiliary arches, whereas the upper vault, the sole purpose of which was to proclaim the monument from afar, was built by means of ribs—too lightly incidentally—one brick thick.

Another novelty to which I have already alluded was the increasing use of glazed tile decoration, which has come to be regarded as the characteristic feature of the Islamic architecture of Iran.

Like most eastern countries, Iran has always esteemed colour in the decoration of its monuments. Think, for example, of the two friezes, of archers and lions, which decorated the Achaemenid palace at Susa (fig. 135) or the spectacle the great ivan of the palace at Ctesiphon must have presented on certain days, the Tāq-i Kisrā, the hall for the Sassanid sovereigns' official audiences. But all that pomp, as Darmesteter said, was only 'royal fantasy'. During the first centuries of Islam colour does not seem to have played a great part in either the Arabian or the Iranian mosques. I am not speaking here of the brutal red and blue lines which sometimes reinforced the architectural design, nor the rudimentary colouring we find in the ninth and tenth centuries on the panels of moulded stucco in the buildings at Nīshāpūr, for example, but of the glazed ceramic decoration which was used systematically and increasingly on both the inside and outside of monuments and became an almost indispensable feature of Iranian religious architecture.

I feel that one can observe the first attempt, or, to put it another way, the first desire to use it, in a building dated to 481 of the Hegira (AD 1088), the Gunbad-i Khākī of the old mosque at Isfahān. Here we find decorating the walls of some flattened niches, clusters of stalactites made of everyday materials of various colours: black stone, grey stone, white stucco and plain brick, once pink perhaps, now yellowish (fig. 196c).

This was clearly an attempt at coloured decoration before the use of glaze. Probably there were others which may be revealed during the restoration of ancient monuments. In any case in 481 of the Hegira, the idea was already launched and glazed tile decoration quickly appeared in Iranian architecture. At first it seems only to have been intended to make the characters of inscriptions on monuments more visible, and thus more legible, for example round the top of the minaret of the Masdjid-i Djāmi' at Dāmghān which we can date to 500 H (AD 1106–1107), round the top of the minaret of the mosque at Sin, near Isfahān, dating from 526 H (AD 1131–1132), in three of the four inscriptions on the Minār-i 'Alī (The Sublime Minaret) (pl. 132) at Isfahān, built between 525 and 550 H (AD 1131 and AD 1155), and in the three inscriptions on the Minār Sariban at Isfahān which are contemporary. A little later and a little further north, in Azerbaidjan, especially at Marāgha, we find a whole series of well-preserved monuments. In them we find some of the best examples of the use of glazed decoration in Iranian architectural decoration. Until then when architectural décor was wanted, the only elements available were unglazed bricks, an excellent specimen of which is the tomb of Ismāʿīl the Samānid at Bukhārā: and the more subtle effects of light and shade which could be produced by decorating the plaster joints between courses of brick with a stamped design at Rubāt Sharaf (fig. 211) for example, i.e. in 508 of the Hegira (AD 1114–1115), already characterize the decorative forms of the monuments to come.

The most ancient of the tombs at Marāgha, the Gunbad-i Surkh, the Red Tomb,[1] is

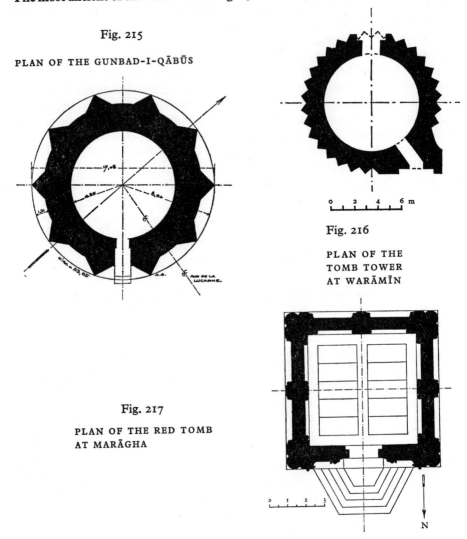

Fig. 215

PLAN OF THE GUNBAD-I-QĀBŪS

0   2   4   6 m

Fig. 216

PLAN OF THE
TOMB TOWER
AT WARĀMĪN

Fig. 217

PLAN OF THE RED TOMB
AT MARĀGHA

N

[1] The primary sense of the Persian *gunbad* is 'dome': from this it was applied to tombs in particular.

a square building containing a single chamber, also square, covered with a dome on stalactite squinches, still well preserved and once surmounted by an eight-sided pyramidal roof of which only the lower part remains (fig. 217).

The main façade of the monument faces north. At the entrance is a flight of five steps, with a sixth and a seventh which form the threshold. Well set off by the sturdy engaged pilasters at the corners of the building (pl. 124), this façade provides a vast and sumptuous framework of the door. The door itself, contained in a finely-proportioned arch, is topped by a panel of geometrical decoration surrounded by an inscription in Kufic characters. Above the arch is another inscription, also in Kufic.

The side and rear walls, between the engaged pilasters at the corners, are each decorated with two arcades and the continuation of the inscription band which crowns the main façade and runs right round the monument.

Below this the capitals of the engaged pilasters at the corners and those of the colonnettes which support the springing of the arches on the three secondary sides are of stone. All the rest is plain brick, admirably dressed, with its red colour set off by a few spots of turquoise blue glaze. There are also a few touches of colour, although they are not very evident, on the engaged pilasters which delimit the main façade.

On the side and rear walls these touches are so modest that they can only be seen if one looks for them. Nothing on the walls and only a few touches on the arches. Nothing on the other two engaged pilasters, except a sort of small blue cartouche some way up.

The glazed decoration on the main façade, also turquoise blue, is a little more abundantly used. It appears above the door, in the panel of geometrical ornaments, and higher still on the two corner-stones which occupy the space between the arch and the band of inscription above. In short not much decoration and scarcely a grand effect, but the beginning of a great art.

According to the upper inscription on its façade 'this tomb was built[1] on the eleventh day of the month of Shawwāl in the year 542', i.e. AD 1147. So it is more ancient than the celebrated mausoleums of Nakhdjuwān (now Nakhichevan in Soviet Azerbaidjan), earlier by forty years than that of Mu'mina Khātūn (fig. 219) and fifteen years earlier than that of Yūsuf ibn Kuthaiyr.

It belongs to a type of building which predominated throughout the north of Iran at this time: a square, polygonal or circular aedicule covered with a dome and topped with a pyramidal roof, most frequently isolated, but sometimes annexed to a sanctuary. Built before it were the Gunbad-i Qābūs, in 397 H (AD 1006–1007) (fig. 215 and pl. 123), the western tower of Rādqān, begun in 407 H and finished in 411 H (AD 1016–1017 and AD 1020–1021), the one at Ladjim, dating from 413 H (AD 1022–1023) and its neighbour, that of Rasgat, a little older, the monument at Dāmghān known as Gunbād-i Pīr-i 'Alamdār, dating from 417 H (AD 1026), the tomb of the Chihil Dukhtarān (the Forty Maidens) also at Dāmghān, dating from 446 H (AD 1054–1055) and the tower of Mahmāndūst, not far from Dāmghān, dating from 490 H (AD 1096–1097).

---

[1] Built, of course, in the sense of 'finished'.

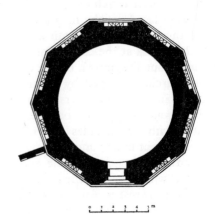

Fig. 218

Fig. 219

PLAN OF THE CIRCULAR TOMB
AT MARĀGHA

PLAN OF THE TOMB OF MU'MINA KHĀTŪN
AT NAKHDJUWĀN (NOW NAKHICHEVAN' IN
SOVIET AZERBAIDJAN)

Also dating from the sixth century of the Hegira, but later than the Red Tomb, are
the Tomb of Yūsuf ibn Kuthaiyr and that of Mu'mina Khātūn (fig. 219) at Nakhdjuwān, dating respectively from 557 H (AD 1162) and 582 H (AD 1186–1187), the circular tower near the Gunbad-i Surkh, at Marāgha, dating from 563 H (AD 1167–1168)
(fig. 218), the tomb at Urmiya known as Sa Gunbad, dating from 580 H (AD 1184–
1185), and the Gunbad-i Qābūd, the Blue Tomb, at Marāgha, dating from 593 H
(AD 1196–1197).

A fairly large number of tombs of this kind belong to the following centuries; they
are situated at Ardabīl (pl. 135), Amul, Bārfurūsh (now Bābul), Bastām, Damāwand,
Kiāw, Kishmar, Qum, Marāgha, Sārī, Eastern Rādqān, Warāmīn (fig. 216 and pl. 138),
Dardjazīn, Abarkūh, Hamadhān, etc.

When comparing these buildings with the Red Tomb at Marāgha, we noted that
coloured decoration was not used prior to it. Neither the Gunbad-i Qābūs, the tomb
towers of Western Rādqān, Ladjim and Rasgat, the tombs of Pīr-i 'Alamdār and the
Chihil Dukhtarān, nor the tower of Mahmāndūst have the least speck of glaze, but
immediately afterwards, its usage seems to have become more or less general.[1] Only
two of the dated monuments which immediately follow the Blue Tomb are not
decorated with it, the mausoleum of Yūsuf ibn Kuthaiyr, at Nakhdjuwān, and the Sa

[1] The tomb tower at Warāmīn, built on an octagonal plan with 32 steppings and topped with a conical
roof, is decorated with glazed bricks (fig. 216 and pl. 138). It dates from the Mongol period (675–688 H,
AD 1276–128), i.e. three centuries after the Gubud-i Qābūs.

Gunbad at Urmiya; but the monument at Nakhdjuwān is only some fifteen years later than the Red Tomb and we may imagine that the remote area of Nakhdjuwān was not very well equipped for that kind of work at the time. As for the edifice at Urmiya, the fact that the characters of its inscriptions and the features of its geo-metrical ornamentation are executed in dressed stone on a brick building, possibly proves that in this part of Azerbaidjan it had already become customary to differentiate the decoration from the actual construction, and that if glazed ornament was not used there, it was not that the means were lacking, as perhaps they were at Nakhdjuwān.

Although it was no doubt the architect of the Red Tomb who thought of embellish-ing his work by adding a few touches of glaze to it, it does not seem to have been his intention to obtain the chief decorative effect in this way. His exquisite ornamental mouldings confirm this. It is not composed in colour, but by the arrangement of planes, and light and shade his predecessors had employed.

The Gunbad-i Surkh at Marāgha therefore marks an important moment in the architecture of Islamic Iran, the moment when glazed ornament appeared in the external decoration of monuments in the north of the country.

The second in date of the Marāgha tombs, the construction of which was finished in 563 H (AD 1167–1168), is a circular tower built of plain bricks (fig. 218) but a rich entrance motif stands out from them (pl. 133). This motif has the same composition as the façade of the Red Tomb—the same moulded framework, the same arch enclosing the door. Above this door there is also a Kufic inscription. Above the door arch there is equally a second inscription, but the powerful moulding of the Red Tomb has here been simplified and flattened in a way which gives pre-eminence to the decorative facing. In addition colour, which played no appreciable role in the 542 building, appears in a better situation here. The letters of the inscriptions and the ornaments which surmount them are of turquoise glazed brick.

The third Marāgha tomb, the Gunbad-i Qābūd, the Blue Tomb, generally passes for the tomb of the mother of the Mongol conqueror Hūlāgū, but the date of its construction, 593 H (AD 1196–1197), demolishes this theory.[1] It belongs to the group of monuments in Azerbaidjan which used nothing but turquoise glaze (pl. 128) and is merely an unfortunate imitation of the Tomb of Mu'mina Khātūn at Nakhdjuwān, which dates from 582 H (AD 1186–1187) (fig. 221).

At that date, 582 of the Hegira, the architecture of Azerbaidjan had developed considerably in relation to what we know of its preceding works. The mausoleum of Mu'mina Khātūn is octagonal, like that of Yūsuf ibn Kuthaiyr, its neighbour, dated 557 H (AD 1162), but its proportions are finer and more graceful. The decoration, a composition of plain dressed bricks, is more skilfully developed and now invades and covers all parts of the building. The plane surfaces of the tomb of Yūsuf are hollowed out in the form of niches the upper part of which is entirely occupied by several series of stalactites. Glazed decoration, which is non-existent on the 557 monument and is only used on the circular edifice at Marāgha to make the inscriptions more visible,

---

[1] Hūlāgū died in 663 H (AD 1265), consequently seventy years after the completion of the Gunbad-i Qābūd.

163. FORTIFICATIONS AT SHĪRĀZ
Zand period (middle of the eighteenth century).
Inside this enclosure Karīm Khān had his residence, his administrative offices and his military headquarters.

164. BAS-RELIEF SHOWING THE IRANIAN HERO RUSTAM SHOOTING WITH BOW AND ARROW
Shīrāz. Zand period.
Today this bas-relief decorates the General Post Office at Shirāz. It was inspired by the Shāh Nāma, the Book of Kings by Firdawsī: Rustam, the Iranian Hercules, shot an arrow at his son Suhrab not recognizing him. Hence the hero's despair when he realized his mistake.

165. MADJNŪN IN THE DESERT, SURROUNDED BY WILD ANIMALS
Zand period.
This carving is on the lower storey of a house of the Zand period at Shīrāz.

166. FARHAD, THE SCULPTOR
Zand period.
This carving forms part of the same composition as that in plate 165.

167. THE PRAYER-HALL IN THE MOSQUE OF THE WAKĪL AT SHIRĀZ
Eighteenth century.
The Mosque of the Wakīl—the mosque of the regent—was built in the reign of Karīm Khān Zand. The roof of the prayer-hall on to which the south ivan opens is covered with small domes supported by five long rows of wreathed columns with capitals of acanthus leaves.

168. THE TOMB OF FATH-ʿALĪ SHĀH AT QUM
First third of nineteenth century.
The oratory adjoins the sanctuary of Qum, one of the holy cities of Shīʿite Islam; Fath-ʿAlī Shāh, who had the dome of the sanctuary covered with gold leaf at his expense, is interred in this oratory beneath a slab of alabaster.

169. THE HALL OF MIRRORS IN THE PALACE OF NIAWARĀN
Near Teheran. Nineteenth century.
Period of Nasr al-Dīn (AD 1848–1896). The plate shows two very typical features of Qādjār decoration: firstly the windows which are partly of stained glass in wooden tracery and secondly the piers between the windows which are decorated with a mosaic of mirror glass.

170. DETAIL OF THE DECORATION OF A SMALL MOSQUE IN THE FORESTS OF GĪLĀN
Beginning of the twentieth century.
Gīlān is a region where wood is particularly abundant, which is not always the case in Iran. This mosque and its decorative features are entirely of wood.

171. DETAIL OF A BAS-RELIEF OF FATH-ʿALI SHĀH HUNTING
This bas-relief is in the mountains, not far from the fortress of Rayy, the ancient Rhages.

165

166

169

spreads over the entire surface of the building, drawing one's gaze to the magnificent design of the great inscription and adding the interest of colour to the felicitously chosen lines of the architecture and the ornamentation.

It must have seemed at this period that it was not possible to go any further in this direction, and yet this is clearly just what the builder of the Gunbad-i Qābūd tried to do. Making use in his own way of the lines and decorative plan of the tomb of Mu'mina Khātūn, he too built a high octagonal tower topped with a band of inscription, a stalactite cornice and a pyramidal roof. He retained the niches on the upper part of the eight faces of the edifice which served as his model and marked off this zone with thin interlaced braids. He then covered the rest of the tower continuously from the braid right down to the stone base with an intricate network of decoration in dressed brick. The whole monument up to the base of the niches literally looks as if it was covered with a single piece of monochrome lace (pl. 128).

The colour lies above the braid, in the zone of the niches, and even higher. It still consists solely of turquoise blue and is only used here for colouring architectural features which could do perfectly well without it. The upper inscription itself, which is too small, is not enhanced by it. In spite of its great pretentiousness this monument of dubious taste seems barbaric compared with the elegant and refined tomb of Mu'mina Khātūn, although the latter is a dozen years earlier.

In short Marāgha gives little information about the history of glazed architectural decoration during the seventh century of the Hegira (thirteenth century AD). It does not seem to have made much progress at this period. However, what we do see in the tombs at Qum, Sawa, Dāmghān, Mashhad and other towns is the use in the interior decoration of these buildings of combinations of star- and cross-tiles at the base of friezes, bands of glazed plaques usually bearing Koranic inscriptions on the upper part of the walls, or those sumptuous mihrābs which were then being made in Kāshān by potters of great talent; Muhammad ibn Abū-Tahir, his son Ali and his grandson Yūsuf.[1]

Some of these star- and cross-tiles and square plaques with inscriptions are very fine (pl. 173). Teheran Museum has a rich collection of them, but they can only rarely be considered as architectural components of the monuments they decorated. They are *objets d'art*, mostly without relation to the general composition of the buildings. Moreover it seems as if the fashion for them soon passed since little remains of them even by Mongol times their use seems to have become less general.

The fourth tomb at Marāgha, the Gunbad-i Ghaffarīya (fig. 220), from the name of a neighbouring school, is that of a Mamluk amir, Shams al-Dīn Qarasunqur, famous as a great builder in Egypt and Syria, who was the Chūkāndār[2] of Sultan Kalā'ūn,

---

[1] Known works by these craftsmen are: Muhammad ibn Abū Tahir: the mihrābs dated 612 H of the Haram of the Imām Riza at Mashhad and the decoration of the tomb of Fatima at Qum, executed between 605 and 613 H. 'Ali ibn Muhammad ibn Abū Tahir: the central part of the mihrab from Qum which is now in Berlin (663 H); the Kevorkian mihrab (663 H) and the undated mihrab of the Haram at Mashhad. Yūsuf ibn 'Ali ibn Muhammad ibn Abū Tahir; the mihrāb in the Hermitage (705 H) and the one in Teheran Museum (734 H).

[2] *Chūkāndār*: literally—the esquire who carries his lord's polo-stick.

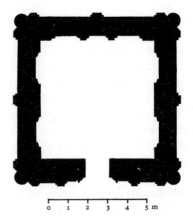

Fig. 220

PLAN OF THE
GUNBAD-I-GHAFFARĪYA

became Viceroy of Egypt under Ladjin, then Viceroy of Syria at the time of the third
accession to the throne of Muhammad ibn Kalāʿūn and took refuge with the Tartars
in 711 H (AD 1311). He died at Marāgha, which had been given him in fief by Sultan
Uldjāitū Khudābanda, where he had built his mausoleum, finished on 27 Shawwāl 728
(September 14, 1328), i.e. during the reign of Sultan Abū Saʿīd Bahādur Khān.

It is a square building of red brick built on a stone substructure which contains a
crypt. Polygonal pilasters tone down the sharp angles of its four corners. On the main
façade an arch in the centre with a two-line inscription above it frames the doorway.
Above the arch is another. Each of the rear and side walls is decorated with two arches,
with a band of inscription at the top.

The general arrangement of this monument therefore is the same as that of the Red
Tomb, its immediate neighbour. However, it is highly possible that it was covered
with a dome both inside and outside, in imitation of the mausoleum which Sultān
Ghāzān Khān had made for himself at Shamb, near Tabrīz. The lettering of the
inscriptions, which is genuine Kufic in the first two Marāgha tombs, the Red Tomb
and the Circular Tomb, and Kufic outside and rounded inside the third, the Gunbad-i
Qābūd, is completely rounded *naskhi* here. Colour, which was scarcely used in the Red
Tomb and then only turquoise, occurs here as at Sultānīya in black, ultramarine and
white, in addition to light blue. The inscriptions are in black on a white ground partially
covered with turquoise floral scrolls. Instead of being blind, like those of the Red
Tomb, the rear and side walls each have two windows, one per arcade, and each window, contained in a rectangular frame, is topped by a very beautiful decorative
composition in a combination of glazed and unglazed brick; above this is a band decorated with three escutcheons with the arms of Shams al-Dīn Qarasunqur.

The Khui Burdj, the last of the five tombs at Marāgha, at the side of the Gunbad-i
Qābūd, is no longer extant. It collapsed early in 1938. This monument was a cylin-
drical tower, like its neighbour the Gunbad-i Surkh, but of more graceful proportions.
It also included a lavishly decorated rectangular appliqué composition serving as a
frame for the door. This entrance composition, entirely executed in stucco and a

mosaic of glazed tiles of such miniature proportions that they stand in complete contrast to the large-scale decoration of the Circular Tomb confirms for us that the Khui Burdj was appreciably more recent. We seem indeed to be able to date its construction, as F. Sarre has suggested, to the second half of the eighth century of the Hegira, i.e. the Tīmūrid period.

The Mongol custom of hiding the burial place of princes was preserved in Persia until the end of the seventh century of the Hegira. 'The tomb of Arghūn,'[1] says the historian Hamd Allāh Mustawfī al-Qazwīnī, 'is in the mountainous massif of Sudjās, where the place was concealed, following the Mongol custom, making the whole mountain into an inviolable sanctuary.' Ghāzān broke with this custom. 'The body of Arghūn,' says W. Barthold, 'was buried in the Sudjās range, south of Sultānīya; later, during Ghāzān's reign, a mausoleum was built there.' I often went there to look for it. However, I found nothing of the kind on the heights or in the plain of Sudjās. Perhaps Ghāzān took the body of his father back to Sultānīya. . . . There was nothing im-probable about the idea. . . . After going to the lengths of extracting him from his hiding-place, it must have been just as easy to remove him from the mountain altogether. . . . After all it was only a matter of a dozen miles or so. . . . One day, while speculating in this fashion on the way back to my camp, I crossed the pass which took me into the valley of Sultānīya. When I was leaving the ravine, just at the moment when the vast plain appeared in its entirety, I noticed a disrupted hillock to the right of my path which looked as if it contained the remains of an ancient building. On approaching, I observed that the place had become a sort of brick quarry. At the foot of the diggings, one could see the first two greenish-blue stone courses, of what had been quite a large monument. This substructure was circular, in other words it must have supported an edifice which was also circular or polygonal. Above was a construc-tion of fine pink brick, decorated with glazed terra-cotta ornaments of ultramarine, light blue and white, exactly the same as those used for the decoration of the tomb which Sultan Ghāzān had built for himself near Tabrīz. So in the past there had been a great monument there, well built and faced with glazed terra-cotta ornaments, prob-ably dating from the time of Sultan Ghāzān.

We can consider the mausoleum of Sultan Ghāzān to have been a dodecagonal tower, some fifty paces in diameter, very high (though far from having been the vast height of 450 feet or so which seventeenth and eighteenth-century travellers attributed to it), covered externally with a dome, the general appearance of which did not differ materially from what we have already seen at Marāgha and Nakhdjuwān. The decoration of glazed and impressed bricks, the way in which the whole building is enhanced with glazed ornaments, the friezes of star- and cross-tiles all formed part of Persian architecture before the Mongol period, but until then we only know examples of turquoise glaze. During the reign of Ghāzān we see the appearance of polychrome: ultramarine, black and white in addition to turquoise.

However, at Zawzan in the east of Iran I have seen on the back wall of the largest of

---

[1] Arghūn, Mongol Khān of Persia, 683–690 H (AD 1284–1291), son of Abāqā (AD 1245–1281) and father of Ghāzān (AD 1295–1304).

the two ivans which form the mosque of Malik Zawzan (fig. 200), a magnificent decorative brick panel dated 616 H (AD 1219–1220), about 42 feet long and more than 16 feet high, on which turquoise and ultramarine glaze occur jointly. On this panel the interior of the central medallion, the lettering of the great inscription and the decoration above it as well, and one in two of the bricks of four small horizontal braids are ultramarine. The filling in of the other medallions, the intermediate decoration and the other bricks of the braids are turquoise.

Confronted with the mausoleum of Sultan Uldjāitū Khudābanda[1] which still stands at Sultānīya, but in ruins (pl. 136), we are no longer impelled to think of earlier monuments in Azerbaidjan, but irresistibly of those of the east, the tomb of Sultan Sandjar at Marw, the domed monument at Sangbast, and especially of the Gunbad-i Hārūnīya at Tūs. It is obvious that the architect of the mausoleum of Ghāzān tried to build a tower higher than the tomb of Sandjar, and that the architect of the tomb of Uldjāitū was impelled to construct a vaster dome than that of the tomb of Sandjar. Thus although these two monuments are not very far apart in time, they differ considerably in spirit and in the tendencies they represent. One lays claim to dominate by means of the elements supplied by the traditional architecture of Azerbaidjan, the other manifests the desire to break away from that architecture and the will to conquer the east with its own weapons.

So once again we have reached an important moment in the history of Iranian art, the one which saw the most enormous dome which that country ever reared into the sky, which would for a time ensure the victory of the constructional point of view over the decorative. Only for a time, of course, for, as I have previously remarked, art, in Persia as elsewhere, under penalty of stagnating in repetition, monotony and finally the sleep of death, must keep on oscillating between the two poles generating its energy—construction and decoration. Movement, this alternating movement, is a vital necessity for it. . . . A little later, under the Safawids, as we shall see, the reaction to this occurred.

The monument at Sultānīya is the tomb of the Mongol Sultan Uldjāitū Khudābanda modified by himself to receive the remains of the Imām 'Alī and his sons, the Imām Husain (fig. 221 and pl. 136). In the past it was surrounded by various dependencies and other establishments contained in a square walled enclosure with a perimeter of 2,000 paces, reinforced with bastions richly decorated with glazed tiling.

Uldjāitū most probably began its construction at his accession, i.e. in 703 H (AD 1304). He became a convert to Shī'ism and conceived the project of transferring the bodies of the two Imāms to Sultānīya; he decided to give up his own mausoleum to them and as a result the buildings under construction were modified. A funerary oratory was added to the tomb on the west side and a mihrāb on the south side. The great hall beneath the dome became a sort of mosque and externally, to emphasize the religious character of the monument, the wall facing the Ka'aba at Mekka was decorated more lavishly.

Restored to its original purpose, when the people of Nadjat and Karbalā refused to

[1] Uldjāitū, son of Arghūn (AD 1304–1316).

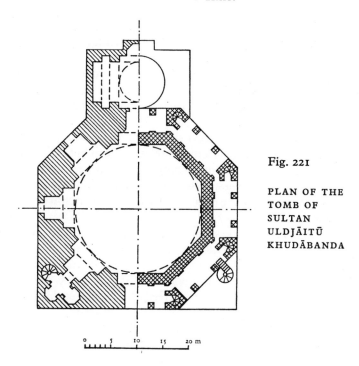

Fig. 221

PLAN OF THE
TOMB OF
SULTAN
ULDJĀITŪ
KHUDĀBANDA

give up the profitable remains of the holy Imāms, then visited and described by many travellers, the Sultan's tomb is well enough known to make another detailed description superfluous. However, I should say that we only find in its ornamentation the decorative elements previously employed, glazed brick with impressed stucco or dressed brick interstices (pl. 137), mosaic of glazed tiles and the imitation mosaic we know from Tabrīz. But colour was used at Sultānīya with a lavishness and force hitherto unknown. It no longer consisted of touches, stippling or agreeable designs, but of powerful combinations of coloured masses. Both in the decoration and the architectural shapes of the monument, the impression of force has been sought for and the graceful and even the elegant rejected. Externally the dome is entirely faced with turquoise faience. At its base a large band decorated with square Kufic characters tones down the contact of this brilliant colour with the ultramarine of the great stalactite cornice. The minarets and the façade of the arcaded gallery are decorated with ultramarine, turquoise and white tracery which allows the golden beige colour of the brick to appear in places. The vaults of the gallery are now decorated with rich designs painted in distemper, of an overall dull red tonality, which have nothing in common with the original monument.

Below, from the bottom of the gallery to the ground, only the natural brick is visible. However, for the reason I have stated, the southern wall especially was decorated with panels of glazed faience. As for the east wall, containing the entrance, it is possible that

it may have included some kind of projecting porch, but today it only shows the remains of a rather dull stucco decoration, contemporary with the Safawid alterations to
the building.

The building thus decorated gives as a whole an astonishing impression of airiness.
On certain days the blue dome, gleaming and flashing in the sun, with its brilliant
crown of minarets, seems to be floating in the sky above its base, which blends with
the fawn colour of the earth and the mountains. And this effect, which was obviously
deliberately sought for, has been obtained so elegantly, so easily, and with so much
skill; in the suppleness of the passage from the intense, deep blue of the cornice to the
natural shade of the bricks there is so much adroitness in the means used to avoid the
insipidity of the great light blue mass of the dome standing out against the paler blue
of the sky that we have to admire the decorative sense of the architect just as much as
his talents as a builder.

Inside the decoration of glazed tile was even richer. Apparently it covered the whole
surface of the walls of the great hall and the dome, for we can see traces of it today.
There was a profusion of inscription—friezes, strapwork, braids, ornamental foliage,
rosettes, stars of stamped brick in a surrounding of glazed brick. 'The whole of the
interior of the mosque,' says Hommaire de Hell, 'is decorated on the principle of
glazed bricks covering certain parts totally and forming designs in others (e.g. the
lower part) by intermingling with the ordinary bricks.'

Unfortunately the magnificent building was altered and restored in the Safawid
period, probably during the reigns of Shāh Ismā'īl and Shāh Tahmāsp I. The oratory
was modified and the interior of the monument covered with a coating of stucco on
which the whole of the Koran was painted and carved. This facing, beautiful as it
must have been shortly after its installation, is now nothing but a dirty grey tattered
coating through the holes in which it is possible to make out a few fragments of the
original decoration. But it is very likely that the major part of the original decoration
would be rediscovered beneath this Safawid plaster work, as well as inscriptions which
could clear up obscure points in the history of the monument, its founder and the art
of Iran in the Mongol period.

We have now come to the moment when colour, having as it were finished its
apprenticeship, sets out deliberately to encompass its aims—or rather those of Islam:
to provide architectural monuments with a covering appropriate to its all-pervasive
role. For three centuries, until the reign of Shāh Abbās I, we shall see glazed faience
covering the internal and external walls of religious monuments more and more completely: mosques, madrasas, khānaqās, tombs, etc. We shall see architecture giving
concrete form, so to speak, to the ancient creation most characteristic of the decorative
sense of the Semites, the pre-Islamic poem.[1]

As early as AD 1313, while Sultan Uldjāitū Khudābanda was still alive, the great
entrance ivan and the one in the courtyard of the sanctuary of Shaikh Bāyazīd Bastāmī
at Bastām were decorated with turquoise glazed panels resembling those on the
mausoleum at Sultānīya. However these were produced in quite a different way.

[1] See pages 259 to 261.

Whereas at Sultānīya the decoration consists of small glazed tesselae, which have been cut up and then assembled according to a certain design, the overall design at Bastām was divided into a certain number of relatively large squares and rectangles with elements in relief which had first been moulded and then glazed. We thus no longer have a mosaic pure and simple but a composition of larger and more elaborate elements, which themselves cannot be split up.

The mosque at Natanz is still more characteristic. It is made up of several parts of different dates (fig. 222). Its construction was begun in the Seljuk period. Then it was no more than an octagonal kiosk against the south wall of a courtyard, in accordance with the usual formula for the kiosk-mosque. According to an inscription on the entrance porch dated 704 H (AD 1304–1305), it was transformed in the Mongol period into a cruciform mosque, with a central courtyard and four ivans. One of these ivans, the north one, dates from 709 H (AD 1309–1310) which must be the date of the termination of the work. Meanwhile in 707 H (AD 1307) the tomb of a celebrated theologian, Shaikh 'Abd al-Samad, was added to the mosque. All these buildings, built of brick, were covered with a coating of white stucco decorated in places, on the

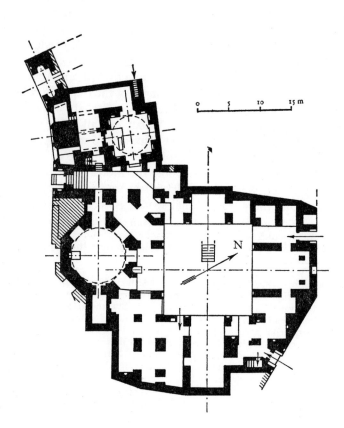

Fig. 222

PLAN OF THE
MASDJID-I
DJUM'Ā
AT NATANZ

vault of the Shaikh's tomb, for example, with stalactites and carved inscriptions on a background of white carved florets.[1]

However, the porch dating from 716 or 717 H which is all that remains of a khānaqā[2] built against the mosque is still profusely decorated with the same panels of blue enamel to be seen at Sultānīya (pl. 137). The frieze which frames this porch is decorated with an inscription in rounded turquoise lettering standing out against a background of small squares of natural-coloured brick.

Fifteen years after the termination of the tomb of Sultan Uldjāitū Khodābanda[3] in 725 H (AD 1325), an excellent small monument at Isfahān, the Imām-Zāda Dja'far, still only makes use of two blues, turquoise and cobalt, together with a pure white, and still turns out to be a masterpiece. It is similar in architecture to the Marāgha monuments, a high tower containing a single chamber. The coloured decoration is a mosaic of glazed faience. At this point it may be a good idea to give a short account of this kind of work.

First of all the artist drew the design of the composition to be realized in glazed faience, joints and cuts included. He did this actual size on one or more sheets of paper. That done, all the lines were pricked with a needle, then the paper was spread on an area of plaster prepared for the purpose and covered with a red or black powder which, passing through the small holes in the paper, reproduced the design on the ground. It then was redrawn strongly incised on the plaster and the original drawing was cut up into as many pieces as there would be bits of mosaic. So far this resembles the fabrication of stained glass in France in the Middle Ages. Each piece of paper was then stuck on to a plaque of glazed faience of the requisite colour. Then by means of a sort of small pick shaped like an adze with very sharp edges, some rasps and files, the *kāshīsaz*, 'the cutter of glazed tiles',[4] cut out all these small pieces and put them glazed face downwards in their right place on the area of plaster. When this part of the work was finished, i.e. when the design on the plaster was completely covered, all that remained was to pour over the whole the mortar needed to join up all the different parts of the panel. When it was dry it was set in its place on the wall to be faced, in such a way that there was a small space between the panel and the actual wall into

---

[1] However, in the past the tomb of Shaikh 'Abd al-Samad contained one of those great glazed terra-cotta mihrābs for which the Abū Tahir family of Kāshān was renowned. Madame J. Dieulafoy and Major P. M. Sykes saw it still *in situ* at the end of the last century. It has since disappeared.

[2] *Khānaqā* means hostelry.

[3] In fact it was in 710 H (AD 1310) that the Sultān, to celebrate the end of the work on the construction of his tomb, invited Shaikh Safī al-Dīn of Ardabil, the ancestor of the first sovereign of the Safawid dynasty, and Sheikh 'Ala al-Dawla of Samnān to a great banquet, about which this story, full of charming hypocrisy, was told: Uldjāitū allowed the great Sheikh Safī al-Dīn of Ardabil to sit on his right and took the great Sheikh 'Ala al-Dawla of Simnan on his left. One of the two ate, while the other touched nothing. When the tables were cleared Uldjāitū said: 'The piety of each of these Sheikhs is pre-eminent, but why does one eat all the dishes while the other eats nothing? If that is allowed, why do they differ? If it is not allowed, why do they not both abstain?' Safī al-Dīn replied: 'His Eminence Sheikh 'Ala al-Dawla is an ocean which nothing may soil', and 'Ala al-Dawla: 'His Eminence Sheikh Safī al-Dīn is a royal falcon who soars above everything'. The Ilkhān, highly pleased with the replies and reciprocal compliments of the two holy men, praised them and rewarded them as a result.

[4] So much was the production of glazed tiles associated with Kāshān that the tiles themselves came to be called *kāshī* (*qāshī*).

which the mortar which would join the panel to the masonry would ultimately be poured.

Naturally when the overall composition was formed of identical elements, each of them could be made separately. In the case of very large elements, or if there were no identical elements in a large composition, the workman arbitrarily divided up the design into several pieces the shape and dimensions of which he himself determined. This type of work demanded both patience and precision, as we see, qualities in which the Iranian workman excelled.

This system of decoration, which had been virtually unknown in the Seljuk period, and which occurs on the Imām-Zāda Dja'far at Isfahan (725 H), was used with more and more skill (pl. 142) right up to the reign of Shāh Abbās I, the great builder, who felt that the process was too slow and too expensive, and replaced it almost entirely by tiles of painted faience (pl. 158) which I shall mention later.

Two more excellent monuments at Isfahan, the Imāmī Madrasa and the Imām-Zāda Qāsim (fig. 223), which are neighbours, were built by a certain Abū'l-Hasan Tālūt al-Dāmghānī in honour of his master, the theologian Muhammad Bābā Qāsim al-Isfahānī,[1] the first during that scholar's lifetime, between 720 and 740 H (AD 1320–1340), the other dating from AD 1341, after his death. Their decoration still only makes use of the two blues, ultramarine and turquoise, white, and for the tomb—more modern than the madrasa—a little beautiful yellow ochre. Yet the decoration of the madrasa was only finished during the reign of the Muzaffarid sovereign Shāh Mahmūd between AD 1358 and AD 1375, at the same time as the madrasa adjacent to the Masdjid-i Djum'ā at Isfahan was being built.

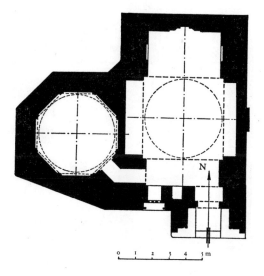

Fig. 223

TOMB OF BĀBĀ QĀSIM
AT ISFAHĀN (ORIGINAL STATE)

0 1 2 3 4 5 m

---

[1] The theologian Muhammad Bābā Qāsim lived at Isfahan at the beginning of the eighth century of the Hegira. His tomb dates from 741 H (AD 1340–1341).

The next Isfahān monument to be discussed, the Darb-i Imām, with its glazed panels in relief and the more supple shapes of its floral decoration, does in fact look forward to Safawid art rather than back to the Muzaffarids. Built over the tombs of two descendants of the Imāms, Ibrāhīm Batha and Zayin al-Abadīn, it was completed in 857 of the Hegira (AD 1453), during the reign of the Qara Qoyūnlū Djahān Shāh.

The main ivan, with a door communicating with the rest of the building which was later walled up in the Safawid period, is certainly one of the masterpieces of coloured architecture in Iran. Its proportions are so right, the design of the decoration, the beauty and distribution of the colours, the delicacy and quality of the work so perfect that one could not experience more pleasure from any other monument of this kind except perhaps the Blue Mosque at Tabrīz, also built during the reign of Djahān Shāh Qara Qoyūnlū. It is an absolute gem.

The Darb-i Imām remained a single chamber preceded by the ivan just described until the time when this entrance hall was transformed into a tomb chamber, i.e. until the reign of Shāh Sulaimān. Previously, under Shāh Abbās I, the outside facing of the dome which covers the main hall had been restored. It has recently been restored again.

The ivan, modified as I have just said, during the reign of Shāh Sulaimān, was also topped by a small dome. It still bears some lines of inscription, the date 1081 H

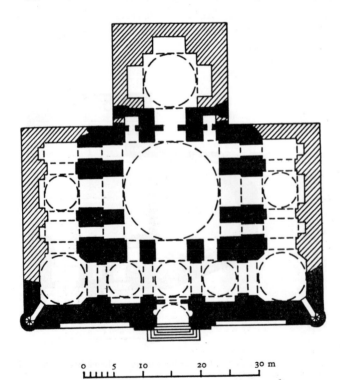

Fig. 224

PLAN OF THE BLUE MOSQUE
AT TABRĪZ

0   5   10   20   30 m

(AD 1670–1671), which clearly belongs to the reign of Shāh Sulaimān (AD 1667–1694), and the name of the writer, Muhammad Riza al-Imāmī.

At about the same time as the completion of the Darb-i Imām at Isfahān, the famous Blue Mosque, the supreme achievement of colour in architectural decoration, was being built at Tabrīz (fig. 224). This monument, dated 870 H (AD 1465), was destroyed by an earthquake which ruined the whole town and killed, so it is said, 70,000 people. All that remains standing of the famous mosque are a few pillars, some sections of the outer wall and the façade which is in a lamentable state. However, what remains is so beautiful and of such interest that the Iranian Department of Antiquities decided to keep it as it is as far as possible. It did not attempt to reconstruct the great dome on inclined pillars which had lost their stability, nor to fill in the gaps in the mosaic of glazed tiles which no modern technique could imitate. It only restored the elements of the building which were still usable, the ancient masonry which thus became the mainstay for the whole but which was not given a new facing of glazed tile mosaic (pl. 145). This difficult task has been successfully completed. What remains of the famous mosque is no longer at the mercy of a minor earthquake. However, it is no good trying to recapture the impression of the original building. The magnificent glazed decoration is now no more than scattered patches of colour, but they are in their right place on the monument, and they only are authentic (plates 145 and 146).

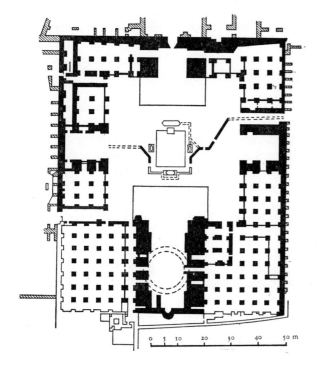

Fig. 225

PLAN OF THE MOSQUE OF
GAWHAR SHĀD
AT MASHHAD

What makes the Blue Mosque at Tabrīz the masterpiece of glazed architectural decoration is the quality of the composition, the design, and the workmanship, but especially the new and varied colours which are employed there. It has tones which give an impression of unrivalled harmony, tones of autumn brown, yellow ochre olive green, colours never seen before in ceramic mosaic. Admittedly in the Tīmūrid period the ceramics of the mosque of Gawhar Shād at Mashhad (fig. 225) already made use of a similar range of colours, but they did not harmonize so well with one another or with the whole building, no doubt because of the importance given to the violent red of the natural brick used as one of the colours in the decoration. The combination of the ultramarine of the background and this red give the whole a most disagreeable deep violet tinge. In the Blue Mosque, the tones, more delicate and better distributed, since the pink of the bricks does not intervene directly in the ceramic decoration, are more pleasing. The design is also much livelier.

During the same period Sultan Djahān Shāh built the winter hall of the Masjdid-i Djum'ā at Isfahān (fig. 196a). Its entrance on the west side of the courtyard is a very beautiful porch which has recently been restored. This entrance composition has no bearing on the date of the other bays of the courtyard, which were executed on the order of a Turkoman prince of the Aq-Qoyūnlū tribe, Uzūn Hasan, 'Hasan the Long', who ruled from AD 1453 to AD 1478.

The Darb-i Kūshk, 'The Gate of Kūshk', Kūshk being the name of an ancient quarter of the town of Isfahān, is all that remains of a *zāwiya*, i.e. an oratory joined to a tomb. This porch, dating from 902 H (AD 1496–1497), is decorated with a ceramic mosaic of the simplest colours; its design appears almost archaic when it is compared with that of the Darb-i Imām, which is nevertheless some forty years older. The sovereign at the time of this reconstruction was Abū'l Muzaffar Rustam Bahādur Khān,[1] grandson of the Uzūn Hasan who built the bays in the courtyard of the Masdjid-i Djum'ā at Isfahān.

In fact, Uzūn Hasan was responsible for a great many important works in the old mosque at Isfahān. According to an inscription of 880 H (AD 1475), situated in the southern ivan of the courtyard, he had the vault of that ivan, which was threatening to collapse, 'renewed', and in a more general way 'restored to order what was in a bad state of this majestic congregational mosque'. The southern ivan and, as I remarked above, the inner façades of the courtyard were repaired at this time and decorated with a magnificent ceramic facing which is still largely in existence. The interior of the ivan contains panels of glazed tile mosaic in relief like those of the Darb-i Imām which are contemporary with it.

The exterior façade was modified by Shāh Tahmāsp,[2] the second monarch of the Safawid dynasty, who replaced the two great inscription-friezes of Uzūn Hasan by others in his own name, one rectangular which runs round the façade, the other, with beautiful light blue medallions, following the curve of the great arch.

The very fine and excellently made mosaic decoration of the façades facing the

[1] Rustam ibn Maqsud ibn Uzūn Hasan (AD 1492–97).
[2] Shāh Tahmāsp, eldest son of Ismā'īl I (AD 1524–1576).

courtyard, has the peculiarity that the large elegant foliated scrolls in it are not glazed but have been cut in panels of natural terra-cotta, the decorative effect of which is very soft and agreeable.

As we see, the decoration which Uzūn Hasan gave to the south ivan and the façades on the courtyard of the mosque seem, like that of the Darb-i Imām, much freer, more supple and more developed, and consequently more recent than that of the Darb-i Kūshk; but art, it must be admitted, does not maintain an even pace in time or space. And again the Great Mosque at Isfahān was a famous monument, cherished by the sovereigns and great personages of the country, imposing in every way beside the simple little *zāwiya* of the suburb of Kūshk. This, of course, must not be taken to mean that the decoration of the *zāwiya* is inferior in beauty to that of the mosque, but only that it was not quite in the fashion of the great monuments of its day and that it obviously seemed a little 'backward' amongst all these rapidly changing schemes of decoration.

Fig. 226   PLAN OF THE SANCTUARY AT QUM

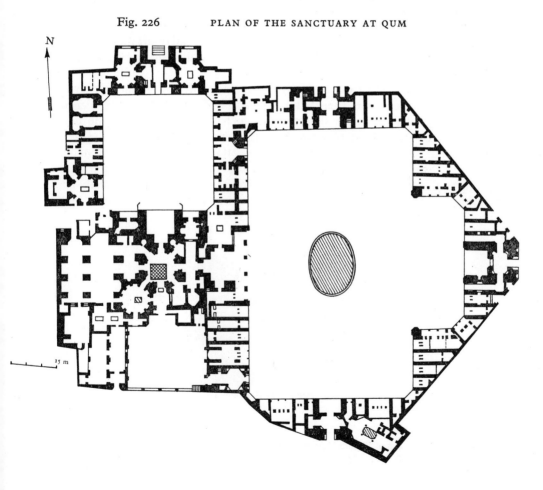

N

15 m

In 918 of the Hegira (AD 1513), 'during the days of Abū'l Muzaffar al-Sultān Shāh Ismā'īl Bahādur Khan',[1] the tomb of Hārūn Wilayat was built at Isfahān. It is said to be the tomb of a holy man whom Muslims, Jews and Christians all lay claim to, although we have no information at all about him. Its interest resides particularly in the great beauty of the ceramic decoration of the porch which gives on to the courtyard. These vibrantly transparent glazes are certainly among the best examples of this art. Possibly less ingeniously composed than those on the porch of the Darb-i Imām, these mosaics surpass them in execution and in that respect are not inferior to those on the Blue Mosque at Tabrīz.

The highly venerated sanctuary at Qum was also built by Shāh Ismā'īl, over the tomb of Fātima, the sister of the eighth Shī'ite Imām, 'Alī al-Riza, and the daughter of the Imām Mūsā al-Qāsim. It is surrounded except on its north side which opens on to the Sahn-i Kuhna, the ancient courtyard, by more recent constructions, some from the Qādjār period which are in less happy taste and others which are still more modern (fig. 226). This very fine north interior façade, dated 925 H (AD 1519), belongs to the period of Shāh Ismā'īl, except that the gold stalactites which adorn the far end of the ivan were added by Nāsir al-Dīn Shāh Qādjār, i.e. at the end of the nineteenth century. The dome was gold-plated by Fath-'Alī Shāh Qādjār[2] half a century earlier (plates 168 and 171).

This part of the edifice was restored in 1937–1938 by the Iranian Department of Antiquities. In the course of this work I photographed a flower of glazed faience which is an exact copy of a much older flower motif which is used elsewhere on the monument (fig. 227). The sort of white framework which demarcates the mass of the petals is in one piece, cut out of a plaque of glazed terra-cotta by means of the only tools at the workman's disposal, a sort of small pick with a horizontal cutting edge, a rasp and some files. The yellow and green petals, cut in the same way and perfectly adjusted, fit inside this framework, as well as the centre of the flower which is in blue, with

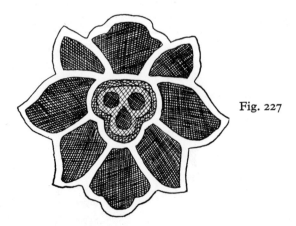

Fig. 227

---

[1] Shāh Ismā'il, the son of Shaikh Hāidar (AD 1503–1524).
[2] Fath-'Alī Shāh (AD 1797–1834), the grandson of Muhammad Hasan.

touches of yellow and red. To make a flower of glazed mosaic like this would take a skilled workman at least a day's work, taking into account the inevitable breakages. We can at once understand why Shāh Abbās replaced ceramic mosaic in his monuments as far as possible by square tiles of painted faience which was then glazed.

Shāh Abbās I,[1] the fifth Safawid monarch, was a zealous builder. It was during his reign, between AD 1587 and 1628, that architectural decoration in glazed faience, which had long been tending to cover the entire surface of the walls of religious monuments, reached its aim or nearly so. But whereas the first monuments of his reign, the Masdjid-i Maqsūd Begh, the Masdjid-i Shaikh Lutfullāh (pl. 150), the porch of the Qaisarīya and even that of the Masdjid-i Shāh (pl. 151) were covered with sumptuous glazed tile mosaics, the interior of the Masdjid-i Shāh was almost entirely faced with painted tiles (pl. 158). Certainly the painted tiles are not as good as the mosaics, but Shāh Abbās did not pay much attention to perfection of detail. What interested him was to face whole monuments with brilliant glazed mosaics. What he wanted to obtain was a general effect and to have buildings being entirely covered with glazed faience of a generally blue colouring; and we must admit that the impression produced is rather satisfying. Besides, the detail, although a little too unvarying and sometimes dull, is carefully done and harmonizes well with the architecture. The use of these thin tiles became almost universal. However, they were only stuck to the walls by gypsum mortar and did not stay there long, falling off and breaking on the ground. Any process which might be able to check this perpetual catastrophe would be so expensive that it would be cheaper to return to the old form of mosaic. We were constantly replacing sections, sometimes quite large parts, of the facing of the mosque of Shāh Abbās and when the repairs had to be done inside the great dome 117 feet above the ground, it was no laughing matter.

'Decrepitude and ruin,' wrote Pierre Loti about 1900, on leaving the madrasa of Shāh Sultān Husain at Isfahān (pl. 162), 'the last mirages of magnificence which will not last now more than a few years; the dome is cracked, the minarets are stripped of their delicate open galleries and the ceramic facing, the colour of which remains as fresh as in the seventeenth century, has fallen in many places, revealing the *grisailles* of the brick. . . . What dismal decay! The black-turbanned mullah who runs this ghost of a school bewails seeing his wonderful mosque turning into dust. "For a long time," he said, "I have forbidden my child to run so as not to shake anything. Every day I hear the tiles falling, falling. . . ." '

By the time Loti visited it, therefore, the monument which Arthur de Gobineau said did not lack a brick in 1855 and was 'as youthful as ever', offered a spectacle of advanced decrepitude less than fifty years later. However, the damage has been cured for a time (pl. 157). The lovely building is once more 'as youthful as ever'. The external facing of the dome has been entirely restored (coloured plate V) and that of the minarets too (pl. 162). But in this madrasa on the Chahār Bāgh,[2] as in the mosque of

---

[1] Shāh Abbās I, son of Muhammad Khudābanda (AD 1581–1628).

[2] The Chahār Bāgh (the Four Gardens) was the name given by Shāh Abbās to the splendid avenue which he laid out and which led up to the mosque of Shāh Abbās in Isfahān.

172. BRONZE PERFUME-BURNER
Gūrgān. Twelfth century. Length: 12 in. Archaeological Museum, Teheran.
This wrought bronze perfume-burner is in the shape of a fantastic animal. An inscription in Kufic lettering on the animal's breast wishes its owner: 'Valour, strength and glory'.

173. FACING TILE IN THE SHAPE OF AN EIGHT-POINTED STAR
Kāshān. Fourteenth century. Diameter: 8¼ in. Musée des Arts décoratifs, Paris.
These glazed faience tiles were fitted together so as to form a continuous facing, which is still intact in a few Iranian monuments. Some Museums (e.g. the Louvre) have succeeded in restoring complete panels of them. The bird on the tile is a pheasant which shows very strong Chinese influence and which, in Persia as well as in China, had come to be identified with the phoenix.

174. GLAZED FAIENCE TOMB SLAB
Kāshān. Fourteenth century. Height: 3 ft. 10⅞ ins. Private collection.
In certain religious monuments these slabs indicate the direction in which to pray. Its shape is that of a mihrab.

175. FRESCO IN THE IMĀM-ZĀDA MĪR BUZURG AT AMUL
Nineteenth century.
This is a fresco panel which most probably depicts Sulaimān (Solomon) on horseback and the djinns he has subdued. The Qur'ān (XXXI-82) does in fact say that the legions of demons obeyed the orders of Solomon.

176. FAIENCE PLATE DECORATED WITH A PALM TREE
Susa. Ninth century. Diameter: 9⅝ in.; height: 3 15/16 in. Archaeological Museum, Teheran.
Here the Mesopotamian palm tree reappears.

177. DEEP BOWL DECORATED WITH LAPIS-BLUE RADIAL STRIPES UNDER A TRANSPARENT GLAZE
Gūrgān. Beginning of thirteenth century. Diameter: 8 9/16 in.; height: 3 9/16 in. Archaeological Museum, Teheran.
This pottery is very light and very delicate. The type has been discovered intact in large jars. The inhabitants of Gūrgān, in terror at the Mongols' reputation for cruelty, seem to have hidden their treasures, especially their pottery, in large jars which they buried, for the most part near religious monuments. Other types of 'Gūrgān' ware include lustre wares and the moulded wares illustrated in plate 178. Interestingly enough it does not seem to have been exported.

178. BOTTLE WITH A HANDLE AND A NECK IN THE SHAPE OF A COCK'S HEAD
Gūrgān. Beginning of thirteenth century. Height: 10⅝ in. Archaeological Museum, Teheran.
Transparent glaze over a white slip with moulded and carved decoration.

179. GOLD MEDAL
Eighteenth century. Diameter: 1⅞ in. Cabinet des Médailles, Bibliothèque Nationale, Paris.
This gold medal was struck at Tabrīz by Tahmāsp Mirzā, one of the sons of Shāh Sultān Husain, who had been proclaimed his heir. But the listless prince did not manage to raise an army. Nādir Quli became his commander in chief and then replaced him on the throne in AD 1731.

174

176

177

178

كيك بارين استخان ايلا كاى	بولوركيم پاپ روان ليكاى	غايت غليب بردى بندى رضون	آنه وغ كشاد خسر درحون
توتون دیک غلیظادوت کبی سرکشی	روان بولدى بى پیاده قتل سنه	الار دين كيم اول ليامش روكم	چه بارتق توكلستيتى كلاس ن تمام
بلا برين ديك كه اوتى چاقلب	تى غسلين كيم كشرار برطيب	گريخه كوك تكبير بحره نكى كيل	سنتى غليدين تا خوديا اسبل
قول يحره بناى كليپ غاد ويك	حيل اغى سنخى جاود ويك	سا پسل بسل ماغند فرشته پر	هلك یى آتش بوست ليان
توروب خسرو چه دعا ايلادى	چوپ ان طريقىن دائلادى	آتين انجمن اجى خبر ن پيان	اتى برم ملى شير درس پيان
	تو كاكلاح دعاچاپتى ملبرتق قمر	انكا دافعى بارتق چاپتى برى برى خیر	

VI. MINIATURE SHOWING A BATTLE SCENE

Herat. Beginning of sixteenth century AD. Width: 7⅞ in.; height: 11 in. Cabinet des Manuscrits, Bibliothèque Nationale, Paris: Turkish supplement, 316, folio 415.

The subject of this battle scene was borrowed from the History of Alexander the Great *by Mīr 'Alī Shīr Naway. The author of this miniature is unknown. According to Blochet, one of the six miniatures in this manuscript was by Bihzād, another by Mīraq. As for the one reproduced here, it belongs to a manuscript, which according to its colophon was executed at Herāt by Ali Hidjrani in AD 1526. Turbans topped by a stick were commonly worn during the reign of Shāh Ismā'īl, the founder of the Safawid dynasty and the father of Shāh Tahmāsp. The artistic conventions which on a first glance seem to idealize the figures and to make them creatures of fantasy, on a closer look astonish by the violence with which the battle is depicted. In an important sense few artistic genres are so lacking in reticence as the post-Tīmūrid miniature.*

The writing of the manuscript is a good specimen of nastalīq, *the last of the great calligraphic scripts to develop.*

Shāh Abbās, we have already had to carry out constant repairs. In some parts of the courtyard we were able to attach firmly to the walls particularly interesting panels of painted tiles; we managed it, but with difficulty, slowness and expense, by somewhat unsatisfactory methods.

After the steady splendid progress of ceramic decoration from the Mongol period until the reign of Shāh Abbās, therefore, we have the sudden cessation and decadence of this art. However, some time later there was a partial return to mosaics. I should say that domes large or small were never completely covered externally with painted tiles, since these are too fragile and unable to resist rain, frost and pigeons' claws. Since the time of their construction they have all been faced with narrow bricks two to two-and-a-half inches thick and pieces of glazed terra-cotta of the same thickness, in other words with real masonry. Meticulously restored, they have once more become splendid airy bubbles, flashing and gleaming in the sky (plates 152 and 156). To tell the truth, they are the most magnificent expression of ceramic architectural decoration in the world.

In the time of Shāh Abbās I the general colour range of the glazes was fairly dark: a lot of ultramarine and turquoise, a little white, yellow and green, very little black and still less red, or none at all. The overall impression was that of a harmonious blue. Under the successors of that monarch this range of colours was considerably modified. In the reign of Shāh Sulaimān there developed enormous foliated scrolls, often out of proportion to their surroundings, in which red, yellow and even a hideous orange play a considerable part.

At the beginning of the eighteenth century, under the last Safawid sovereign, Shāh Sultān Husain,[1] the dimensions of these decorative features, which had become exaggeratedly large, diminish—one might even say that their structure diminishes—and colour, abandoning red, makes increasing use of a very cheerful clear yellow, often in association with a stately blue (coloured plate V). The façade of the madrasa on the Chahār Bāgh (pl. 162) and the west ivan of the Masdjid-i Djum'ā at Isfahan, which is a Seljuk structure but was redecorated by Shāh Sultān Husain, are particularly typical of this period. Obviously there is some decadence in relation to works of the age of Djahān Shāh, Uzūn Hasan and even of Shāh Abbās I, but there is still much nobility and a very pure sense of architectural decoration. The porch of the madrasa of Shāh Sultān Husain which faces on to the Chahār Bāgh is still a masterpiece (pl. 157). Some people even prefer it to other works of the Safawid age.

The foliated scroll, misused under Shāh Sulaimān,[2] virtually disappeared. A return was made to geometrical compositions and to the sort of mosaic in which the main role was played by small glazed bricks rectangular or square and dressed as little as possible. However, painted tiles, as fragile as in the day of Shāh Abbās, and ornamented with the same designs coloured in the same way, were still used.

After the Safawids, the Afghans, who dominated Iran for some years, confined themselves, as regards ceramic architectural decoration, to producing inscription friezes, nearly always decorated with simple florets of no great interest.

[1] Shāh Sultān Husain II, son of Tahmāsp II (AD 1753).
[2] Shāh Sulaimān I, son of Abbās II (AD 1666–1694).

Under the Zands, during the second half of the eighteenth century, the large composition went out of fashion. On large panels of glazed ceramic tiles with a white ground we see—quite independently of the architecture they are supposed to decorate—official personages lined up as if on parade and the exploits of Rustam, the national hero. Or again, when this type of composition rapidly declined into insignificant anecdote, hunting or love scenes, Shīrīn bathing, Bahrām Gūr and Azadi, or so-called landscapes in the European manner on tiny ceramic panels.[1]

A little later, at the beginning of the Qādjār period, the early nineteenth century, a rather interesting local school of ceramic decorators appeared at Shīrāz. Shīrāz, the garden of roses, painted, *ad infinitum*, roses, pink carnations and violet irises with their long green leaves. Decorators produced very pleasing decorative compositions with them for the Khān madrasa, the mosque of the Wakīl (pl. 167) and other monuments. Obviously they have not much connection with the buildings to which they belong, but being gay and charming they were at least superior to anything of this kind which was made in the rest of the country during the nineteenth century.

Fig. 228

---

[1] During the Zand period similar subjects were treated in bas-reliefs (see plates 164, 165 and 166).

In fact the painted ceramics of the Qādjār period are for the most part very impoverished. They are an inferior reproduction of the achievements of the previous
period. At the same time Nāsir al-Dīn Shāh[1] sent painters to study the museums of
Rome and Paris. But whereas some artists progressed and produced works full of
promise, the production of ceramics, which remained in the hands of simple craftsmen, did not fare so well.

Fig. 229

However, it kept up to date, at least in its own view. At the doors of government
departments life-size sentries, of painted tiles, saluted (fig. 228) and young and elegant
secretaries were depicted on the way to their offices. On the porch of a military college
cannon, guns, pyramids of cannon balls and extraordinary machine guns could be seen.
On the door of another school there was a wretched, badly dressed individual 'illiterate'
on one side and on the other side a handsome young man 'literate', sitting in state in a
superb barouche.

Modernized versions of the old Iranian legends were represented on the walls of the
royal palaces (fig. 229).[2] Architectural decoration which had been so magnificently
treated over several centuries now evinced a total lack of brain and talent.

[1] Nāsir al-Dīn, son of Muhammad ibn Abbās Mirza ibn Fath-ʿAlī (AD 1848–1896).
[2] Figure 229 shows Prince Khusraw coming upon Shīrīn bathing.

How did it happen? How is it that one can still find an excellent *ustād* (craftsman) in the bazaars of Isfahān who is capable of repairing and restoring the glazed mosaic decoration of ancient monuments, and can even reconstruct it faultlessly when only a few traces remain, as if he himself was a contemporary? How is it that these intelligent and capable men have shown themselves incapable of developing, creating and modernizing themselves in the line of their traditions? We have here the whole tragedy of Iranian art of the end of the nineteenth and beginning of the twentieth century, not only in the field of ceramics, but also in the spheres of painting, building, carpet weaving, and so on. Perhaps the following considerations may help us to understand why.

Until the beginning of this century the Iranian foreman was a mason who had become an *ustād*—a master in his calling.[1] He was entirely responsible for the building of the edifices ordered from him, the composition of their plans, as well as their realization and decoration. He knew nothing outside his calling of mason, had no trace of general culture, no professional library and would reply quite openly to anyone who asked that he could not make what he had never seen. His only documentation consisted of a roll of paper which he would proudly flourish containing, according to him, all the wisdom in the world: some traditional drawings of arches and vaults and some set formulae; for example, one which has caused a certain number of disasters: *The perimeter of the ground base of a minaret is equal to its height.* As if the ground's resistance to pressure was always and everywhere the same!

When he was commissioned to build a house, he would go to the site, accompanied by his client, a sack of plaster under his arm, he would choose the most suitable of the plans he knew for the particular job, then, piercing a hole in the sack he carried, he would draw the plan of the future building with a little trail of white powder. Since everything followed more or less automatically, both façades and interior arrangements, the make-up and even the design of the garden, it is hardly surprising that the architecture of Iran stayed Iranian for such a time. Western objects only appeared in it in the shape of lithographs or coloured engravings, framed and introduced into the decoration of the public rooms. Sometimes, too, the ceilings, which were composed of multiple small compartments, were decorated with landscapes of cottages which recall Europe.

When the lounge suit and the stiff collar appeared in Iran, and European fashions were introduced to the country by the young men who returned after completing their studies of medicine or law, the master-mason, like the tailor, had to westernize himself. Ignorant of the new techniques and materials, not even knowing what modern books to read, all he had to consult, in the absence of technical works and art reviews written in Persian which did not yet exist, were catalogues of European houses. So, torn between his traditions, his Iranian calling and his desire to Europeanize himself, the ceramic decorator, for example, rejecting the flowers and arabesques, decorated constructions with the European things he saw around him: the ravishing ladies in

[1] There is no equivalent to the word 'architect' in Persian. We only find the 'muhāndiz', engineer, and the 'bannā', mason.

crinolines, the cannon, the guns, that wonderful barouche. The master-mason built fire-places because he had seen them in some picture, although often they had no chimney to let the smoke away, and cornices in the 'Renaissance style' with small pot-bellied cherubs *à l'Italienne*. I have even seen metal beams, made by eye and not resistant enough, which had been reinforced with the trunks of young poplars.

How could it have been otherwise? Why should we be astonished at the oddity and incoherence of Iranian art at the end of the last century? In fact it has had to undergo a terribly difficult period of adaptation to the new ideas.

That time is over. The master-mason is now a master-mason and nothing more. Young Iranians, architects, painters, sculptors, decorators, pursue proper studies in Iran itself and Europe, where they are taught not only modern shapes and techniques but also their purpose and history. They are addressed about art in general and com-position in general, without confining these topics to the frontiers of one country or another, to the West rather than the East or vice-versa. They are supplied with the means of viewing the problems of their time with completely open minds and of solving them from their store of knowledge, relying on their own talent.

Iran now has real architects, real engineers and real decorators. The best of them, fully aware of the ancient traditions of their country, will be able to modernize them without slavishly imitating either Europe or ancient Iran. They will be the masters. To them will fall the honour of extending the continuous thread which from Antiquity right up to the present has led and still leads Iranian art, sometimes visibly, but often hidden, towards its destiny. Others will fail for art is the privilege of a few. But these few can suffice to guide the masses and make their age distinguished.

The minor arts of Iran have keenly interested the west. The art of carpet-making so captivated the Europeans that even in the fifteenth century we find those meticulous reproductions of oriental carpets with which Flemish painters decorated the handsome interiors they liked to depict. We learn from inventories that Jean, duc de Berry, and Catherine de Medici, among others, possessed oriental carpets in their palaces. Later Rembrandt copied Indian miniatures from the court of the Great Moguls. But East-West relations developed most intensively from the second half of the sixteenth century as a result of the numerous stays by Europeans in the East which created closer con-tacts between these two worlds.

If I have given a comparatively reduced place to the so-called minor arts in this work, the reason is precisely because they have been known in Europe for so long. This has made it possible for them to be studied intensively.

Persian painting could not be more intensively or better studied that it has been by Basil Gray, Stchoukine, Robinson and other scholars. Their conclusions in this field would appear to be of lasting importance.

Similarly many pieces of pottery have been and continue to be collected. These pro-vide the necessary basis for the systematic studies now in progress. And if the study of carpets has been less intensive, it is because we only possess a small number of items earlier than the sixteenth century and it is difficult to add to the inventories which have been established.

However, I have felt it necessary to say a few words about the painting, carpets and numismatics in Iran in the Islamic period, trying hard, as I have done throughout this book, to show the links which unite the art of one period of Iranian history to the art of the preceding periods.

PAINTING

Ever since man has appeared on the earth, he has tried to express his fears and desires by drawing. Today we can still admire the decoration of the Lascaux caves, although it dates from 15,000 BC. The road has been a long one, events have succeeded each other in a series of which we barely know the last terms. And yet we cannot say that the talent displayed by a prehistoric painter has been surpassed by a modern painter: the work of the former is still valid for us.

The few caves in Iran which have been explored by specialists have so far only produced limited archaeological results. No mural decoration has been found.

Some still visible traces of colour have survived on the sculptures at Persepolis, proving that the Achaemenids, like the Greeks of the same period, decorated their statues in the primary colours and, on occasion, with jewels and precious stones. But polychrome sculpture is not painting, and in addition the Achaemenids do not seem to have tried to glorify the personality of their heroes, even the royal ones: majesty, splendour, power, seemed more important to them than individualities.

The Hellenistic and then the Parthian period introduced to Iran a taste for the portrait, the representation and expression of a humanity differentiated by age and conditions according to the generations. But if ancient Iran has not yet yielded frescoes like those at Mari, for example, that does not mean that they did not exist. On the contrary it is scarcely plausible that a country which showed so much creative ingenuity could not express itself by painting from earliest Antiquity. Outside Iran, the Syrian caravan town of Doura Europos decorated its famous synagogue with frescoes, some of which, such as the vision of Ezekiel, depict characters dressed like Persians. The same is true of the frescoes at Sāmarrā (figs. 182, 183 and 184) which enable us to see the persistence of Sassanid civilization during the Abbāsid Caliphate. We may even suppose the panels in the Capella Palatina at Palermo to be influenced by Sassanid art. The fragments of painting found at Nīshāpūr dating from the ninth century, when the Sassanids ruled Iran, prove that painting existed and was used then in the mural decoration of palaces.

China always enjoyed privileged treatment in Iran: its pottery was as much admired as its painting, it was copied and imitated, but Iranians never managed to achieve the quality of its material and the purity of its paste; the same was true of painted decoration.

From AD 1038 to 1157 the Seljuk Turks governed Iran: China retained its prestige. However, the first illuminated manuscripts which have come down to us, of the botanical treatises of Dioscorides, among others, still show the power of ultimately Sassanid tradition. One of the centres of manuscript illumination appears to have been at

Mosūl, which was one of the Capitals of the Caliphate and this produced manuscripts as magnificent as the Galen, which is preserved in Vienna. The Pierpont-Morgan collection also possesses a work dated AD 1298, written in Persian and executed at Marāgha. Naturalism and archaism combined in this to produce a remarkable bestiary.

Then came the *Djāmi al-Tawārikh* (Collection of Histories), Rashīd al-Dīn's universal history the decoration of which is very much under Chinese influence.

In the fourteenth century Demotte *Shāh Nāma*, preoccupation with the dramatic is always obvious. Gold and blue skies distinguish the vigorous style of this work which scholars agree to date from the middle of the fourteenth century. A character in the foreground is often used in it as a sort of foil; the 'Combat of Iskandar' (Alexander the Great) is perhaps the most striking miniature in this series. It belongs to the Boston Museum of Fine Arts.

We can fix the beginning of the school of truly Iranian painting during the reign of Abū Sa'īd (AD 1317–1335). The Djalā'irids of Baghdād and Tabrīz were the Maecenases at the turn of a century which saw the appearance of the menacing figure of the victorious Tīmūr who took Baghdād in AD 1393. A *Kalīla and Dimna* very similar in composition to that of the Demotte *Shāh Nāma* is now in the library of Istanbul University. The page entitled 'The king of the monkeys throwing figs to the tortoise' is splendid: the drawing of the trees, which is done with great picturesqueness, overflows into the margin.

We now come to an important stage in the history of the Iranian book: the calligrapher Mīr 'Alī Tabrīzī invented the *Nastalīq* script which was used increasingly from now on. The famous manuscript of Khwādju Kirmānī is one of the greatest monuments of Iranian painting. The paintings are attributed to Djunaid.[1] His name appears on a miniature depicting the marriage of Humāy and Humāyūn. By exceptional good luck, because Iran is the country where good and evil are in constant strife, the most savage and destructive invasions have always been followed by a long period of time when the descendants of the terrible conquerors have once again become lovers and patrons of art. This indeed is how Prince Bāysunqur, the grandson of Tīmūr the destroyer, turned out to be. Among the manuscripts of his time which have been preserved is a *Kalīla and Dimna*, a collection of ancient fables which inspired La Fontaine, and a *Shāh Nāma*, in which the name of Bāysunqur frequently appears and which was certainly supervised during its writing and illumination by the prince. Bāysunqur himself was a celebrated calligrapher. He is considered to be the author of a monumental Qur'ān of which pages are preserved in the museum of the Sanctuary at Mashhad in Khurāsān. He is also supposed to have written the great inscription on the mosque of Princess Gawhar Shād, herself the daughter of Tīmūr, at Mashhad which dates from AD 1418.

The *Anthology of Sultān Iskandar* (i.e. Alexander the Great) belonging to the Gulbenkian Foundation, dated AD 1410, gives a glimpse of a world of charming sirens in bikinis; while on the other hand Abraham, intrepid although surrounded by a circle of fire, shows his heroic virtues by supporting the ordeal with rare stoicism.

---

[1] On the subject of Djunaid and the Djalā'irids of Baghdād, see p. 246.

Shīrāz showed great activity in the production of manuscripts during the fourteenth century, under the government of the Indjūs and the Muzaffarids. Slightly less than a century later a son of Shāh Rukh, Sultān Ibrāhim, came to power in Shīrāz. He was one of the great patrons of the Timurid period, like his brother Bāysunqur. However, the productions of Herāt during the first half of the fifteenth century seem to me to reach the apogee of an art which in fact only had three centuries of existence. A *Shāh Nāma* produced at Shīrāz *c.* AD 1444 which represents a banquet in a small, rather Chinese-looking Iranian courtyard shows the eclecticism and good taste which the period had acquired. In it white and blue Ming pottery, as well as carpets with geometrical designs, are depicted.

Mīrak, the famous painter and calligrapher, is believed to have brought up and trained Bihzād, who has come to be recognized as the greatest of the Iranian painters and miniaturists. Mīrak illustrated a manuscript of the *Khamsa* of Nizāmī containing thirteen miniatures on which Bihzād may well have collaborated. Bihzād's artistic expression, at once sensitive and familiar, can be studied in the illustrations of a Nizāmī manuscript which belongs to the British Museum. One of the most vivid pages depicts the construction of the castle of Khawarnaq. It was executed at Herāt *c.* AD 1494. Incidentally, the fact that a manuscript is catalogued as 'the work of Bihzād' does not guarantee that the famous miniaturist ever collaborated on it. Often the mention 'painted by Bihzād' only indicates that the illustration of the work seemed so excellent to one of its owners that he added what was merely an opinion to it.

Shāh Tahmāsp, the second of the Safawid sovereigns, decided to abandon the role of protector of the arts which he had held up to the middle of the sixteenth century or so. However, the love of fine manuscripts was too firmly rooted in the population (coloured plate VI) for this defection to be very appreciable.

There was a veritable industry, or in any case a well organized group of craftsmen, at Shīrāz and this produced large-scale works, especially copies of the *Shāh Nāma*; however, by the end of the sixteenth century these products had given way to the stereotyped repetition of the same motifs.

Generally speaking the seventeenth century was much less addicted to book illustration. Instead the sovereigns and great lords had the walls of the palaces they built at Isfahān and Qazwīn decorated with frescoes. Unfortunately European influences had a bad effect on Iranian production and altered its character. Nevertheless the seventeenth century had its skilled draughtsmen including the painter Riza-i Abbāsī and his disciple Mu'īn. Riza-i Abbāsī sometimes illustrated even small-scale manuscripts with great charm. One of these is now in the collection of the Teheran Museum.

There is no doubt, however, that the reign of Shāh Abbās was the end of the brilliant period of the Persian miniature. It had a renaissance at the court of the great Moguls in India, but we would be straying from our terms of reference to talk about this here.

However, under the Zands and the Qādjārs, the end of the eighteenth and the first half of the nineteenth centuries proved to be favourable times for artists. With the seventeenth century came the fashion of decorating reception or living rooms with frescoes: during the nineteenth century the fashion for portraits spread and an interest

O

in nature appeared in Iranian painting. One of the most skilful painters of the nineteenth century, Abū'l Hasan Ghaffarī, whose fame asserted itself towards the middle of the century, produced a large number of portraits of an astonishing purity of line, done in pencil with a touch of gouache.

CARPETS

Woven carpets appear to have existed in Egypt as early as the second millennium BC, but it is only during the first centuries of the Christian era that we have evidence for the manufacture of *knotted* carpets in this part of the world. The Soviet finds at Pazyryk in Siberia confirm the opinion that the knotted carpet existed in Antiquity as early as in the fifth century BC. The Soviet scholar Rudenko has studied various examples of these,[1] which insulating layers of ice had preserved up to our own day. Since Rudenko is inclined to attribute their origin to Iran, we may perhaps suppose similar carpets to have been made from the Achaemenid period onwards. However, it must be said that this is the only evidence we have.

The famous Sassanid fabric called *The Springtime of Khusraw*, which the Arabs carried off in AD 637, is said to have been a gold brocade with a powdering of precious stones, pearls and various kinds of appliqué work; it seems to have been sumptuous embroidery on a particularly rich ground, but not a carpet.

One of the pieces of Sassanian silverware, in the former Stroganov collection, we should note, is a dish representing a sovereign sitting in oriental style on a fabric which could be a carpet.

A little later, Surah XV of the Qur'ān assures the faithful that 'they will rejoice, reclining on green cushions and beautiful carpets'.

Shortly after the Hegira, during the seventh century AD, the celebrated Chinese pilgrim Huan Tsang travelled on the borders of the Iranian plateau and expressed in his *Memoirs* deep admiration for Iranian craftsmen, both as carpet-makers and weavers of silk.

Of the Arab geographers who visited Iran during the first centuries of the Hegira, some speak of the carpets which come from the province of Fārs, while others mention the carpets of Azerbaidjan. Ibn Battūta, who went to Izzadj, not far from present-day Mālamīr, spoke of carpets also made there.

These testimonials are sufficient to show that the manufacture of carpets was current practice in Iran at the very latest from the beginning of the Islamic period. At the same time the Armenian carpets of the Caucasus and those of Asia Minor as well appear to have enjoyed the highest repute because of the fineness of the wool used and the beautiful deep red they were dyed.

The close connection between the arts of the carpet, polychrome mosaic and the miniature is obvious. The manuscript of Khwādju Kirmānī dated AD 1396 and belong-

---

[1] Published in S. I. Rudenko, *The Culture of the Population of the Central Altay in Scythian times.* Moscow-Leningrad 1960 (in Russian) [Publications of the Archaeological Institute of the Academy of Sciences of the U.S.S.R.].

ing to the British Museum is decorated with carpets depicted with such accuracy that there can be no doubt about their reality. This also holds good for the Tīmūrid period, that is, in the fifteenth century. The mosaics which decorated the porches and walls of the religious buildings of the Safawid period might have served as a model for magnificent carpets, as plates 157 and 158 show.

In miniatures, the decoration of carpets had been geometrical for a long time; it ceased to be so in the sixteenth century.

Carpet-making occupied the leisure time of the women, whose life was otherwise rather dull and empty. The carpets of the tribe known by the name of *Bībībaf* which means 'woven by the ladies' are highly esteemed by connoisseurs. Iranian nomads have always made brightly coloured carpets for their tents. I once heard one of them say to someone who asked him where he lived: 'My dwelling is where my carpet is . . .' That is to say, the carpet represents for them comfort, security and luxury.

Iranian carpets are made to fit the dimensions of living or reception rooms, and if some of them seem very elongated to us it is because Iranian architecture was circumscribed by the necessarily short beams supporting the roofs of both palaces and dwelling houses. In contrast to the nomads, Persian taste was not in favour of geometrical decoration; it preferred carpets with garden and hunting scenes, themes much employed in silverware and miniatures, and in pottery as well. Some of these hunting carpets have come down to us and figure among the most precious items of our collections. The one in the Poldi Pezzoli Museum at Milan may be regarded as one of the most striking of its kind, being both dated and signed. The carpet of which we reproduce a part in colour (coloured plate IV) belongs to the Musée des Arts Décoratifs, Paris. This sixteenth century carpet, probably made at Kirmān, is decorated with hunting scenes, the subjects of which are borrowed from the works of the poet Nizāmī.

Tavernier, the seventeenth-century French traveller, visited the royal carpet workshops at Isfahān and described them as occupying the space between the 'Alī Qapū (plates 148 and 149) and the Chihil Sutūn (Forty Columns), two of the imperial pavilions of the Safawid period, which represents an enormous ground area. Chardin tells us how the royal warehouses reserved the finest wool from selected flocks, as well as silks, gold and silver thread, and so on, for the use of the court manufacturers.

The making of carpets remained a tradition in Iran until the beginning of the nineteenth century. The skill of the workmen, which was quite the equal of what it had been in the past, went so far that some fifty years ago some Tabrīz craftsmen, advised by a connoisseur, forged magnificent carpets which they artificially aged and then tried to pass off as sixteenth- and seventeenth-century carpets. One has to be a real expert, especially in dyeing techniques, to detect the fraud.

At the beginning of the nineteenth century, European firms set up branches in Hamadhān, Kirmān and Isfahān where they produced carpets, using manpower which at the time was cheap and abundant. They worked for large organizations responsible for furnishing government offices, grand hotels for travellers and other administrative buildings and their manufacture had to meet the demands of a specific clientele. These foreign firms subsequently were virtually forced to abandon the traditional craft and replace the old designs and the old colours by a decoration which was often quite different in type.

The future of the knotted carpet therefore is threatened.

Manpower has now become very expensive and the social laws are such that the children once employed on making carpets now do so less and less, which is only to be praised. Moreover, it is no longer indispensable even in Iran to cover the floor with expensive carpets. Marble, ceramic or other tiles already replace them, creating a different style.

COINS

When the Arabs entered Iran, bringing Islam with them, the coinage of the country was still using the human face in its design. The Muslims for a time followed this practice, confining themselves to supplementing the head of the Sassanian king with a short Arabic inscription.[1] However, as the stock of Sassanid coins became exhausted, they replaced them by others which bore Islamic formulae, the name of the Prophet, that of the Caliph of the period, the date of issue and the mint. But human pride, always so powerful, was quick to add as well the name of the sovereign which had struck the coinage and the titles which had been conferred on him. Such was the case with the Būwayhids, the Ghaznawids and the Seljuks.

Towards the sixth century of the Hegira, the Kufic script which had been used at first was abandoned and replaced by the *naskhī*, *thulth* and *nastaʿlīq* scripts during the following centuries.

The last Safawid sovereign who actually reigned, Shāh Tahmāsp II,[2] had a very interesting gold medal struck in AD 1722 (1135 H), after the deposition of his father, Shāh Sultān Husain, by the Afghans, at what he thought was to be the beginning of his reign. The obverse and reverse of it appear on fig. 230 and pl. 179 respectively.

Having seen something of the artistic development which this book has attempted to chronicle one cannot but hope fervently that the country and art of Iran may long continue to live their individual life!

Our period may indeed be exciting; but it is also the creator of an *angst* which is universally felt. All countries, large and small, are aware of the limit of their strength and know the impoverishment which national egoism represents. The famous towers of San Giminiano once housed brothers who warred against each other; now men are trying to divide the whole world into hostile camps. The Sorcerer's Apprentice has let events get well beyond his control

Teheran, which I knew when it was protected by its gardens, can only regret the proliferation of incongruous skyscrapers. Baked or sun dried brick, long thin poplar beams and sheet metal are giving way to concrete, steel and wired glass. And as a result of the high cost of construction, speculation in property and the frightening increase in size of the urban populations, families have to be packed into dwellings

---

[1] Hence the name Arabo-Sassanid which is sometimes given to these coins.
[2] Shāh Tahmāsp II, the son of Shāh Sultān Husain I (AD 1722–1731).

which do not satisfy the elementary rules of hygiene. The evil seems to have no remedy. However, the Iranian government is trying to give the greatest possible number of titles to property by supplying people with a roof and a few rooms, with water and electricity laid on. These indispensable social measures call for considerable efforts on the part of town planners, architects and engineers to make such an overall programme successful.

If these efforts are continued, a state of well-being which a people made healthy and happy could appreciate would finally result. We may hope that the country will be better balanced and organized in all classes of the population. All who have lived in the shadow of the ancient Iranian monuments and devoted a great part of their life to them will wish this with all their hearts.

Fig. 230

NOTE TO PART FIVE

SUNNISM AND SHI'ISM[1]

For Islam the Qur'ān is the expression of the divine will dictated to the Prophet Muhammad, who in his turn created the *Sunna*, i.e. the Law which subsequently was to direct by way of tradition the life of all believers. Thus, Allah is linked to the community by his Book, Muhammad by the Sunna.

For their part the companions of the Prophet reported his actions and deeds and eventually became propagators of the Sunna. From the complex of these revealed documents and the hadīths or traditions added by the companions of Muhammad was created the Sunnite doctrine, the orthodox expression of the Islamic religion.

It is well known, however, that Iranians are practising Shī'ites. 'Shī'ite' is a word the general sense of which applies to a large group of very diverse Islamic sects who take as their point of departure the recognition of 'Alī, the cousin and son-in-law of the Prophet Muhammad, as the legitimate Caliph after the death of the founder of Islam. The miserable fate of 'Alī and his son Husain was to draw the attention of Islam to their descent and provoke the flowering of a legitimist sect which claimed the Caliphate as the hereditary right of the family of the Prophet. Theological views mainly worked out in Iranian circles were then added to the political aspirations of the 'Alids. The most impressive of these conceptions is that of the *Mahdi*, a demi-prophet who is to reappear and make the world a better place. This rather Messianic belief in a man pre-destined to assure the kingdom of God upon earth became the essential idea of the Shī'ites. In another way this doctrine met with success because it did away with the despair of the 'Alids, who saw the line of 'Alī disappearing as a result of the constant executions of his descendants. The legitimist position of the Shī'ites consisted in preaching that the pontifical quality of the Caliphate, namely the Imamate, was passed from father to son in the line of 'Alī. Up to the sixth descendant of 'Alī the majority of Shī'ite sects are agreed in according pre-eminence to these descendants of the Prophet's son-in-law. However, the sixth Imām had two sons, Ismā'īl and Musa, and it was at that point that the gravest schism occurred. Some claimed that the Imamate was transmitted in the line of Ismā'īl, they are the *Ismā'īlites* of *the people of the Seven Imāms*. But other Shī'ites were worried by the fact that Ismā'īl died before his father, and transferred the title of Imām to his brother Musa and the Imamate continued via the line of the latter. The twelfth Imām, who was called Muhammad, is supposed to have disappeared at an early age in rather mysterious circumstances: his adherents, the *Imāmites* or *the people of the Twelfth Imām* agree in asserting that he will reappear. He is in a state of absence, and it is he the *master of the hour*, the *awaited Imām*, who one day is to return to earth.

When Islam was imposed by the Arab conquest, Iran took refuge in the practice of the Shī'ite creed which has left no uncertain mark on it.[2] It has given the Iranians the taste for misfortune, for desperate emotion, and for dissimulation too, for it was long

[1] The best treatment of Shī'ism is by H. Corbin: *Histoire de la Philosophie Islamique*, Vol. I. Gallimard Paris, 1964.

[2] The Sunna, with the addition of the cult of the twelve Imāms, still remains the basis of the Shī'ite doctrine.

persecuted. Islam inculcated resignation in Iran, the feeling that everything is written, that God alone is powerful, that his will alone shall prevail. Such sentiments do not drive people to action, but often to distrust. Only the Muslims are pure and none but the Shī'ites practise the true religion in which 'Alī, the revered head of the Holy Family, is elevated to almost divine rank. The Shī'ites revere extraordinary qualities in every one of 'Alī's descendants and consecrate them martyrs or witnesses to the faith.

BIBLIOGRAPHY

I. ANCIENT IRAN

AMIET, P.: *La glyptique mésopotamienne archaïque*, Paris, 1961.

BARNETT, R. D.: 'The Nimrud Ivories and the Art of the Phoenicians', *Iraq II*, (London), 1935.

BARNETT, R. D.: 'The treasure of Ziwiye', *Iraq XVIII*, 1956, p. 2.

BARNETT, R. D., and WATSON, W.: 'Russian Excavations in Armenia', *Iraq XIV*, 1952, pp 132–47.

BOSSERT, H. TH.: *Altanatolien*, Berlin, 1942.

CAMERON, G.: *History of Early Iran*, Chicago, 1936.

CAMERON, G.: 'Données permanentes de l'histoire iranienne', in *La civilisation iranienne*, Paris, 1952, pp. 32–42.

CHILDE, V. GORDON: *The Most Ancient East*, London, 1929.

CONTENAU, G.: *Manuel d'archéologie orientale*, 4 volumes, Paris, 1927–1947.

CONTENAU, G.: *L'art de l'Asie occidentale ancienne*, Paris-Brussels, 1928.

CONTENAU, G.: *L'archéologie de la Perse des origines à l'époque d'Alexandre*, Paris, 1931.

CONTENAU, G.: *La civilisation des Hittites*, Paris, 1948.

CONTENAU, G.: *La civilisation d'Assur et de Babylone*, Paris, 1951.

CONTENAU, G.: 'L'Iran avant les Indo-Européens', in *La civilisation iranienne*, Paris, 1952.

CONTENAU, G., and GHIRSHMAN, R.: *Fouilles de Tépè Giyan*, Paris, 1935.

CONTENAU, G., and GHIRSHMAN, R.: *Fouilles de Tépè Giyan, près Nehavand, 1931–1932*, Paris, 1935.

DELAPORTE, L.: *Catalogue des cylindres orientaux du Musée Guimet*, Paris, 1909.

DELAPORTE, L.: *Catalogue des cylindres orientaux de la Bibliothèque Nationale*, Paris, 1910.

DELAPORTE, L.: *Catalogue des cylindres orientaux du Musée du Louvre*, Paris, 1934.

DELAPORTE, L.: *La Mésopotamie*, Paris, 1923.

DELAPORTE, L.: *Le Proche-Orient asiatique*, Paris, 1948.

DESHAYES, J.: *Les outils de l'âge du bronze, de l'Indus au Danube*, Paris, 1960.

FORBES, R. J.: *Metallurgy in Antiquity*, Leyden, 1950.

FRANKFORT, H.: *Cylinder-seals*, London, 1939.

FRANKFORT, H.: *The art and architecture of the Ancient Orient*, London, 1959.

GHIRSHMAN, R.: *Fouilles de Sialk*, 2 volumes, Paris, 1938–1939.

GHIRSHMAN, R.: *Iran: From the Earliest Times to the Islamic Conquest*, Harmondsworth, Middlesex, and Baltimore, Md., 1954.

GHIRSHMAN, R.: 'Trésor de Sakkez', in *Artibūs Asiae*, Ascona, Switzerland, 1950.

GHIRSHMAN, R.: *Iran: From the earliest times to Alexander the Great*, London, 1964.

HALL, H.: *The ancient history of the Near East*, London, 1924.

HERZFELD, E.: *Archaeologische Mitteilungen aus Iran*, 9 volumes, Berlin, 1929–1938.

HERZFELD, E.: *Iranische Denkmäler*, volume I, *Vorgeschichtliche Denkmäler*, Berlin, 1932.

HERZFELD, E.: *Archaeological History of Iran*, London, 1935.

HERZFELD, E.: *Iran in the Ancient East*, London-New York, 1941.

HUART, C., and DELAPORTE, L.: *L'Iran antique. Elame et Perse et la civilisation iranienne*, Paris, 1952.

HUSING, G.: *Der Zagros und seine Völker (Der alte Orient)*, Leipzig, 1908.

HUSING, G.: *Die einheimischen Quellen zur Geschichte Elams*, Leipzig, 1916.

KÖNIG, F. W.: *Geschichte Elams (Der alte Orient)*, Leipzig, 1931.

KRAMER, S. N.: *History Begins at Sumer*, New York, 1959.

LE BRETON, L.: 'The early periods at Susa', *Iraq XIX*, 1957.

MACCOWN, D. E.: *The comparative stratigraphy of early Iran*, Chicago, 1942.

MALLOWAN, D. E.: *Twenty-five years of Mesopotamian discovery (1932–1956)*, London, 1958.

MAXWELL-HYSLOP, K. R.: 'Urartian bronzes in Etruscan tombs', *Iraq XVIII*, 1956, 2.

Mémoires de la Délégation archéologique française en Perse, Paris, 1921–1939.

MINNS, E. H.: *The Art of the Northern Nomads*, London, 1942.

MORET, A.: *Histoire de l'Orient*, 2 volumes, Paris, 1929–1936.

MORET, A., and DAVY, G.: *Des clans aux empires*, Paris, 1923.

MORGAN, J. DE: *L'humanité préhistorique*, Paris, 1921.

MORGAN, J. DE: *La préhistoire orientale*, 3 volumes, 1929–1936.

NEGAHBAN, E. O.: 'The wonderful gold treasures of Marlik', *The Illustrated London News*, 28 April and 5 May, 1962.

PARROT, A.: *Sumer: the Dawn of Art*, New York, 1961.

PARROT, A., and LAMBERT, M.: *Glyptique mésopotamienne*, Paris, 1954.

PERKINS, ANN-LOUISE: *The comparative Stratigraphy of Early Mesopotamia*, Chicago, 1949.

PERROT, G., and CHIPIEZ, C.: *Histoire de l'art dans l'antiquité*, volume V, Paris, 1890.

POPE, A. U.: *A Survey of Persian Art from Prehistoric Times to the Present*, volume I, New York-London, 1938.

PORADA, E.: *Corpus of Ancient Near Eastern seals in North American Collections*, Washington, 1948.

RUTTEN, M.: *Musée du Louvre. Guide des antiquités orientales*, Paris, 1934.

RUTTEN, M.: *Arts et styles du Moyen-Orient*, Paris, 1950.

SARRE, F.: *L'art de la Perse ancienne*, trans. Paul Budry, Paris, 1921.

SCHAEFFER, C.: *Stratigraphie comparée et chronologie del'Asie occidentale (IIIe et IIe millénaires B.C.)*, London–New York, 1948.

SCHMIDT, E.: *Excavations at Tépé-Hissar*, Damghan, Philadelphia, 1937.

STEIN, SIR AUREL: *Old Routes of Western Iran*, London, 1940.

VAN BUREN, E. DOUGLAS: *The flowing vase and the gods with streams*, Berlin, 1933.

VAN BUREN, E. DOUGLAS: 'The dragon in Ancient Mesopotamia', *Orientalia*, Rome, 1939.

VAN DEN BERGHE, L.: *Archéologie de l'Iran ancien*, Leyden, 1959.

WILKINSON, C. K.: 'The art of the ancient Near East', Metropolitan Museum of Art Bulletin, New York, March 1949.

II. ACHAEMENID IRAN

CHARDIN: *Voyages du Chevalier Chardin en Perse et autres lieux de l'Orient*, L. Langlès edition, 10 volumes, Paris, 1811.

CHRISTENSEN, A.: *Die Iranier* (Handbuch der Altertumswissenschaft, III), Munich, 1933.

CONTENAU, G.: *Manuel d'archéologie orientale*, 4 volumes, Paris, 1927–1947.

DALTON, C. M.: *The Treasure of the Oxus*, London, 1926.

DIEULAFOY, M.: *L'art antique de la Perse*, 5 volumes. Paris, 1884–1885; volume II is devoted to the monuments of Persepolis and volume III to Persepolitan sculpture.

DIEULAFOY, M.: *L'acropole de Suse*, Paris, 1890.

FLANDIN, E.: *Relation du voyage en Perse*, 2 volumes, Paris, 1851–1852.

FLANDIN, E., and COSTE, P.: *Voyage en Perse*, 8 volumes, Paris, 1843–1845.

GODARD, A.: 'L'art de la Perse ancienne', in *Nouvelle histoire universelle de l'art*, Paris, 1932.

HERODOTUS: *The Histories*.

HERZFELD, E.: 'The pre-Achaemenian and the Achaemenian epochs', in *Archaeological History of Iran*, London, 1935.

HERZFELD, E.: *Archaeologische Mitteilungen aus Iran*, 9 volumes, Berlin, 1929–1938.

HERZFELD, E.: *Iran in the Ancient East*, London-New York, 1941.

HUART, C.: *La Perse antique et la civilisation iranniene*, Paris, 1925.

KENT, R. G.: *Old Persian*, 2nd edition, New Haven, Conn., 1953.

KING, L. W., and THOMPSON, R. C.: *The sculptures and inscriptions of Darius the Great on the rock of Behistun in Persia*, London, 1907.

KÖNIG, F. W.: *Alteste Geschichte der Meder und Perser (Der alte Orient)*, Leipzig, 1934.

MEILLET, A. M., and BENVENISTE, E.: *Grammaire du vieux-perse*, Paris, 1932.

NOELDEKE, TH.: *Etudes historiques sur la Perse*, trans. O. Wirth, Paris, 1896.

NYBERG, H. S.: *Die Religionen des alten Iran*, Leipzig, 1938.

NYBERG, H. S.: *Das Reich der Achämeniden* (Historia mundi, volume III), Berne, 1954.

OLMSTEAD, A. T.: *History of the Persian Empire*, Chicago, 1948.

PERROT, G., and CHIPIEZ, CH.: *Histoire de l'art dans l'antiquité*, volume V, *La Perse*, Paris, 1890.

PORTER, R. KER.: *Travels in Georgia, Persia, Armenia, etc.*, 2 volumes, London, 1821.

RADET, G.: *Alexandre le Grand*, Paris, 1931.

ROSTOVTZEFF, M.: *Iranians and Greeks in South Russia*, Oxford, 1922.

SACY, SILVESTRE DE, A. I.: *Mémoires sur diverses antiquités de la Perse*, Paris, 1793, new edition, Paris, 1840.

SARRE, F.: *L'art de la Perse ancienne*, trans. Paul Budry, Paris, 1921.

SARRE, F., and HERZFELD, E.: *Iranische Felsreliefs*, Berlin, 1910.

SCHMIDT, E.: *Flights over Ancient Cities of Iran*, Chicago, 1940.

SCHMIDT, E.: *The Treasury of Persepolis and other Discoveries in the Homeland of the Achaemenians*, Chicago, 1939.

SCHMIDT, E.: *Persepolis*, volume I, Chicago, 1953.

STEIN, A.: 'An archaeological Tour in Ancient Persia', *Iraq III*, No. 2.

STOLZE, F. and ANDREAS, F. C.: *Persepolis*, Berlin, 1882.

A Survey of Persian Art, 6 volumes, volume I, text, volume IV, plates. Oxford, 1938.

TEXIER, C.: *Description de l'Arménie, la Perse et la Mésopotamie*, 2 volumes, Paris, 1842–1852.

III. SELEUCID AND PARTHIAN IRAN

ALTHEIM, F.: *Weltgeschichte Asiens im griechischen Zeitalter*, I, Halle, 1947.

ALTHEIM, F.: *Alexander und Asien*, Tübingen, 1953.

ANDRAE, W.: *Hatra, nach Aufnahmen von Mitgliedern der Assur-Expedition der deutschen Orient-Gesellschaft*, parts 1 and 2, Leipzig, 1908.

BIKERMAN, E.: *Institutions des Séleucides*, Paris, 1938.

BOUCHE-LECLERC, A.: *Histoire des Séleucides*, 2 volumes, Paris, 1913.

BOUCHE-LECLERC, A.: 'L'Iran séleucide et parthe', in *La civilisation iranienne*, Paris, 1952, pp. 75–119.

CHRISTENSEN, A.: *L'Iran sous les Sassanides*, 2nd edition, Copenhagen, 1944 (in the introduction: 'Résumé de la civilisation iranienne avant l'avènement des Sassanides').

DEBEVOISE, N. C.: *A political history of Parthia*, Chicago, 1938.

GABRIEL, A.: *Die Erforschung Persiens*, Vienna, 1952.

GUTSCHMID, A. VON: *Geschichte Persiens zur Zeit der Seleuciden und Arsaciden*, Leipzig, 1894.

HERZFELD, E.: *Archaeological history of Iran*, 'The Hellenistic period', pp. 44–76, London, 1935.

HERZFELD, E.: *Iran in the Ancient East*, pp. 275–306, London-New York, 1941.

JONES, A. H. M.: *The Greek City*, Oxford, 1938.

JOUGUET, P.: *L'impérialisme macédonien et l'hellénisation de l'Orient*, Paris, 1926.

KÜHNEL E., and WACHTSMUTH, F.: *Die Ausgrabungen der Zweiten Ktesiphon Expedition (Winter 1931–1932)*, Berlin, 1933.

MORGAN, J. DE: *Manuel de numismatique orientale*, 2 volumes, Paris, 1923.

Neue deutsche Ausgrabungen im Mittelmeergebiet und im Vorderen Asien, Berlin, 1959.

NEWELL, E. T.: *The coinage of the Eastern Seleucid mints*, New York, 1938.

OSTEN, H. H. VON DER, and NAUMANN, R.: *Takht-i Sulaimān*, Berlin, 1961.

REUTHER, O.: 'Parthian architecture', in *A Survey of Persian Art*, volume I, 1938, pp. 411–444.

ROSTOVTZEFF, M. I.: 'Dura and the problem of Parthian art', in *Yale Classical Studies*, volume V, 1935, pp. 155–304.

ROSTOVTZEFF, M. I.: *Social and economic history of the hellenistic world*, volume I, Oxford, 1941.

SARRE, F.: *L'art de la Perse ancienne*, 'L'art de la période séleucide et de la période parthe', trans. Paul Budry, Paris, 1921, pp. 21–28, pl. 58–61.

TARN, W. W.: *The Greeks in Bactria and India*, 2nd edition, Cambridge-New York, 1951.

IV. SASSANID IRAN

BENVENISTE, E.: *Les mages dans l'ancien Iran*, Paris, 1938.

BROWNE, E. G.: *A literary history of Persia*, volume I, New York, 1925.

CHOISY, A.: *Histoire de l'architecture*, volume I, Paris, 1955, pp. 100–123.

La civilisation iranienne, Paris, 1952, 'L'Iran sassanide', pp. 120–167.

CHRISTENSEN, A.: *L'Empire des Sassanides*, Copenhagen, 1907.

CHRISTENSEN, A.: *L'Iran sous les Sassanides*, 2nd edition, Copenhagen, 1944.

DARMESTETER, J.: *Coup d'oeil sur la histoire de la Perse*, Paris, 1885.

DARMESTETER, J.: *Le Zend-Avesta*, Paris, 1892–1893.

DIEULAFOY, J.: *La Perse, la Chaldée et la Susiane, Relation du voyage en Perse*, Paris, 1887.

DIEULAFOY, M.: *L'art antique de la Perse*, 5 volumes, Paris, 1884–1885.

DUCHESNE-GUILLEMIN, J.: *Zoroastre*, Paris, 1949.

FIRDAWSĪ: *Le Livre des rois*, trans. J. Mohl, 7 volumes, Paris, 1876.

FLANDIN, E., and COSTE, P.: *Voyage en Perse*, 8 volumes, Paris, 1843–1845.

GEIGER, W., and KUHN, E.: *Grundriss der iranischen Philologie*, 2 volumes, Strassburg (Leipzig), 1895–1904.

GHIRSHMAN, R.: *Bîchâpour*, volume II, Paris, 1956.

GHIRSHMAN, R.: *Persian Art: the Parthian and Sassanian Dynasties*, London-New York, 1962.

GODARD, A.: 'Voûtes iraniennes', in *Athār-é Iran, Annales du Service archéologique de l'Iran*, Teheran, 1949.

HENNING, W. B.: *Zoroaster, politician or witch-doctor?* London–New York, 1951.

HERZFELD, E.: *Am Tor von Asien*, Berlin, 1920.

HERZFELD, E.: *Paikuli: Monuments and Inscriptions of the Early Sassanian Empire*, 2 volumes, Berlin, 1924.

HERZFELD, E.: 'La sculpture rupestre de la Perse sassanide', in *Revue des Arts asiatiques*, volume V, pp. 129–142.

HERZFELD, E.: *Archaeological history of Iran*, London, 1935.

HERZFELD, E.: *Zoroaster and his world*, volumes I-II, Princeton, N.J., 1947.

HONIGMANN, E. and MARICQ, A.: *Recherches sur les 'Res Gestae divi Sapores'*, Brussels, 1953.

HUART, C.: *La Perse antique et la civilisation iranienne*, Paris, 1925.

JACKSON, W.: *Zoroaster*, New York, 1927.

LABOURT, J.: *Le christianisme dans l'Empire perse*, Paris, 1904.

MARQUET: J.: *Eransahr . . .*, Berlin, 1901.

MORGAN, J. DE: *Manuel de numismatique orientale*, Paris, 1923.

MOULTON, J. H.: *Early Zoroastrianism*, London, 1913.

NOELDEKE, TH.: *Etudes historiques sur la Perse ancienne*, trans. O. Wirth, Paris, 1896.

ORBELI, J., and TREVER, C.: *Orfèvrerie sassanide*, Moscow-Leningrad, 1935.

ORBELI, J.: 'Sassanian metalwork', in *A Survey of Persian Art*, volume I, Oxford, 1938.

PÉZARD, M.: *La céramique archaïque de l'Islam*, Paris, 1920.

PUECH, C. H.: *Le manichéisme*, Paris, 1950.

SACY, SILVESTRE DE, A.I.: *Mémoires sur diverses antiquités de la Perse*, 1793, new edition, Paris, 1840.

SARRE, F.: *L'art ancienne de la Perse*, trans. Paul Budry, Paris, 1921.

SARRE, F., and HERZFELD, E.: *Iranische Felsreliefs*, Berlin, 1910.

SMIRNOFF: *Argenterie orientale*, St Petersburg, 1909 [in Russian].

TEXIER, C. F. M.: *Description de l'Arménie, la Perse et la Mésopotamie*, 2 volumes, Paris, 1830 and 1842-1852.

UPHAM POPE, A., ed.: *A Survey of Persian Art*, volume I, London–New York, 1938–1939, pp. 498–830.

ZAEHNER, R. C.: *Zurvan*, Oxford, 1935.

V. ISLAMIC IRAN

ARNOLD, T. W.: *Painting in Islam*, Oxford, 1928.

Ars Islamica, Ann Arbor, Mich., 1934–1951, continued as *Ars Orientalis*, 1954 onwards.

Athār-é Iran. Annales du Service archéologique de l'Iran, Teheran, 1936–1949.

BARTHOLD, W.: *Turkestan down to the Mongol Invasion*, trans. H. A. R. Gibb, 2nd revised edition, London, 1958.

BERCHEM, M. VAN.: 'L'Architecture musulmane de la Perse' in *Journal des Savants*, February 1911, p. 59.

BERCHEM, M. VAN: 'The Mosaics of the Dome of the Rock at Jerusalem and the Great Mosque at Damascus', in K. A. C. Cresswell, *Early Muslim Architecture*, Oxford, 1932.

BLOCHET, E.: *Les enluminures des manuscrits orientaux—turcs, persans, arabes—de la Bibliothèque Nationale*, Paris, 1926.

BLOCHET, E.: *Musulman Painting*, trans. C. M. Binyon, London, 1929.

BODE, W.: *Altpersische Knüpfteppiche*, Berlin, 1904.

CHARDIN: *Voyages du Chevalier Chardin en Perse at autres lieux de l'Orient*, ed. L. Langlès, 10 volumes, Paris, 1811.

CHOISY, A.: *Histoire de l'architecture*, 2 volumes, Paris, 1955.

La civilisation iranienne, Paris, 1952: 'L'Iran musulman du VIIe aus VX siécle; pp. 168–211; 'Des Safavis aux Pahlavis', pp. 212–234.

COHN-WIENER, E.: *Turan, Islamische Baukunst in Mittelasien*, Berlin, 1930.

CORBIN, H.: *Terre céleste et corps de résurrection de l'Iran mazdéen a l'Iran shî'ite*, Paris, 1960.

CORBIN, H.: *Histoire de la philosophie islamique*, Paris, 1964.

COSTE, P.: *Monuments modernes de la Perse*, Paris, 1867.

CRESSWELL, K. A. C.: *Early Muslim Architecture*, 2 volumes, Oxford, 1932–1940.

DIEZ, E.: *Churasanische Baudenkmäler*, Berlin, 1918.

DIEZ, E.: *Iranische Kunst*, Vienna, 1944.

DIEZ, E:. *Islamische Baukunst in Khurasan*, Hagen-i-W, 1923.

DIMAND, M. S.: *A Handbook of Mohammedan Decorative Art*, 3rd Edition. New York, 1958 (the illustrations are taken almost entirely from objects in the collection of the Metropolitan Museum).

EDHEM, H., and STCHOUKINE, I.: *Les manuscrits orientaux illustrés de la bibliothèque de l'Université de Stamboul*, Paris, 1933.

ETTINGHAUSEN, R.: *Arab Painting* (Treasures of Asia), Cleveland, Ohio, 1962.

FLURY, S.: *Islamische Schriftbänder*, Basle-Paris, 1920.

GARDIN, J. C.: Lashkari Bazar, Les Trouvailles, DAFA, volume XVIII, Paris, 1963.

GODARD, A.: *Les Monuments de Marâgha*, Paris, 1934.

GOLDZIHER, I.: *Le dogme et la Loi de l'Islam*, trans. F. Arin, Paris, 1920.

GRAY, B.: *Persian Painting* (Treasures of Asia), Cleveland, Ohio, 1961.

HANGELDIAN, A. E.: *Les Tapis d'Orient*, Paris, 1962.

HERZFELD, E.: 'Khurasan: Denkmalsgeographische? zur Kulturgeschichte der Islam in Iran', *Der Islam*, 1921, volume XI (for list of dated monuments up to AD 1316).

HERZFELD, E.: *Die Malereien von Sāmarrā*, Berlin, 1927.

Historical Monuments of Islam in the U.S.S.R., ed. the Editorial Department of the Moslem Religious Board of Central Asia and Kazakhstan, Tashkent, 1962 (text in English, French, Russian and Arabic).

HOMMAIRE DE HELL: *Voyage en Turquie et en Perse*, Paris, 1853–1860.

HOWORTH, H. H.: *History of the Mongols*, volume 3, *The Mongols of Persia*, London, 1888; volume 4, supplement and index, London, 1927.

KÜHNEL, E.: *Islamische Kleinkunst*, Berlin, 2nd revised edition, 1963.

KÜHNEL, E.: 'Dated Persian Lustre Pottery', *Eastern Art*, volume 3, 1931.

LANE, A.: *Early Islamic Pottery*, London, 1947, New York, 1948.

LEWIS, B.: *The Arabs in History*, revised edition, London, 1958, New York, 1960.

LE STRANGE, G.: *The Lands of the Eastern Caliphate—from the Moslem conquest to the time of Timur*, Cambridge, 1905.

MARÇAIS, G.: 'L'art de l'Islam' in *Nouvelle Histoire Universelle de l'art*, volume 2, pp. 305–330, Paris, 1932.

MARICQ, A., and WIET, G.: 'Le minaret de Djam—la découverte de la capitale des Sultans Ghorides' (12–13e siècles), in *Mémoires de la délégation francaise en Afghanistan*, volume XVI, Paris, 1959.

MARTIN, F. R.: *The miniature painting and painters of Persia, India and Turkey from the eighth to the eighteenth century*, 2 volumes, London, 1912.

MASSIGNON, L.: 'Les méthodes de réalisation artistique des peuples de l'Islam', *Syria II*, 1921.

MIGEON, G.: *Manuel d'art musulman*, volume II, *Arts plastiques et industriels*, Paris, 1927 (this forms the second volume to SALADIN, 1907, qv).

NICHOLSON, R. A.: *A Literary History of the Arabs*, New York, 1907.

OLEARIUS: *Relation du voyage de Adam Olearius en Moscovie, Tartarie et Perse*, 2 volumes, Paris, 1866.

ROBINSON, B. W.: *A Descriptive Catalogue of the Persian Paintings in the Bodleian Library*, Oxford, 1958.

RUSKA, J., SARRE, F., and WINDERLICH, R.: 'Orientalische Steinbücher und persische Fayence-technik' in *Istanbuler Mitteilungen*, Heft 3, Istanbul, 1935.

SALADIN, H.: *Manuel d'art musulman*, volume I, *L'architecture*, Paris, 1907.

SARRE, F.: *Denkmäler persischer Baukunst*, 2 volumes, Berlin, 1901–10.

SARRE, F.: *Seldschukische Kleinkunst*, Leipzig, 1909.

SAUVAGET, J.: 'Observations sur quelques mosquées seldjoukides', *Annales de l'Institut des études orientales*, IV, 1938, for further observations on the koisk-mosque theory.

SCHLUMBERGER, D.: Lashkari Bazar, une residence royale ghaznéride: DAFA, Paris, 1965.

SPULER, B.: *Iran in früh-islamischer Zeit*, Wiesbaden, 1952.

SPULER, B.: *Die Mongolen in Iran*, AD 1220–1350, revised edition, Berlin, 1955.

STCHOUKINE, I.: *La peinture iranienne sous les derniers Abbâsides et les Il-Khans*, Bruges, 1930.

STCHOUKINE, I.: *Les peintures des manuscrits safawis de 1502 à 1587*, Paris, 1959.

STRZYGOWSKI, J.: *Altai-Iran und Völkerwanderung*, Leipzig, 1917.

STRZYGOWSKI, J.: *Asiens bildende Kunst*, Augsburg, 1930.

UPHAMPOPE, A., ed.: *A Survey of Persian Art*, 6 volumes, London–New York, 1938–1939.

USEINOV, M. A.: *Monuments of Azerbaidzhan*, Moscow, 1951 (in Russian).

VIOLLET, H., and FLURY, S.: 'Un monument des premiers siècles de l'Hégire en Perse—la mosquée de Nayin', in *Syria II*, 1921.

WILBER, D. N.: *The Architecture of Islamic Iran—the Il-Khānid period*, Princeton, N.J., 1955.

INDEX

FRANCOIS CHAMOUX

THE CIVILIZATION OF GREECE

F'cap 4to   About 75s net

Throughout many centuries the individual Greek found a favourable environment for the development of his life and the fulfilment of his dreams within the narrow limits of the city-state. From one end of the ancient world to the other, little states came into existence, in which a single people, scattered yet conscious of its unity amid all its jealousies and quarrels, led an adventurous existence, abounding in unforeseen vicissitudes, bold action and creative energy. They brought virgin soil under cultivation, established trade routes, determined new political and social forms, and created models for the thought, literature and art of the western world.

   In order to present a civilization whose legacy remains essential for our age, Francois Chamoux, archaeologist, historian and Hellenist, has chosen several themes which seemed to him of primary importance: war, the gods, the city-state, the birth of literary forms, the role of the artist and his position in society. In discussing each of these topics, the author has made every effort to extract the material for a provisional synthesis from literary sources and monuments, making use of the contributions of recent researches. It is to be hoped that this exposition will make the origins of our culture more familiar and accessible to the traveller, the student and the general reader curious about the remote past of the Greek world. The abundant illustrations will no doubt rightly attract and hold the reader's eye.

J. EDWARD KIDDER

THE BIRTH OF JAPANESE ART

10 in. $\times$ 11$\frac{1}{4}$ in.   £6 6s net

Japan's archaic sculpture is the original art of a country which was later overwhelmed by the cultural influences of China, Korea and even more westerly parts of Asia. The tomb-figures of the Jomon period, which came to light only a generation ago, can be dated to the third millennium B.C., while the *haniwa* sculpture belongs to the first 400 years of our era. The expressive strength and simplicity of the work of these two periods have exerted great influence on modern western art and are therefore of exceptional interest today.

   Professor Kidder, a recognized authority on early Japanese art, has in this book enabled the English-speaking reader to examine this rare material in the light of modern scholarship. The well-known photographer, Kenishi Ozawa, has travelled extensively with the author throughout Japan to obtain the series of unrivalled photographs which accompany the text.

GEORGE ALLEN AND UNWIN LTD

GEORGE ALLEN & UNWIN LTD
London: 40 Museum Street, W.C.1

Auckland: 24 Wyndham Street
Bombay: 15 Graham Road, Ballard Estate, Bombay 1
Bridgetown: P.O. Box 222
Buenos Aires: Escritorio 454–459, Florida 165
Calcutta: 17 Chittaranjan Avenue, Calcutta 14
Cape Town: 68 Shortmarket Street
Hong Kong: 44 Mody Road, Kowloon
Ibadan: P.O. Box 62
Karachi: Karachi Chambers, McLeod Road
Madras: Mohan Mansions, 38c Mount Road, Madras 6
Mexico: Villalongin 32–10, Piso, Mexico 5, D.F.
Nairobi: P.O. Box 4536
New Delhi: 13–15 Asaf Ali Road, New Delhi 1
Ontario: 81 Curlew Drive, Don Mills
Philippines: 7 Waling-Waling Street, Roxas District, Quezon City
São Paulo: Caixa Postal 8675
Singapore: 36c Prinsep Street, Singapore 7
Sydney: N.S.W.: Bradbury House, 55 York Street
Tokyo: 10 Kanda-Ogawamachi, 3-Chome, Chiyoda-Ku